Heidegger's Religious Origins

Indiana Series in the Philosophy of Religion
Merold Westphal, general editor

Heidegger's Religious Origins

Destruction and Authenticity

Benjamin D. Crowe

INDIANA UNIVERSITY PRESS
BLOOMINGTON AND INDIANAPOLIS

Indiana University Press
601 North Morton Street
Bloomington, IN 47404-3797 USA

http://iupress.indiana.edu

Telephone orders   800-842-6796
Fax orders   812-855-7931
Orders by e-mail   iuporder@indiana.edu

© 2006 by Benjamin D. Crowe

The paper used in this publication meets the minimum require-
ments of American National Standard for Information Sciences—
Permanence of Paper for Printed Library Materials, ANSI
Z39.48-1984.

MANUFACTURED IN THE UNITED STATES OF AMERICA

Library of Congress Cataloging-in-Publication Data

Crowe, Benjamin D., date
    Heidegger's religious origins : destruction and authenticity / Benjamin D. Crowe.
        p.   cm.   — (Indiana series in the philosophy of religion)
    Includes bibliographical references and index.
    ISBN 0-253-34706-8 (cloth : alk. paper) — ISBN 0-253-21829-2 (pbk. : alk. paper)
    1. Heidegger, Martin, 1889–1976—Religion. I. Title. II. Series.
    B3279.H49C76 2006
    193—dc22

                                                        2005025808

1 2 3 4 5   11 10 09 08 07 06

To my wife, Kristin:

Volo ut sis.

To my grandmother Mary, whose life and stories

are inseparable from the history that I am.

Contents

ACKNOWLEDGMENTS / ix

ABBREVIATIONS OF PRINCIPAL WORKS / xi

Introduction / 1

PART ONE. HEIDEGGER'S ORIGINS: A THEMATIC SKETCH

1. Heidegger's "Religion" / 15

2. Luther's *Theologia Crucis* / 44

PART TWO. HEIDEGGER'S MOTIVES

3. Inauthenticity / 69

4. The Language of Inauthenticity / 101

5. The Roots of Authenticity / 134

6. Authenticity / 162

PART THREE. HEIDEGGER'S "METHOD"

7. Heidegger on the "How" of Philosophy / 207

8. Destruction / 231

NOTES / 267

REFERENCES / 283

INDEX / 291

ACKNOWLEDGMENTS

Something I have learned during the process of carrying out this project, something that Heidegger knew well, is that intellectual work is never purely private, but takes place only within a community. The community of generations of Heidegger scholars constitutes the real foundation of the present work, and I cannot begin to enumerate my debts here. There are, however, many individuals who made up the more proximate community of scholarship and comradeship, without whom none of what is present in this book would have the form it does today.

Professor Michael E. Zimmerman, Ph.D. (Tulane University) mentored me through years of study and has done much to influence the lenses through which I view Heidegger's work. He has also exemplified for me what it means to be a scholar. Special thanks are also due to Professor Ronna C. Burger, Ph.D. (Tulane University), and Professor Paul A. Lodge, Ph.D. (Oxford University). Professor Burger taught me the art of reading texts, and Professor Lodge offered numerous criticisms and suggestions, without which I would never have been able to arrive at the conclusions that I have.

Many others have provided useful guidance and criticism during various stages of this project. During the earliest stages, I was assisted by Professor John Van Buren, Ph.D. (Fordham University), who encouraged the project and who generously provided me with material on both Heidegger and Luther. Professor Theodore Kisiel, Ph.D. (Northern Illinois University), shared his own vast archival knowledge with me in many e-mail exchanges and generously provided me with copies of some of his own works in the area. To Professors Frank Schalow, Ph.D. (University of New Orleans), and Professor Thomas Sheehan, Ph.D. (Stanford University), I owe the insights gained through rich conversations about Heidegger's life and work.

During part of the writing of this text, my work was supported by a Graduate Fellowship from the Center for Ethics and Public Affairs, a division of the Murphy Institute for Political Economy at Tulane. I am particularly grateful to Richard F. Teichgraeber III, Ph.D., director, and Margaret M. Keenan, Ph.D., program coordinator, for their friendship and support during this process.

Special thanks are also due to my family, my mother, father, and brother, for the constant encouragement I have received along the way. This project is the ultimate fruit of my parents' attempts to instill in me the values of learning, reason, and scholarship. To my wife, Kristin, I am particularly indebted for her steadfast love and for countless conversations along the way, which deepened and enriched my understanding of many things, including the ideas found in this book. Without her support, none of this would have been possible.

Finally, I owe many thanks to Professor Merold Westphal, Ph.D. (Fordham University), for his enthusiastic reception of my work and his comments on earlier drafts. Thanks also to an anonymous reviewer. In addition, I want to thank Dee Mortensen and others at Indiana University Press for all their guidance and assistance.

ABBREVIATIONS OF PRINCIPAL WORKS

The following list provides abbreviations of works cited in parentheses in the body of the text. The references are given to the original language version and, where applicable, to the corresponding English translation. These two references are separated by a "/". In most cases, I have employed the relevant English translations without alteration. I have translated passages that appear only in the German.

General Abbreviations

KNS   *Kriegsnotsemester* 1919
SS   Summer Semester
WS   Winter Semester

Works by Heidegger

BZ   1989. *Der Begriff der Zeit.* Tübingen: Max Niemeyer./William McNeill, trans. 1992. *The Concept of Time.* New York: Blackwell.

G1   1978. *Gesamtausgabe,* vol. 1: *Frühe Schriften.* Frankfurt: Vittorio Klostermann.

G7   2000. *Gesamtausgabe,* vol. 7: *Vorträge und Aufsätze.* Frankfurt: Vittorio Klostermann.

G9   1976. *Gesamtausgabe,* vol. 9: *Wegmarken.* Frankfurt: Vittorio Klostermann./William McNeill, ed. 1998. *Pathmarks.* Cambridge: Cambridge University Press.

G14   1985. *Gesamtausgabe,* vol. 14: *Zur Sache des Denkens.* Frankfurt: Vittorio Klostermann.

G15   1986. *Gesamtausgabe,* vol. 15: *Seminare.* Frankfurt: Vittorio Klostermann.

G16   2000. *Gesamtausgabe,* vol. 16: *Reden und andere Zeugnisse eines Lebensweges (1910–1976).* Frankfurt: Vittorio Klostermann.

G17   1994. *Gesamtausgabe,* vol. 17: *Einführung in die phänomeno-*

	logische Forschung. Frankfurt: Vittorio Klostermann. (Marburg: WS 1923–1924).
G20	1979. *Gesamtausgabe*, vol. 20: *Prolegomena zur Geschichte des Zeitbegriffs.* Frankfurt: Vittorio Klostermann./Theodore Kisiel, trans. 1985. *History of the Concept of Time: Prolegomena.* Bloomington: Indiana University Press. (Marburg: SS 1925).
G24	1975. *Gesamtausgabe*, vol. 24: *Die Grundprobleme der Phänomenologie.* Frankfurt: Vittorio Klostermann./Albert Hofstadter, trans. 1982. *The Basic Problems of Phenomenology.* Bloomington: Indiana University Press. (Marburg: SS 1927).
G26	1978. *Gesamtausgabe*, vol. 26: *Metaphysische Anfangsgründe der Logik im Ausgang von Leibniz.* Frankfurt: Vittorio Klostermann./Michael Heim, trans. 1984. *The Metaphysical Foundations of Logic.* Bloomington: Indiana University Press. (Marburg: SS 1928).
G27	1996. *Gesamtausgabe*, vol. 27: *Einleitung in die Philosophie.* Frankfurt: Vittorio Klostermann. (Freiburg: WS 1928–1929).
G29/30	1983. *Gesamtausgabe*, vol. 29/30: *Die Grundbegriffe der Metaphysik. Welt-Endlichkeit-Einsamkeit.* Frankfurt: Vittorio Klostermann./William McNeill and Nicholas Walker, trans. 1995. *The Fundamental Concepts of Metaphysics: World, Finitude, Solitude.* Bloomington: Indiana University Press. (Freiburg: WS 1929–1930).
G39	1999. *Gesamtausgabe*, vol. 39: *Hölderlins Hymnen "Germanien" und "Der Rhein."* Frankfurt: Vittorio Klostermann. (Freiburg: WS 1934–1935).
G40	1983. *Gesamtausgabe*, vol. 40: *Einführung in die Metaphysik.* Frankfurt: Vittorio Klostermann./Gregory Fried and Richard Polt, trans. 2000. *Introduction to Metaphysics.* New Haven: Yale University Press. (Freiburg: SS 1935).
G42	1988. *Gesamtausgabe*, vol. 42: *Schelling: Vom Wesen der menschlichen Freiheit* (1809). Frankfurt: Vittorio Kostermann. (Freiburg: SS 1936).
G56/57	1987. *Gesamtausgabe*, vol. 56/57: *Zur Bestimmung der Philosophie.* Frankfurt: Vittorio Klostermann./Ted Sadler, trans. 2000. *Towards the Definition of Philosophy.* London: Athlone Press. (Freiburg: KNS 1919, SS 1919).
G58	1993. *Gesamtausgabe*, vol. 58: *Grundprobleme der Phänomenologie.* Frankfurt: Vittorio Klostermann. (Freiburg: WS 1919–1920).
G59	1993. *Gesamtausgabe*, vol. 59: *Phänomenologie der Anschauung und des Ausdrucks. Theorie der philosophischen Begriffsbildung.* Frankfurt: Vittorio Klostermann. (Freiburg: SS 1920).
G60	1995. *Gesamtausgabe*, vol. 60: *Phänomenologie des religiösen*

Lebens. Frankfurt: Vittorio Klostermann. (Freiburg: WS 1920–1921, SS 1921).

G61   1985. *Gesamtausgabe,* vol. 61: *Phänomenologische Interpretationen zu Aristoteles. Einführung in die phänomenologische Forschung.* Frankfurt: Vittorio Klostermann./Richard Rojcewicz, trans. 2001. *Phenomenological Interpretations of Aristotle: Initiation into Phenomenological Research.* Bloomington: Indiana University Press. (Freiburg: WS 1921–1922).

G63   1988. *Gesamtausgabe,* vol. 63: *Ontologie (Hermeneutik der Faktizität).* Frankfurt: Vittorio Klostermann./John Van Buren, trans. 1995. *Ontology: Hermeneutics of Facticity.* Bloomington: Indiana University Press. (Freiburg: SS 1923).

G65   1989. *Gesamtausgabe,* vol. 65: *Beiträge zur Philosophie (Vom Ereignis).* Frankfurt: Vittorio Klostermann.

G66   1997. *Gesamtausgabe,* vol. 66: *Besinnung.* Frankfurt: Vittorio Klostermann.

G67   1999. *Gesamtausgabe,* vol. 67: *Metaphysik und Nihilismus.* Frankfurt: Vittorio Klostermann.

HB   1989. Martin Heidegger and Elisabeth Blochmann, *Briefwechsel, 1918–1969.* Edited by Joachim W. Storck. Marbach am Neckar: Deutsche Schillergesellschaft.

HJ   1990. Martin Heidegger and Karl Jaspers, *Briefwechsel 1920–1963.* Edited by Walter Biemel and Hans Saner. Frankfurt: Vittorio Klostermann.

HL   1990. "Drei Breife Martin Heideggers an Karl Löwith." In Dietrich Papenfuss and Otto Pöggeler, eds. *Zur philosophischen Aktualität Heideggers,* vol. 2: *Im Gespräch der Zeit.* Frankfurt: Vittorio Klostermann, 27–39.

HR   2002. Martin Heidegger and Heinrich Rickert, *Briefe 1912 bis 1933 und andere Dokument.* Edited by Alfred Denker. Frankfurt: Vittorio Klostermann.

NB   1989. "Phänomenologisiche Interpretationen zu Aristoteles (Anzeige der hermeneutischen Situation)." *Dilthey Jahrbuch für Philosophie und Geschichte der Geisteswissenschaften* 6: 228–274/John Van Buren, trans. 2002. "Phenomenological Interpretations in Connection with Aristotle: An Indication of the Hermeneutical Situation (1922)." In *Supplements: From the Earliest Essays to "Being and Time" and Beyond.* Edited by John Van Buren. Albany: State University of New York Press, 111–146.

S   2002. *Supplements: From the Earliest Essays to "Being and Time" and Beyond.* Edited by John Van Buren. Albany: State University of New York Press.

SZ   1977. *Gesamtausgabe,* vol. 2: *Sein und Zeit.* Frankfurt: Vittorio

Klostermann./John Macquarrie and Edward Robinson, trans.
1962. *Being and Time*. New York: Harper and Row.

US   1959. *Unterwegs zur Sprache*. Pfüllingen: Gunther Neske.

ZS   1987. *Zollikoner Seminare, Protokelle—Gespräche—Briefe*. Edited by Medard Boss. Frankfurt: Vittorio Klostermann./Franz Meyer and Richard Askey, trans. 2001. *Zollikon Seminars: Protocols, Conversations, Letters*. Evanston: Northwestern University Press.

Works by Luther

LW25   1972. *Luther's Works*, vol. 25: *Lectures on Romans: Scholia and Glosses*. St. Louis: Concordia Publishing House.

LW29   1968. *Luther's Works*, vol. 29: *Lectures on Titus, Philemon, Hebrews*. St. Louis: Concordia Publishing House.

LW31   1957. *Luther's Works*, vol. 31: *The Career of the Reformer I*. Philadelphia: Muhlenberg Press.

WA1   1883. *D. Martin Luthers Werke, Kritische Ausgabe*, vol. 1. Weimar: Hermann Bohlaus.

WA56   1883. *D. Martin Luthers Werke, Kritische Ausgabe*, vol. 56. Weimar: Hermann Bohlaus.

WA57/3   1883. *D. Martin Luthers Werke, Kritische Ausgabe*, vol. 57/3. Weimar: Hermann Bohlaus.

Works by Dilthey

GS1   1959. *Gesammelte Schriften*, vol. 1: *Einleitung in die Geisteswissenschaften*. Stuttgart: B.G. Teubner./Rudolf A. Makkreel and Frithjof Rodi, eds. 1989. *Wilhelm Dilthey, Selected Works*, vol. 1: *Introduction to the Human Sciences*. Princeton, N.J.: Princeton University Press.

GS2   1957. *Gesammelte Schriften*, vol. 2: *Weltanschauung und Analyse des Menschen seit Renaissance und Reformation*. Stuttgart: B.G. Teubner.

GS5   1957. *Gesammelte Schriften*, vol. 5: *Die Geistige Welt: Einleitung in die Philosophie des Lebens, Erste Hälfte: Abhandlungen zur Grundlegung der Geisteswissenschaften*. Stuttgart: B.G. Teubner.

GS6   1958. *Gesammelte Schriften*, vol. 6: *Die Geistige Welt: Einleitung in die Philosophie des Lebens, Zweite Hälfte: Abhandlungen zur Poetik, Ethik, und Pädagogik*. Stuttgart: B.G. Teubner.

GS7   1958. *Gesammelte Schriften*, vol. 7: *Der Aufbau der geschichtlichen Welt in den Geisteswissenschaften*. Stuttgart: B.G. Teubner./Rudolf A. Makkreel and Frithjof Rodi, ed. 2002. *Wilhelm*

Dilthey, Selected Works, vol. III: *The Formation of the Historical World in the Human Sciences.* Princeton, N.J.: Princeton University Press.

GS8   1960. *Gesammelte Schriften*, vol. 8: *Weltanschauungslehre: Abhandlungen zur Philosophie der Philosophie.* Stuttgart: B.G. Teubner.

Heidegger's Religious Origins

Introduction

For it is written, "I will destroy the wisdom of the wise, and the discernment of the discerning I will thwart."

(1 Corinthians 1:19)

The Theme of This Study

European intellectual history bears witness to the fact that times of social, cultural, and political uncertainty often serve as the occasion for intellectuals to think through the implications of their positions in society and to seek an articulation of their more general responsibility for society. The beginning of the twentieth century was such a period of social, political, and cultural turbulence, particularly in Germany. The horrors of World War I had discredited the platitudes of "progress" and "civilization" for a whole generation of sensitive individuals. The dissolution of the Hohenzollern Empire, the Russian Revolution, and the Communist revolutions in Munich and elsewhere fatally undermined the political certainties of an earlier age. This was a time of ideological warfare as well, exemplified in the anti-modernist controversy in the Catholic Church. All these events combined with unprecedented cultural and intellectual ferment in the arts (futurism, expressionism), in philosophy (popular "philosophy of life," Nietzsche, and the rediscovery of Kierkegaard), and in theology (Schweitzer, Barth, Bultmann). This was the situation in which young Martin Heidegger began to attempt to understand his own personal vocation as a philosopher.

In Heidegger's case, clarity about his own social role as an intellectual could only be found by coming to grips with his own religious upbringing, with his theological education, and with his own religious convictions. From his student days to his old age, Heidegger always recognized the way religion and philosophy have interacted to shape the unique cultural and intellectual heritage of Europe. At the same time, this heritage was a matter of profound *personal* import for Heidegger. Thus, for him, the articulation of the social role of the intellectual had to occur in dialogue with the religious traditions of Europe. He puts the matter so in a letter to his friend and mentor Engelbert Krebs from January 1919:

> I believe that I have the inner calling to philosophy and, through my research and teaching, to do what stands in my power for the sake of the eternal vocation of the inner man, and *to do it for this alone,* and so justify my existence [*Dasein*] and work ultimately before God. (S 70)

Like many people in his generation, Heidegger was contemptuous of what he perceived to be the sterility and irrelevance of the dominant trends in academic philosophy. He struggled to find a way in which the philosopher, *qua* philosopher, could address the situation of the times. As he reflected on his own religious convictions and on the course of Western intellectual history, he found a figure who pointed the way toward such an engaged philosophy, Martin Luther. Luther was a man who, by vocation, was never anything but a professor of biblical theology, who spent most of his days in the classroom, and who, contrary to romanticized myths, accomplished his most revolutionary work with a pen and a specially printed Bible. Part of Luther's genius lay in his ability to resurrect ancient traditions and to transform them into powerful catalysts for change in the present.

As I will show, Heidegger learned a great deal from the example of Luther. In particular, he found especially compelling Luther's ability to transform the past into both a critical measure of the present and living possibility for the future. Heidegger himself cultivated this ability and attempted to articulate both its ultimate meaning and the conditions for its possibility throughout the 1920s. He chose a name for it which itself reflects the importance of Luther to his thinking: '*Destruktion,*' a Germanized version of the term '*destructio,*' used quite frequently in Luther's early writings. Destruction became Heidegger's response to his own situation, his own unique answer to the question of the role and responsibility of the intellectual in society.

No one denies that destruction is one of the central ideas in Heidegger's work. Few, however, have attempted to come to a thorough understanding of it, and fewer still have succeeded in the task. By and large, the term "destruction" (or some other translation of Heidegger's term '*Destruktion*') either receives little comment or is used by commentators as if its meaning were obvious.[1] My general aim in this study is to correct this situation. In so doing, I hope to articulate an understanding of "destruction" that does justice to Heidegger's work as an attempt to respond to the social, political, and cultural situation of his time. The purpose of this is not to relativize Heidegger to a bygone era. Instead, by explicating the meaning of "destruction" as a response to its time, I want to clear the way for both an accurate understanding of Heidegger's thought *and* the possibility of appropriating destruction in the present. My thesis is that when viewed through the lens of Luther's influence on Heidegger, it becomes clear that the ultimate motivation for engaging in this practice of destruction is the value of an "authentic" way of life. That is, destruction is a philosophical practice that aims at cultivating authenticity as a concrete possibility for individual men and women.

Clarifying the Project

By any reckoning, Heidegger's philosophical corpus is an exceptionally fertile field for scholarship, as well as for original work in philosophy and a host of other disciplines. His essays and lectures encompass virtually the entire history of philosophy, not to mention philosophical disciplines as diverse as logic, philosophy of science, ontology, and philosophical theology. Moreover, the controversial nature of both his life *and* his work continues to motivate both sober analysis and impassioned polemic.

With regard to any subject matter, but particularly one as vast as Heidegger's philosophy, one must always begin the examination from a definite point of view. This is a point that Heidegger himself, and his student Gadamer, have made into something like a philosophical principle. One cannot simply presume to treat the entirety of a thinker's work without further ado. Indeed, a fruitful study of a philosophical corpus as complex and voluminous as Heidegger's necessitates a host of prior decisions about the sources, scope, aims, and assumptions that guide the investigation. It is, therefore, important that I make my own prior decisions as explicit as possible.

Sources and Chronological Scope

The focal point of this study is the theory and practice of destruction in Heidegger's work. This focus dictates the sources and the chronological scope of the discussion. The primary sources of my study are drawn from a decade-long period at the start of Heidegger's independent career (roughly 1917–1927). The term "destruction [*Destruktion*]" first appears in Heidegger's lecture course for WS 1919–1920. By the time *Being and Time* is published in 1927, its meaning is more or less fully articulated, and Heidegger has drawn out all the systematic connections between destruction and other ideas integral to his thought. After SS 1927, Heidegger uses the term less and less frequently. In SS 1928, when discussing the historical orientation of philosophical activity, he does not use it at all (G26 197/155). The following semester, he prefers the language of "confrontation [*Auseinandersetzung*]" (G27 9–10). Around 1930, one begins to catch a glimpse of an idea that will come to fruition at the end of the decade as the "history of being." By the late 1930s, "destruction" only shows up in retrospective accounts of his work, where Heidegger argues for the primacy of something else called "confrontation" (G66 67–68). What is true of "destruction" is no less true of other key terms used in this study, e.g., "authenticity" (and its cognates) and "inauthenticity" (and its cognates). After about 1930, these terms, and the ideas they designate, rarely appear except in brief, retrospective treatments.

While I do not want to take any position here on the much-debated issue of the "turn" in Heidegger's thought in the 1930s, I do think it can be uncontroversially asserted that some of the terms, ideas, and concerns that characterize his work between 1917 and 1927 are de-emphasized and overshadowed by new terms, ideas, and concerns. While the latter are, no doubt, "organic" outgrowths of Heidegger's earlier work, ideas like the "history of being" and "poetic dwelling" are different enough, and complex enough, to warrant their own treatment. Thus I will restrict my sources to correspondence, essays, and lecture notes from the period up to and including *Being and Time*, while fully recognizing that it would be a worthwhile project to trace out the further development of the ideas examined in this study.[2]

Aims

In a perceptive and entertaining essay, "A Paradigm Shift in Heidegger Research," Thomas Sheehan provides a penetrating characterization of various approaches to Heidegger scholarship.[3] In the present study, I am self-consciously aligning myself with what Sheehan calls the "center right." What this entails is that my overriding concern here is with *getting Heidegger right*. While others endeavor to evaluate Heidegger's work and its legacy, to critically expose its putative flaws, or to adapt Heideggerian ideas to contemporary debates in various disciplines, I aim to understand Heidegger's work in its own right and, at least immediately, for its own sake. My project is to determine what Heidegger thinks by carefully considering what he says (or, in some cases, leaves unsaid), and to determine, as far as possible, why he thinks what he does. To this end, I employ a two-sided strategy of (1) close textual exegesis and (2) historical examinations of Heidegger's times and of various important influences on his work (especially Luther and Dilthey).

While it may appear that "getting Heidegger right" is a more or less antiquarian, or even altogether pedestrian, project, I submit that this is not at all the case. Heidegger remains, without a doubt, one of the most influential thinkers of the past century. His work has irrevocably defined the discourse in "Continental" philosophy for generations and will doubtless continue to do so for the foreseeable future. It is also worth noting that the work of a number of American scholars (e.g., Dreyfus and Dahlstrom) has also made it clear that Heidegger has plenty to say to philosophers more rooted in the Anglo-American traditions of "analytic" philosophy. Heidegger's direct and indirect influences on other disciplines like theology, religious studies, art criticism, cultural theory, clinical psychology, and even architecture also continue to be felt. The continued publication of the "Collected Edition" of Heidegger's works will most likely serve to kindle the interest of future scholars while keeping older flames burning brightly.

Given that all of this is true, the project of "getting Heidegger right" becomes more than a matter of simply shedding light on a relatively obscure bit of intellectual history. To the contrary, in view of Heidegger's past and present influence, this project is a matter of self-understanding. To borrow a pithy turn of phrase from the man himself, Heidegger is a part of the history that we *are*. Getting him right is a matter of coming to terms with one of the richest and most powerful sources for contemporary intellectual discourse. That said, it should be made clear from the outset that the aim of this study is not to enter directly into the long-standing debate about the darker sides of Heidegger's thought, to say nothing of the less palatable aspects of his personal character. My contention is that such a debate can only move forward on the basis of a clear, accurate, and comprehensive grasp of the man's work as it is in itself.

Reading Heidegger

This study is, as I have already made clear, concerned with a particular, but vitally important, aspect of Heidegger's thought during a particular, but vitally important, period of his career. This restriction of scope is mandated by a self-imposed demand for rigorous exegesis and comprehensive treatment. At the same time, it is obvious that any study of any element of a thinker's work, particularly one as elemental as destruction in Heidegger's thought, is always oriented ahead of time by a set of assumptions about his work as a whole. My own assumptions will, no doubt, be made explicit at numerous points during the discussion. However, it is worthwhile to spell out a few of my most global assumptions about Heidegger's work and to show why I think they are warranted.

First of all, it should be clear that I want to steer away from an abiding tendency in Heidegger studies to privilege *Being and Time* as *the* definitive statement of Heidegger's thought. This is a tendency that not only flies in the face of Heidegger's own explicit statements about this work (e.g., in SS 1936, G42 111), but also, more importantly, impairs the project of understanding his work by unintentionally sidelining alternative formulations of key ideas found in *Being and Time*. Indeed, the illegitimacy of this tendency is something that has become increasingly clear to many students of Heidegger's work during the past decade. John Van Buren's detailed exposition of the "young Heidegger's" letters, lectures, and essays, along with Theodore Kisiel's invaluable and painstaking archival work on this same period, have together dethroned *Being and Time* from its putative status as *the* book by Heidegger. Indeed, as Van Buren says, with warranted hyperbole, "there never really was *a* 'text' called 'Being and Time.' "[4] What this means for this study, in concrete terms, is that while passages from *Being and Time* are by no means excluded from consideration and sometimes constitute the linchpin of particular arguments, the bulk of the material from which I draw my conclusions comes from other parts of Heidegger's corpus.

Secondly, an attentive reader will quickly notice that "Being" hardly makes an appearance at all in this study, whereas it is generally a principal cast member in much of the relevant literature on Heidegger. This apparently curious omission is in fact based on what I take to be the sound conclusions arrived at independently by a number of judicious commentators in recent years. John Van Buren, for example, concludes from his reading that Heidegger "so radically transformed the traditional being-question that he eventually stopped using the term 'being' as a designation for what he was ultimately aiming at," and later that "Heideggerians in their search for 'Being' have for years been after the wrong thing."[5] Thomas Sheehan, who has actually been arguing this point for decades, ultimately gives this sound piece of advice to scholars: "Since Heidegger's focal topic never was 'being' in any of its forms, and since the term 'being' is plagued by so much confusion and absurdity, we would do well to follow Heidegger's example and abandon the word 'being' as a marker for *die Sache selbst*."[6]

What, then, is *die Sache selbst* for Heidegger? After 1919, his lifelong project is to explicate that which comes before "Being" and "beings," i.e., the dynamic unfolding (*Ereignis*) of a "world" or "clearing [*Lichtung*]" of meaning within the everyday course of human life. Theodore Kisiel has captured the subject matter quite clearly, and so it is worth quoting his remarks in full:

> All these things (books, pens, cars, campus, trees, shade, etc.) give themselves directly out of the immediate context of meaning encompassing us which we tend to call the "world." Much like [Emil] Lask's objects known only through the constitutive categories in which we live, such things receive their significance from that meaning-giving context encompassing us, whose activity can then be described as "worlding." [. . .] the true locus of our experience is not in objects or things which "in addition are then interpreted as signifying this or that," but rather the signifying element itself now dynamized and set in motion, the "It" that "worlds."[7]

What interests Heidegger is the way, *before* theory, *before* categories, human life is *already* meaningful. What fascinates him is that there are "categories" that are "alive" in life itself at the most immediate level (G61 88/66). Over the years, Heidegger gives lots of different names to this topic—"life," "factical life-experience," "it worlds for me," the "worlding of the world," "being-in-the-world," "Dasein," "transcendence," the "truth of being," "*Seyn*," the "event," "dwelling," and many more. All are attempts to get at how a context of meaning is immediately given in human life such that one can make *sense* of oneself, of other people, and of things in the workshop, the studio, the cloister, and the laboratory. These ideas constitute the theoretical horizon in which Heidegger's views on destruction and authenticity have an integral role to play.

Organization of This Study

My argument about the origins, nature, and goals of destruction in Heidegger's early work proceeds in three stages, each of which consists of a number of distinct steps. The first stage is the concern of Part One, "Heidegger's Origins: A Thematic Sketch." This consists of chapters 1 and 2 and is designed to provide what Heidegger called a "preliminary sketch [*Vorzeichnis*]" of my basic claim, i.e., that Heidegger's religious "origins," in particular his study of Luther, decisively shaped his conception of the nature and goals of philosophy.

In chapter 1, I undertake to clarify Heidegger's philosophical position on the importance of religion and theology not only for Western intellectual history as a whole, but also for his own philosophical project. In examining what Gadamer called the "religious dimension" of Heidegger, I reject attempts to either *reduce* Heidegger's work to a "secularization" of religious ideas or to evade the ambiguities of the issue by offering a merely sociological and biographical *explanation* of it. I show that Christianity has an abiding importance in Heidegger's project of a "hermeneutics of facticity." While Heidegger rejected "natural theology," he was nonetheless convinced that Christian religiosity in its historical expressions had a feeling or sense for life that, understood properly, could ground a more adequate understanding of life in its immediacy. I argue that Luther's "theology of the cross" was, for Heidegger, one of the most significant articulations of this Christian "basic experience." For this reason, the influence of Luther on Heidegger's thought can hardly be overestimated.

Having shown the significance of Luther for Heidegger's work, I turn in chapter 2 to the task of examining one particular aspect of it, viz., the role his study of Luther played in the development of Heidegger's conception of philosophy as destruction. The term *'Destruktion'* enters Heidegger's vocabulary in 1920, a year which also marks the beginning of his lifelong interaction with Luther's thought. The term itself is a Germanization of Luther's Latin *'destructio,'* which, along with its cognates, plays a central but heretofore unexamined role in his "theology of the cross." Focusing on Luther's lectures and other writings between 1515 and 1518, I explicate the meaning of *'destructio'* (and its cognates) by examining its usage. Two distinct but interrelated usages occur here. First, Luther uses *'destructio'* to refer to what he elsewhere calls the "alien work [*opus alienum*]" of God, i.e., the humiliation of human self-righteousness that is aimed at uprooting the corruption of human nature, which is, paradoxically, an act of grace. Second, Luther also uses this term (and synonyms) to describe what he regards as the proper way of doing theology. Luther holds that the Aristotelian theology of his predecessors and the policies of the institutional Church only fuel humanity's natural tendency toward smugness and self-righteousness. Hence, Luther argues that true theologians must join Paul in preaching the "foolishness" of the cross. As I will argue in more detail in chapters 7 and 8, these senses survive Heidegger's translation of Luther's *destructio* into philosophical *Destruktion*.

Part Two, "Heidegger's Motives," consisting of chapters 3 through 6, is concerned with the elaboration of one of the points that emerges during Part One, viz., that Heidegger's conception of philosophy is a *motivated* conception. In other words, the aim of this stage of the argument is to establish the "values" or ideals that motivate Heidegger's way of doing philosophy. The most familiar names for these ideas are "inauthenticity" and "authenticity." In the process of establishing the nature of these ideas and their importance in Heidegger's work, I will also provide a fresh and more accurate reading of them.

In chapter 3, I undertake to give a thorough account of Heidegger's conception of an "inauthentic" way of life. This chapter is an examination of "inauthenticity" *per se*, and itself consists of two stages. First, I will briefly consider the nature of Heidegger's views against the background of moral theory in order to clarify what Heidegger is concerned with and to respond to some long-standing worries about his position. Here I argue that Heidegger maintains a species of "perfectionism," i.e., a kind of moral theory that sketches out valuable ways of life rather than duties. Second, I will examine the "categories" that define the contours of an inauthentic life in Heidegger's account. This latter discussion will be an explication of what "inauthenticity" means. "Inauthenticity" is not a term that refers to a univocal concept, but is instead a provisional, revisable way of indicating a certain pattern of life that Heidegger thinks it worthwhile to be concerned with. Hence, the five "categories" of inauthenticity I describe are not constitutive of a *definition* of a *concept*, but are rather interrelated features of a way of life that Heidegger picks out to delineate its boundaries.

In chapter 4, I examine Heidegger's views about the way public discourse, particularly intellectual discourse, is oftentimes complicit in an inauthentic way of life. This mode of discourse is the ultimate target of Heidegger's practice of critical destruction. Here, I will explore in more detail Heidegger's views about tradition, history, and discourse as these relate to the topic of inauthenticity. Tradition is the immediate context of meaning within which individuals undertake to interpret their own lives and the world around them. Heidegger argues that tradition tends to "fade" or "decline," to become superficial and restrictive, and to thus foreclose "genuine" possibilities of meaning. This tendency is concretized in "idle talk," a mode in which public discourse operates. The hallmark of "idle talk" is that words simply get passed along from person to person, without any sort of attempt at understanding. Public discourse as "idle talk" also exercises a sort of unconscious tyranny over individuals by shaping their values and desires. The tendency of individuals to seek the path of least resistance feeds into "idle talk" in such a way that public discourse serves to provide people with "masks" and "disguises" that allow them to abdicate self-responsibility. Like Luther and other religious thinkers, Heidegger also holds that *educated* discourse is too often complicit in this sort of self-abdication. He singles out philosophy, historical consciousness, and religious discourse for a scathing critique.

The aim of chapter 5 is to begin moving toward an understanding of "authenticity." This move is necessary because my guiding thesis is that philosophy, as destruction, is supposed to contribute to or foster an authentic way of life. Hence, we need to know what Heidegger means by an "authentic" way of life. The problem, however, is that it is hard to spell out just what Heidegger has in mind. While partially a function of the oft-discussed obscurity of his language, the elusiveness of authenticity has a deeper philosophical motive. As I show in chapter 4, Heidegger is particularly wary of attempts to dictate the ultimate "meaning" of life or to prescribe a "world-view" for the salvation of "culture." Furthermore, as I hope to show in more detail, authenticity is an ideal that is importantly linked with a more general commitment to the unique individuality of each human life. For these reasons, Heidegger is deliberately reticent about the idea.

In light of this difficulty, I propose a two-pronged approach, one that combines straightforward textual analysis with historical reflections on the tradition within which the ideal of authenticity has been articulated. The purpose of chapter 5 is to accomplish the latter account. Following Charles Taylor, I maintain that "authenticity" is an idea deriving from the Romantic personalist tradition. I then show how features of Heidegger's view manifest an obvious affinity for this tradition, particularly as articulated by Schleiermacher and Dilthey. Dilthey's work was an especially important influence on the development of Heidegger's ideal of authenticity. Dilthey maintained that "primitive Christianity" is the origin of modern historical consciousness and of modern personalism. Heidegger appropriated this thesis and actively attempted to breathe new life into the personalist tradition by examining primitive Christianity in detail. The result of this investigation was Heidegger's own notion of an "authentic life," which, while rooted in Romantic personalism, owes even more to primitive Christianity.

Chapter 6 builds on the previous chapter. In chapter 6, I present an explication of Heidegger's conception of an "authentic life" by focusing on his works before and including *Being and Time*. During this period, Heidegger uses a rich and variegated vocabulary with the intention of suggestively intimating or "formally indicating" his own idea of the good life. Heidegger wants to avoid deploying a rigid taxonomy here, one that might suggest a clearly defined *concept* of an authentic life. The reason for resisting the latter impression is that, as Heidegger makes clear, authenticity is always a matter of *individual concern* rather than of general theoretical determination. This point is something that must be kept in mind when talking about Heidegger's position with respect to moral theory. His commitment to Romantic personalism precludes him from making straightforward normative pronouncements. All the same, no one can deny that he embraces a moral ideal of authenticity.

The chapter begins with an examination of three influential and important readings of authenticity. The first, called the "ontological," interprets authenticity as a kind of *cognitive achievement* such that one gains a better appreciation for or understanding of one's true human nature. I argue that this reading is too *theoretical* in its orientation and that the notion of "human nature" or the "true self" is foreign to Heidegger's thinking. The second reading, called the "narrative," holds that authenticity is a *style* of life characterized by wholeness and coherence. I suggest that this approach presents significant advantages but is a bit too reductive and fails to capture the richness of Heidegger's discussions. Finally, I consider an "emancipatory" reading, according to which Heidegger's concern is to proclaim the value of individuals and of individual ways of life over anonymous conformity and the hegemony of various ideologies. While I worry about some of the details of this view, I nonetheless find it to be correct and illuminating in many respects.

Having thus clarified what I think "authenticity" does *not* mean, I then begin to define what it does mean by examining Heidegger's vocabularies before *Being and Time*. At an early stage, one finds Heidegger embracing a version of Romantic personalism in the form of an ideal of "life-intensification" or a "vehement life" of personal vocational commitment. I describe Heidegger's guarded appreciation for the "Free German Youth" and other neo-Romantic cultural tendencies of the time, which reveal a good deal about his own thinking on the subject of the good life. In the early 1920s, the vocabulary shifts to talk of *Existenz* and "resolve," of "distress" and "anxious worry." In his essays and lecture notes before 1922, Heidegger further develops an ideal in which life has been shocked out of its complacency and has taken responsibility for itself by staking itself on a vocation. In 1923, the vocabulary changes once again, this time to the manifestly Christian language of "wakefulness." Heidegger mentions artists like Van Gogh and Dostoyevsky and religious figures like Paul, Luther, Pascal, and Kierkegaard as paradigms.

In *Being and Time*, Heidegger finally settles on the more familiar vocabulary of "authenticity," "conscience," "resolve," and "repetition." I show how the term "conscience" evolves in Heidegger's work after 1922, from a general indication for authenticity as such to a more specialized designation for a particular element of his overall moral vision. In *Being and Time*, the "voice of conscience" is a formal catchall designation for moments of "intensity" that break in on one and make possible a kind of reorientation. "Resoluteness," as Heidegger calls one's response to these moments, is best understood as a kind of vocational commitment. As such, resoluteness is diametrically opposed to the sort of complacency and conformity that characterize an inauthentic way of life. This commitment involves the appropriation of possibilities inherited from one's tradition. "Repetition" is Heidegger's term for the attempt to explicitly model one's life on an exemplary individual or life-pattern received from one's cultural inheritance.

A further aspect of authenticity that is explored in *Being and Time* is *social*. Heidegger stresses that an authentic individual, while breaking out of the dictatorship of the anonymous public, nonetheless remains very much a part of the web of social relations that help to constitute human identity. This is especially true in the case of one's "generation," i.e., that group of people with whom one has a particularly close bond in virtue of a common history and common formative experiences. It is within the "generation" that the authentic individual finds the tasks and problems that must be faced in her own way. Heidegger also envisions a community of authentic individuals, in which each is committed to the authenticity of the other. On Heidegger's account, these relations are not predicated on common beliefs or on authority, but rather on a shared commitment to fostering an authentic way of life in each person. Such a community eschews paternalism for "dialogue" and "communication," forming what Heidegger calls a "community of struggle [*Kampfgemeinschaft*]."

Part Three, "Heidegger's 'Method'," comprises the final two chapters, chapters 7 and 8. This is the culminating stage of my argument. In these two chapters, I articulate Heidegger's general notion of the practical role of philosophy in human life, and I go on to offer a detailed, comprehensive analysis of the ideal of destruction [*Destruktion*] that lies at the very heart of Heidegger's more general conception of the nature of philosophical activity.

Having laid the groundwork for understanding the meaning of "destruction" in chapters 1 through 6, I begin an explicit examination of the nature of Heidegger's conception of philosophy in chapter 7. This discussion begins with an overview of the main ideas about the nature and tasks of philosophy that were circulating in Germany in the early twentieth century, as viewed by Heidegger. I identify two basic tendencies: (1) "scientific" philosophy, and (2) "world-view" philosophy. The former refers to a sort of dysfunctional family of views that attempt to align philosophy, in one way or another, to the mathematical natural sciences. The most prominent member of this family, as far as Heidegger was concerned, is neo-Kantianism. "World-view" philosophy is used here as a catchall term for various reactions against "scientific" philosophy, many of them inspired by Nietzsche, whose watchwords were "life," "feeling," "spirit," and the like. I describe how Heidegger rejects both of these alternatives and instead attempts to steer a path for philosophy between the arid abstraction of "scientific" philosophy and the superficial moralism of "world-view philosophy."

I then describe how this project was motivated by Heidegger's concern with concrete life, with the real personal issues that faced men and women, particularly intellectual men and women, in the aftermath of World War I. For Heidegger, *the* fundamental issue was the need for each individual to achieve an *authentic* way of life. This concern with the value of an authentic life is the catalyst that drives Heidegger's deepest reflections on the nature and tasks of philosophy. Next, I examine the way Heidegger hoped to practice philosophy in such a way as to remain true to his values. Philosophy, on his view, has the duty of "making things hard" for people by refusing them the luxury of ideo-logical hiding places and "metaphysical tranquilizers."

Chapter 8 is the culmination of my argument. Up to this point, I show the following four claims to be true of Heidegger's early thought: (1) primitive Christianity, particularly as exemplified by Luther, is a decisive influence; (2) Heidegger embraces an ideal of authentic selfhood, which he contrasts with a kind of complacent self-abdication called inauthenticity; (3) he regards public intellectual discourse, especially in philosophy, as being complicit in an inau-thentic way of life; and (4) he articulates a vision of a way of doing philosophy that is motivated by a concern with fostering authenticity by challenging indi-viduals to break out of their complacent conformity. Beginning in WS 1919–1920, Heidegger began to call this practice 'Destruktion,' borrowing a term from Luther's early thought. The goal of chapter 8 is to arrive at a detailed understanding of the meaning of "destruction" in Heidegger's thought. Having demonstrated the real importance of destruction for Heidegger, I then proceed to examine the *development* of his use of this term during the 1920s to provide an accurate *and* comprehensive picture of what it means.

The first stage in this development comes in SS 1919, where Heidegger uses the phrase "phenomenological critique" to designate the practice he even-tually calls 'Destruktion.' The latter term appears for the first time in WS 1919–1920. Here, Heidegger makes it clear that this practice is absolutely integral to his own unique phenomenological way of doing philosophy, and he tries to articulate its sense by drawing an analogy between it and Hegel's dialectic. In SS 1920, he attempts to give this term a more precise determination.

After examining the earliest stages in the development of the use of 'De-struktion,' I next go on to explicate the mature conception of philosophy as destruction from the second half of the 1920s. I show how a crucial stage in the process of the development of this idea was Heidegger's confrontation with philosophical debates about historical consciousness. This confrontation issues in Heidegger's own conception of history that has been freed from historicist strictures about "objectivity" and from neo-Kantian concerns about relativism and validity. Once this conception of history is firmly in place in Heidegger's philosophical vocabulary, he is able to develop a practice of destruction as at once a critical liberation *from* the past and a positive liberation *of* the past as a possibility for the future.

PART ONE. HEIDEGGER'S ORIGINS: A THEMATIC SKETCH

Heidegger's "Religion"

Without this theological origin I would have never arrived at the path of thinking.

(US 96)

Whoever wants to philosophize with Aristotle without danger must first of all become a fool in Christ.

(WA1 355)

My argument about the relationship between destruction and authenticity in Heidegger's early work is predicated upon a more fundamental claim regarding the general role played by *religion* in his thought. Throughout the remainder of this study, I will make constant reference to Heidegger's discussions of religious ideas and religious figures, as well as to his own indications of the importance of these ideas and figures for his fundamental philosophical project. Accordingly, the aim of this chapter is to provide what Heidegger would call a "preliminary sketch [*Vorzeichnis*]" of the role that religion in general, and Christianity in particular, play in his work.

The theme around which the present discussion will revolve is that of Heidegger's religious "origin [*Herkunft*]." In the passage quoted above, taken from a text composed in the 1950s, Heidegger explicitly highlights his own estimation of the importance of this "origin." I have two principal theses with respect to this thematic issue. First, I contend that religious life, particularly Christian religious life, exemplifies a "basic experience [*Grunderfahrung*]" of human life in general, which, when sufficiently "formalized" in the notion of authenticity, provides Heidegger with a starting point for his phenomenological investigations into the pre-theoretical sense of "factical life-experience," as he was wont to call his topic in the early 1920s. Second, I claim that in the early 1920s, Heidegger began to craft a conception of doing philosophy that aimed at cultivating, preserving, and staying loyal to this "basic experience." Taken together, these two theses encompass the central claim of this study, viz., that Heidegger's conception of philosophy as destruction is ultimately motivated by his concern with an authentic way of life. In chapters 3 through 8, I will fill in the details of this account. What I want to accomplish in this chapter, and in the next, is to establish the *prima facie* plausibility of my general approach and to provide necessary background material for a thorough understanding of Heidegger's religious "origins." Along the way, I hope to provide a more satisfying account of the religious aspects of Heidegger's work.

The "Religious Dimension" of Heidegger

Among the most enduring questions that has been posed by students of Heidegger's thought is the question of what Hans-Georg Gadamer called the "religious dimension."[1] This is the question, or group of questions, concerning the relations between religion, theology, and philosophy in Heidegger's life and thought. Heidegger began his intellectual life as a seminarian, and continued, albeit with some degree of ebb and flow, to discuss religious themes and to converse with theologians for the remainder of his life. The facts are now all quite well-known, thanks largely to the work of scholars in the past decade.

There is, unfortunately, no univocal reading of this mass of biographical evidence, for Heidegger's relationship to religion, though intimate, was ambivalent. The new direction taken by Heidegger in philosophy immediately following the First World War corresponded to a painful break with his Catholic faith.[2] At nearly the same time, Heidegger began to invoke the "atheism" of philosophy (e.g., G61 197). Near the end of his tenure at Marburg, Heidegger stressed to his friend Elisabeth Blochmann that "[r]eligion is a basic possibility of human existence of a completely different sort than philosophy" (HB 25). In this same letter, Heidegger at one and the same time describes his theological period at Marburg as a thing of the past while admitting that he has not achieved the proper standpoint from which this issue can be adequately investigated.

In the 1930s, Heidegger's interpretive efforts were directed much more frequently at Nietzsche, Hölderlin, and the pre-Socratics than at Luther or the New Testament. Yet during this same period, Heidegger often spent weeks in retreat at the Benedictine monastery of Beuron, not far from his hometown (see HB 31f., 40f.). Beginning in WS 1934–1935, Heidegger also begins a decades-long engagement with Hölderlin's poetry, in which the latter's religious discourse, and religious conception of the poetic vocation, plays a large role (see G39). In an unpublished text from the late 1930s, Heidegger offers his most lengthy reflections on matters of divinity since his WS 1920–1921 lectures on Paul, while at the same time sharply criticizing the "Jewish-Christian" conception of God (G66 225–256). In another text from this same period, one finds Heidegger offering the following observations about his own work:

> But who could deny that a confrontation with Christianity discreetly accompanied the whole path up to this point?—A confrontation which was not and is not some "problem" that was latched onto, but rather at *once* the preservation [*Wahrung*] of my own origin—of the parental house, homeland, and youth—and a painful separation from it. Only someone thus rooted in a really vital Catholic world could have an inkling of the necessities that exerted an effect on the path of my questioning up to this point like subterranean earthquakes. (G66 415)

Not surprisingly, the evaluations of Heidegger's "religious dimension" reflect the ambiguities of the matter. Some of the earliest scholars to receive Heidegger's work in the English-speaking world were theologians, most of whom tended to give a narrowly theological reading of Heidegger in which "Being" was equated with God. A version of this reductive tendency that is less sympathetic to Heidegger can be seen in the commentaries of his students Karl Löwith and Hans Jonas, who read Heidegger's philosophy in a critical vein as crypto-Christianity or crypto-Gnosticism.[3] The problem with these readings lies precisely in their *reductive* quality. They fail to do justice to the ambiguities of Heidegger's life and thought, to the balance between resistance to and enthusiasm for religion and theology. Such a reduction also manifestly falsifies the sheer breadth of Heidegger's work, the variety of (non-religious) influences on it, and, most importantly, his virtual silence on obviously theological issues of a systematic nature (e.g., Trinity, soteriology, etc.).

Among more sympathetic readers, a kind of "disciplinary" explanation has been offered for the ambiguities of Heidegger's biography. Some commentators recognize the impact of Christian religiosity on Heidegger's philosophy, yet are faced with the challenge of Heidegger's silence on many theological questions and of his insistence on the incommensurability of philosophy and theology. Commentators as diverse as Rudolf Bultmann and Jeffrey Barash maintain that this situation can be explained with reference to Heidegger's starting point in "philosophy" as opposed to "theology."[4]

While this is certainly an improvement over the reductive approach, the terms of this explanation remain unclarified. What is to be understood by the alleged distinction between "philosophy" and "theology"? Is this simply an institutional or sociological distinction? If so, does it rule out a more genuinely philosophical or doxographical explanation of Heidegger's "religious dimension"? Surely not, especially since Heidegger himself regarded the interpenetration of philosophy and theology to be a philosophical issue of paramount importance. Is the distinction between "philosophy" and "theology" a more substantive one, perhaps along the lines of the traditional distinction between reason and faith? If this is indeed the case, then this explanation is even more problematic, for it fails to include an adequate account of what *Heidegger* took to be the substance of the distinction between philosophy and theology.[5]

One might be tempted at this point to relegate this entire issue to the realm of *biography* rather than *philosophy*. Indeed, some of the best evidence for Heidegger's "religious dimension" comes not from his published works or lecture courses, but from the facts of his education.[6] This move is, however, out of keeping with the philosophical significance that Heidegger himself attached to this "religious dimension," as the quote at the beginning of this chapter indicates. The project of finding a *philosophical* answer to the question of the "religious dimension" remains important.

Among recent commentators, there are several who have gone the farthest toward providing such an answer: John Van Buren, Theodore Kisiel, and István Fehér. Fehér approaches the issue through Heidegger's self-interpretation as a philosopher, arguing that Heidegger "transposes" a specific interpretation of theology onto the "level of philosophy."[7] That is, his very conception of what it means to do philosophy rests upon a view about what it means to do theology. The nature of this antecedent interpretation of theology can be seen clearly in Heidegger's 1927 essay "Phenomenology and Theology" (G9 45–78/39–62). What Fehér establishes is that there are substantive doxographical issues involved in the question of Heidegger's "religious dimension."

Van Buren's *The Young Heidegger: Rumor of the Hidden King* provides a detailed treatment of Heidegger's theological interests. Most of the facts of the case are also presented by Theodore Kisiel in *The Genesis of Heidegger's Being and Time*. Heidegger was of the opinion that a unique intellectual breakthrough had occurred in early Christianity and that it was subsequently concealed by the importation of Greek metaphysics by the Fathers.[8] Heidegger was an avid reader of thinkers like Meister Eckhart, Luther, and Kierkegaard, whom he regarded as men who had revived the spirit of original Christianity.[9] Van Buren describes the results in this way:

> He took the Christian experience of such realities as mystery, Parousia, Kairos, wakefulness, and falling to be a specific "ontic" model from which to read off and formalize general and ontically noncommittal "ontological" categories that would make up his new beginning for phenomenological ontology.[10]

As Van Buren convincingly argues, it was an important part of Heidegger's project to "save" this original Christianity from its subsequent falsification.[11] He describes Heidegger's work as a "creative reinscription" of the basic "intentional configuration" of primal Christianity as the basis for a new kind of "metaphysics."[12] According to Van Buren, Heidegger's famous critique of the metaphysical tradition was self-consciously modeled on its earlier foes, such as Luther and Kierkegaard.[13]

As for the more negative side of Heidegger's relation to Christianity, Van Buren and Kisiel are also in agreement. Van Buren argues that Heidegger eventually came to abandon his earlier project of retrieving original Christianity, turning instead to the "Greco-German axis" of the pre-Socratics, Nietzsche, and Hölderlin.[14] Kisiel locates Heidegger's break with Christianity much earlier, around 1922, and argues that Heidegger's interest in religion was always really "philosophical."[15] While Van Buren seems to lament Heidegger's turn away from original Christianity, Kisiel seems to view Heidegger's "Christian" period as a time well-lost, and as one that impairs the alleged universality of Heidegger's fundamental ontology.[16]

While both Van Buren and Kisiel have shed some much-needed light on Heidegger's "theological origin," their accounts need to be modified in several important respects. First of all, nothing that Heidegger says clearly indicates that he wanted to give a formal or "neutral" version of Christian faith, one acceptable to "mere reason," in the way that previous philosophers like Kant or Hegel had. To the contrary, Heidegger seems to have rejected the traditional notion of "objectivity" altogether, along with the companion idea that there are timeless truths of reason. He denounces both the paradigmatic status of timeless and dispassionate mathematics for philosophy, as well as the widespread "demand for observation which is free of standpoints" (G63 72/56, 82/63).[17]

Thus there is no indication from Heidegger that his interests in early Christianity were purely "philosophical," as this view suggests. Nor is there any reason to think that Heidegger's aim was to articulate some sort of universal philosophical religion, or that he was skeptical about the core doctrines of Christianity.[18] For example, in a 1951 seminar, Heidegger tells a questioner that faith has no need of philosophy (G15 435f.). Indeed, unlike Kant, Heidegger never once objects to Christianity on *epistemic* grounds. His occasional denunciations of "religious ideology and fantasy" and "fanaticism" are not suggestive of some more global doubt about the rationality of religious belief. Indeed, such denunciations are fully compatible with a robust Christian faith.[19]

Heidegger's outspoken critiques of religion and theology are always aimed at narrow confessionalism and at an "inauthentic" faith that dodges tough questions (e.g., G40 5f., 80, 132). In a letter to Heinrich Rickert dated February 27, 1917, during a period recognized as lying prior to his "break" with Christianity, Heidegger claims never to have aligned himself with the "narrow [*engen*]" Roman Catholic standpoint, and to profess a more liberal "free Christianity" (HR 42). As in his earliest period, Heidegger continued to maintain later that theology, as it has developed throughout the course of European civilization, was infused with metaphysical assumptions that are fundamentally opposed to the spirit of original Christianity (G65 411; G67 155). Such claims certainly imply a rejection of theology *in its present form*, but are completely consistent with an attempt to provide a new philosophical ground-work for the conceptual articulation of faith. Heidegger himself clarifies the situation in a 1943 essay on Nietzsche:

> For Nietzsche, Christianity is the historical, secular-political phenomenon of the Church and its claim to power within the formation of Western humanity and its modern culture. Christianity in this sense and the Chris-tian life of the New Testament faith are not the same. [. . .] a Christian life is not necessarily in need of Christianity. Therefore, a confrontation with Christianity is by no means an absolute battle against what is Christian, no more than a critique of theology is a critique of the faith for which theology is supposed to be the interpretation. (G5 219f./164)

Further, in his *Letter on Humanism* of 1947, Heidegger discusses the religious and theological import of his inquiries into being in a way strongly reminiscent of his views in the early 1920s, though in different language (G9 161/252f., 169/258). In 1951, he told participants in a seminar that he was still "inclined" to write a theology, and that were he to do so, he would purge it of the taint of metaphysics (G15 436).

Van Buren's thesis that Heidegger sought a "retrieval" of original Chris-tianity must be extended beyond the early 1920s to encompass the whole of his career. A further question lingers, however. Given that this thesis is a sustain-able one, what does it mean to "save" primitive Christianity? This question becomes more urgent when one turns to the work of Heidegger's colleague Rudolf Bultmann. Bultmann's theology of "de-mythologizing" the New Testa-ment proclamation is aimed at a reassertion of original Christianity in lan-guage that can be appropriated by citizens of a post-Enlightenment world. Criticisms notwithstanding, Bultmann's work preserves some of the essential doctrinal content of historical Christianity, such as the resurrection and justifi-cation by faith.[20] If Bultmann's work is taken as a model for "saving" primitive Christianity, then it is hard to see how this project can be genuinely ascribed to Heidegger. One searches in vain for anything like the doctrines of traditional Christianity in Heidegger's thought.

Heidegger's project of "saving" primitive Christianity was not something that could be recognized as being part of the traditional theological disciplines of dogmatics and apologetics. Indeed, Heidegger's understanding of the "athe-ism" of philosophy signifies that a philosopher, even as a Christian philoso-pher, simply cannot proclaim a "world-view." Furthermore, the historical in-terpenetration of metaphysics and theology led Heidegger to be extremely reticent about speaking as a "theologian." What Heidegger's project amounts to is a critique of what he called "onto-theology" that points the way to the experience of faith.[21]

During WS 1921–1922, Heidegger records some thoughts "on introduction [*zur Einleitung*]" (G61 197/148). The core of his philosophical approach is the "actualization of questionability," not in the sense of arid skepticism, but in such a way that "it alone might lead to a situation of religious decision" (G61 197/148). To "save" Christianity, for Heidegger, is not to defend or to clarify the dogmas of a historical faith, but rather to lead into [*einleiten*] the experience that is and remains the essence of religion. If Heidegger's work does not belong to dogmatics or to apologetics, perhaps one could say that it is a sort of "homiletics."

Ultimately, however, Heidegger appears to have been convinced that philosophy alone could not decide the issue. That is, one cannot *reason* one's way to faith. Instead, faith as the acknowledgment of revealed truths provides what Jeffrey Stout has called a "context of reasons" *within which* the intellectual endeavors of theology can be carried out.[22] On Heidegger's view, Christian life only gets under way with the reception of the "proclamation" (G60 116). In a deep sense, then, Christianity is an achievement that is beyond the power of human beings (G60 122). The "proclamation" is the message of the "cross," or of the "crucified God" (G60 144). Heidegger's gloss on Galatians 5:11 is especially revealing with respect to his views on this issue: "*to skandalon tou staurou:* That is the authentic foundation of Christianity, *in the face of which there is only faith or unbelief*" (G60 71, emphasis added).

Scholars have shown that the ideas and experiences of original Christianity were of decisive importance for the development of Heidegger's thought. Let us, then, take the old Heidegger seriously when he says, "Without this theological origin I would have never arrived at the path of thinking." What is distinctive about this path of thinking, and in what sense can it be said to have originated in theology? In asking this question, one must put aside biography for a moment (it is, after all, obvious that Heidegger began to study philosophy in seminary) and search for a philosophical sense of the word "origin." My contention is that such a sense can be discerned in Heidegger's hermeneutical methodology. Heidegger asserts at numerous points that his investigations always take their point of departure from life as it is concretely lived. It is here that primitive Christianity becomes Heidegger's philosophical "origin."

Heidegger's Project

In this section, I will explain in general terms Heidegger's philosophical project and his chosen methodology. This methodology is not a technical calculus for generating truths, but it is nevertheless an identifiable practice that Heidegger not only engages in but also explains in considerable detail. The method belongs to a "hermeneutics of facticity," i.e., an attempt to articulate the immediate, pre-conceptual meaningfulness of human life. This articulation begins with what Heidegger calls a "basic experience [*Grunderfahrung*]," a sense of life as a whole that allows one to gain a purchase on the phenomena. Though Heidegger maintains that everyday existence can yield such "basic experiences," he is nevertheless committed to the view that primitive Christianity is a paradigmatic instance.

Hermeneutics of Factical Life-Experience

By all accounts, Heidegger found his philosophical voice during the War Emergency Semester of 1919.[23] It was here that he began the break with the synthesis of neo-Kantianism and scholasticism that had defined his earliest work. Before an audience of recently returned war veterans, Heidegger enacts a quest for a science of the "pre-theoretical" sphere of life (G56/57 74–76). The problem Heidegger faces is how to avoid the "de-historicizing" deformations that seem to inevitably stalk attempts at grasping life in a scientific fashion (G56/57 89). How, Heidegger asks, can philosophy achieve a genuine "sympathy for life [Lebenssympathie] (G56/57 110)"? Heidegger gives his answer at the end of the course:

> The gripping [bemächtigende] experiencing of lived experience that takes itself along is the understanding intuition, the hermeneutical intuition, the originary phenomenological back-and-forth formation of concepts from which all theoretical objectification, indeed every transcendental positing, falls out. (G56/57 117/99)

"Hermeneutical intuition" is the name of the method Heidegger proposes for articulating the immediate sense of life without theoretical distortion. The "intuition" of concrete, lived experience is not carried out from a third-person perspective, but is itself supposed to be a kind of lived experience. Articulate philosophical ideas arise out of this experience, rather than being imposed upon the stream of life "from above." In this way the procedure is hermeneutical. Heidegger hopes to avoid what he calls "transcendental positing," i.e., the attempt to explain the lived immediacy of life by means of a priori concepts. This is why he calls his method hermeneutical intuition. He has no interest in the constructions of transcendental philosophy. Rather, he wants to "read" life, to let it speak for itself, as it were, and to articulate the sense immanent to it.

In the following semester (SS 1919), Heidegger first names his style of philosophy "phenomenological hermeneutics" (G56/57 131). A contemporaneous remark from Heidegger's projected course on medieval mysticism helps to concretize this method of research:

> The analysis, i.e. hermeneutics, works within the historical I. Life is already there as religious. It is not such as a natural consciousness of a subject matter might analyze; rather, the specific determination of sense is attended to [herauszuhören] in everything. Problem: intuitive eidetics is, as hermeneutical, never theoretically neutral, but itself only has "eidetically" [illegible words follow] the vibration [Schwingung] of a genuine life-world. (G60 336)

The character of Heidegger's hermeneutics emerges quite clearly in this remark. In a concrete investigation, one takes up what is given in life as a starting point. Each "life-world," or specific, concrete form of life in general, has its own "determination of sense." Heidegger's conviction is that ordinary human life has meaning and that this meaning is not *conceptual*. The passage quoted here clearly illustrates this idea. A hermeneutics of religious life starts with life as *already* religious. Religious life is itself structured by an autonomous web of practices and beliefs that provide its specifically "religious" sense. The task, then, is to make this sense *explicit*. In the long passage quoted above, Heidegger expresses a degree of reticence about the Husserlian notion of phenomenology as an "eidetic" discipline, i.e., one that defines the transcendental "forms [eidē]" of pure consciousness. For Heidegger, there just is no such pure consciousness, except as an abstraction motivated by a theoretical bias. Instead, there is only the "historical I," the finite, historically conditioned, immediately meaningful perspective "behind" which one cannot go.

Heidegger gives voice to this basic conviction quite early, during KNS 1919: "Life as such is *not* irrational (which has nothing whatever to do with 'rationalism'!)" (G56/57 219/187). Or, as he puts it in supplementary remarks during the winter semester of 1919–1920, "Life is not a chaotic confusion of dark torrents, not a mute principle of power, not a limitless, all-consuming disorder, rather *it is what it is only as a concrete meaningful shape*" (G58 148). Yet in order to arrive at an explicit understanding of this "sense," one cannot simply "observe" a life-world from a theoretically neutral standpoint. On the contrary, "hermeneutics," Heidegger says, "works within the historical I." This is a matter of "sympathetically" following along with concrete life-experience, allowing it to speak for itself and formalizing categories only after having heard what it says.

It is easy to mistake what Heidegger is trying to accomplish here. The best way to avoid such a mistake is to get clear about how his project differs from what has traditionally been called "metaphysics." This term can be understood in two ways: (1) a pre-Kantian or "pre-critical" sense, according to which concepts have a purchase on objective reality; (2) a post-Kantian or post-critical sense, according to which concepts have a purchase on the *a priori* conditions for objective knowledge. In both cases, the goal is to construct, through theoretical reason, an all-embracing explanatory framework. For a pre-critical metaphysician like Descartes, our metaphysical concepts (e.g., "substance") pick out the fundamental structures of reality, which in turn make up the deep explanatory ground for reality as a whole. For a post-critical metaphysician like Kant, our concepts tell us about how rational beings *must* think about the world in order to have objective knowledge of the whole of reality.

A look at Heidegger's remarks throughout the early 1920s reveals that his own project has nothing whatsoever to do with either kind of metaphysics. A letter to Karl Jaspers dated June 27, 1922, reveals Heidegger's attempt to differentiate his project from both varieties of traditional metaphysics. "The old ontology (and the categorial structure that emerges from it) must be rebuilt from the ground up [. . .]" (HJ 27). This has nothing to do with resurrecting Greek metaphysics, or with some kind of antiquarian eulogy on the grandeur of Greek thought. "What is required is a critique of ontology up till now, in its roots in Greek philosophy, in particular in Aristotle, whose ontology (already this concept is not suitable) is just as much alive in Kant and Hegel as in medieval Scholasticism" (Ibid.). True to his word on this point, Heidegger spends most of the rest of his life in successive confrontations with metaphysics in all its forms, with Aristotle as well as with Kant.

During the early 1920s, Heidegger was particularly occupied with neo-Kantianism. The work of philosophers like Wilhelm Windelband and Heinrich Rickert dominated the German intellectual scene. In the summer semester of 1919, Heidegger devotes considerable space to the "critical" neo-Kantian understanding of the "categories" (G56/57 160f./135). For Windelband and Rickert, despite their other differences, a "category" is a "synthetic form of consciousness" (G56/57 160/136). These "categories," along with the synthesizing consciousness itself, form the bedrock of explanation in neo-Kantian theories of knowledge. Rickert, in particular, maintains that reality is an irrational continuum of individuals that can only be understood when it is conceptually grasped (G56/57 171f./145). Heidegger also devotes considerable attention to the neo-Kantian position in the summer semester of 1920. Again, "categories" are the forms under which sensibly given material is synthesized by the spontaneity of the understanding (G59 25). Everything that is "known," whether scientifically or on the more primitive level of "natural knowledge," is made up of material that has been "formed" by "rules" built into the understanding (G59 25).

According to Heidegger, the link between the post-critical work of the neo-Kantians with the pre-critical thought of Aristotle and Descartes is the dominance of the "theoretical attitude." Beginning in the War Emergency Semester of 1919, Heidegger traces out the genesis of this "theoretical attitude" through the "de-vivification" of the immediate lived experience of the world (G56/57 73f./61). "De-vivification [*Ent-leben*]" is Heidegger's term for the process in which the immediate involvement of human beings in the world is gradually reduced to the point at which it has been transformed into mere "looking," i.e., detached observation. Heidegger illustrates this with the example of entering a classroom and looking at the lectern. When he himself enters the room, he does not see "sense-data" that has been conceptually synthesized. Instead, he sees a particular object that is intelligible to him by virtue of its place within a web of practical relationships. For example, it appears to him as the place from which he is to speak, but which is too high for him (Heidegger was a relatively short man). He tries to get his students to examine their own immediate experience of the lectern as well, and he imagines what it would be like to a farmer from the Black Forest or a native from Senegal. The meaning the lectern has is, Heidegger concludes, not *concep-*

tual, but instead rests upon the concrete relationships that permeate human experience on the most immediate level.

The "theoretical attitude," by abstracting away from this immediate "environmental experience," is forced to reconstruct it by appeal to the synthetic activity of concepts on raw "sense-data." The privileging of this attitude ultimately leads to what he regards as an "obsession" with "explanation through dismemberment" (G56/57 88/74). The privileging of the "theoretical attitude" is the all-pervasive characteristic of Western philosophy. On this assumption, all knowing is taken to be *conceptual* knowing. Concepts either grasp the objective nature of things (pre-critical metaphysics) or they capture the necessary structures of the "spontaneity" of the understanding.

The philosophical project that Heidegger assigns to himself is one of *articulating* or making explicit the structure of this immediate, meaning-laden experience of the world. "The understanding of life," Heidegger tells us, "is *hermeneutical intuition* (making intelligible, giving meaning)" (G56/57 219/187). Several semesters later, he characterizes the project as one of bringing "to light [*zu Tage*]," "exhibiting [*am Tage*]," or placing "into the light of day [*Täglichkeit*]" the "categories" that are "*alive in life itself* in an original way" (G61 62/47; 88/66). These "categories" that Heidegger is after are neither the objective features of reality as it is cognized (Aristotle, Descartes), nor are they the *a priori* forms of understanding (Kant). They are not "concepts" that are imposed upon "sense-data" by the spontaneity of the understanding in order to yield objective knowledge, but are the structures and relations that constitute our most immediate experience of the world as meaningful.

Heidegger articulated many of these ideas in an essay written between 1919 and 1922, which was meant to be a critical review of Karl Jaspers's recent book *Psychology of Worldviews*. As he would continue to do throughout his career, Heidegger here attributes the first "breakthrough" in phenomenology to Husserl's *Logical Investigations* (G9 34–5/30). He is, however, critical of the "theoretical" orientation of Husserl's work.[24] On Heidegger's view, to carry the phenomenological program to its completion, it is not enough to simply extend Husserl's methodology into other realms of experience such as art or religion. "Rather, we need to see that experiencing in its fullest sense is to be found in its authentically factical context of enactment in the historically existing self" (G9 35/30). Heidegger goes on to describe the "method" that accords with the basic character of life-experience as "the method belonging to our interpretive, historically enacted explication of concrete and fundamental experiential modes of having-oneself in a factically and anxiously concerned manner" (G9 36/31). The interpretation of life-experience is "historically enacted"; it is a peculiar way life-experience "has" itself as an object.

Heidegger means to draw a contrast here between the quietist theoretical perspective that he regards as the hallmark of Western metaphysics since its inception in Greek thought and the kind of "knowing" that is actively engaged in the historical unfolding of its object. In hermeneutics, life-experience is not an "object" that stands over against a cognizing subject. As Heidegger puts it in his famous "Aristotle Introduction" from 1922, this sort of "fundamental research" is "the *phenomenological hermeneutics* of facticity," in which the genitive is to be read both *objectively* and *subjectively* (NB 16/121). That is to say that hermeneutics is *about* life-experience *and* belongs to it. Hermeneutics is the lived experience of lived experience.

Hermeneutics as such forms one of the central themes of Heidegger's lecture course during the summer semester of 1923, entitled "Ontology: The Hermeneutics of Facticity." Here he gives the following "definition" of hermeneutics: "a definite unity in the actualizing [*Vollzugs*] . . . of the *interpreting of facticity* in which facticity is being encountered, seen, grasped, and expressed in concepts" (G63 14/11).[25] Heidegger's method is, put simply, the conceptual articulation of life-experience by life-experience itself. A bit later in the text of this lecture course Heidegger presents a kind of prospectus of the ultimate goal or success condition for a hermeneutical investigation:

> Hermeneutics has the task of making the Dasein which is in each case our own accessible to this Dasein itself with regard to the character of its being, communicating Dasein to itself in this regard, hunting down the alienation from itself with which it is smitten. In hermeneutics what is developed for Dasein is a possibility of its becoming and being for itself in the manner of an *understanding* of itself. (G63 15/11)

Hermeneutics is seamlessly intertwined with facticity itself, in that it helps bring to fruition the tendency of facticity to understand itself and to discourse about itself.[26] It seeks to do so in a way that does not involve the imposition of some conceptual framework "from above," which only serves to alienate facticity from itself (G63 15/12). In the final analysis, hermeneutics is successful if it makes an articulate self-understanding possible. Whether or not it gives us a theory that can be usefully applied to every area of inquiry is not what is ultimately at issue. Thus, Heidegger asserts, "Hermeneutics is itself not philosophy" (G63 20/16). It does, however, bear a kinship to "philosophy" as it has been known traditionally in that it seeks the categorial structures of a particular subject matter [*Sache*]. It is still "ontology" (NB 16/121), even to the point of being "fundamental ontology" (SZ 13 f.). Heidegger nevertheless recognizes a certain strangeness about his work in comparison with the philosophical tradition. He writes:

> I think that hermeneutics is not philosophy at all, but in fact something preliminary which runs in advance [*Vorläufiges*] of it and has its own reason for being: what is at issue in it, what it all comes to, is not to become finished with it as quickly as possible, but rather to hold out in it as long as possible. (G63 19/15)

The Hermeneutic Circle

What can Heidegger's method tell us about the philosophical importance of religion in his thought? In order to arrive at a clear answer to this question, it is necessary to probe more deeply into the nature of his hermeneutics. Hermeneutics is a particular way of carrying out what Heidegger calls *understanding* [*Verstehen*]. By this, Heidegger does not mean cognitive activity in general, but rather a more basic disclosure of a human being's "ability to be [*Seinkönnen*]" (SZ 144). Heidegger's point is that the things we encounter in any of our activities take on a certain significance, a kind of ground-level intelligibility, as a result of our prior "projection [*Entwurf*]" of some possibility or other, be it a career, a momentary project, or some grander vision of the purpose of human life as such. On the basis of this projected significance, we can then develop more explicit kinds of understanding in which we actually express and conceptualize the things in question (SZ 148 ff./188 ff.). It is this explicit articulation of what has already been opened up for us in understanding that Heidegger calls "interpretation [*Auslegung*]" (SZ 148/188).

To say that "having an understanding" is an "ontological" feature of human life is simply to say that life is always already meaningful, even at its most immediate level. This primary meaning is, according to Heidegger, available to us in our knowing our way about the world, rather than in any explicit knowing *about* the world. To "understand," in this sense, is to be familiar with a pre-reflective context of practical relations and linguistic usages. To "interpret," then, is to make this context, or rather some aspect of it, *explicit*. Heidegger maintains that this can occur through simply engaging in some activity, and so wordlessly "articulating" our pre-reflective understanding of the world. Alternatively, interpretation may involve actually *saying something* about the world as refracted by this immediate context of meaning. Philosophical hermeneutics is an activity of interpretation in this latter sense.

It is against the background of these claims that the nature of Heidegger's hermeneutics can be brought into more precise relief. According to Heidegger, interpretation is only possible on the basis of "pre-intention [*Vormeinung*]," a kind of antecedent familiarity with a given object or situation.[27] This point is made in numerous places throughout Heidegger's works, and it gradually reaches its most developed and articulate form in *Being and Time*. One of the earliest applications of this theory to hermeneutics can be found in Heidegger's review of Jaspers's book.[28] Much of Heidegger's review is devoted to uncovering the assumptions that guide Jaspers's investigations. This project is predicated on a more general view about the role that background assumptions play in human understanding:

> What these problems indicate and lead us to acknowledge is that preconceptions "are" at work "everywhere" in the factical experience of life (and therefore also in the sciences and in philosophizing), and that what we need

> to do is simply, as it were, join in the experience [*mitzuerfahren*] of these
> preconceptions wherever they operate, as they do, for example, in providing
> direction for any fundamental type of knowledge about something. (G9 9/8)

Here Heidegger celebrates what he eventually comes to call the "herme-neutical circle." On his view, all intellectual inquiry operates with some pre-suppositions. Indeed, it is precisely these presuppositions that open up the possibility for achieving the conceptual articulation of a subject matter. It is only when one tries to ignore one's own presuppositions, or when they turn out to be inadequate to the subject matter at hand, that this circularity becomes a definite problem. There is no way, on his view, for one to stand outside of the circle, to light upon some presuppositionless starting point for theorizing, or to find the final "justification" for a given theory. What can, and should, be done is that presuppositions should be questioned, modified, or abandoned if what results from them either fails to "ring true" or else breaks down on some other level.

Heidegger not only highlights the inevitability of presuppositions, but he also counsels their *cultivation*. A cautious investigator will always explicitly articulate the assumptions that guide her inquiry. If she follows Heidegger's recommendations, she should "project" or "sketch out in advance" a general picture of the subject matter under consideration. This initial "projection" is not fixed or final, but is instead a wholly revisable *hypothesis* about the mean-ing of that which is to be investigated. Heidegger contends that this initial hermeneutical hypothesis must, on pain of being arbitrary, have its roots in an actual familiarity with the subject matter. He calls this initial familiarity a "fore-having" or "having in advance [*Vor-haben*]." This is the "bedrock" of an interpretation. This ground-level familiarity is what allows one to be confident that the more general hermeneutical hypothesis is not arbitrary.

In hermeneutics of facticity, as in any other interpretation, one must secure an initial purchase on the phenomenon in question. This is something that is "constitutive—and indeed in a decisive manner—of interpretation" (G63 16/13). Heidegger quotes a passage from Kierkegaard's journals as a kind of graphic illustration of his claim about the necessity of a fore-having: " 'Life can be interpreted only after is has been lived, just as Christ did not begin to explain the Scriptures and show how they taught of him until after he was resurrected' " (quoted at G63 16–17/13).

In *Being and Time*, Heidegger also addresses the charge of "circularity" that might be leveled against this picture of human epistemic activity. For Heidegger, this is motivated by a desire to maintain a pre-existing ideal of knowledge at all costs, regardless of the "facts" of the case (SZ 153/195). For Heidegger, "[w]hat is decisive is not to get out of the circle but to come into it in the right way" (SZ 153/195). Indeed, the attempt to escape the circle amounts to a denial of a basic ontological feature of human existence. Instead, one must realize, says Heidegger, that it is precisely this "circle" itself that makes explicit understanding possible. He then adds suggestively, "In the circle is hidden a positive possibility of the most primordial kind of knowing" (SZ 153/195).[29] The circle of understanding does not present an impediment to philosophical knowledge, provided it is entered into in the appropriate way. This means that the "pre-intention" of a given interpretation must not "be presented to us by fancies and popular conceptions, but rather . . . in terms of the things themselves" (SZ 153/195). This is precisely where the "fore-having" is supposed to help. A hermeneutical hypothesis not grounded in the "things themselves" risks swinging free of them, i.e., it risks being uprooted from any connection with the matter under consideration.

"Basic Experience [*Grunderfahrung*]"

Later in *Being and Time*, Heidegger suggests how this kind of "pre-intention" might be secured. Heidegger argues that it must be secured "in a basic experience [*Grunderfahrung*] of the 'object' to be disclosed, and in terms of such an experience" (SZ 232/275). This is where Heidegger's project of giving a "fundamental ontology" links up with a fundamentally *practical* concern with *authenticity*. Heidegger asserts that "authenticity," a way of being a self (see chapter 6), is a "presupposition" for phenomenological investigation:

> But does not a definite ontic interpretation of authentic existence, a factical ideal of Dasein, underlie our ontological interpretation of the existence of Dasein? Indeed. But not only is this fact one that must not be denied and we are forced to grant; it must be understood in its *positive necessity*, in terms of the thematic object of our inquiry. Philosophy will never seek to deny its "presuppositions," but neither may it merely admit them. It conceives them and develops with more and more penetration both the presuppositions themselves and that for which they are presuppositions. (SZ 310/358)[30]

In what sense can "authenticity" be said to form a "presupposition"? Clearly not in the sense that it is a principle or a proposition from which other propositions are derived *more geometrico*. Authenticity is the kind of presupposition that belongs to a hermeneutics *of* facticity, i.e., it is a concrete experience that provides the hermeneutician with a purchase on the phenomenon that is to be interpreted; it is, Heidegger says, an "understanding projection" (SZ 314/362). Authenticity, then, is an experience of human life that allows for the phenomenologist to get an immediate, pre-theoretical purchase on it. Heidegger's hope is that once this has been accomplished, the hypothesis or set of hypotheses that guides his interpretation will reflect an actual familiarity with his subject matter. The key, then, to getting the proper "fore-having" in place is locating the right "basic experience."

The notion of a "basic experience" is by no means new to Heidegger's thought with its appearance in *Being and Time*. The idea that life contains moments that, despite their rarity and strangeness, provide insight into the basic character of life is one that can be called Heidegger's most fundamental assumption.[31] It emerges clearly time and again in his correspondence and in his lectures. Perhaps one of the earliest and most interesting statements of this view occurs in Heidegger's letter to Elisabeth Blochmann of May 1, 1919. Here, he talks about "graced moments" of life, which are not simply there for our aesthetic enjoyment, but rather present an opportunity to bring our lives as a whole into focus (HB 14). These "graced moments" are "basic experiences" in which "we feel ourselves belonging immediately to the direction in which we live," experiences of "understanding having-of-oneself [*verstehende Sichselbsthaben*]" (HB 14).

More concretely, Heidegger tells Blochmann that he is especially thinking of her "clear commitment [*Verhaftetsein*] in scientific work" (HB 14).[32] Heidegger has in mind those moments when we have a special sense of who we are, where our life is going, what we want to make of ourselves, or, more colloquially, of the "meaning of life." It is vital that these are moments of "understanding," not of vague sentimentality. These are moments of explicit familiarity with our own lives, which Heidegger takes to be promising points of departure for a hermeneutics of facticity.

In a contemporaneous lecture course, Heidegger also describes the "intensities" or "intensifications" of life as opportunities for getting a purchase on the structure of the "I-self, the 'historical I'" (G56/57 208/175).[33] According to Oskar Becker's transcript of this lecture course, Heidegger is interested in avoiding the "'de-historicization of the I'" and cultivating a "primordial science" (G56/57 206/174, 207/145). One key element in this lies in attending to "genuine life-experiences" (G56/57 207/175). Presumably, it is in these experiences that one gains a kind of understanding access to the living, historical "I" without "objectifying" it. Heidegger's suggestion is that such phenomena grant the phenomenologist a unique window into the structure of life.

During the following semester, WS 1919–1920, Heidegger returns to these ideas once more. A recurring question in this lecture course concerns the grasping of an "experiential ground" for a "primal science of life in and for itself" (G58 80). In every science, including phenomenology, the object of research must be "pre-given" in a pre-scientific fashion (G58 70, 76, 79, etc.). Phenomenology must take its point of departure from life itself, not from some limited "extract" of life (G58 79). Accordingly, it is crucial to secure a "basic motivational experience" as way of preparing the "experiential ground" for phenomenological research (G58 94–95). Heidegger identifies this "basic experience" as the "experience of the self-world" in its "standing out [*Abgehobenheit*]" (G58 101). This is a *special style* of experience (G58 101).

This "style" of experience is one that occasionally emerges in our daily activities (G58 33). Indeed, Heidegger describes these "fleeting" encounters with ourselves through some concrete examples, such as hiking in the woods, listening to a broken clock-tower, and regretfully reflecting on some careless remarks (G58 96–97). In certain cases, "factical life 'can' be centered in an especially accented way on the self-world" (G58 57). Heidegger goes on to designate this phenomenon as the "intensifying concentration [*Zugespitzt-heit*] towards the self-world" (G58 59). In a supplemental remark, Heidegger notes that "this does not take place in a deliberate way, the self does not consciously observe itself, rather it lies in the factical flow [*Ablauf*] of life itself" (G58 206). In other words, moments of intensified reflection on life are *not* necessarily instances of the "theoretical attitude" at work. Heidegger is interested in a more immediate kind of familiarity with life, which, he suggests, can be detected in autobiographies and in religious confessions. It is the task of the phenomenologist to follow up on and interpret the inexplicit "forms of expression" contained in this unique phenomenon. This particular "style" can be seen in significant individuals (Heidegger mentions "artists, scientists, saints"), everyday situations, and in works of literature (G58 85). The task is, of course, to follow up on this, to found a science upon it (G58 86–87).

The precise nature of a "basic experience," and its role within the project of hermeneutics of facticity, receives another treatment in Heidegger's review of Karl Jaspers's *Psychology of Worldviews*. I have already shown how, in this text, Heidegger calls attention to the ubiquity of presuppositions in science and in philosophy. He glosses the relevant presuppositions as "basic experiences [*Grunderfahrungen*]" (G9 3–4/3). Heidegger argues that the "basic experience" that lies at the very roots of Jaspers's theory of human existence is a "basic aesthetic experience [*ästhetische Grunderfahrung*]" (G9 23/20). This "basic experience" is mostly characterized by the "relational sense" that belongs to it, i.e., that of merely "gazing upon something" (G9 23/20). The core of Heidegger's critical review is that the enactment of this kind of experiential foundation ultimately fails to do justice to the "things themselves," in this case, human life. Securing the proper "basic experience" is not a trivial matter, for it is here that one finds the object in question "initially given" (G9 24/21). That is, it is precisely the "basic experience," structured in advance in a definite way, which constitutes the pre-intention of any interpretation.

At this point, Heidegger proposes an alternative "basic experience" as the beginning for a hermeneutics of facticity. We have already met with this possibility as the "highly-strung intensities of life," the "intensifying concentration toward the self-world," and the non-objectifying "having" of the self. Here Heidegger contends that an understanding of the "I" is gained not through theoretical reflection, but rather through "enacting the 'am'" (G9 29/25). Heidegger explicitly designates this kind of "having" of the self as a "basic experience" (G9 29/25). Because it is not a mute intake of "data," this experience is one that can be interrogated, interpreted, and explicated. That is, it is just the kind of thing that grants a hermeneutician the necessary sort of purchase on an object of investigation. Heidegger describes the experience in question as one of "having" the self in an "anxiously concerned" manner (G9 30/26). Heidegger then echoes the comment he made to Blochmann in May 1919:

> It is itself not something extraordinary and removed; rather, it has to be enacted in our factical experience of life as such and appropriated from out of such factical experience. And this is supposed to happen not merely once in a momentary and isolated fashion, but rather again and again in a constant renewal of anxious concern that is of necessity motivated by concern for the self as such, and is moreover oriented in a historical manner. (G9 33/28)

Heidegger goes on to give this "basic experience" the resonant designation "conscience" (G9 28/33). This term is perhaps more familiar from its usage in §§54–60 of *Being and Time*. There Heidegger uses it as a "formal indication" for any experience that interrupts the normal trajectory of an "inauthentic" life, thereby enabling a kind of clear-sighted vocational commitment that he calls "authenticity." I will return to these ideas in more detail in chapters 5 and 6. Here, notice needs to be taken of the role that a certain experience of the self plays in grounding Heidegger's "hermeneutics of facticity." Such an encounter with life must form "the starting point of our approach to philosophical problems" (G9 35/30). For Heidegger, hermeneutics stands or falls with the ability to gain an adequate grasp on this phenomenon in a concrete kind of appropriation. For present purposes, it is clear that Heidegger regards a "basic experience" as the *conditio sine qua non* of phenomenological hermeneutics. It is only by means of the actual enactment of a certain experience that Heidegger hopes to avoid the pitfalls of the traditional approach to understanding human existence as an "object."

Primitive Christianity

The Methodological Role of Primitive Christianity

How does this exposition of Heidegger's methodology provide the basis for a *philosophical* understanding of the "religious dimension" of his thought? The answer lies in the notion of "basic experience" that is so integral to Heidegger's vision of his own philosophical project. Particularly during the earliest period of his work, Heidegger was intrigued by the hermeneutical potential of "primitive Christianity [*Urchristentum*]." Primitive Christianity provided just the kind of "basic experience" that was needed for a radical re-envisioning of philosophy by providing an initial purchase on the phenomenon of life. Moreover, this was a concrete "basic experience" into which Heidegger did not have to artificially insert himself, for he was quite familiar with the "life-world" of faith.

I have chosen to use the phrase "primitive Christianity" here because it was Heidegger's view that the life of the early Christian community, as expressed in the New Testament, was *the* definitive historical form of Christianity. At the same time, he also held that this basic "life-experience" is expressed occasionally during later periods, in the works of Augustine, Bernard of Clairvaux, Luther, the Spanish mystics of the Counter-Reformation period, and Schleiermacher. Since Heidegger seems to have held that all these various historical expressions could be reasonably regarded as expressions of an identifiable life-experience, the phrase "primitive Christianity" can be used to refer to the content of each. Moreover, as I will show (chapter 8), a "life-world" like primitive Christianity is *not* something that lies in an inaccessible past, but rather is a *possibility* that is capable of being creatively re-enacted, and, indeed, has been thus re-enacted already.

It is, of course, certainly true that primitive Christianity was not the only paradigm for a "basic experience" that Heidegger explored in his career, even during the 1920s. Aristotle's practical philosophy, poetry, art, and Kant's ethics all at one time or another found their way into Heidegger's hermeneutical project. In the 1930s and beyond, Heidegger focused his gaze more intently on early Greek philosophy and dramatic poetry, on Nietzsche, and on poets like Hölderlin, Rilke, and Trakl. Even quite early Heidegger is adamant that "[t]he primordial region of philosophy is no final statement, no axiom. It is also not the idea of pure thinking (as intended by H. Cohen and Natorp). It is also nothing mythical or mystical (i.e., only experienceable in a religious way)" (G58 203). Nonetheless, it is the case that life *can* be experienced "in a religious way" and that Heidegger found such experiences of life to be especially significant and interesting. Indeed, "primitive Christianity" has a kind of paradigmatic status for Heidegger, both as a "basic experience" and as an exemplar of what he comes to call an "authentic" way of life (chapter 6). All the same, Heidegger is something of a committed pluralist with respect to the ways valuable insights into human life can be had. Religious experience is by no means the only one that interested him. Nonetheless, the "basic experience" of religious life had the most profound and long-lived effect on his intellectual development. This is precisely what he urges us to consider when he writes, "Without this theological origin I never would have arrived at the path of thinking. Yet, the origin ever remains that which is to come."

Heidegger's lifelong fascination with religious experience is motivated by a variety of commitments. First of all, it is clearly motivated by Heidegger's own deeply held religious beliefs. Heidegger counsels his friend Blochmann that "primal religious experience [*religiösen Urerlebnis*]" must form the basis for all theorizing (HB 10). His letter to Father Krebs, announcing his break with Catholicism, and his letter to Karl Löwith, announcing his self-conception as a "Christian theo-*logian*," all testify to his concrete religious life. In a loose page contained in his manuscript for the lecture course of WS 1921–1922, Heidegger reveals his struggle for a kind of authentic religiosity (G61 197–8/148).

Furthermore, Heidegger's focus on Christian experience is also motivated by his understanding of the cultural history [*Geistesgeschichte*] of European civilization. Time and again he illustrates how the situation of the present times has been decisively shaped by the complex intertwining of Christianity and Greek metaphysics. These reflections take a concrete form in Heidegger's brief "conceptual history [*Begriffsgeschichte*]" of the concepts of "life" and "man" (NB 21ff./125; G63 21–29/17–24). Heidegger often viewed this relation in a negative light, accusing Greek philosophy of a "disfigurement [*Verunstaltung*]" of original Christianity (G59 91).[34] He remarked on the connections between the great period of German Idealism and theology on more than one occasion (G59 95, 141; G61 7/7). Heidegger also makes reference to Wilhelm Dilthey's "theological origins" and comments at length on the significance of this bit of intellectual history (S 151f.). Heidegger seems to have been particularly impressed with Dilthey's work on the "young Hegel," which showed just how deeply Hegel was motivated by theological issues. It is also worth noting here that Heidegger's favorite poetic conversation partner, Hölderlin, shared the same theological milieu as Hegel and Schelling.[35] Heidegger clearly viewed himself as part of this larger tradition of nineteenth-century German philosophy, a tradition that takes seriously the cultural and intellectual significance of Christianity. All of the major figures mentioned and studied by Heidegger from this tradition—Kant, Hegel, Schelling, Nietzsche, Dilthey—struggled to come to terms with the legacy of Christianity or to articulate philosophically defensible versions of it.

It was Heidegger's view that this cultural history impacts contemporary philosophy in ways that are often overlooked. Moreover, consistent with what Heidegger comes to call the "thrownness [*Geworfenheit*]" of human existence in *Being and Time*, it is this cultural history that makes the contemporary situation what it is and makes us who we are. One cannot simply leap out of history, but must instead come to a reckoning with it. This point is born out by Oskar Becker's transcript of Heidegger's concluding remarks on February 25, 1921, during the WS 1920–1921 lectures on Paul:

> Only a *particular* religiosity (for us the Christian) yields the possibility of its philosophical apprehension. Why precisely *Christian* religiosity constitutes the focus of our reflection is a difficult question, which can only be answered by a solution to the problem of our *historical* connections. It is the task of arriving at a *genuine* relationship to history, which is to be explicated from our *own* facticity. The question is what the sense of history can mean for us such that the "objectivity" of the historical "in itself" disappears. For there is a history only when it stems from a present, our present.[36]

Heidegger's claim here is that a constructed *theory* of religion can never provide a genuine foundation for philosophy of religion. Instead, only concrete, historically particular [*jeweilig*] religious *experience* can become the basis for a theory of religion. In this case, the primary reasons for the focus on Christianity are *historical* and *factical*. On the former point, Christianity is part of the history "that we ourselves are." For Heidegger, historical understanding in philosophy has as its chief task the achievement of a self-understanding on the part of historical individuals at a particular time. For Heidegger in the

1920s, it is "our" (European) present, the present shaped by the Greco-Christian tradition, which demands this kind of historical understanding. This is what Heidegger means when he says that "[i]t is the task of arriving at a *genuine* relationship to history." His remark about "our *own* facticity," which calls to mind the previously mentioned letter to Karl Löwith, uncovers the other dimension of Heidegger's interest in "primitive Christianity," i.e., his attempt to appropriate anew the roots of his own concrete, factical life-experience of Christian faith.

It should be clear, then, why *Christianity* is so important for Heidegger's project. The nature of its importance, however, is the crucial point. A letter to Rudolf Bultmann from December 31, 1927, provides a clear confirmation of the role of Christianity as a basic hermeneutical experience.[37] He tells Bultmann that his "ontology" begins with a proper understanding of the "subject," taken as "human Dasein." He points out that "Augustine, Luther, Kierkegaard are *philosophically* essential for the cultivation of a more radical understanding-of-Dasein." The claim here is precisely that primitive Christianity is essential for doing philosophy properly. That is to say, primitive Christianity is the crucial "basic experience" that provides the "fore-having" of hermeneutics.

Heidegger seems to have first gained an intimation of this possibility during the First World War. Around 1917, he was interested in Schleiermacher and the "free Christianity" movement inspired by him.[38] Indeed, he credits Schleiermacher with the rediscovery of primitive Christianity (G56/57 134/114). Theodore Kisiel has painstakingly documented Heidegger's first steps toward taking up Christianity as a "basic experience." Notes from 1917 through 1919 reveal Heidegger's growing interest in primitive Christianity in addition to mysticism, as well as his interest in Paul. Moreover, Heidegger seems to have paid attention to traditional devotional literature during these studies.[39] In a letter to Elisabeth Husserl from April 14, 1919, Heidegger seems to identify an "authentic" life with a religious life of some sort:

> We must again be able to wait and have faith in the grace that is present in every genuine life, with its humility before the inviolability of one's own and other's experience. Our life must be brought back from the dispersion of multiple concerns to its original wellspring of expansive creativity. Not the fragmentation of life into programs, no aestheticizing glosses or genial posturing, but rather the mighty confidence in union with God and original, pure, and effective action. Only life overcomes life, and not matters and things, not even logicized "values" and "norms."[40]

It is in the experience of religious faith, lived with total dedication, that life is "intensified" and brought to a point. It is here that an experience of the self is gained, the sort of experience that, as I have already shown, provides the "fore-having" for Heidegger's radical hermeneutical project. This emerges clearly in the lecture course from WS 1919–1920, "Basic Problems of Phenomenology." One section of this lecture is entitled "Christianity as the historical paradigm for the shift of emphasis of factical life to the self-world" (G58 61). Heidegger articulates his view thus:

> The self-world as such enters into life and is lived as such. What is present in the life of the original Christian community signifies a radical inversion of the direction of the tendency of life—one has in mind particularly world-denial and asceticism (*the thought of the kingdom of God, Paul* (cf. Ritschl)). Herein lives the motive for the development of a totally new context of expression which life itself produces and which we today call *history*. (G58 61)

Heidegger recognizes primitive Christianity as a genuinely unique achievement in the intellectual and cultural history of the Western world. It is here that a new "context of expression" emerges from a total inversion of life's usual tendency. This idea of "inversion" or "counter-movement" will appear again later in connection with Heidegger's conception of authentic existence. As will become clear in subsequent discussions, it is precisely the character of this "basic experience" as a reversal of life's tendency to conceal itself that makes it particularly important for Heidegger's hermeneutical project. Also significant here is Heidegger's revisiting of Dilthey's thesis about the origins of historical consciousness in Christianity. Heidegger places his own particular spin on this thesis, clearly identifying "history" with the life of the self. I will examine Dilthey's views, and their influence on the young Heidegger, in more detail in chapter 5.

Heidegger goes on to argue that this novel achievement was subsequently covered over by the predominance of Aristotle's philosophy in Christian dogmatics and theology.[41] The "inner experiences" and "new attitudes of life" belonging to the earliest era of Christianity were thus "constrained" by Greek ontology (G58 61). Heidegger claims that it is one of the most important tasks of contemporary phenomenology to overcome this process of obfuscation and decline (G58 61). This task is certainly facilitated by historical retrievals of primitive Christianity, including the work of Augustine and the "the practical guidance of life" (G58 62). Heidegger points to "medieval mysticism" here, including Bernard of Clairvaux, Bonaventura, Eckhart, Tauler, and Luther in this movement.[42] He then returns to Augustine, whom he regards as a kind of phenomenological mentor. "*Crede, ut intelligas*: really live your self, and then build knowledge for yourself on this experiential basis, your ultimate, complete experience of self" (G58 62). Later, in the main text of the lecture, one finds Heidegger again discussing a "practical" or "intensified" sense of experience. The latter is simply identified with "religious experience: being troubled or concerned in the innermost self. Not only is what is experienced available, but the self is 'immediately itself' available" (G58 68).

Given Heidegger's position during WS 1919–1920, one should not at all be surprised that he turned to religion explicitly one year later. During WS 1920–1921 and SS 1921, Heidegger delivered his now famous lectures on Paul and Augustine. One important aspect of these lectures is their attempt to get clear about the "basic experience" that Heidegger finds so promising for his hermeneutical project. A few remarks from Heidegger's lectures on Paul will suffice to make this clear. During the course of his discussion of Paul's epistle to the Galatians, Heidegger attempts to pinpoint the experience of "having the self" in Paul's work: "The basic comportment of Paul is to be compared against Philippians 3:13: self-certainty of position in his own life—break in his existence—primordial historical understanding of himself and of his existence" (G60 73–74). Heidegger's position emerges much more clearly later when he presents two preliminary theses that will guide his reading of Paul's letters:

> 1. Primal Christian religiosity lies in factical life-experience. Corollary: it is authentically life-experience itself.
> 2. Factical life-experience is historical. Corollary: Christian experience lives time itself ("live" understood as a *verbum transitivum*). (G60 82)

All of this suffices to show that much of the significance of religion for Heidegger lies in its ability to provide a suitable "fore-having" for the hermeneutics of facticity. In primitive Christianity Heidegger sees a genuine instance of living self-understanding that does not privilege a theoretical relation to the subject matter. Thus, it can provide a starting point for a hermeneutics of facticity that avoids the deformations that, for Heidegger, characterize the vast majority of philosophical inquiries into human existence. This does not, however, exhaust the significance of Christianity in Heidegger's thought. As has already been shown, Heidegger held that the "basic experience" that burst forth onto world history in the first decades of the common era was subsequently obscured and misunderstood. It was one of his projects, during the 1920s, to provide the conceptual tools needed to retrieve this experience, not only for the sake of developing a hermeneutics of facticity, but also for breathing new life into theology. During SS 1920, Heidegger repeatedly remarks that the ultimate terminus of his efforts lies in a renewal of theology (G59 12, 91, 95). The kind of theology that Heidegger envisions here must be a *hermeneutical* one, i.e., one that originates in a "basic experience" and then proceeds to develop an explicit conceptual articulation the "context of expression" contained within it.

Philosophy beneath the Cross

The preceding sections have shown that the significance of religious experience for Heidegger lies in its hermeneutical role. The task faced by the hermeneutician is to secure this "basic experience" and to continually return to it in the development of articulate philosophical expressions. The "basic experience" in question is not some inarticulate reception of sense-data, but rather a concrete way of experiencing one's own life. It is a way of being a self that Heidegger will eventually come to call "authenticity." How, then, can it be secured? In trying to answer this question, Heidegger developed his conception of the nature of philosophy. As István Fehér has suggested, this conception developed in concert with Heidegger's study of theology. Fehér does not, however, provide an account of the specific brand of theology that Heidegger turns to for guidance.

It is, I submit, the theology of *Luther* which provides Heidegger with the basis for his own conception of hermeneutics. As I will argue in more detail later (chapter 2), a central aspect of Luther's early thought is focused around the use of the term '*destructio*' and its cognates. *Destructio* is a name for a way of doing theology that attempts to block the influence of humanity's pervasive urge for self-glorification on the concrete experience of religious life. As I will show (chapters 7 and 8) Heidegger transcribes this program into his own philosophical outlook by developing a practice of "*Destruktion*," which, like Luther's *destructio*, attempts to counter the tendencies toward complacency and conformity that encroach upon an individual's attempts to live an "authentic" life.[43]

At this point, however, I merely want to lend these claims some initial plausibility by following up on and developing a suggestion first made by Fehér in a recent article. Many of these points will reappear in a later part of this study, but it is important to briefly mention them here. One can look to Heidegger's lecture course on Paul from WS 1920–1921 to find a confirmation for Fehér's thesis about the development of Heidegger's conception of *philosophy*. The greater part of the introduction to his concrete exposition of Christian facticity in Paul's letters is taken up by questions regarding the nature and essence of philosophy.

Philosophy may be a science, says Heidegger, but the usual, commonplace conceptions of what it is to be a science should in no way be allowed to dictate the essence of philosophy (G60 6). Rather, the self-understanding of philosophy can only be reached through philosophizing itself (G60 8). For this reason, it is especially important to Heidegger that one avoid taking over the unclarified "scientific conception [*Auffasung*] of philosophy" (G60 8). For Heidegger, philosophy should be defined in relation to its object, factical life-experience. "The problem of the self-understanding of philosophy is always taken too lightly. Should one take up this problem in a radical way, one would find that philosophy springs from [*entspringt*] factical life-experience. And then it leaps back into factical life-experience itself" (G60 8). It is in factical life-experience that the "inversion" leading to philosophy must take place (G60 11).

Heidegger continued to wrestle with the question of the nature of philosophy in the coming years. In the famous "Natorp Report" from 1922, which contains interesting hints about Heidegger's theological motivations, the primary characteristic of philosophy is its difficulty. First of all, Heidegger argues that philosophy can never relieve future generations of "the burden and the anxious worry [*die Last und die Bekümmerung*] about radical questioning" (NB 3/113). It does not pass down a "system" of results, but instead a context of fundamental questions. All of this accords with the fundamental difficulty of life itself; the best manner of access to this "object" is, accordingly, that of "making things hard [*Schwermachen*]." This is the "duty [*Pflicht*]" of philosophy. Heidegger castigates the way philosophy all too often conspires with life in its tendency to flee its difficulty:

> All making things easy, all the tempting flattery about yearnings, all the metaphysical tranquilizers prescribed for problems which have for the most been derived from mere book learning—the basic intention of all this is from the start to give up with regard to the task that must in each case be carried out, namely, bringing the object of philosophy into view, grasping it, and indeed preserving [*behalten*] it. (NB 4/113)

I have already described the way a "basic experience" forms the starting point of Heidegger's hermeneutics. This experience of "having the self" provides the initial purchase on the phenomenon of personal life, which then opens the way for conceptual articulation. Given the significance of this "basic experience," it is little wonder that Heidegger views one of the tasks of philosophy as holding this in an "authentic safekeeping [*eigentliche Verwahrung*]" (NB 21/124). This requirement emerges still more clearly in Heidegger's conception of philosophy as always already "applied," as seamlessly interwoven with the actual course of a specific style of life: "As such, [philosophy] co-temporalizes [*mitzeitigt*] and helps to unfold the concrete and historically particular [*jeweilige*] being of life itself, and it does this in its very enactment, and not first by means of some subsequent 'application' to life" (NB 5/114).

All of these features of philosophy can be found in Heidegger's 1927 essay "Phenomenology and Theology": (1) it begins and ends in "factical life," (2) it accentuates the inherent "difficulty" of life, (3) it preserves a special possibility of human existence, and (4) it is always already "applied" to life. The significant point of difference, however, is that these features are attributed *not to philosophy, but to theology*. And, as I will now show, the view of theology expressed by Heidegger is thoroughly *Lutheran*.

One of the primary issues faced by both philosophy and theology during the first part of the twentieth century was the question of whether or not these disciplines were "scientific." The problem itself had its roots in the middle part of the nineteenth century, when the philosophical mood in Europe shifted away from the sort of speculative metaphysics that characterized the zenith of German Idealism. Side by side with this shift came new developments in the special sciences of chemistry, physics, and biology, all of which only served to convince more intellectuals that idealist "science [*Wissenschaft*]" was a relic from a more naïve age. In this situation, the natural problem on many minds concerned the nature and rights of philosophical inquiry. In philosophy, there were two basic attempts to answer this question. Some argued that philosophy must model itself in one way or another on the mathematical sciences (positivism, neo-Kantianism, Husserl). Others cast off the mantle of science altogether, opting instead for an enthusiastic "philosophy of life" that tried to address perennial questions of "world-view." In theology, there was a parallel attempt to secure "scientific" credentials through critical textual analysis and a new orientation toward the study of the history of religion. Heidegger's own views on philosophy and theology are deeply shaped by this intellectual situation.

In the 1927 essay, Heidegger claims that theology is a science, yet it should not be determined as such via the concepts of other sciences like physics or psychology: "In no case may we delimit the scientific character of theology by using an *other* science as the guiding standard of evidence for its mode of proof or as a measure of rigor of its conceptuality" (G9 60/49). According to Heidegger, the distinctiveness of theology is that it originates in faith and participates in the existential struggle to maintain faith. Heidegger writes, "Furthermore, faith not only motivates the intervention of an interpretive science of Christianness; at the same time, faith, as rebirth, is *that* history to whose occurrence theology itself, for its part, is supposed to contribute" (G9 54/45). By its very nature, theology is "applied" to life. Utilizing the same vocabulary that he had applied to philosophy during WS 1920–1921, Heidegger states that theology "springs from faith [*aus dem Glauben entspringt*]" (G9 55/46). Furthermore, its task is always to "cultivate [*auszubilden*]" faith (G9 55/46). This does not, of course, mean that theology is supposed to make faith easy:

> Likewise, the theological transparency and conceptual interpretation of faith cannot found [*begründen*] and secure faith in its legitimacy, nor can it in any way make it easier to accept faith and remain constant in faith. Theology can only render faith more difficult, that is, render it more certain that faithfulness cannot be gained through the science of theology, but solely through faith. (G9 56/46)

What is Heidegger's conception of the faith that forms the factical starting point for theology, the faith that it at once preserves and renders more difficult? Faith is determined, for Heidegger, by what is revealed to it, and this is the "crucified God" (G9 52/44). This revelation is an address; it has a specific "direction of communicating [*Mitteilungsrichtung*]" that calls one to participate in the salvation occurrence (G9 52–53/44). This participation is best understood, says Heidegger, as a kind of "rebirth" (G9 53/44). "Rebirth" means enacting the history that begins with the event of salvation and has a definite "uttermost end" (G9 53/44).

A careful reading uncovers the fact that Heidegger's claims about the meaning of faith and the nature of theology are permeated by manifestly Lutheran commitments. For example, the Lutheran formula "the crucified God" is used to designate the object of faith. The claim that theology cannot *construct* faith, but must instead take its cue *from* faith, is one of the hallmarks of Luther's polemic against late scholastic theology. These links are by no means speculative, for Heidegger quotes Luther as an authority on the conception of faith which he employs in this essay: "Luther said, 'Faith is permitting ourselves to be seized by the things we do not see' (*Werke* [Erlangen Augsgabe], vol. 46, p. 287)" (G9 53/44).[44] Heidegger no doubt drew this quotation from the texts of Luther that he had received as a gift some years before. It is, however, not only this conception of faith that betrays the influence of Luther. Indeed, the entire "ideal construction" of theology presented by Heidegger, according to which theology is not a contemplative science on the model of Aristotelian *theoria*, but rather a concrete struggle within and on behalf of faith, clearly has much in common with Luther's "theology of the cross."

John Van Buren has clearly shown Heidegger's abiding interest in Luther, illuminating the way his studies of Luther played a large part in the development of Heidegger's self-understanding as a thinker in his own right.[45] For present purposes, it will suffice to draw attention to Heidegger's own remarks concerning Luther in his lecture courses and published works. His identification of "genuine" theology with the work of Luther is evident in a remark from the introductory part of *Being and Time*:

> *Theology* seeks after a more original interpretation of the being of man, sketched out in advance by the meaning of faith and remaining within it. It is slowly beginning to understand once again Luther's insight that its dogmatic system rests upon a "foundation" that has not arisen from a primarily faithful questioning [*glaubenden Fragen*], and that its conceptual apparatus is not only inadequate for the theological problematic, but it also conceals and distorts it. (SZ 10/30)

This remark is very much of a piece with the conception of theology as the conceptual articulation of faith, found in the essay "Phenomenology and Theology." Here, in *Being and Time*, the insight that theology must have a "factical" origin and must avoid the imposition of "system" is attributed directly to Luther. That Luther was, however, Heidegger's source for much more than this conception of theology emerges from two explicit acknowledgments of the importance of Luther for the project of hermeneutics (G61 182; G63 5). Part of this significance surely lies in Luther's revolt against the encroachments of Greek metaphysics onto the "basic experience" of Christian faith (G60 97).

By far the most frequent allusions to Luther occur in connection with the idea of the "eruption" of a new form of life-experience in primitive Christianity. The claim that Luther represents one such "eruption" seems to have been made first of all in WS 1919–1920, where, as I have already pointed out, Heidegger develops the idea of the "basic experience" required for the development of hermeneutics (G58 62, 205). In some supplemental remarks, found in Oskar Becker's transcript of the course on Augustine from SS 1921, Heidegger develops this thesis in connection with Luther's "Heidelberg Disputation" of 1518, an early presentation of the "theology of the cross," as well as with Romans 1:19 (G60 282). Heidegger seems to have been familiar with Luther's lectures on Romans (recently unearthed at the time), as evidenced by a direct reference to the discovery of this text (G58 204) as well as to the editorial introduction to it by Johannes Ficker (G60 308–309). There are a number of other points during his lectures where Heidegger describes the "breakthrough" achieved by Luther (G60 310; G61 7; G17 118). Finally, in *Being and Time*, Heidegger makes reference to Luther's work in connection with the phenomenon of anxiety (SZ 190n4).

Perhaps the most telling piece of evidence here is that Heidegger actually lectured on Luther on two occasions. One of these was in a seminar, co-taught with Julius Ebbinghaus, on the theological origins of Kant's position in *Religion Within the Limits of Reason Alone* (1793). The second instance was Heidegger's guest lecture on Luther in Bultmann's course on the ethics of Paul. The text of the latter has recently come to light, and it reveals the depth of Heidegger's knowledge of Luther. Heidegger freely moves the length and breadth of Luther's corpus and manifests a keen sensibility for the Reformer's theological position.

As Heidegger reads Luther, the latter's whole theological position begins *in concreto*, i.e., with the experience of sin (S 105). Heidegger tries to show how this is true both in Luther's early, pre-Reformation period and in his later work. He begins with one of Luther's lesser-known works from 1516. Heidegger outlines Luther's position as follows: "Man is seized by *horror* [horror] that is based in *quarere iustitiam suam* [seeking his righteousness]. There thus arises *desperatio spiritualis* [spiritual despair], despair before God [. . .] because of the *affectus horrens peccatum* [affect of being horrified at sin]" (S 106).

Here Heidegger clearly finds a model for an intellectual discipline that begins its investigations in the thick of "factical life-experience," where theoretical cognition is not privileged over affect and emotion. As he puts it a bit later, Luther's ideal of a "theology of the cross" is of a discipline that "takes its point of departure only from the actual matter (*dicit id quod res est* [it says what the matter actually is])" (S 107). A discipline that begins in this way must, on Heidegger's view, also reach its terminus in "factical life-experience." In this seminar paper, Heidegger attributes this position directly to Luther:

> The fundamental requirement for all theology is thus to interpret man's being in the world in such a way that he can get out of this being and come to God. Thus this being may not be presented as something good, for here he does not learn to love God; rather, man must be brought to the point where he grasps his being as a persisting in the world that affords not glories but adversities. God has in His mercy shattered man's *quarere suam iustitiam* [seeking his righteousness], so that he now knows "I have nothing to expect from the world." Thus Luther [. . .] arrives at a proposition quite the reverse of Scholasticism: *corruptio amplificanda est* [corruption is something to be amplified]. (S 106)

Luther is, for Heidegger, a paradigm of a thinker whose problematic was motivated not by theory but by concrete human life, by the "basic experience" of being a fallen, corrupted human being. Luther's *theologia crucis* aims at opening up the possibility of an alternative mode of existence through relentlessly exposing the corruption of human nature. As I will argue in the following chapter, one of the central terms employed by Luther in connection with this conception of theology is *'destructio,'* a term that, Germanized as *'Destruktion,'* plays an equally central role in Heidegger's thought.

Luther's *Theologia Crucis*

As for me, I said in my prosperity, "I shall never be moved." By your favor,
O LORD, you had established me as a strong mountain; then you hid
your face; I was dismayed.

(Ps. 30:6–8)

In the preceding chapter, I established that primitive Christianity and
certain kinds of theological reflection were both pivotal influences on Heidegger's early intellectual development. Heidegger enlists primitive Christianity
in his "hermeneutics of facticity" as a "basic experience [*Grunderfahrung*],"
i.e., as a concrete, pre-theoretical configuration of life that is used to furnish
hermeneutics with a basic orientation that is largely free of conceptual distortions and that is able to provide him with a purchase on the immediacy of
meaningful life. At the same time, Heidegger discerned paradigms in theology
that helped him to craft his own vision of philosophy as a discipline that not
only grows out of the immediacy of lived experience but also holds open the
possibility of a special, valuable way of life. At the conclusion of the last
chapter, I showed how Heidegger took Luther's theology to be an exemplification of both of these moves. This can be seen in Heidegger's 1924 guest lecture
on Luther, as well as in his brief discussions of Luther's theological anthropology during SS 1923 (G63 27ff./22ff.). Heidegger shows how the Reformer takes the concrete experience of human corruption as his starting
point, then proceeds to develop a theological system that serves grace by

means of an unflinching portrayal of the corruption of human existence. The remainder of this study is aimed at working out the details of this preliminary thematic sketch.

Recent scholarship has clearly shown the importance that Luther had in Heidegger's intellectual development. Nonetheless, one of the central ideas to emerge from Heidegger's conversation with Luther has received insufficient attention. The idea in question belongs to the very heart of Heidegger's philosophical project, and he tellingly employs the term '*Destruktion*,' a Germanized version of the Latin '*destructio*,' in order to capture it. While it has been noted that the latter term is used by Luther and that this is the likely source of Heidegger's term '*Destruktion*,' no account of what Luther means by this term has been given, either by Heidegger scholars or by Luther scholars.[1] The purpose of the present chapter is, then, to fill in these lacunae in the interests of gaining a better understanding not only of Luther, but more importantly of Heidegger.

My analysis will, accordingly, be devoted to working out the meaning of the term '*destructio*' in Luther's theology. I will argue that this term has two distinct yet complimentary meanings. First, '*destructio*' is a term Luther uses to describe what he also calls the "alien work [*opus alienum*]" of God. The latter is a descriptor for an element in the process of salvation or "justification," in which the false self-estimation of human beings is obliterated so that God may effect His "proper work [*opus proprium*]," the shaping of a person into a "new creation." Second, '*destructio*' is a term used by Luther to articulate the basic task of theological reflection. Like his model Paul, Luther aims to render foolish the "wisdom of the wise," to expose the "prudence of the flesh" and its articulation in "heathen" metaphysics. In this sense, '*destructio*' is a name for a way of doing theology that participates in God's "alien work" by castigating the hedonistic longing for quietude and by denouncing the false theology that is more or less complicit in it.

Luther and the Aristotelian Tradition

As Van Buren and others have clearly shown, part of Heidegger's affinity for Luther arose from the latter's virulent assault on the theological system of medieval Aristotelianism. Luther's critique of what he called the "theology of glory" seems to have resonated particularly strongly with the young Heidegger. Heidegger saw his own work as bringing to completion the dismantling of the metaphysical tradition that began with Luther. Inspired by Luther, Heidegger undertook a critique of the "aesthetic" orientation of Greek metaphysics toward static presence.[2] Luther's emphasis on the concrete experience of Christian life under the cross, afflicted by *Anfechtung*, and his critique of the pride (*superbia*) of metaphysical speculation, exerted a powerful influence over Heidegger's new hermeneutics.

As I will show more fully in subsequent chapters, Heidegger largely shares

Luther's conviction that intellectual discourse is mostly complicit in a sort of complacent, self-congratulatory way of life (chapter 4). The direct targets of Heidegger's critique were, of course, not the same as Luther's antagonists; Heidegger reserves his most bitter polemics for neo-Kantianism and vulgar "life-philosophy." Nonetheless, Luther's attack on scholasticism clearly had a deep impact on Heidegger's own critical theorizing. And, like Luther's *theologia crucis*, Heidegger's philosophical brand of *destructio* is both negative and positive. Heidegger's more negative or critical work serves a more positive or constructive goal of preserving what he regards as a valuable way of life against its many foes.

For Luther, the principal enemy was nominalist theology and its use of Aristotelian concepts to account for the salvation of souls. What was it about Aristotle that so vexed the young Luther? It was not philosophy *per se* that troubled him.[3] Nor was Luther exercised by some particular metaphysical problem of the kind, which, in the century after his Reformation, brought about the demise of Aristotelianism. Moreover, it is surely anachronistic to read Luther as a critic of metaphysics after the twentieth-century style, a sort of Derrida born out of season. Luther's concerns were, in fact, soteriological. That is, Luther's worries were focused on the doctrine of salvation or "justification" offered by many late medieval theologians. B. A. Gerrish has made this point convincingly in his study of Luther's attitude toward reason, and this judgment is shared by a number of scholars.[4] Luther's position, stated in the most general terms, was that the infiltration of Aristotelian and neo-platonic philosophy into Christian doctrine led directly to a host of incorrect, confusing, and ultimately un-Christian ideas about the order of salvation. To borrow from Heidegger, Luther was concerned with a "deformation [*Verunstaltung*] of Christian existence" (G59 90).

It is worthwhile to briefly discuss, in outline, the theological position to which Luther opposed his own evangelical theology. Karl-Heinz zur Mühlen has argued that in the dominant strands of medieval theology, reason, as *recta ratio* (correct reasoning), was viewed as having a crucial role to play in soteriology.[5] Grace, in conjunction with *recta ratio* and *bona voluntas* (good will), serves to direct humanity toward a blessed future. Understood metaphysically, justification is the self-movement of the soul toward a more complete participation in God. This movement receives its motive force from the will, which is in turn directed by reason. In the divine economy of the universe, this movement, modeled on the Aristotelian ideal of human self-realization through moral praxis, is a condition for the imputation of grace.[6]

This theory was current amongst the theologians of the *via moderna*, whose works formed the bulk of Luther's own theological education. This theory began with a distinction between two powers of God, the absolute and the ordained. The first designates God's absolute freedom to elect to create any possible thing (save a contradiction), while the latter designates the self-imposed limitation involved in the choice of a certain set of possibilities. On the basis of these ideas, the "nominalists" developed a covenantal soteriology according to which the moral actions of human beings, though of little intrinsic value, could, by virtue of God's ordained power, merit grace. God had ordained from eternity that the gift of grace followed of necessity on certain actions being performed. Such a theological scheme clearly lacks the Christological focus that became the hallmark of evangelical thought.[7] According to Alister McGrath, this covenantal scheme relied heavily on Aristotle's conception of justice as mediated through the Roman legal tradition.[8]

It was, in particular, the late medieval theory that a human being can, by his or her own power, produce an act of love for God above all things, which then merits saving grace, which Luther found repellent.[9] It was precisely here that Luther discerned the pernicious influence of Aristotle on medieval theology. In particular, it was the conceptualization of the economy of salvation on the model of Aristotle's ethics that Luther saw as the crux of the problem. Gerhard Ebeling has provided an excellent discussion of this part of Luther's thought.[10] Ebeling points out that the medieval doctrine of faith was set within the context of a definite view of human nature. Faith was viewed as a kind of *virtus*, albeit a supernatural one. As such, faith was understood as a *habitus*, a disposition, rather than as an *actus*. For Aristotle, these ideas were situated within the context of an understanding of human nature according to which a human being attains the perfection of the essence of humanity through self-realization. It is the *actus*, the "work," which brings about the fulfillment of the essence. In this schema, *actus* precedes *habitus*. Moral praxis is not the externalization of an already complete being, but a way a being is first realized. According to Karl-Heinz zur Mühlen, Luther did not seek to challenge this theory at all when it came to accounting for human moral activity. What he protested was, rather, the interpretation of the message of the Gospel in these Aristotelian terms.[11] In Luther's mind, this entire scheme smacked of the "righteousness of man."

Luther's critique of philosophy, which he almost always identified with Aristotle, was thus circumscribed quite narrowly. In Luther's works there is nothing like a global denunciation of philosophy as such. Rather, it is late medieval soteriology, and its complicity with human presumption and legalistic self-righteousness, that is the object of Luther's destructive project. Over against this, Luther championed the idea that faith is not a *virtus* in the sense of a "disposition," but rather, that it possesses *virtus*, the power to save humanity.[12] Human salvation is not the achievement of a person aided by grace, but is a *potentia realis passiva*, a possibility that is only really a possibility for God.[13]

That Luther's critique of metaphysics is set firmly within a soteriological, or practical, context will prove to be an important clue for understanding the way Heidegger uses the term '*Destruktion*.' By and large, scholars have held that this theme belongs to the *theoretical* sphere.[14] That is, *Destruktion* is taken to be an activity that is primarily aimed at helping secure the proper *theory* about human life by critically examining traditional ideas. As I will show (chapter 8), this reading overlooks the deep motivations of Heidegger's work, motives he makes explicit at a number of points. By taking up Luther's terminology in this way, Heidegger clearly intended to preserve *something* of the original meaning. In Luther, '*destructio*' is a term that sometimes refers to the critical work of a "theologian of the cross." This work is not motivated by a theoretical concern with truth so much as a by a practical concern with the human good, i.e., salvation. This concern survives Heidegger's translation of '*destructio*' into '*Destruktion.*'

The following discussion of *destructio* in Luther will proceed in a chronological manner through some of his most important works during the period between 1515 and 1518. The reason for this restriction is that Heidegger himself notes that it was the "young Luther" who had the most significant influence on his work in the early 1920s (G63 5/4). First to be examined is Luther's *Lectures on Romans*, delivered during the years 1515 and 1516. Next, the *Lectures on Hebrews* from 1517 and 1518 will be discussed. Finally, the analysis of *destructio* will conclude with a discussion of two of Luther's more well-known academical writings from 1518, the "Explanations of the Ninety-five Theses" and the "Heidelberg Disputation." All four of these texts have been selected not only for their important place in the story of Luther's development, but also for the frequency with which '*destruere*' and '*destructio*' are mentioned. A close study of these texts yields a thorough, practicable understanding of these ideas.

Lectures on Romans

At the beginning of the previous century, the world was presented with a critical edition of Luther's nearly legendary lectures on Paul's epistle to the Romans. It was in these lectures, held between 1515 and 1516, that Luther began to solidify his decisive break with the nominalist theology in which he was trained.[15] This work is, therefore, indispensable to anyone who seeks to understand the development of evangelical theology in the sixteenth century. More germane to the present study is the frequent use of '*destruere*' and its cognates in these lectures. These lectures were certainly familiar to Heidegger, and, as John Van Buren has suggested, played a significant part in the development of his own thought.[16] Accordingly, these lectures will receive particular focus in the present investigation. My exposition begins with a sketch of Luther's dark portrait of human life under sin and of the complicity of philosophy and theology in this fallen state. After this discussion, I will explicate the term '*destructio*' as it is used in these lectures.

For Luther, the root of humanity's fallen state, the so-called "tinder of sin," is concupiscence (LW25 259).[17] Contrary to the opining of many unsympathetic critics of Luther's thought, concupiscence has nothing to do with intemperance or sexual desire.[18] On the contrary, concupiscence designates a much more radical flaw in human nature than occasional lapses in moral judgment.

Concupiscence is basically the quality of being obsessively centered on one's self: "For man cannot but seek his own advantages and love himself above all things. And this is the sum of all his iniquities. Hence even in good things and virtues men seek themselves, that is, they seek to please themselves and applaud themselves" (LW25 222). The condition of unredeemed humanity is one of egocentric blindness, of a hunger for glory and temporal security rather than for the "righteousness of God." Here "we are turned in upon ourselves and become ingrown at least in our heart, even when we cannot sense it in our actions" (LW25 245).

According to Luther, this fundamental "crookedness" of human nature manifests itself in many ways. One of its most frequent manifestations is in the sin of pride (*superbia*). In his comments on the opening of Paul's epistle, Luther points to the self-aggrandizing motive that perverts the knowledge of God innate in all human beings.[19] In his interlinear gloss on Romans 1:20, Luther describes the effects of sin on metaphysical speculation:

> They became vain and worth nothing, although in the eyes of people they became great and wise as if they knew everything, *in their thoughts*, that is, in their studies, wisdom, and speculations [*studiis, sapientiis, speculationibus*], *and their senseless minds were darkened*, on account of the blindness of their state of mind [. . .]. (LW25 20/WA56 13)

Instead of leading to humble thanks and worship, this knowledge of God led instead to pride in the powers of human thought (LW25 10). Luther clarifies Paul's point later, in the scholia, by arguing that "they did not worship this divinity untouched but changed and adjusted it to their desires and needs" (LW25 10). The pride of humanity in its own intellect leads to an understanding of God in anthropocentric, rather than theocentric, terms (LW25 157). Heidegger makes reference at one point to Luther's "Disputation Against Scholastic Theology" from 1517, where a similar point is made. In Heidegger's paraphrase, Luther holds that "man cannot of himself want God to be God; rather, man wants to be God. And this is precisely the essence of sin [. . .]" (S 106). In his usual colorful manner, Luther laments the perversion of the truth of God by the crooked minds of human beings: "But alas, even now many people think in an unworthy way about God and claim in bold and impudent treatises that God is this way or that way. . . . they so raise their opinion to the skies that they judge God with no more trouble or fear than a poor cobbler judges his leather" (LW25 167).

In these remarks, one can detect anticipations of Heidegger's own critiques of what he calls "onto-theology." "Onto-theology" does not refer to theism as such, but to a very specific version of it. Here, "God" serves as a justification for human pride and presumption, a kind of clandestine self-congratulation. "God" serves, in an onto-theological scheme, to ground an all-embracing explanation of reality, a project which has little to do with proclaiming an experience of salvation.[20] The root of the problem, as Luther sees it, is that metaphysics elevates humanity to divine status, thus effacing the distinction between God and humanity. This same worry reappeared in the work of "dialectical theologians" like Karl Barth at the beginning of the twentieth century. Another clear statement of this idea can be found in Franz Rosenzweig's 1914 essay, "Atheistic Theology." Rosenzweig sums up the problem with contemporary Jewish and Christian thought in a way that echoes Luther's critique of scholasticism: "The distinction between God and man, this frightful scandal for all new and old paganism, seems to be removed; the offensive thought of revelation, this plunging of a higher content into an unworthy vessel, is brought to silence."[21]

A more obvious manifestation of pride, and the one that Luther expends most of his energy attacking, is pride in the moral accomplishments of human beings. It is also here that Luther finds the most pernicious point of contact between Aristotelian philosophy and medieval theology. For Luther, the nominalist soteriology of *facere quod in se est* is simply the latest incarnation of the "righteousness of works" against which Paul preached in so many of his letters. Heidegger draws attention to this feature of Luther's thought as well, making reference to a contemporaneous text called "*Quaestio de viribus et voluntate hominis sine gratia*" from 1516 (S 105). In Luther's words, "The principle of works necessarily puffs us up [*inflat*] and makes for glorying, because he who is righteous and fulfills the Law doubtless has something of which to glory and exalt himself" (LW25 251/WA56 263). Luther's position is that this pride (*superbia*) is rooted in the false presumption (*presumptio*) that one is righteous in the eyes of God (LW25 233). Like the more abstract kinds of "speculation" and "pagan" wisdom, the problem with the "righteousness of works" lies in the note of self-congratulation that it sounds.

In addition to pride and presumption, one other primary manifestation of human concupiscence is the continual longing for temporal security. This, too, was an aspect of Luther's thought that Heidegger seems to have found interesting. He examines Luther's discussion of humanity's fear and flight from God in the 1544 lectures on Genesis (S 109). As I will show below, Heidegger regards longing for security as a central feature of an "inauthentic" life (chapter 3). Luther notes in this regard how many people engage in religious observances merely "because they delight us and quiet the fears of our heart, because we are praised by men, and thus we do them not for the sake of God but for ourselves" (LW25 245f.). It is no surprise to Luther that "many give themselves up to laziness [*torporem*] and security [*securitatem*] [. . .]" (LW25 267/WA56 280).

Continually attacking hedonism, Luther emphasizes that temporal peace is never the lot of the righteous (LW25 286). He castigates the "hypocrites" who venerate alleged relics of the True Cross and yet "flee from and curse their sufferings and adversities" (LW25 289). They rant about the so-called "enemies of the cross," i.e., non-Christians, and yet they are the true enemies of the cross, who hate tribulation and suffering and seek only to flatter and coddle the people of God (LW25 289f.). This sort of pseudo-religiosity reaches its apogee in the more extreme of the indulgence preachers, such as Luther's bitter foe Tetzel. As with prideful "wisdom" and the "righteousness of works," Luther's worry concerns the tendency to feed humanity's natural complacency, to fuel the compulsion to glorify oneself at the expense of a life of humble striving.

Another aspect of sin that is of particular importance for the soteriological scheme of Luther's lectures on Romans is the so-called "prudence of the flesh." Luther goes so far as to identify this *prudentia* with concupiscence, describing it as a kind of exaggerated self-love (LW25 348). The "light" of nature, says Luther, is truly "darkness," for it turns all things inwards toward itself (LW25 346). The prudence of the flesh, properly speaking, designates the false self-understanding of human beings and all that accompanies it. Here, humanity views itself through the eyes of the world (*coram mundo*), rather than through the eyes of God (*coram Deo*). In the eyes of the world, of course, everything is as it should be, provided that one is "doing what lies in him [*facere quod in se est*]." As long as the balance sheet of right and wrong stays in the black, there is no reason not to think of oneself as wise, righteous, and secure. Luther argues that, in Romans 8:7, the phrase "wisdom of the flesh" would be better rendered as "prudence of the flesh," for "there is general agreement that the term prudence is used by all people to apply to our actions while wisdom is applied to our thinking" (LW25 350).

In Luther's scheme, there are two possibilities open to a human being. There is, on the one hand, the path of identification with this world, with what is visible, and this is the "wisdom of the flesh." On the other hand, there is the possibility of identification with what is not of this world, with what is invisible, and this is the "wisdom of the spirit" (LW25 68f.). One can, like Mary, cling to the one thing needful, or, like Martha, trouble oneself over the things of this world (LW25 352). The radical nature of Luther's theory lies in the fact that these possibilities are not qualities that can be added to or subtracted from the substance of the person, but are instead totally distinct ontological orders. When God redeems a human being, there is truly a *creatio ex nihilo*.

It is the "prudence of the flesh" that is most closely identified with philosophy and scholastic theology by Luther in his Romans lectures. As Heidegger notes, a similar link is made in the Heidelberg Disputation of 1518 (S 107). For Luther, Scotus and Occam "speak in the manner of Aristotle in his *Ethics*, when he bases sin and righteousness on works, both their performance or omission" (LW25 261). In particular, Luther aims his invective at the view that original sin can be entirely removed in this life. "O fools, O pig-theologians!" he cries (LW25 261).

In Luther's view, Aristotle's conception of righteousness "comes from blindness of the mind or from human wisdom which is concerned only with temporal matters [. . .]" (LW25 410f.). In basing their soteriology upon such a teaching, Luther feels that his predecessors are complicit in the depravity of the "prudence of the flesh." Their theology is merely a self-justification for lukewarm spirituality and complacency. We will all eventually "snore in our smugness" as a result of doctrines such as these (LW25 495). Luther views this position, perhaps unjustly, as outright Pelagianism.[22] In a remark that looks ahead to the controversy over indulgences, he writes:

> And thus the most pestilent class of preachers today is that group which preaches about the signs of present grace, so that it makes men secure, when in fact the very best sign of grace is that we fear and tremble, and the surest sign of God's wrath is to be smug and self-confident. (LW25 498)

In addition to Aristotle's ethics, the source of this sophisticated version of the "prudence of the flesh" also lies in a mistaken understanding of original sin. For Luther's opponents, original sin is a property of the will such that it lacks original righteousness (LW25 299). Luther, however, argues that the scriptural understanding of original sin is much more radical, "a total lack of uprightness and of the power of all the faculties both of body and of soul and of the whole inner and outer man" (LW25 299).

The less radical view characteristic of the scholastics lends support to the soteriological position mentioned at the beginning of this chapter. There, I described the soteriological consensus that existed amongst many theologians prior to Luther. On this view, justification consists in a state of character achieved through habituation which in turn merits divine grace. Such a view only makes sense if original sin is more or less an adventitious property, as opposed to a radical flaw in created nature as such. Luther argues that the import of the scholastic teaching is to increase presumptuous pride. Indeed, this is the core of Luther's objection to scholastic theology: its doctrines promote hypocrisy and pride through a misinterpretation of Christian ideas through Greek metaphysics, logic, and ethics. Later in his commentary, Luther directly attributes this perversion to the influence of Aristotle (LW25 338). "For this reason philosophy stinks in our nostrils, as if our reason always spoke for the best things, and we make up many stories about the law of nature" (LW25 344).

Scholastic theology is also complicit in a false self-understanding on the part of human beings. In his comments on Romans 3:7, Luther argues that we are like the patient in a story from Percius, who refused to recognize his illness. We condemn God when He calls us sinners, for we are righteous in our own estimation. It is God's revelation of our sinfulness that enables us to gain self-knowledge (LW25 203 ff.). This is not, however, simply a matter of acquiring some new properties, but of being radically transformed in the very depths of our being (LW25 213). Through the creative power of God's Word, affirmed in faith, human nature is renewed.

A major part of our false self-understanding, according to Luther, is the idea that spiritual perfection can be achieved through our own efforts in this very life. This actually falsifies the truth of the matter, for "the condition of this life is not that of having but of seeking God" (LW25 224). The greatest danger is to assume that we are completely righteous before God (LW25 243f.). Luther summarizes the situation of those infected by the "prudence of the flesh" as follows:

> They do not do these works, therefore, in order to seek justification, but that they may glory in the righteousness which they already possess. Therefore, after they have performed these works, they come to a stop, as if, now that the Law has been entirely fulfilled, no other justification were necessary. And surely this is a proud and arrogant attitude. (LW25 252)

Luther continues to attack this understanding in his scholion on Romans 5:2, attributing it particularly to "hypocrites and legalists," but also to those who ascribe to mystical theology. The latter are presumptuous in their assumption that one can attain union with God apart from God's own saving deed (LW25 287f.). Luther likens all this to a "spiritual sleep" of false complacency (LW25 478). In his mind, "to stand still on the way to God is to retrogress, and to advance is always a matter of beginning anew" (LW25 478). Thus, anyone who claims to possess knowledge and virtue has not even begun to gain possession of these goods.

As I will show in a succeeding discussion (chapter 4), Heidegger shares Luther's misgivings about intellectual discourse in both philosophy and theology. While not particularly exercised by issues like original sin, Heidegger nonetheless shares Luther's conviction that philosophical discourse is too often complicit in a life of fugitive self-abdication and hyperbolic excess. Like Luther, he tries to articulate a vision of intellectual activity that is radically different, hoping to avoid the failings of the common fare. The task of a philosopher, in particular, is to resist the tendency to take over traditional opinions as self-evident and to construct grand world-views designed to guide the lives individual men and women or to solve social problems. Heidegger was certainly well aware of Luther's similar concerns. He notes that Luther's position is "quite the reverse of scholasticism: *corruptia amplificanda est* [corruption is something to be amplified]" (S 106). That is, the job of the intellectual (whether a philosopher or a theologian) is to challenge and criticize traditional opinions and to continually expose the superficiality and hypocrisy of dominant modes of public discourse.

The "prudence of the flesh" is, then, the false self-estimation of humanity, rooted in selfish concupiscence. One takes up a human understanding of virtue and of righteousness and assumes that this is the same as virtue and righteousness *coram Deo*. This sinful "prudence" manifests itself in the scholastic theology against which Luther so vehemently objected. It distorts the truth of human life, duping humanity into complacent self-satisfaction and ignoring the reality of radical sin and the temporal finitude of existence. The most dangerous outcome of the attitude engendered by this "prudence" is its perversion of Christian teaching, i.e., in the claim that sin can be overcome by one who "does what lies in him." Luther makes this point in a striking analogy in his comments on Romans 3:20:

> A monkey can imitate the actions of people, but he is not a man on that account. But if he should become a man, this doubtless would not take place by virtue of these actions, by which he has imitated a man, but by some other power, namely, God's; but then having become a man, he would truly and rightly perform the actions of a man. (LW25 235)[23]

It is against the background of this radical soteriology that the idea of "destruction [*destructio*]" in Luther can be best understood. How, Luther asks, is the required transformation of human identity to be achieved, if not by human efforts? The "good news" that he found proclaimed by Paul is that this transformation is a work of God, lacking any inherent relation to human conceptions of worth or desert. This saving act eliminates the "prudence of the flesh," stymies its quest for temporal security and self-satisfaction, and, ultimately, utterly transforms the very existence of humanity. God's deed has, for Luther, both a negative and a positive side. Only faith is capable of seeing the intrinsic unity of these apparent opposites.

In his lecture course on Romans, Luther most frequently uses the verb *'destruere'* to describe the negative side of this activity. It was this fateful choice of words that, four centuries later, took hold of the mind of Martin Heidegger and spurred him on toward a radical new beginning in philosophy. In his 1924 lectures on Luther, Heidegger describes this feature of his thought as it appears in a little-known text from 1516. He describes what Luther eventually calls *'destructio'* in the Romans lectures and shows how this is *both* an act of God and a way theology can participate in this act:

> The fundamental requirement for all theology is thus to interpret man's being in the world in such a way that he can get out of this being and come to God. Thus this being may not be presented as something good, for here he does not learn to love God: rather, man must be brought to the point where he grasps his being as a persisting in the world that affords not glories but adversities. God has in His mercy shattered man's *quarere suam iustitiam* [seeking his righteousness], so that he now knows "I have nothing to expect from the world." (S 106)

Not only in the lectures under consideration, but also in Luther's other writings during the period from 1515 to 1518, there are two distinct, yet closely related, meanings given to the terms *'destruere'* and *'destructio.'* Heidegger clearly refers to both in the passage quoted above. The first, and from Luther's point of view the most important, refers to the "alien work" of God whereby the "old man" is slain and the way is cleared for salvation. The second, which is perhaps more significant from the point of view of this study, refers to an element of evangelical theology, of the "theology of the cross." For Luther, theology, as the guardian and interpreter of the Word, must participate in the struggle against sin and must, through reason and rhetoric, denounce theories that prevent this struggle. Both of these usages can be found in Luther's lectures on Romans, and I will describe them successively in what follows, beginning with the term's use in connection with divine action.

In his comments on Romans 1:1, Luther argues that it is God's will that everything that is ours be completely unmade for the sake of His new creation. He quotes Jeremiah 1:10 to the effect that "[t]o pluck up and to break down, to destroy [*destruas*] and to overthrow" all our own righteousness and wisdom is integral to God's saving act (LW25 136/WA56 158). This, says Luther, is the meaning of Nebuchadnezzar's vision, interpreted with help from Daniel, of the stone that "shattered [*destruente*]" the statue, i.e., the idol of our own self-estimation. To clear the way for the "foreign" righteousness of God, our own must be "plucked up [*evelli*]." Christ desires that we be "stripped down [*exutum*]," denuded of our own righteousness and wisdom, so that we simply wait upon the "naked mercy of God" (LW25 137/WA56 159). In this lies the undoing of humanity's corrupt identity and the creation of a "new man." Luther explains this clearly in his remarks on Romans 3:7:

> Therefore, to become a sinner is to destroy this way of thinking [*hunc sensum destrui*] by which we believe tenaciously that we are living, speaking, and acting in a good, pious, and righteous way, and to adopt another mode of thought [*alium sensum*] (which comes from God) whereby we believe from the heart that we are sinners, that we are acting, speaking, and living wickedly, that we are astray, and thus we come to blame ourselves, to judge, condemn, and hate ourselves. (LW25 218/WA56 233)

The first "way of thinking [*sensus*]" described in this passage is none other than the "prudence of the flesh." As I have already explained, this is Luther's designation for a corrupted mode of human existence that is ruled by self-satisfaction and complacency. The alternative he proposes is to "become a sinner," a turn of phrase that at first glance appears puzzling. Luther clearly does not mean that one ought to embrace an immoral or "unrighteous" way of life. Instead, he urges that one recognize and own up to being corrupted and fallen.

Luther tells us that the "power of God," whereby this destruction of the "old man" is carried out, is the Gospel (LW25 149). The one who hears the Gospel becomes "weak and foolish before men, so that he may be strong and wise in the power and wisdom of God [. . .]" (LW25 150). God's Word is what reveals the truth about the human condition *coram Deo*, i.e., that the soteriological resources of human beings are simply non-existent.[24] For this reason, it necessarily seems like foolishness to the prudence of the flesh, so accustomed to regard itself as sufficient for all things. In a corollary to his main remarks on Romans 7:6, Luther writes that "[the Gospel] does nothing else than to destroy [*destruit*] those who are presumptuous concerning their own righteousness to make room for grace, that they may know that the Law is fulfilled not by their own powers but only through Christ, who pours out the Holy Spirit in our hearts" (LW25 326 f./WA56 338). As the active power in the negative side of Luther's soteriological scheme, the Word carries out the task of "tearing down" and "doing away with" the "wisdom of the flesh" (LW25 399).

Once again, Heidegger explicitly discusses this element of Luther's position, commenting this time on the 1544 lectures on Genesis. He writes:

> And this situation of man is effected by God, insofar as it is the *summa gratia* [highest grace] that he did not remain silent after the Fall but *loquitur* [speaks]. What also needs to be taken into account is how the being of God is always conceived of as *verbum* [word], and the fundamental relation of man to him as *audire* [hearing]. (S 110)

Heidegger clearly took Luther's theology of the Word seriously. This accounts for his early interest in Karl Barth, who also attributes a pivotal role to *revelation* in the drama of salvation. As I will show (chapters 5 and 6), Heidegger maintains that the move from an inauthentic to an authentic life requires a moment of "intensity," an experience that interrupts the course of life as it is normally lived and so makes possible a kind of reorientation. In *Being and Time*, he uses the phrase "the voice of conscience" to formally indicate the meaning of such experiences. Much earlier, however, during WS 1920–1921, he explicitly attributes similar qualities to the "proclamation" of the New Testament (see chapter 5).

It is in his remarks on Romans 10:15 that Luther most clearly describes the activity of the Word of God. In his mind, "heretics" are those who preach a word that conforms to their own understanding rather than to the Word of God. As I have already shown, the natural state of human understanding is that of the corruption of the prudence of the flesh. Therefore, the true Word "does not allow our thinking to stand, even in those matters which are most sacred, but it destroys [*destruit*] and eradicates and scatters [*dissipat*] everything, as Jer. 23:29 says, 'Is not My Word like fire, says the Lord, and like a hammer which breaks the rocks in pieces?'" (LW25 415/WA56 423). This image recalls Luther's earlier discussion of the stone that smashes the idol in Nebuchadnezzar's dream. The idol that is destroyed by the flame of God's Word is our own false self-understanding.

Luther concludes this passage with an excellent summation. Several noteworthy points are found in these remarks, most importantly Luther's insistence on the *critical* function of the Word. This is an idea one can also find sharply expressed in the work of "dialectical theologians" of the post–World War I era, such as Karl Barth. Indeed, the latter represents a reassertion of this radical Pauline-Lutheran message. Once again, this accounts for much of the interest that Heidegger had in early dialectical theology. Evidence abounds of his interest in radical theologians like Overbeck, Schweitzer, Barth, Gogarten, and Bultmann, most of whom called upon Luther as an ally in their assault against self-congratulatory liberal Protestant culture. Luther's statement of the ideas is as follows:

[T]he Word of God "breaks the rocks in pieces" and destroys [*destruit*] and crucifies whatever in us is pleasing to us and does not allow anything to remain in us except that which is displeasing, in order that it thereby may teach us to have pleasure, joy, and confidence only in God, and outside ourselves pleasure and happiness in our neighbor. (LW25 415/WA56 423)

In Luther's thought, there is most certainly an experiential dimension to this activity of the Word. The experiences of awe before the power of God, and of heart-wrenching *Anfechtung*, are vital to Luther's understanding of salvation.[25] This part of Luther's position no doubt had a strong influence on Heidegger's well-known discussions of *Bekümmerung* and *Angst*. It is through the "fire of tribulation [*per tribulationibus ignem*]" that God reveals to us the depravity of human nature (LW25 291/WA56 304). *Destructio* is as much an experience as it is a vital part of the theory of justification. Luther explains:

Therefore suffering comes, through which a man is made patient and tested; it comes and takes away everything he has and leaves him naked and alone, allowing him no help or safety in either his physical or spiritual merits, for it makes a man despair [*desperare*] of all created things, to turn away from them and from himself, to seek help outside of himself and all other things, in God alone [. . .]. (LW25 292/WA56 305)

Lennart Pinomaa has argued that Luther's theology is "the theology of the afflicted [*angefochtenen*] conscience."[26] *Anfechtung*, the concrete experience of the wrath of God, places one into the situation of religious decision and affects the entire person.[27] In Luther's mature thought, this experience is not merely a stage on the way to beatitude, but rather a negative expression of one's relationship to God. Moreover, it is this experience that distinguishes Luther's conception of faith.[28] Mere natural knowledge of God, attained through reason, collapses in the face of the onslaught of *Anfechtung*.

It is important to realize that Luther's soteriology of *destructio* is dialectical. That is, there is a dialectic between God's condemnation of human pride and self-will, concretely experienced in *Anfechtung*, and God's creation of the "new man." One and the same act of God is both *destructio* and *aedificatio*. "The righteous person . . . understands that even the severity of God is good for his salvation, for it breaks him down and heals him. 'The Lord kills and brings to life' (1 Sam. 2:6)" (LW25 176). Luther often describes the situation in terms of a dialectic between deformation and formation, between tearing down and building up. One example of this way of speaking can be found in his remarks on Romans 6:17, where he argues that "the wisdom of the flesh" must "give up its form and take on the form of the Word" (LW25 317).

Elsewhere, Luther puzzlingly refers to the authority of philosophy to make this point: "As the philosophers say: a thing is not brought into form unless there is first a lack of form or a change of previous form; again, a 'potential idea' does not receive a form unless at its inception it has been stripped of all form and is like a *tabula rasa*" (LW25 204). Luther also describes this dialectic in a discussion of Romans 8:3, first of all pointing out that "the Spirit kills [*occidet*] the 'wisdom of the flesh' and makes the inner man alive and causes men to despise death and to give up life and to love only God above all things [. . .]" (LW25 349/WA56 359). Later he explains further that Paul "says that God has damned and destroyed [*destruxit*] the sin in our flesh, but He causes us to destroy [*destruere*] it through His Spirit, who is poured out by faith into our hearts" (LW25 349/WA56 360).

The saving work of God is, according to Luther, always hidden under its opposite (*sub contrario*). This is another way Luther presents the claim that one act is both *destructio* and *aedificatio*. Indeed, the notion of the "hiddenness" of God's saving action is a crucial theme in the "theology of the cross." Foolish people flee from the "works" of God, wishing to form themselves rather than to be formed by Him. This is because these works are always hidden under what is contrary to our expectations. This is clear in the example of Jesus, whose disciples longed for his exaltation, which actually only took place after his humiliating death. Luther also points to the example of Augustine's youthful intemperance (LW25 366f.). "We ask for salvation," Luther says, "and [God], to save us, increases our damnation and hides his answer under this kind of thunder" (LW25 370). Of God's will, Luther says that "while doing us evil it does us good; while most unacceptable to us it is most acceptable; while it destroys [*destruit*] us, it perfects us" (LW25 443/WA56 450).

In addition to the conception of *destructio* as part of the divine economy of salvation, there is, as I have already mentioned, a second major way this idea is employed. This usage is very much continuous with the one discussed above. In Luther's view, a theology that is based on the Gospel, rather than on the "prudence of the flesh," must participate in the struggle on behalf of faith and against sin. As I have already discussed, the primary sin, for Luther, is concupiscence, which manifests itself primarily in pride and in the haughty self-estimation of human beings. Thus, an evangelical theology, which Luther eventually comes to call *theologia crucis*, also has as its duty the critique of the "prudence of the flesh" in all its forms.

Luther self-consciously chooses Paul as his model for a theological *destructio*. The scholia begin with the announcement that "[t]he chief purpose of this letter is to break down, to pluck up, and to destroy [*destruere*] all wisdom and righteousness of the flesh. This includes all the works which in the eyes of people or even in our own eyes may be great works" (LW25 135/WA56 159).[29] Our inner self-satisfaction [*affectu et complacentia interiori*] must be destroyed [*destruatur*] (LW25 136/WA56 159). This is the aim of true theology, as opposed to the tempting flattery of Occam and his disciples. Luther makes this strikingly clear in his remarks on Romans 3:13:

> Because such teachers do not bite [*mordent*], therefore they do not chew and grind [*ruminant et conterunt*], that is, do not criticize [*arguunt*] people, do not pull them down [*destruunt*] and break [*fraguunt*] them. (LW25 229/WA56 243)

Such are the teachers that flee the "cross" and "suffering." Instead of teaching people to trust only in the naked mercy of God, they "only soften the heart of men to be pleased with themselves [. . .]" (LW25 230). For Luther, this is the practical effect of interpreting Christian soteriology through the lens of Aristotelian virtue theory. The false understanding of original sin is particularly culpable in the corruption of theology. Those who maintain the scholastic teaching "become smug [*securi*] in that they have attained righteousness and are at rest and relaxed [*et manibus remissis quieti*]," while in truth "we are not called to ease [*ocium*] but to a struggle against our passions" (LW25 338f./WA56 350).

The real task of a theologian, accordingly, is to "strangle 'the prudence of the flesh'" (LW25 372). This is carried out through preaching "hard sayings" like the doctrine of predestination. Of this doctrine in particular Luther says that "no words are more effective than these for terrifying, humbling, and destroying [*destruendem*] our arrogant presumptuousness regarding merits" (LW25 377/WA56 386). It is the task of the preacher and theologian to participate in God's *destructio* of the "old man," not to edify this false self-understanding through flattering theories of virtue. "For while the hearer sits quietly and receives the Word, the 'feet' of the preacher run over him, and he crushes him to see if he can make him better" (LW25 417). For the young Heidegger, Luther's *destructio* of scholastic theology was a paradigm of a responsible intellectual discipline, one committed to the radical and concrete transformation of people's lives. In chapter 4, I will show in more detail how Heidegger shared Luther's worries about the complicity of intellectuals in an irresponsible and complacent way of life.

Lectures on Hebrews

Beginning with his lectures of 1515 and 1516 on Paul's epistle to the Romans, Luther worked out, in increasing detail, a revolutionary soteriology, a soteriology of *destructio* and *aedificatio* in which humanity is saved by grace through faith. As the crisis over indulgences began to boil over, Luther continued to develop these ideas in his lectures of 1517 and 1518 on Hebrews.[30] Here we find a critique of scholastic theology that closely parallels the one worked out two years before. Moreover, Luther elaborates on his conception of God's saving deed as a *destructio* of the "prudence of the flesh." Finally, Luther adds to his critique of scholasticism a new conception of faith. Each of these ideas will be briefly described in this section.

As he had in his lectures on Romans and in academical writings such as the Heidelberg Disputation of 1518, Luther vehemently argues that concupiscence, the fundamental flaw of human nature, infects all moral activities (LW29 120). He continues his Pauline polemic against the "righteousness of works" and the Pelagian soteriology undergirding it (LW29 208f.). A new element of this polemic, reflected in Luther's more famous public activities during this period, concerns the penitential system of the Middle Ages. This part of Luther's nascent theology received its most renowned expression in the "Explanations of the Ninety-five Theses." But here, in the quiet of the lecture hall, Luther still manages to inveigh against what he regards as a theological abomination:

> But that endless tradition of decretals, decrees, statutes, etc., has multiplied us work-righteous hypocrites like "locusts out of the smoke," as Rev. 9:3 writes, and thus has darkened for us the sun of the completely pure faith, so that the spirit also sobs anew for the church, as in Ps. 12:1: "Save me, O God; for there is no longer any that is godly, for the faithful have vanished from among the sons of men." (LW29 232f.)

As in his Romans lectures, Luther also criticizes the philosophical and theological substructure of this system. Rather than targeting Aristotle's ethics in particular, Luther now focuses his attention on speculative knowledge of God and on the sort of "faith" involved in it. Luther counsels his students to abandon "human metaphysical rules" concerning the knowledge of God and instead to cling to the humanity of Christ. "For it is exceedingly godless temerity that, where God has humiliated Himself in order to become recognizable, man seeks for himself another way by following the counsels of his natural capacity" (LW29 111).[31] The natural knowledge of God, the possibility of which Luther is fully prepared to recognize, is no substitute for faith in the humanity of Christ. For one thing, such knowledge is totally impotent from a soteriological point of view. No human doctrine, says Luther, "can direct man and make him upright, since it leads only so far that it established good behavior, while man remains as he has been of old" (LW29 118). In his remarks on Hebrews 6:13, Luther asserts a connection between the impotence of legalism and this inadequacy of natural knowledge:

> Furthermore, to learn to know God as a dog learns to know its master or in the way the philosophers learned to know His power and His essence, as is recorded in Rom. 1:20, is not enough. For this is sensual, crude knowledge that is harmful to those who have it. (LW29 185)

Luther expounds upon the idea of "human faith" to further illustrate the inadequacy of natural knowledge of God. Nominalist theologians held, famously, that one who does "what lies in him" will be given the gift of justifying grace due to the ordained power of God. In theory, pre-Christian philosophers had met this covenantal requirement by arriving at a species of the love of God through natural reason. Luther argues, however, that this brand of "human faith" is soteriologically impotent. It arises not from the merciful gift of God's grace, but from the conceit of human reason. As such, its failure is inevitable. Luther writes:

> "To believe that God exists" seems to many to be so easy that they have ascribed this belief both to poets and to philosophers, as the apostle asserts

in Rom. 1:20. In fact, there are those who think that it is self-evident. But such human faith [*fides humana*] is just like any other thought, art, wisdom, dream, etc. of man. For as soon as trial assails, all those things immediately topple down. (LW29 235/WA57/3 233)

Eduard Ellwein, in his study of these lectures, notes that, for Luther, "we cannot speak about faith abstractly, but rather, in the highest degree, only concretely and existentielly."[32] Faith must be a personally appropriated commitment, or else it is simply not faith. As for the "human faith," Luther writes that it is "[f]or this reason [that] the apostle James calls this faith 'dead' (2:17), and others call it 'acquired' faith [*fides acquisitam*]" (LW29 235/WA57/3 233). The scholastic view that faith is a quality of the soul that must be "formed" by love to be effective is explicitly rejected by Luther (LW29 237).[33] Faith is the very "life of the heart." True faith alone, a gift of God and not a human acquisition, is soteriologically efficacious (LW29 123).

As in his lectures of 1515 and 1516, Luther argues that the "alien works" of God are essential to the process of finally receiving the gift of justifying faith. Here again, the Gospel serves as the agent of this painful transformation. Luther writes:

> And thus the Gospel preserves nothing of the old man but destroys [*destruit*] him completely and makes him new, until hatred of himself utterly roots out love of himself through faith in Christ. Therefore all boasting of erudition, wisdom, and knowledge is useless; for no one is made better by these, no matter what good and laudable gifts of God they are. (LW29 119/WA57/3 109)

Luther's discussion here also adds a new element to the soteriology of *destructio*. In keeping with the Christocentric tone of Hebrews, Luther comes to understand the "alien works" of God as a kind of historical *imitatio Christi*. Just as "death and all the works of the devil have been destroyed [*destructa*] in Christ," this must also occur in all of his "members" (LW29 136/WA57/3 129). God's will is to "destroy [*destruere*]" these things through Christ (LW29 136/WA57/3 129). Luther describes the wondrous nature of God's saving deed in Christ. It is through death itself that humanity is freed from death. "And in this way God destroys [*destruit*] the devil through the devil himself and accomplishes his own work by means of an alien work [*alieno opere*]" (LW29 136/WA57/3 129).

In introducing the concept of the "alien work" of God, Luther harks back to the dialectic of *destructio* described earlier in the Romans lectures. Commenting on Hebrews 2:9, he argues that "it is necessary that 'the body of sin' and the law of the flesh 'be destroyed [*destrui*]'" (LW29 130/WA57/3 129). This comes about through all kinds of trials, tribulations, and *Anfechtungen*. But God's ultimate purpose can be discerned with the eyes of faith: "God kills in order to make alive; He humiliates in order to exalt, etc." (LW29 130). Later, in his comments on Hebrews 3:6, Luther uses a striking metaphor to describe this dialectic. Paul tells us that we are the "house" built by Christ. Yet the "construction [*fabricacio*]" takes place in "tension, pressure, and in every way the cross and sufferings that are in Christ" (LW29 146/WA57/3 141). Just as the frame of a house is supported by the tension exerted by the beams upon one another, so also the spiritual "house" of the "new man" is only constructed by means of the destruction inflicted upon the "old man" by God.

In his lectures on Hebrews, Luther continued to develop the theology first glimpsed in the years 1515 and 1516. He writes of the inadequacy of contemplative theology and contrasts its theoretical understanding of God with the true faith that is forged in the furnace of *Anfechtung*. He focuses particular attention on the Christological dimension of *destructio* as the "alien work" of God. All these teachings were to have a profound impact on the young Heidegger as he began to formulate his own philosophical position in dialogue with Luther and others. Luther's critique of Greek metaphysics, his Pauline anti-hedonism, and, above all, the concept of *destructio* all receive a new embodiment in Heidegger's thought during the 1920s and early 1930s.

Destructio in Luther's Academic Writings

In the year 1518, at the same time he was lecturing on Hebrews, Luther produced two of his most important works. The first is the "Heidelberg Disputation," composed on the occasion of the general chapter of the German Augustinians, at the request of Luther's fatherly friend Johannes von Staupitz. This is a series of theses in support of the new evangelical theology that had recently begun to gain a hold on the faculty of the University of Wittenberg. The second work is the "Explanations of the Ninety-five Theses," also known as the "Explanations of the Disputation Concerning the Value of Indulgences." This work was published a few months after Luther's return from Heidelberg. It was subsequently sent to his superiors, including Pope Leo X. In both of these writings, Luther adumbrates what he calls the "theology of the cross." The concept, and practice, of *destructio* are central to this new theology.[34]

The "Heidelberg Disputation" also figures prominently in Heidegger's discussions of Luther. He first mentions it in his lectures on Augustine from SS 1921. In this text, according to Heidegger, Luther opens up a "new understanding of primitive Christianity" (G60 282). He goes on to enlist some of the theses from Luther's "Heidelberg Disputation" in his own attack on Augustine's neo-platonic tendencies. This text surfaces again several years later, in Heidegger's guest lecture in Bultmann's seminar at Marburg. "Here," Heidegger writes, "Luther very clearly characterizes the task of theology by contrasting two theological points of view [. . .]" (S 107). Heidegger paraphrases Luther's main argument: "This Greek point of view of Scholasticism makes man proud; he must first go to the cross before he can say *id quod res est* [what the matter actually is]" (S 107). In case there are any doubts about the importance that Heidegger attaches to this text, he adds, "In the 'Heidelberg Disputation,' we surely find the most pointed formulation of Luther's position in his early period" (S 107).

The "Heidelberg Disputation" of 1518 contains forty theses, twenty-eight of which are "theological," while twelve are designated "philosophical."[35] Luther advertises these theses as continuous with the thought of both Paul and Augustine (LW31 39). The influence of these thinkers is evident from Thesis 18, which proclaims Luther's unequivocal break with the theology of the *via moderna*: "It is certain that a man must utterly despair [*desperare*] of his own ability before he is prepared to receive the grace of Christ" (LW31 40/WA1 354). The theological position that accords with this "certainty" is explained by Luther in the "proofs" to selected theses. In his proof of Thesis 4, Luther provides a systematic presentation of the notion of the "alien works" of God, already familiar from previous discussions. He writes:

> That the works of God are unattractive is clear from what is said in Isa. 53 [:2], "He had no form of comeliness," and in 1 Sam. 2 [:6], "The Lord kills and brings to life; he brings down to Sheol and raises up" [. . .] And that it is which Isa. 28 [:2] calls the alien work of God [*opus alienum Dei*] that he may do his work (that is, he humbles us thoroughly, making us despair [*desperantes fasciens*], so that he may exalt us in his mercy, giving us hope), just as Hab. 3 [:2] states, "In wrath remember mercy." (LW31 44/WA1 357)

This passage neatly summarizes the dialectic between the wrath of God, experienced in *destructio*, and the mercy of God, experienced in *iustificatio*. This is a dialectic that can be discerned in many of Luther's works from the period under discussion. To borrow the language of Karl Barth, the divine "No!" is at once a divine "Yes!" That is, the judgment of all human righteousness and wisdom by God is, when properly received by faith, the fulfillment of humanity.

This is, says Luther, something that is always overlooked and obscured by the "enemies of the cross of Christ," whom Luther often calls the "theologians of glory" (LW31 53). The friends of the cross see that it is a good thing, for only by it can the "old Adam" be destroyed [*destruuntur*] (LW31 53/WA1 362). He stresses that the hankering after wisdom and "glory" can never be satisfied. "In other words, he who wishes to become wise does not seek wisdom by progressing toward it but becomes a fool by retrogressing into seeking folly" (LW31 54). Only thus can one begin to recognize that it is truly God's grace that accomplishes all things in us (LW31 55).

As in his contemporaneous lectures on Hebrews, Luther finds fault with the quietistic, contemplative knowledge of God available to reason unaided by grace. The mere "recognition [*cognita*]" of goodness, virtue, or wisdom does not impart these qualities to a person (LW31 52/WA1 361). This is why God chose to reveal himself in humility, "hidden in suffering" (LW31 52). Reason, by itself, cannot make the transition from cognitive apprehension of some fact or other to existential commitment. To use Luther's words, "[n]ow it is not sufficient for anyone, and it does him no good to recognize God in his glory and majesty, unless he recognizes him in the humility and shame of the cross. Thus God destroys [*perdit*] the wisdom of the wise, as Isa. [45:15] says, 'Truly, thou art a God who hidest thyself'" (LW31 53/WA1 362).[36] The scandal of the death of God on the cross is of such magnitude, according to Luther, that reason is at a loss to discern the mercy of God within it, let alone His glory. Only faith, the appropriation of God's personal assistance, can see God's "proper work" hidden in this "alien work." Yet even then the hiddenness of God always provokes doubt, trial, and *Anfechtung*.[37]

Luther's "Explanations of the Ninety-five Theses" provides further clarifications of the "theology of the cross" and the importance of *destructio* within its soteriological scheme. Here again, one finds strongly worded critiques of the Aristotelianism of medieval theology. In this case, it is Aristotle's hedonistic eudaimonism that Luther's finds to be completely out of place in Christian theology. Luther goes so far as to attribute the more intemperate theological views on indulgences to this influence:

> The theologian of glory, however, learns from Aristotle that the object of the will is the good and the good is worthy to be loved, while the evil, on the other hand, is worthy of hate. He learns that God is the highest good and exceedingly lovable. Disagreeing with the theologian of the cross, he defines the treasury of Christ as the removing and remitting of punishments, things which are most evil and worthy of hate. (LW31 227)

Here Luther charges his theological opponents with complicity in fallen humanity's lust for *securitas*. According to the indulgence preachers, the "treasury of Christ" was a kind of supernatural storehouse of merits which, for a fee, could be imparted to souls both on earth and in Purgatory who were languishing from canonical obligations. Luther, of course, finds such teaching completely out of place in a genuinely evangelical theology, for "it is evident that the cross continues until death and thereby to entrance into the kingdom" (LW31 89). In Luther's mind, the scholastic theology is the "deceiving [*illusoria*]" theology—"for that is the meaning of the word in Greek" (LW31 225/WA1 613). Luther no doubt has in mind the word '*scholastikos*,' meaning originally "to be at leisure" or "lazy." Under the influence of Aristotelian eudaimonism, the indulgence preachers had become preachers of smugness, of self-righteousness, and of flight from suffering, rather than preachers of Christ crucified.

Contrary to this "deceiving theology," Luther argues that the merits of Christ carry out God's "alien work," i.e., "the cross, labor, all kinds of punishment, finally death and hell in the flesh, to the end that the body of sin is destroyed [*destruantur*] [. . .]" (LW31 225/WA1 613). As in his lectures from 1515 and 1516, Luther states that it is the Gospel that "destroys [*destruit*]" that which exists, that which is strong and wise in its own estimation

(LW31 232/WA1 617). Indeed, the Gospel destroys precisely those "enemies of the cross," those who flee from the "hard saying" that reveals their own soteriological impotence. Instead, they are comforted by what Luther regards as the Pelagian doctrines of his contemporaries. They fail to see that it is only in putting the "old man" to death that God brings forth His new creation in our hearts. Luther writes:

> So it seems to me, and I declare: When God begins to justify a man, he first of all condemns him; him whom he wishes to raise up [*aedificare*], he destroys [*destruit*]; him whom he wishes to heal, he smites; and the one to whom he wishes to give life, he kills, as he says in 1 Kings 2 [1 Sam. 2:6], and Deut. 32 [:39], "I kill and I make alive, etc." (LW31 99/WA1 540)

In the "Explanations," Luther puts particular emphasis on the *experience* of *destructio*. His vivid descriptions of the torments of an afflicted conscience have been regarded as one of Luther's greatest self-confessions.[38] There are some, says Luther, who have experienced in this life the "flight [*fugam*]" and "anxiety [*angustias*]" that characterize the torments of hell (LW31 126/WA1 556; LW31 127/WA1 556). Luther finds the writings of the mystic Johannes Tauler particularly important for his discussions of this point (LW31 128f.). "At such a time," Luther writes, "there is no flight, no comfort, within or without, but all things accuse" (LW31 129). *Destructio* goes far beyond intellectual doubts about articles of faith; it is experienced as a genuine demolition of everything that one has, up to that moment, identified with. Here, the faulty self-understanding of a person, *coram mundo*, is confronted with the terrifying reality of that person's life *coram Deo*. The futility of human efforts is revealed in one shattering moment. Luther concludes his description thus:

> All that remains is the stark-naked desire for help and a terrible groaning, but [the soul] does not know where to turn for help. In this instance the person is stretched out with Christ so that all his bones may be counted, and every corner of the soul is filled with the greatest bitterness, dread, trembling, and sorrow in such a manner that all these last forever. (LW31 129)

It is now abundantly clear that the term '*destructio*' has an absolutely crucial role to play in Luther's early theology (1515–1518).[39] The theological revolution that occurred during these years is best understood not as a rejection of authority or as an attack on institutional corruption, but as a reconceiving of fundamental issues in Christian soteriology. It is not without warrant that "justification by faith" is viewed as the cardinal Lutheran doctrine. *Destructio* is integral to the new theological position propounded by Luther.

Indeed, it can be said that one of Luther's primary difficulties with late medieval soteriology was its failure to include a proper appreciation for the reality designated by this term. The ethos of *facere quod in se est* holds no place for the humiliating revelation of human corruption and impotence. For

Luther, it is precisely this revelation that is required if the "old man" is to be truly vanquished. '*Destructio*' is Luther's name for God's dismantling of the idols of human egotism. This act is concretely experienced in spiritual trial, in the pangs of conscience, and, ultimately, in total despair. It is only when all confidence in human faculties and in the world has been lost that faith, filial trust in the goodness of a gracious God, is able to take possession of the heart.

Luther also gives the name '*destructio*' to his own polemics against the faulty soteriology and anthropology of scholastic theology. This theology speaks the language of the "prudence of the flesh," rather than of the crucified and hidden God. All of Luther's polemics against scholasticism, Aristotle, reason, and philosophy amount to his own attempt, as a custodian of the Word of God, to participate in the *destructio* of the "old man." It is this vision of the role of theology that came to intrigue Martin Heidegger. Heidegger shared, for the most part, Luther's pessimistic assessment of the human condition. Yet, like Luther, he was aware of what to him was a more authentic mode of living. Accordingly, he began to conceive of philosophy not merely as a handmaiden to the sciences (positivism), or as a construction of *a priori* values (neo-Kantianism), or even as the proclamation of ideology (philosophy of life), but as a comrade in the struggle against inauthenticity. Learning from Luther, Heidegger called this philosophy '*Destruktion.*'

PART TWO. HEIDEGGER'S MOTIVES

Inauthenticity

Indeed, all of us are convinced that for the moment almost everything is ordered as neatly as possible [. . .]. In this domain, there is not only complacency, but even joy and delirium.[1]

In chapter 2, I argued that Luther's primary problem with scholastic theology and its dependence on the concepts of Aristotelian philosophy is *soteriological*. Luther contends that scholasticism not only fails to convey the "good news" of free grace in Christ, but that it is actually *complicit* in a sinful life of self-satisfaction. The "theology of the cross," which Luther offers as a more appropriate alternative, is ultimately anchored not in a *theoretical* problem but in a *practical* one. My thesis, which has yet to be completely supported at this point, is that Heidegger, too, anchors the very meaning of philosophical activity in a consideration of a *practical* issue. To see how this might be true, it is of course imperative that Heidegger's explicit comments about the nature and tasks of philosophy be thoroughly explored. Equally important, however, is the task of coming to understand *what is at issue* ('*was es kommt darauf an*,' to borrow a Heideggerian turn of phrase) in the attempt to make philosophy practical. The question is, what value or set of values informs Heidegger's conception of the nature and tasks of philosophy?

In 1921, Heidegger responded to a letter from his student Karl Löwith in which Löwith had related a debate between himself and Oskar Becker regarding the most attractive features of Heidegger's thought. Becker, a mathematician, naturally appreciated the *wissenschaftlich* side of Heidegger, while Löwith gravitated toward his existential "pathos." In his response, Heidegger tells Löwith that his work cannot be reduced to either extreme. To quote his revealing response in full:

> I work concretely and factically out of my "I am," out of my intellectual and wholly factic provenance [*Herkunft*]—milieu—context of life [...]. To this facticity of mine belongs—to put it briefly—the fact that I am a "Christian theo*logian.*" This involves a particular radical anxious worry about oneself [*Selbstbekümmerung*], a particular radical scientificity, a strict objectivity *in* the *facticity* [...].[2]

It is precisely this rare mixture between academic philosophy and existential "pathos" that accounts for much of the continuing appeal of Heidegger's philosophy. Similar thinkers, such as Kierkegaard, Nietzsche, and Rosenzweig, undertook their work outside the university and all were quite critical of institutionalized intellectual life. Heidegger shared many of their attitudes toward the "business [*Betrieb*]" of philosophy, yet he remained a professional philosopher for his entire life. Heidegger, the sharp critic of academic "bustle," was never anyone besides Heidegger, the professor of philosophy. His goal remained the reinvigoration of intellectual life from within the university. Heidegger's ultimate practical concern, however, extends well beyond the walls of the lecture hall. For Heidegger, *the* issue of human life as such is what sort of life it is going to be. There are two possibilities: "inauthenticity" and "authenticity." One is characterized by complacency, distraction, and selfconcealment, while the other is marked by commitment, struggle, and sober responsibility for oneself. One kind of life is, ultimately, a failure to "own up" to oneself [Un-*eigentlichkeit*], while the other is a life of profound honesty.

The idea that life can be either "authentic" or "inauthentic" is certainly not Heidegger's invention. As I will describe below (chapter 5), Heidegger's thoughts on this issue have their proximate roots in the tradition of Romantic individualism. At the same time, as the passage quoted above from a letter to Löwith suggests, Heidegger's thought is also deeply shaped by theology. Thus, the values that motivate his thought, including his concern with the pervasiveness of "inauthenticity," reflect his own blend of Christian theology and Romantic personalism. The spirit of Romanticism was once again making itself felt during the early twentieth century. The proliferation of "philosophies of life," of anti-bourgeois youth movements, and the cult of the artist as a higher type of human being all testify to this.

Heidegger drank deeply from the wells of Romanticism, and his vision of an authentic life clearly attests to this. At the same time, Heidegger's view bears the stamp of a particularly German sort of neo-Romanticism that eventually issued, after the collapse of the Hohenzollern empire, in a movement known as the "Conservative Revolution." Heidegger's discussions often involve attacks on public opinion and modern mass society, sharing many points of contact with other intellectuals of the Conservative Revolution in Germany during the 1920s and 1930s.[3]

Much has been written about the idea of inauthenticity in *Being and Time*, while comparatively little has been said about it in Heidegger's writings and lectures leading up to the publication of his *magnum opus*.[4] This is due, no doubt, to the privileged status enjoyed by *Being and Time* in anglophone Heidegger scholarship in particular. The bulk of the present chapter will be made up of an analysis of Heidegger's work prior to *Being and Time*. However, given that Heidegger's more polished discussions in *Being and Time* often lend more systematic clarity to his thoughts on these matters, I will naturally include this material in my discussion. Nonetheless, I do hope to move the state of the current discussion beyond the scholarly fixation on *Being and Time*, which has been rightly challenged by the work of Van Buren and Kisiel. This chapter is an examination of "inauthenticity" *per se*, and itself consists of two stages. First, I will briefly consider the nature of Heidegger's views against the background of moral theory in order to clarify what Heidegger is concerned with and to respond to some long-standing worries about his position. Second, I will examine the "categories" that define the contours of an inauthentic life in Heidegger's account. This latter discussion will be an explication of what "inauthenticity" means.

Reading Heidegger on Inauthenticity

The Basics of Inauthenticity

Throughout the 1920s, Heidegger developed a critical analysis of a particular mode of human life. What is distinctive about Heidegger's views, compared to those of his contemporaries on both right and left, is that his belong to a unique philosophical project. In 1923, Heidegger called this project the "hermeneutics of facticity," and in *Being and Time* he calls it the "existential analytic of Dasein." The project is to "bring to the light of day" the categorial structures that make life, and its manifold relations to the world, the meaningful and intelligible things that they are (see chapter 1). A variety of general terms are employed to characterize what eventually comes to be called, in *Being and Time*, "inauthenticity." Prior to this work, Heidegger more often employs terms such as "lapse" or "decline [*Abfallen*]," "collapse [*Sturz*]," "falling [*Verfallen*]," and "ruinance [*Ruinanz*]." The more familiar terminology of *Being and Time* takes shape during SS 1925. It is, however, in *Being and Time* itself that this early nomenclature comes to be explicitly linked to inauthenticity.[5]

It is difficult to find anything like a single general characterization of inauthenticity in Heidegger's works. In the text for WS 1920–1921, we find the following: "A formally indicative definition would therefore determine ruinance as follows: the movedness of factical life which it 'enacts' and is *in* itself, *as* itself, *for* itself, and, in all of this, *against itself*" (G61 131/98). The significance of this very formal characterization is that it links a "fallen" or "inauthentic" life with Heidegger's more general view of human selfhood. To put it briefly, Heidegger views selfhood as a *process* rather than as a *presence*. One way to express this is by talking about the "movedness [*Bewegtheit*]" of life, as Heidegger does in this passage. The clear sense of these remarks is that inauthenticity, here called "ruinance," is a *way* of being a self.

In *Being and Time*, there are several candidates for a general description. Perhaps the clearest comes in §38, where Heidegger writes, "Just as little does 'inauthenticity' mean something like 'no longer being-in-the-world,' but it amounts to a distinctive being-in-the-world, that is completely benumbed [*benommen*] by the 'world' and the co-Dasein of others in the 'one'" (SZ 176/220). If we look at both of these characterizations together, we see that a basic trait of this way of life, whether we call it "ruinance," "falling," or "inauthenticity," is that of a kind of abdication of self. This is formally indicated in the first quote by the locution "*against itself*," while it is given a bit more content in Heidegger's depiction of the benumbed state of Dasein in *Being and Time*. Put simply, an inauthentic life is one that is not lived by itself.

Heidegger is also clear regarding what we ought *not* to think about inauthenticity. First of all, it does not signify some sort of metaphysical deficiency or some failure to realize the essence of humanity. Heidegger makes this explicit in his discussion of the "one-self," a central feature of this way of existing. "This way to be [*Weise zu sein*] does not signify a diminishing of the facticity of Dasein, and just as little is the 'one,' as the 'nobody,' a nothing. On the contrary, in this kind of being Dasein is an *ens realissimum*, provided that 'reality' is understood as a Dasein-like way of being" (SZ 128/166). Heidegger reiterates this point later in his discussion of "falling," reminding his readers that "[i]n no way do 'in-' or 'non-authentic' signify 'really not,' as if in this mode of being Dasein would altogether forfeit its being" (SZ 175/220).

Second, Heidegger also wants us to avoid thinking about inauthenticity as a psychological feature that belongs to particular individuals or groups of individuals. The point is made in Heidegger's 1924 lectures on Dilthey at Kassel. Here, Heidegger explains the related terms "the one [*das Man*]" and "idle talk," both of which figure large in his more well-known analysis in *Being and Time*. At the end of the discussion, he remarks, "Here we are not discussing acts or experiences of consciousness, but certain ways of being-in-the-world" (S 165). In other words, Heidegger is not giving us an *a priori* psychology nor simply a phenomenological description of what goes on in our minds, but is rather attempting to elucidate the structures that make up the "primary reality of human Dasein" (S 164). "Human Dasein" is not a metaphysical "nature" or "essence" that determines the course of thought and action, but is simply the fluid web of meaningful relations in the midst of which our actions make sense to us and to others.

That "inauthenticity" and its cognates are not *psychological* can be further illustrated by a consideration of the early Christian idea of the *"world,"* which Heidegger acknowledges as a source for some of his own ideas. "World," for the writers of the New Testament, is a "how" of human existence that is contrasted with the "age to come" (G26 222/173; G9 143 f./112). World does not mean, to borrow Wittgenstein's memorable phrase, the totality of what is the case, but is instead a way of life, including both a web of values and patterned responses to it. In the Johannine writings, for example, "world" describes the state of humanity in its separation from God, a state that is set into apocalyptic conflict with Jesus Christ (G9 144/113). Clearly, it is inappropriate to reduce inauthenticity to a psychological category. Given the link that Heidegger explicitly draws between his analysis of inauthenticity and the Christian-prophetic critique of the "world," it stands to reason that "inauthenticity," like "world," is not the name of a psychological category.

Inauthenticity in Moral Theory

At this point, however, a question arises regarding the goals of Heidegger's analyses. He is emphatic in his avoidance of "matters better left to the preacher" (G61 165/124). At the same time, it is hard to see how attacks on inauthentic complacency, the bankruptcy of culture, and the shallowness of dogmatic religiosity could be construed otherwise than as instances of Weimar *Kulturkritik*, albeit of a brilliantly intellectualized sort. The ambiguity of Heidegger's conception of philosophy is clearly brought out by a note later added to the lecture notes for WS 1919–1920:

> Philosophy—neither mere investigation of a subject matter or an object (validity of propositions)—nor sermonizing, practical directing or regulation—rather, understandingly leading [*Führung*];—not the practical usefulness of norms,—but rather genuine possibilities of leading and of formation [*Bildung*]. (G58 150)

What could it mean to "lead" without somehow lapsing into "sermonizing, practical direction, or regulation"? This is one of the central dilemmas that Heidegger faces. I will show in more detail below (chapter 4) how Heidegger is critical of ideology, world-view, and moral theory for contributing to an irresponsible and complacent way of life. Like Luther, Heidegger aimed at "destroying" these tendencies. This critical project takes precedence over any more "positive" or "constructive" theorizing about values. The motto of Heidegger's thought, as of Luther's, could well be *"corruptio amplificanda est."* Heidegger is thus faced with the difficult situation of having values so fragile that they are undermined by the kind of direct presentation characteristic of most moral theory.

Another kind of concern has been offered by Hubert Dreyfus in *Being-in-the-world*. Dreyfus sees two versions of "inauthenticity" or "falling" in *Being and Time*, one that is "structural," or built in to human existence, and another that is "motivational," and hence avoidable. The result of these two accounts, according to Dreyfus, is that "inauthenticity becomes both inevitable and incomprehensible."[6] The charge of "inevitability" is directed at Heidegger's alleged "hermeneutics of suspicion," which, according to Dreyfus, is meant to undermine the "obviousness" of our everyday mode of existence. That is, according to Dreyfus, Heidegger is trying to call into question everything from our everyday practices to our most rarefied reflections by showing how these arise from a seemingly inescapable and lamentable feature of human life. The "inevitability" of inauthenticity, however, seems to make Heidegger's account of authenticity strangely inconsistent, for why would something inevitable in this way be worth criticizing? The "incomprehensibility" of a "motivated" account of inauthenticity, on the other hand, stems from the intrinsic satisfaction and consequent desirability of an authentic life. Why, Dreyfus asks, would anyone be inauthentic? Moreover, how do these two accounts, the "structural" and the "motivated," fit together?

The alleged "inevitability" of inauthenticity is something that must be more closely considered in the light of Heidegger's thought as a whole. First of all, Dreyfus's criticisms seem to rest upon a robust metaphysical conception of Heidegger's categories in *Being and Time*, one which fails to take into account Heidegger's explicit formulations of what his philosophy amounts to: he has no pretensions to "absolute knowledge" or "objectivity" (cf. G29/30 28f./19).[7] "Philosophy," he tells us, "is what it can be only as a philosophy of 'its time.' 'Temporality.' Dasein works in the how of its *being-now*" (G63 18/14). A philosophical "concept" is not a representation of the timeless reality of something, but is "a meaning drawn out of something" (G63 16/12). Philosophy is "historical" knowing of life, not ahistorical metaphysical contemplation (G61 2/3). Rather than passing down truths for posterity, philosophy must confront its own situation: "The situation is not a safe harbor, but rather the leap into a moving boat, and it all depends on getting the line for the sail in hand and looking to the wind" (G61 37/29). It seems, then, that one ought not to read Heidegger's existential analytic as a catalogue of necessary truths about the human condition. In this way, Dreyfus's talk about the "structural" account of inauthenticity needs to be qualified. Heidegger is not to be taken as giving us a story about human nature, or as presenting us with fixed, necessary "transcendental" concepts. Instead, Heidegger is trying to intimate the pre-theoretical meaning of life in a provisional and revisable way. The ubiquity of "fallenness," something that Heidegger certainly describes, should not be mistaken for a claim about *necessity*.

Perhaps more importantly, one might well wonder why the "inevitability" of inauthenticity represents a significant problem at all. The problem, one will recall, seems to be that the inevitability of inauthenticity seems to render *authenticity* impossible, thus calling into question the whole project of articulating an alternative. Yet, it is surely not the case that the possibility of moral perfection is a necessary condition for moral improvement, or, for that matter, of moral exhortation. Were it so, Heidegger would certainly not be alone in facing Dreyfus's worry. Indeed, every moral theory that is tied to a realistic depiction of human life would seem to be subject to this sort of objection. Luther's influence on Heidegger's work can help us understand the position more clearly. As Heidegger was well aware, Luther took sin to be a *basic* feature of human existence.[8] As such, only God's creative righteousness is capable of removing this stain on our lives. For Luther, the scholastics' more liberal understanding of human nature is such that it renders the basic truths of Christianity superfluous. Heidegger seems to have been cognizant of this: "The more one fails to recognize the radicalness of sin, the more redemption is made little of, and the more God's becoming man in the Incarnation loses its necessity" (S 106). Moreover, Luther taught that while we are accounted righteous by faith in Christ's atoning sacrifice, *actual* righteousness is something that stands under an "eschatological proviso." That is, it is only in the end-time consummation of God's promise of salvation that human beings will be definitively without sin.[9]

The neo-orthodox revival that occurred in the 1920s involved a forceful reassertion of these ideas. Heidegger was familiar not only with their biblical and Lutheran sources, but also with the work of these young theologians.[10] Perhaps the most influential and most uncompromising statement of this position is Karl Barth's *Der Römerbrief*. Here, Barth advocates a "crisis" theology, according to which all of human culture stands under judgment. Historically, the target of Barth's polemic in this work is the liberal optimism of nineteenth-century theology, which, following Kant, tended to identify the kingdom of God with the moral and intellectual perfection of an enlightened society. There is nothing obviously "incoherent" about the neo-Lutheran view. In holding that moral, cultural, or spiritual perfection is beyond the grasp of humanity due to sin, one is not thereby committing oneself to holding that moral imperatives are meaningless or that moral *improvement* is impossible.

The point of Heidegger's warnings about his own notion of inauthenticity parallels this theological position. Inauthenticity or "fallenness [*Verfallen-heit*]" is not some accidental, adventitious feature of certain people's lives. Instead, it is the *de facto* starting point of all human activity (which is not to say it is a metaphysical "property" that belongs to "human nature"). A number of passages in *Being and Time* make this clear. "*Authentic being a self* is not based upon an exceptional condition of the subject, detached from the 'one,' but rather *is an existentiell modification of the 'one' as an essential existential*" (SZ 130/168). That is to say, inauthenticity is a basic "category" that articulates an important element of the pre-conceptual meaningfulness of human life.[11] Further, just as inauthenticity is not adventitious, so also authenticity is not some pristine state of existence that is achieved once and for all.[12] The point, then, of cautioning against a certain reading of inauthenticity is to keep a critical distance from precisely those kinds of moral and religious complacency that best characterize it. To quote one of Luther's favorite sayings, "to cease wanting to be good is to cease being good altogether."

As for the "incomprehensibility" of inauthenticity, one needs only to look to both Heidegger's own conception and to its theological roots. Recall that, on Dreyfus's reading, the "motivational" account of inauthenticity is "incoherent," since the intrinsically satisfying nature of an authentic life would seem to preclude the possibility of anyone's opting for a lesser alternative. However, this reading must be revised by a consideration of the *sources* of Heidegger's notion of inauthenticity. In his exposition of Pauline Christianity, Heidegger stresses the intrinsic distress and insecurity of Christian life, in contrast to "poor mysticism" (G60 99 f.).[13] Luther, too, cautioned against hedonistic readings of Christian life. For Heidegger, then, an authentic life is one that is only contingently related to pleasure or satisfaction. While it is certainly clear that Heidegger *values* an authentic way of life, this does not entail that he regards it as *satisfying*. Moreover, Dreyfus gives us no reason to think that, on Heidegger's view, value is always a matter of preference satisfaction. Unless Heidegger is somehow committed to such a view, there would seem to be no problem with his holding that authenticity is both valuable and *unsatisfying*.

My response to Dreyfus's worries regarding inauthenticity rests, in part, upon a conception of Heidegger's work as a species of moral theory. It makes little sense, after all, to bring in considerations about moral improvement when the matter under discussion is not even a moral issue. Quite aside from objections of the kind that Dreyfus presents, or from those offered by critics of Heidegger who take their lead from his later involvement with Nazism, my reading of Heidegger as a moral theorist faces the challenge of Heidegger's explicit warnings against such readings. Yet I think that the only way to make sense of his talk of "inauthenticity" and "authenticity" is to think of them as part of a kind of moral theory. The task, then, is to show what kind of moral theory it is, and then to explain Heidegger's reticence about this view.

Much of the following remarks are necessarily provisional, since I have yet to examine the alternative to inauthenticity, i.e., authenticity. Thus, the story I am offering here comes with a promissory note attached. That said, Heidegger's view can be characterized as a species of *perfectionism*. Taken most broadly, perfectionism is a general type of theory concerning the human good. It differs from other theories of the good, e.g., utilitarian ones, in that the good in question is not pleasure or happiness. Perfectionist theories tend to offer a picture of human flourishing couched in terms of the full and unimpeded exercise of basic human capacities. A classic example is Book X of Aristotle's *Nicomachean Ethics*, in which the human good is identified with the perfect exercise of human reason in the theoretical sphere. Some perfectionist theories are theories about the value of self-realization, but this is not essential to this type of view.

Heidegger's theory is perfectionist in the sense that he clearly thinks there is a valuable way of life called "authenticity" that is not to be identified with pleasure or happiness. At best, pleasure is only contingently related to living an authentic life. However, this is not an ethic of self-realization. This is true for two reasons: (1) Heidegger offers no theory of "natural" human capacities; and (2) Heidegger explicitly denies the possibility of a human life ever being "realized" or "complete" in a teleological sense.

Heidegger's view also differs from other perfectionist ones in that there is no worked-out value theory to accompany it. Again, Aristotle's *Nicomachean Ethics* can serve as a guide; in Book I, Aristotle clearly ranks the values of pleasure, of social interaction, and of knowledge, and presents *eudaimonia* as something like the ultimate human good. Heidegger has no value theory, and is, moreover, sharply critical of the prevailing theories of the time (neo-Kantianism). Thus, there is no assertion to the effect that authenticity is the "best" life for a human being, nor that it is the ultimate value that must be promoted. Furthermore, as Karl Löwith has argued, authenticity is something of an ideal without content.[14] This could be true in several senses. First, there is no explicit paradigm of "the" authentic person. In addition, Heidegger does not spell out in detail any constraints, of either an axiological or deontological character, on living an authentic life. "Authentic" seems like a value that belongs to a life as a whole, and hence to particular choices, values, and so forth insofar as they are parts of such a life.

While these features certainly make Heidegger's view a peculiar kind of moral theory, the real problem lies in his explicit disavowal of offering a moral theory at all. Is Heidegger simply being disingenuous? Is he offering a contentious moral theory, only to pull back from it rather than face philosophical questions? Again, a full answer to this question can only really come after *both* inauthenticity *and* authenticity have been explicated. I think, though, that Heidegger's reticence about proclaiming his view as a moral theory is not only consistent with the kind of value he is endorsing, but also with some of his commitments concerning the nature of philosophical discourse.

Beginning around WS 1919–1920, Heidegger developed the idea of "formal indication."[15] Heidegger developed this idea under pressure to create a mode of philosophical discourse adequate to capture the meaning of pretheoretical life. Important influences on this conception seem to have included Kierkegaard and Aristotle. For Heidegger, if philosophy is to fulfill the project of the "hermeneutics of facticity," then it must face the fact that it "would thus be deprived of its most traditional entitlements as a regal, superior occupation" (G56/57 11/10). Part of the traditional "occupation" of philosophy has been, to use Nietzsche's terms, the erection of a "table of values." Heidegger abdicates this much of the philosophical peerage, not because he wants to avoid thorny issues, but because he thinks this project is profoundly misguided. Rather than present the objective "answers" to life's questions, Heidegger wants a discourse that merely amounts to "calling something to the attention of others" (G9 6/5). "This," he says, "is ultimately the predicament of all philosophizing regarding its intention of having an effect on the world of others" (G9 6/5). This kind of provisional discourse is ultimately one that is rooted in experience, in the "poverty" of the philosophizing individual. "One can call something to the attention of others, and compel them to engage in reflection, only by traveling a stretch of the way oneself" (G9 42/36).

A formal indication in Heidegger is often more of a question than an answer. It is a kind of discourse that is aimed at throwing the individual back upon herself. Heidegger's clearest statement to this effect comes from WS 1921–1922:

> The formal indication of the "I am" [. . .] becomes methodologically effective by being brought into its genuine factical actualization, i.e., by becoming actualized in the demonstrable character of the *questionability* ("restlessness") of factical life as the concretely historical question, "Am I?" [. . .]. The peculiarity of the actualization of this question is precisely the fact that, as a matter of principle, it does not answer the question with a pure, simple, and perfect "yes," which would then obviate any further discussion of life, or with that kind of "no." (G61 174f./131f.)

Heidegger's presentation of the ideal of authenticity is a formal indication *par excellence*. This, of course, should not be surprising, since the whole idea of authenticity is of a life that owns up to itself and that resists the pull of complacency. We could hardly expect someone who found this to be valuable to be offering us practical prescriptions on how we ought to live. Instead, the aim of Heidegger's discourse is, at least in part, to "hint" at or point to factical possibilities that only become meaningful when they are realized by a concrete individual existing at the particular time. Formal indication is clearly not the *only* way to go about doing moral theory. It might not even be the best way, though it seems to be the only reasonable approach in light of some of Heidegger's basic commitments about the problems of traditional moral theory.

"Categories" of Fallen Life

In the absence of anything approximating a general definition of inauthentic, "fallen" life, the only way to come to terms with it is by examining its various features. For brevity, I refer to these as the "categories of fallen life." Focusing on "falling" is more appropriate here, since the actual term "inauthenticity" does not emerge as a designation for this phenomenon until the period immediately preceding the publication of *Being and Time*. During the early 1920s, terms like "falling" and "ruinance" are far more common in Heidegger's discourse.[16] There are five general features of a fallen life that recur throughout Heidegger's discussions of this issue. [1] Heidegger often begins his discussions of this theme by describing an "inclination," "propensity," or "proclivity" toward fallenness. [2] Closely linked with this is a tendency to "take it easy," and the consequent complacency and "numbness." [3] Along with this comes a kind of dispersion, a kind of distracted existence that lacks focus. [4] Heidegger also often describes what he at one point terms the "hyperbolic" tendency of life, that manifests itself in ambition, presumption, and a drive to manipulate or calculate one's own life and that of others. [5] The category that Heidegger devotes most attention to involves a tendency toward self-concealment. This shows up as a lack of "anxious worry [*Bekümmerung*]" about oneself, hidden behind a spurious kind of self-interest. Also characteristic of Heidegger's discussions here is the notion of *fleeing* from oneself, of "masking" or hiding from oneself, and ultimately of forfeiting one's own existence to a kind of anonymous public identity.

The Temptation

Heidegger often begins his discussions of inauthenticity by describing its "tempting" quality. Heidegger conceives of the self as a kind of *movement* or *process*. A life has a kind of temporal trajectory, oriented toward activities that form the core of an identity. This trajectory is not something that one consciously wills most of the time, but instead has the character of a "pull." For the most part, we are pulled into a kind of average, public way of thinking and acting. As I will describe later (chapter 6), authenticity involves a resistance to this pull.

Heidegger succinctly characterizes this feature of life in the "Natorp Report," written in 1922. Heidegger describes the *"proclivity [Geneigtheit]* toward the world, which takes the form of a *propensity [Hang]* toward becoming absorbed in it [*zum Aufgehen in ihr*], to letting oneself be taken along by it" (NB 9/117). In colloquial English, we might refer here to our tendency to be "sucked in" by particular issues or concerns. Heidegger goes on to state that this propensity is an "expression [*Ausdruck*]" of another, more basic tendency of life. This is nothing other than the "basic factical tendency in life toward *falling away [Abfallen]* from itself and, in this, toward *falling into [Verfallen]* the world and thereby itself *disintegrating [Zerfall]*" (NB 9/117).[17]

As I have already mentioned, this propensity toward falling into ruin is not some accidental feature of life. Rather, it is "the most profound *fate [Verhängnis]* which life factically has to endure within itself" (NB 9/117). It is for this reason Heidegger goes on to condemn the "eschatological illusion" of utopianism. The attempt to "approach human Dasein" on the basis of some reinstatement of a pristine existence, or some ultimately paradisiacal stage of culture, are precisely symptoms of this tendency toward falling into ruin.[18] This movement of falling is, according to Heidegger, something that is *"tempting [versucherisch]"* to life (NB 10/117). This is because it constantly offers up the "path of least resistance," the easy road in which life becomes simply a matter of calculating manipulation.

In a roughly contemporaneous text, the lecture course from WS 1921–1922, Heidegger provides a more detailed discussion of our "inclination" toward fallen life. Again, he proposes that the basic "relational sense" of life is caring [*Sorgen*], which is related to the objects in the world as "meaningful" or "significant."[19] Taken broadly, then, the basic feature of life is "care about one's 'daily bread'" (G61 90/68). After developing this idea and sketching out some of the implications of it that will become famous in the opening sections of *Being and Time*, Heidegger turns to the task of explicating the basic categories of this relational sense. The first one he describes is *"conative inclination [Neigung],"* a feature that "imparts to life a peculiar weight, a direction of gravity, a pull toward something" (G61 100/75).[20] Life is pulled in a certain direction, led onto the path of a certain way of living. This comes to fruition in a "propensity [*Geneigtheit*]" (G61 100/75). It is here that life begins to take on the specific modality that we can clearly associate with inauthenticity. Heidegger writes:

> This propensity forces [*drängt*] life into its world, takes it captive [*hält es darin fest*], temporalizes a petrification [*Festigung*] of the direction taken by life. It genuinely finds itself where its ownmost propensity captures it; and life takes from there its direction in relation to itself, i.e. in relation to its dealings with its world, and also takes from there the "representation" which it develops of itself (i.e. the world). (G61 100f./76)

The distinction between "conative inclination" and "propensity" is not particularly precise. It is useful to remember, however, that these terms do not refer to *concepts*. Instead, they are formal indications that are meant to articulate the inchoate meaningfulness of human life. In the passage quoted here, Heidegger is once again attempting to intimate a common feature of everyday life. Life can easily be drawn into certain ways of doing things, and, as a result, can become "petrified" or "set in its ways." A person might begin to identify herself with a particular way of doing things. For example, one often hears people explaining their views and values by relating their personal histories, family backgrounds, and so forth. Contingent modes of behavior thus become "the way it's always been," to employ a common phrase. As I will show in chapters 5 and 6, the implication of this "petrification" for Heidegger is that an "authentic" way of life only becomes possible if one experiences some kind of radical "interruption" of the normal course of life. Life, therefore, "finds" itself already in a world, i.e., already involved in particular propensities and meaningful relations. "In propensity, life itself is experienced essentially as world; i.e., life itself, in facticity, exists always in the form of its world, its surrounding world, its with-world, its self-world; every life is in the form of my, yours, his, her, their world; our life, our world" (G61 101/76).

In carrying out our concerns on the path that is more or less predetermined by our propensities, we encounter ourselves already in the midst of daily activities. As Heidegger puts it in this lecture course, "life . . . offers itself to itself in a worldly way . . ." (G61 119/88). He formulates this point in a slightly different way in *Being and Time*: "Dasein finds 'itself' proximally in *what* it does, uses, expects, avoids—in the things environmentally handy with which it is *proximally* concerned" (SZ 119/155). "Life," Heidegger says, "reflects light back on itself." One's engagement with the world is always oriented toward one's own specific concerns, projects, and habits. This means we tend to identify with these practical concerns, to become absorbed in them. We encounter ourselves in being occupied with things (cf. G63 99/76); life "approaches itself and addresses itself in a worldly manner" (G63 102/79). As Heidegger puts it, "That which factical life cares about at any particular time in its world encounters it from this concern as care" (G61 119/89). Heidegger terms this complex phenomenon "relucence [*Reluzenz*]" (G61 119/89). Here again, the idea is that people come to identify themselves with their everyday concerns, particularly when these are accompanied by stable ideas about how to fulfill them.

Since the meaning of life is experienced in terms of the daily projects that it is pulled into, life "measures itself" and gives itself direction via the world that is "relucently" experienced in terms of concernful manipulation. "Life builds itself from out of this world and for it" (G61 119/89). Life establishes itself in terms of a definite "prepossession," i.e., its familiarity with itself and its world as items of concernful manipulation. "In caring, it is always constructing in advance [*vorbauend*], in its relucence it is *at the same time prestructive* [*prästruktiv*]" (G61 120/89). Our relucent "images" of ourselves tend to become fixed and to be transformed themselves into objects of active concern. This can be either an individual project or it can become communal, as in the maintenance of cultural assets. Heidegger's view is that the particular concerns, ideals, and beliefs that people identify themselves with are elevated to the status of valuable commodities that have to be defended and nurtured. As he sees it, this tendency lies at the root of neo-Kantian "philosophy of culture," which attempted to ground endeavors in science, morality, and religion by positing *a priori* values. This "prestructive" tendency of life thus culminates in an attempt to secure everyday values by removing them altogether from the vicissitudes of temporal reality.

As part of Heidegger's "hermeneutics of facticity," all these ideas are not elements of a general description of the more or less familiar "facts" about human life. Heidegger is attempting to illuminate the basic structures of everyday life in its pre-conceptual meaningfulness. An important component of this immediate lived experience is the tendency to become absorbed by or caught up in our day-to-day affairs. Jobs, chores, and other tasks have a *weight* that pulls us toward them. The consequent movement of our lives is *relucent*; we see ourselves "in light of" what we care about, of what concerns us. The primitive values and concepts with which we make our lives meaningful, such as "success" or "failure," emerge out of our absorption in daily activities. Sometimes, "worldly" values can take on a life of their own as cultural goods. Our "images [*Bildern*]" of ourselves, and the web of practices and concepts linked to them, then become swept into a further tendency of life.

Taking It Easy

Daily practices and concerns tend, then, to pull us in, to drag us down, and to rigidify into a particular way of thinking and acting. As early as 1920,

Heidegger begins to develop a deeper analysis of the motivating factors that lend force to the "pull" of this average, everyday way of existing. Life involves a strong drive toward security, toward peace and quiet amidst the struggle for one's "daily bread." The restless movement of life, its temporal incompleteness, is disquieting. Particularly disturbing is that all our struggles ultimately terminate in the nothingness of death. There is, then, a deep longing for *presence* amidst the temporal flow of life, for something to cling fast to. On Heidegger's account, this shows up in our tendency to gravitate, in an unreflective way, toward average ways of existing, toward social conventions and deeply entrenched ways of thinking about ourselves and the world.

During WS 1920–1921, Heidegger reflects on the problem of the "historical" and its position in contemporary philosophy. He observes that historical consciousness has, in general, a disquieting effect on culture (G60 33). This observation certainly accords with the effects of historicism on German life and thought in the years immediately prior to and following World War I. An increasing trend toward relativism, skepticism, and irrationalism was greeted with alarm by figures as diverse as Husserl, the neo-Kantians, and the *magesterium* of the Catholic Church. Heidegger describes a variety of responses to this disquieting nature of historical consciousness (G60 38 ff.). What he concludes, following a brief survey of some of these trends, is that no one has made that which seeks security in the face of historical consciousness into an explicit philosophical problem (G60 50). It is only in the life-philosophy of Simmel and Dilthey that we begin to get a glimmer of the real issue, namely *life*. It is human life itself, "human Dasein in its anxious concern about itself," that is disquieted by the historical (G60 50 f.). The dominant trends of contemporary philosophy (in 1920) simply translate this anxious worry into some transcendent framework, thereby failing to really address the nature of life itself. Heidegger sets himself the task of examining this anxious worry on its own terms (G60 51).

It is with this project in mind that Heidegger eventually turns to the examination of primitive Christianity in connection with Pauline epistles. Particularly in Paul's eschatological ideas, Heidegger finds that Christian existence does not hide from the anxious worry of life, but instead heightens it into an "absolute affliction" or "distress" (G60 97 f.). Thus Paul cautions the Thessalonians against the longing for worldly peace and security that impels their contemporaries into idolatry (G60 103). Such people find peace in the world, they are "attached to the world [*an diese Welt hängen*]" because it offers them this kind of peace and security. Paul metaphorically describes the situation of these people as "darkness" and "drunkenness," drawing on the apocalyptic language of Second Temple Judaism.[21] When the sudden "day of the Lord" comes, these people are caught unawares. "When they say, 'There is peace and security,' then sudden destruction will come upon them, as labor pains come upon a pregnant woman, and there will be no escape!" (1 Thess. 5:3). Heidegger glosses these passages as follows: "They [who say "peace" and "security"] are caught up by what life offers them; they are in darkness with respect to self-knowledge. The faithful are, on the other hand, sons of light and of the day" (G60 105). The wakeful urgency of the Christians' expectation of the Parousia is thus contrasted with the somnambulant complacency of the majority of humanity. The latter fall prey to a basic tendency in life, namely the drive toward peace and security.

Similar features can be found in Augustine's discussion of *gaudium veritate* in *Confessions* X, which forms the topic of Heidegger's lecture from SS 1921. People have a kind of "inauthentic" love of the truth, one that, for Augustine, only serves to entrench their bondage to error (G60 200f.). Such people love truth when it enlightens them, when it gives them useful information about something, but they hate it when it accuses them. They love truth only when it can be taken in at a glance in quietist, aesthetic enjoyment, but when it attacks them or puts a claim on them, they hate it. "When it bears on them and shakes them up, when it places their own facticity in question, then it is better that they shut their eyes in a timely fashion, and take their delight in incensed choral litanies" (G60 201).

In the Natorp Report from 1922, Heidegger provides a general characterization of this tendency. He writes:

> A characteristic of the being of factical life is that it finds itself hard to endure. The most unmistakable manifestation of this is the fact that factical life has the tendency to make things easy for itself. In finding itself hard to endure, life is difficult in accord with the basic sense of its being, and not in the sense of a contingent feature. (NB 31/13)

This passage more or less speaks for itself. It represents, however, a distillation of Heidegger's contemporaneous thoughts on this and related issues, which can be found in the lecture course from WS 1921–1922. Here, we find that one of the primary categories of life is "the easy [*das Leichte*]" (G61 108/81). As in the Natorp Report, it is Aristotle's practical philosophy that forms the point of reference for Heidegger's reflections, though this is an Aristotle that has been refracted through the lens of Luther's early theology.[22] Heidegger begins by quoting *Nicomachean Ethics* B 5, 1106b28ff.[23] This passage on practical reasoning highlights the true difficulty of acting appropriately. Heidegger, of course, is more interested in the general message here about life itself, rather than in Aristotelian moral philosophy. "Factical life is," he says, "always seeking the easy way; conative inclination follows the direction in which it is pulled and does so by itself, readily" (G61 108/81). Following Aristotle's discussion, Heidegger goes on to relate this tendency to further aggravations of complacent existence: "Thereby arises a directionality toward possible mistakes as such, mistakeability, lapsing [*Abfall*], making things easy for oneself, fooling oneself, fanaticism [*Schwärmen*], exuberance" (G61 109/81). This remark points ahead to Heidegger's conception of the role of philosophy and religion in securing a complacent, carefree way of existing, which will be discussed in the next chapter (chapter 4).

The category of "the easy," the longing for tranquillity, involves a pull toward the path of least resistance. Everything must be accomplished "without further ado" (G61 108/81). Life gravitates toward tranquil convenience [*Bequemlichkeit*] (G61 108/81). As I have already pointed out, though, the basic sense of daily life, i.e., care, is such that this kind of tranquillity proves to be perennially elusive. The struggle for one's "daily bread" does not end, despite our attempts to achieve total self-security. Thus it becomes necessary that life actually actively avoid itself in order to satisfy this craving for peace and security. "Life seeks to secure itself by looking away from itself" (G61 109/81). The difficulty of life is then viewed solely in terms of concernful manipulation. One's relation to oneself at this level is best characterized by "self-seeking [*sich . . . Versuchung*]," a kind of "carefreeness [*Sorglosigkeit*]" (G61 109/81). Everything is available, everything is as it should be. The disturbing quality of the movement of life vanishes from view.

Heidegger expounds on this dimension of carefreeness toward the end of his lecture course from SS 1923. "Care," he writes, "disappears in the habits, customs, and publicness of everydayness—and this does not mean that it comes to an end, but rather that it does not show itself any longer" (G63 103/80). Everything is there, it seems, just as it should be. Everyday existence, while of course still fundamentally determined as practice, i.e., as care, takes on the quality of "carefreeness" (G63 103/80). The world is encountered as something "self-evident." Echoing Paul, Heidegger tells us that "care is asleep" (G63 103/80). The Pauline resonance of these remarks is even more evident in Heidegger's claim that "the possibility ever remains that distress will suddenly break forth in the world [cf. 1 Thess. 5:3]" (G63 103/80, reference added).

In some writings closer in time to *Being and Time,* new dimensions of "taking it easy" emerge in Heidegger's discussions. The lecture course for SS 1925 contains much of the terminology that soon finds its way into Heidegger's first treatise. The theme of the "one [*das Man*]," which first clearly emerges in SS 1923, receives a more extended treatment here. Some of the material from SS 1925 eventually becomes §§26–27 of *Being and Time.* I will have more occasion to focus on the notion of the "one" later. What is of more immediate interest is the idea that our anonymous public existence "unburdens [*entlastet*]" us, or releases us from responsibility (G20 340/247). The public talks everything over at the most superficial level, and precisely tries to avoid getting deeper into the issues. "The public is involved in everything but in such a way that it has already always absolved itself" (G20 340/246f.). One is thus relieved of the task of taking responsibility for thinking and acting for oneself. Thus, our public mode of existence accommodates the previously mentioned tendency to "take it easy."

In §38 of *Being and Time,* Heidegger revisits the categories of "fallen" life that he had initially described during WS 1921–1922. He highlights a number of essential features of the distinctive movement of "falling." Of most interest here is what he calls "tranquillity [*Beruhigung*]" (SZ 177/222). As in SS 1925,

Heidegger maintains that public ways of thinking and acting are bound up with a deep urge to make everything available as a matter of course. The tendency is, he says, to want to "guarantee the security, genuineness, and fullness of every possibility of its being for Dasein" (SZ 177/222). There is no need to look further, no need to worry oneself, everything is as it should be. It is simply supposed that one is leading a more or less full and genuine life. All doors are open, everything is readily available (SZ 177/222). For this reason, falling is "tranquilizing [*beruhigend*]" (SZ 177/222).[24]

A clear manifestation of this tendency lies in everyday attitudes toward death. Death is a well-known occurrence, something that is not "there" yet, and hence poses no problem. Heidegger finds this attitude expressed in everyday reasonings such as this: "One of these days one will die too, in the end; but right now it has nothing to do with us" (SZ 253/297). When our neighbor is dying, we console him by saying that he will soon enough return to "the tranquilized everydayness of the world of his concern" (SZ 253/297). Nothing is allowed to disturb our tranquillity, especially not the thought that death is our own ultimate destination. "Indeed the dying of others is seen often enough as a social inconvenience, if not even a downright tactlessness, against which the public is to be guarded" (SZ 254/298). Here Heidegger cites Tolstoi's *The Death of Ivan Ilyich* as a literary presentation of this way of dealing with death. Ivan's daughter, for example, finds it altogether tactless of her father to die before she is married. Death, for Heidegger, signifies the ultimate disquietude of our existence, for our mortality means, from the perspective of the individual, that our lives are never complete, never "there all at once."

Dispersion

As in each of the categories of fallen life I have described so far, the third, that of *dispersion*, is first discussed in the religion courses of 1920–1921. Our tendency to take a self-avoidant, complacent plunge into everyday ways of thinking and acting manifests itself in the dispersed, random quality of day-to-day existence. Heidegger's view is that we try to distract ourselves from our own lives. Recall that, for Heidegger, human selfhood is a matter of *process* rather than *presence*. Identity cannot be accounted for by positing a substance that endures through time. Instead, on Heidegger's view, the cohesiveness of a life stems from one's repeated *identification* with inherited possibilities of thinking and acting. One *understands* oneself ahead of time *as* a particular sort of person. This *understanding* provides a revisable framework within which our past and future can be rendered intelligible to us.

In many of his writings from the 1920s, Heidegger describes the way selfhood is affected by "fallenness." As I have already discussed, one of the principal features of a "fallen" life is that, impelled by a drive for security, it tends to slip into the path of least resistance. One symptom of this is that a "fallen" life tends to lack *focus*. An "inauthentic" life suffers "disintegration" or "decomposition [*Zerfall*]." We find ourselves pushed about by a host of contradictory beliefs, practices, and projects. For Heidegger, this betrays an attempt to distract ourselves from the difficulty of life and to take refuge in the everyday world in which things are a matter of course.

Again, this dispersed and distracted mode of life is first discussed by Heidegger in his religion course of WS 1920–1921.[25] Here, Paul contrasts the present life of the community, which is focused on God and anxious expectation of the Parousia, with the idol worship and polytheism they practiced prior to receiving Paul's proclamation (G60 95). This contrast is found even more starkly in Augustine's *Confessions*, which, as already mentioned, formed the topic for Heidegger's lectures in SS 1921. In Book IV, Augustine chastises the wayward heart of his youth, "glued fast" to sensible things that "rend my soul with death-dealing desires."[26] He counsels it to "fix [its] dwelling" on one thing alone, namely God. "Stand with him and you will stand firm, rest in him and you will find peace. Where are you going, along your rough paths? Tell me, where are you going?"[27] Later, Augustine writes, "A human being is an immense abyss, but you, Lord, keep count even of his hairs, and not one of them is lost in you; yet even his hairs are easier to number than the affections and movements of his heart."[28]

The theme of distraction or of a dissipated life also occupies Augustine in Book X, and it is this material that Heidegger focuses on in his own discussion. Here, in describing the virtue of *continentia*, Augustine writes, "By continence the scattered elements of the self are collected and brought back into the unity from which we have slid away into dispersion."[29] Heidegger glosses this as follows in his lecture notes: "we dissolve [*zerfließen*] into multiplicity and come apart into dispersion. You command the countermovement against this dispersing" (G60 205). In keeping with the neo-platonism that so profoundly influenced his thought, Augustine clearly views multiplicity as an evil and unity of soul as a virtually unsurpassed good. Our ordinary lives, however, are characterized by *defluxus* or "dissipation" (G60 206f.). We are dissipated into our concerns for the multitude of things amongst which we dwell. Lacking any real unifying identity, we fall victim to the whims and passions of the moment.

Heidegger discusses this same tendency more formally during WS 1921–1922. Under the heading of the "conative inclination" that I have already treated above, Heidegger explains that the "relation of care," or "life in the world," comes to be "*dispersed* [*zerstreut*]" (G61 101f./76). The propensities that follow upon the heels of such inclinations hold life in these "dispersions [*Zerstreuungen*]" (G61 102/76). That is, life is pulled in a multitude of directions in daily activities. "The how of life is a being played out in its world, 'in whatever the day might bring [*in den Tag hinein*]'" (G61 102/76). This amounts to a kind of loss of identity, a complacent manner of being carried along by whatever comes one's way, that Heidegger calls "self-satisfaction [*Selbstgenügsamkeit*]" (G61 102/76). We come to conceive of ourselves not in terms of a stable identity but rather in terms of the daily projects that sweep us along. Ultimately, this means that we have no clear conception of ourselves, no real substantial core of identity.

This point emerges more clearly in §75 of *Being and Time*, where Heidegger contrasts the "loyalty" of an authentic person to herself with the distracted, dissipated, evanescent quality of everyday, fallen existence. "Everyday Dasein," Heidegger tells us, "is dispersed into the multiplicity of that which daily 'comes to pass'" (SZ 389/441). One's "fate," or sense of identity, is given not by the resolute projection of an inherited possibility of existence, but by the "opportunities and circumstances" we reckon with in our daily activities (SZ 390/441). We drift about aimlessly in our daily "affairs [*Geschäften*]" (SZ 390/441). An authentic existence is one that struggles to "pull itself together" from out of this distracted, dispersed mode of everyday existence. As inauthentic, one focuses only on the "today," on the next new thing, forgetting the continuities that exist between this and what has gone before (SZ 391/443). "Blind for possibilities, the 'one' is not able to repeat what is already [*Gewesenes*], rather it only retains or receives the 'actual' that has been left over from what is already world-historical, the remnants, the information about them that is objectively present" (SZ 391/443).[30]

Underlying these assertions is the claim that historical meaning derives from the horizon of expectation of an individual carrying out his or her projects. That is, that which belongs to the "past," over and above the *facts* about what happened, is opened up for the present by its direction into the future.[31] Wolfhart Pannenberg has explored this idea extensively. In his work on the concept of revelation, Pannenberg argues that "[h]istory is not composed of raw or so-called brute facts. As the history of man, the history of revelation is always bound up with understanding, in hope and remembrance."[32] This conception of historical meaning is illustrated for Pannenberg in the context of textual interpretation, or the hermeneutical dimension of the historical sciences. He makes the seemingly obvious point, which has nevertheless eluded generations of theoreticians in history and in the other human sciences, that the meaning of history, above and beyond "what really happened," is relative to the present time and its horizon of expectation. Thus, "[i]f one describes the Greek tragedies of the 5th century exclusively as an expression of the history of this classical period, one has obviously not touched the artistic truth of the works of Aeschylus or Sophocles, which speak to man regardless of his time or place."[33]

In *Being and Time*, Heidegger brings this conception of historical meaning to bear on his description of the category of dispersion in fallen life. Completely occupied by the demands of the moment, by the "business" of life, one not only loses a unified identity but also loses touch with the meaningful possibilities contained in the cultural tradition that one has inherited. The richly complex web of relations that lie in the background of inherited practices and ways of thinking becomes constricted, disappearing behind the pressing throng of tasks and affairs of the day. In SS 1920, Heidegger describes this process as the "fading of significance." The web of meanings in one's socio-linguistic inheritance is reduced to simple availability or usefulness for one's present project. In *Being and Time*, this process is described as "leveling" (SZ 127/164f.). Everything has long been known, everything has a place in the scheme of one's daily affairs. Thus, by bringing about this fading of signifi-cance, the tendency toward dispersion feeds back into the drive to "take it easy," to have everything at one's fingertips. One already knows what "such and such" is all about; it can either be used and enjoyed or discarded as a mere relic of the past.

Hyperbolic Life

In keeping with our tendency to identify with our daily projects and activities and to seek out security and comfort in them, there is also a tendency to make everything available for our use. In the busy world of struggle for one's "daily bread," this requires a superficial familiarity with things in which they can be rendered more readily available. Heidegger describes a way this process can be aggravated by our failure to take note of the limits of our superficial familiarity with the world. This is often linked with an excessive presumptive-ness about the validity of this superficial familiarity. On Heidegger's view, we actively seek to maintain the availability of things for our use, further en-trenching the horizon of meaning of everyday life.

Heidegger's descriptions of this tendency begin during SS 1921, in his discussion of Augustine's notion of "worldly ambition [*ambitio saeculi*]." On Augustine's account, this is the third kind of trial that plagues human life, one of many which render Augustine questionable to himself. Our basic manner of relating to the world is fundamentally self-regarding [*eigenwillig*] (G60 226f.). We are, as Luther later taught, "curved in" upon ourselves. According to Heidegger, what all the forms of trial or temptation share is the absence of any real self-identity; the self is "lived by the world" (G60 227). In the third form of temptation, *ambitio saeculi*, the self is actually the subject of attention, though in an "inauthentic" way. "What is at issue is the value of the self in factical experience, i.e. in the with-worldly contexts of life, but also, ultimately, in the self-worldly context" (G60 228). This is perhaps most evident in our attempt to seek honor and affection from other people. Our concern is with achieving a certain position in our social milieu, or "with-world." The "self-world," i.e., our way of conceiving of and of encountering ourselves, is carried along by this, so that we see ourselves in terms of this position in the with-world (G60 229). Language plays a crucial role here, insofar as it is what one *says* about us that is the object of concern (G60 230). For Heidegger, the philo-sophically salient point here is that *ambitio saeculi* helps to constitute our everyday "horizon" of meaning, which is closely linked with our membership in a community.

A key motivating factor here is our sense of "self-importance [*Selbst-*

wichtignahme]" (G60 232). For Augustine, when we yield to the force of this motive, the directions in which we seek satisfaction of our desires are fundamentally altered (G60 223). Specifically, our self-important worldly ambition blocks the way to our loving God with "chaste fear [*timor castus*]" (G60 233). "God himself," glosses Heidegger, "is no longer taken to be something decisively important" (G60 233). That is, one loves God not for His own sake, but for our own gratification. This sort of self-aggrandizement fails to recognize that whatever might be good and praiseworthy about a person is a gift from God (G60 234f.).

Augustine goes on to distinguish between use [*uti*] and enjoyment [*fruitio*] (G60 271ff.). The latter is the appropriate attitude toward God, the *summum bonum*. Human concupiscence, however, is warped and seeks in worldly things the enjoyment that can only be found in God. Our lives are thus filled with a presumptuous lack of measure, even in relation to ultimate things. For Augustine, this is particularly clear in magic and divination. Here, the end of our desire is a *perversa scientia* (G60 224). "God must lapse, must become a factor in human experimentation. He must give an answer to an inquisitive, self-important, pseudo-prophetic curiosity, i.e. a curious looking around related to Him which is *not* fitting to his objective meaning" (G60 224). Even the love of God ultimately degenerates into a self-regarding curiosity.

The guiding characteristic of this multifaceted phenomenon is clearly that of *presumption*, of failing to grasp the measure appropriate to life. Everything becomes available as an object of use. Everything is sucked into a self-regarding mode of calculation, even God, the "highest good," that which is beautiful and good in itself. Whatever is not simply available, there for the taking, is of no interest (G60 198). Hence, people fall away from the "one thing needful," the one thing really capable of fulfilling the restless desires of the human heart (God), into lust for the things of the world. The uncertainty of life, the reality of our struggle for goods, becomes a mask for gluttony and presumptive desire (G60 215).

Our tendency to transgress measures in daily activities also forms part of Heidegger's discussion of the basic "relational sense" of life in WS 1921–1922. In our caring for things, there is always a certain "distance," we always have something "before" ourselves in our practical dealings (G61 103/77). That is to say, human practical activity is *futural*. There is always something still outstanding, something incalculable, a "not yet" that hovers just beyond our reach in historical experience.[34] In our "ruinous" mode of caring, however, this "before" is abolished. Heidegger explains:

> In its actual propensity and dispersion, life does not maintain this distance; it commits an oversight [*es versieht sich*]. Distance as such is not explicitly there in dispersed thrusting aside of the "before." This becomes even less explicit in proclivity; in the enactment of experience, life passes over it. In oversight with regard to distance, life misses itself; it makes an error with respect to the measure appropriate to it. (G61 103/77)

One fails to grasp one's own finitude, fails to see that there is always something still outstanding, something "before." Instead, everything is taken to be available or to be completely in one's reach.[35] At the same time, part of the mismeasurement of life involves being intent on one's position within the world. While overlooking distance, one simultaneously tries to establish distances within the social world and with respect to the world of things. One is intent on "rank, success, position in life (position in the world), superiority, advantage, calculation, bustle, clamor, and ostentation" (G61 103/77). The possibilities for gratifying these intentions multiply themselves endlessly. "Life, in its inclination to disperse its relationality into self-distantiation, is *hyperbolic*" (G61 104/78). These possibilities and their availability become objects of deep concern, of "care that this multiplicity is always available, does not run out, is present in ever new modes" (G61 104/78). The incompleteness of life, its constant "unrest," the ineradicable "distance" between what it is and what it could be, is subtly transformed into care about one's position in the social world. The horizon of meaning of everyday life is reduced to a superficial, businesslike hustle and bustle.

This trait of fallen life appears again throughout *Being and Time*. Life in the public world is characterized by "distantiality [*Abständigkeit*]," by the constant concern over one's position vis-à-vis others, by constant attempts to secure one's status. In our social life, we are concerned with "averageness [*Durchschnittlichkeit*]," with assimilating everything exceptional, strange, or challenging into the domain of familiarity and mediocrity (SZ 127/164f.). "Everything achieved through struggle [*Erkämpfte*] becomes manipulable. Every secret loses its power" (SZ 127/165). One leaps from fashion to fashion in distracted curiosity (SZ 172/216f.). "Not only does everyone know and discuss what is at issue or what occurs, but everyone already knows how to talk about what ought to happen first, about what is not yet at issue but must 'really' be done" (SZ 173/213). One quickly passes on to the next new thing, so that whatever might count as a genuine achievement soon becomes out of date (SZ 174/218). The result is that one is constantly committing oversights [*versieht sich*] in one's daily projects. One is constantly out for something, addicted to being "lived" by whatever the latest possibility might be (SZ 195/240). One is impelled along by urges that *must* achieve what they are after, no matter the cost (SZ 195/240).

Heidegger's descriptions of hyperbolic life clearly resonate with both Christian and Aristotelian analyses of excessive pride. Nevertheless, the uniquely Heideggerian point here is that these features of life are not adventitious properties, but are instead elements of the basic pre-conceptual meaningfulness of life. In our drive toward security, we want to make everything available to ourselves. For Heidegger, this means we overstep the bounds of our finitude by attempting to turn everything into something that can be easily controlled and manipulated. The proclivities that suck us into ordinary ways of thinking and acting, and scatter our identities amongst a multiplicity of affairs, also compel us toward excessive desires. We strive for self-aggrandizement in our social lives just as much as we strive for technical mastery in our practical occupations. Like Augustine, Luther, and others, Heidegger views this as a symptom of a fundamental blindness regarding the human condition. It is this self-concealing blindness that makes up the fifth feature of fallen life.

Self-Abdication

In our plunge into daily affairs, our tendency to seek out security and comfort, and our drive to overstep our own limits, we nevertheless are always concerned with ourselves. Life is "in each case mine [*je meines*]," regardless of whether I own up to that fact or not. One is always somehow or other familiar with oneself. "Fallenness" is one way to characterize the way we most often have possession of ourselves. Yet the paradox of this way of existing is that it is a flight from ourselves. We are, for Heidegger, fugitives from the worry of having to take responsibility for our lives, from our mortality, and from the fluidity and incompleteness of human life itself. Ultimately, we find our refuge in a kind of anonymous public existence that presents us with opportunities to conceal the disturbing movement of life. In effect, we no longer live our own lives, but are lived by the ways of thinking and acting that we have grown accustomed to.

It is a basic tendency of our lives that we tend to "conceal [*verdeckt*]" ourselves from ourselves (G60 15). Heidegger suggests that we try to understand Christian life and Christian doctrine within the context of a struggle against this tendency. It is from this worry about life, about salvation, that Christianity can best be understood (G60 69). Paul refers to the negative tendencies in life either as "flesh" or, borrowing from apocalypticism, as "darkness." I have already described how a fundamental feature of this way of living, for Paul, is that of complacency (G60 103). People who have been swept along by this tendency experience the "day of the Lord" as one of utter ruin. Their expectations are completely focused on what might come to pass *within* the sphere of their daily affairs, rather than with what will ultimately come to pass *in spite of* it (G60 103). For these people, meaning lies only in the horizon of everyday life. "They cannot rescue themselves," glosses Heidegger, "because they do not have themselves, they have forgotten their own selves; because they do not have themselves in the clarity of authentic knowing" (G60 103). They are, says Paul, "in darkness" (1 Thess. 5:4). The Christians, though, are not "in darkness," so that this day might suddenly overtake them (G60 104). They are "sons of the light." Heidegger summarizes the contrast a bit later: "They [non-Christians] are caught up by what life offers them; they are in darkness with respect to self-knowledge. The faithful are, on the other hand, sons of light and of the day" (G60 105).

What is the relevant sense of "self-knowledge," which those outside the early Christian community seem to lack? We can begin to understand this by considering Heidegger's gloss on Paul's response to the Thessalonians' question about when to expect the Parousia, in which Paul irritatingly turns the question back on them. "Now concerning the times and the seasons, brothers, you do not need to have anything written to you. For you yourselves know very well that the day of the Lord will come like a thief in the night" (1 Thess. 5:1–2). Heidegger claims that the self-knowledge that is operative here is a knowledge of their "having become" (G60 94). That is, the community knows itself in its *history*, in the *history of God*, which began for them with the reception of the proclamation in "great tribulation," and which is consummated in the end-time Second Coming of Christ (G60 94f.). Heidegger diagrams this "knowing" and "having become" for his students.[36] The diagram represents the *ongoing history* of the community in its struggle against idolatry and in its perseverance in hope. The life of the community is one of constant trial, constant affliction, and anxious worry, suspended between promise and fulfillment. They relate to themselves in anxious worry, not in complacent self-satisfaction. Thus the "darkness" that those outside the community inhabit is a fugitive way of existing that takes refuge from the tribulation of the eschatological drama of human history in the affairs of the moment.[37]

In Book X of his *Confessions*, Augustine also uses metaphors of "light" and "darkness" to describe the situation of humanity apart from God. As in Paul's epistles, "darkness" is a metaphor for the common tendency to become engrossed in worldly things and to exaggerate one's distance from God (G60 199). Things that we find meaningful in our daily, practical lives become surrogates for the truth (G60 200). Augustine's general term for this state of depravity, which Luther also employs, is concupiscence. Heidegger abstractly explains what this term designates: "*Con-cupiscere*: to crave all together [*zusammen-begehren*], a sort of concentration, though one in which what is concentrated upon is the 'objective'-worldly, into which the self is drawn" (G60 211).

Augustine's biblical source of this idea is 1 John 2:15–17, where the writer counsels against the "love of the world" in all its forms. Another biblical term used to describe this mode of existence is the "flesh." Heidegger glosses: "'*in carne*,' in an abstracted, ungodly, unspiritual orientation towards the *beata vita*, one that is not *anxiously worried in an existentiell manner*" (G60 218, emphasis added). In our crooked desire for worldly gain and satisfaction, we fail to see the basic character of our lives as *molestia* [trouble, affliction, distress], as the "threat [*Gefährdung*] of having a self" (G60 244). This threat, the danger of having to live before God, is dimmed down or concealed by our worldly occupations. Life must be lived by us alone, and we can so easily go wrong. "In anxious worry about the self, the self develops—in the how of its ownmost being—the radical possibility of lapsing [*Abfall*], but also that of achieving the right 'opportunity'" (G60 245). The basic idea is that the nature of life is such that two possibilities are open to each and every individual: (1) acceptance of the "danger" or "threat" of living one's own life, or (2) abdication of self-responsibility through identification with "worldly" concerns and occupations. Life is *tentatio*, a trial with two possible outcomes: self-forgetfulness and self-realization (G60 246).[38] Thus, as he had done the previous semester in his exposition of 1 and 2 Thessalonians, Heidegger finds Augustine presenting his reader with a choice between two fundamentally opposed ways of life. In *Being and Time*, Heidegger employs the terms "inauthenticity" and "authenticity" to formally indicate roughly the same options. As I will show in more detail in chapters 5 and 6, he uses Christian metaphors of "darkness" and "light," of "sleep" and "wakefulness," of drunken "numbness" and "sobriety," to intimate the ways of life that are of concern to him.

Heidegger discusses the possibility of abdicating self-responsibility in this way once more during WS 1920–1921. One of the principal categories is what Heidegger calls "barricading [*Abriegelung*]" (G61 105/79). In our relations of caring for the world, we stand "before" something, before a situation, and we experience ourselves in this relation. Under the influence of our propensities, however, the possibility of genuinely appropriating this "before" fades from view (G61 106/79). What Heidegger has in mind for a genuine appropriation is left unclear in this discussion. Its opposite, however, clearly involves some kind of a failure to own up to the situation, to take over one's life in the "here" and "now."

Essential to this tendency is that one tries to avoid oneself, tries to avoid the demands of the situation that bear upon one's identity. This involves a kind of "unworriedness," a "non-caring" about oneself (G61 107/80). Life tries to escape from itself, though this is, strictly speaking, impossible. Thus, the kind of "escape" involved here is more of a "concealment" or "disguising." This is brought out by Heidegger's remarks in the following passage:

> The more life increases its worldly concern and the "before" is lost in the increased proclivity and expulsion of distance, all the more certainly does life then have to do with itself. In caring, life barricades itself off from itself, and yet, in so doing, precisely does not get loose from itself. In its constant looking away toward new things, life is always seeking itself, and indeed does encounter itself where it least expects—i.e., for the most part in its disguises (larvance). (G61 107/80)

This description certainly calls to mind that of the previous semester, in which the topic is Augustine's picture of the way our natural love of truth and desire for happiness become perverted by worldly propensities. It is important to note here that "barricading" ourselves off from ourselves is still a way of *being ourselves*. Heidegger calls it "larvance [*Larvanz*]," from the Latin '*larva*,' meaning both "mask" and "ghost." In "barricading," we meet up with ourselves in disguises that have been thrown up to conceal the difficulty of life in its temporal movement. We "barricade" ourselves off from the difficult reality of life, condemning ourselves to a spectral existence in which we drift about from day to day, failing to fully own up to ourselves.

Later in these lectures, Heidegger returns to the category of "barricading" once more, this time focusing on the "movement" involved in it. Clearly, what predominates is a movement "away from" oneself. Yet in this movement away from oneself, one encounters oneself again in the "ghostly" form of one's disguises (G61 123/91 f.). "Out of this flight before itself, life acquires the modes in which it deals with its world and *with itself*"(G61 123/92, emphasis added). Life is concerned with maintaining these disguises, and so tends to become set in its ways (G61 124f./91 f.). One way Heidegger offers for conceiving of this turns on the notion of "formation," "development," or "construction [*Bildung, Ausbildung*]" (G61 128/95). Life gives itself "structure [*Gebilde*]" according to an "image [*Bild*]" that it, no doubt, acquires from its social milieu. What this means is that our way of relating to ourselves and of maintaining a certain conception of ourselves emerges during the course of our fugitive plunge into daily activities, and then becomes entrenched. For Heidegger, "what is at issue is not primarily the figure of what has been formed but the temporalization as such—*struere* ['to construct']" (G61 128/95). That is, the particular conceptions of ourselves that emerge from our relations to the world and to other people are not so much the issue as is the *way* these come to be and the way they function as "disguises."[39]

Perhaps the most influential and well-known formal indication that Heidegger gives for this sort of "disguise" is the "one [*das Man*]."[40] This idea emerges first in SS 1923 in connection with what Heidegger there calls the "today [*das Heute*]," the public consciousness of a time. This public domain is precisely that wherein everything is held to a kind of averageness, a notion that has already been discussed (G63 31/26). This public domain has the manner of being of "the one": "one says that . . . , one has heard that . . . , one tells it like . . . , one thinks that [. . .]" (G63 32/26). "This 'one' is precisely *the* 'no-one,' which circulates in factical Dasein and haunts it like a specter, a how of the fateful undoing [*Verhängnisses*] of facticity to which the factical life of each pays tribute" (G63 32/26). The identity of the individual is haunted by the public in such a way that it is ultimately relinquished; this is what Heidegger means when he says that the "one" is *the* "no-one." Heidegger uses a clearly "political" metaphor here, that of "paying tribute," to intimate the way this category of the "one" functions in everyday life. The "one," the anonymous public *status quo*, exercises a despotic domination over individuals. At the same time, people are generally willing subjects, as is often the case in societies ruled by oppressive or tyrannical regimes.[41] On Heidegger's view, this is primarily motivated by a desire for "security" or "tranquillity."

The "one" appears again later in the discussion, following Heidegger's analysis of contemporary philosophy and historical consciousness. Heidegger is concerned here with the project of explicating the basic categories of life in its "everydayness." "What belongs to everydayness is a certain averageness of Dasein, the 'one,' in which the fact that Dasein is 'our own' and the possibility of authenticity keep themselves covered up" (G63 85/65). The "one" is a way of being a self that is utterly delivered over to social life, to one's position vis-à-vis others (G63 94/72). In our everyday dealings with other things and other people, we are constantly pursuing this "one-self," i.e., "one's status, reputation, accomplishments, successes and failures among the others" (G63 99/76). Thus, one's life ultimately is no longer one's own, but is "owned" by the public world of superficiality and mediocrity.

The claim that life constructs "masks" to conceal its difficulty appears once again during SS 1923. Heidegger's description of this phenomenon is particularly incisive:

> Dasein speaks about itself and sees itself in such and such a manner, and yet this is only a *mask* that it holds up before itself in order not to be frightened by itself. The warding off "of" anxiety. Such visibility is the mask in which factical Dasein lets itself be encountered, in which it comes forth and appears before itself as though it really "were" it—in this masquerade of the public manner of being-interpreted, Dasein makes itself present and puts itself forward as the *height of living* (i.e. of industriousness). (G63 32/26)

Immediately following these remarks, Heidegger presents what appears to be a counter-example by way of illustration. He quotes part of a letter from Vincent van Gogh to his brother, dated October 15, 1879, in which the artist writes, "I would rather die a natural death than be prepared for it at the university" (G63 32/26). And so, instead of taking refuge in the common run of "opportunities" available to him, van Gogh "went mad in the course of this intense confrontation with his own Dasein" (G63 32/27). Clearly Heidegger is not advocating mental illness as a practical ideal. Instead, what the illustration is supposed to show is that we so often take refuge behind the possibilities offered up by the public domain. Heidegger's alternative is a life that *confronts* itself, owns up to itself, and is earnestly dedicated to its possibilities.[42] The contrast is between a fugitive, dissembling mode of life and one that meets life head-on in all its difficulty.

As Heidegger continued to work toward the publication of *Being and Time*, these ideas began to take a more systematic shape. By the time this work appeared, Heidegger had settled upon the "one" as an umbrella term for many of the features of fallen life I have examined up to this point. Much of the discussion in *Being and Time* is prefigured by Heidegger's essays and lectures from 1924 and 1925. Particularly notable in this regard are his 1924 address to the Marburg Theological Society, his guest lecture on Dilthey in Kassel, and the lecture course of SS 1925, *Prolegomena zur Geschichte der Zeitbegriffs* (G20). Here, I will be concerned with the more polished presentation of these ideas in *Being and Time*.

The self forms one of the core philosophical concerns of *Being and Time*, beginning at the outset of the work with Heidegger's formal discussion of the *in each case mineness* [*Jemeinigkeit*] of Dasein (SZ 12/32 f.; 42/67). This formal designation for a basic feature of human life is what is at issue in Heidegger's later analyses of the "who" of Dasein (§§25 ff., 63). The indexical pronoun "I" is, of course, the natural way to refer to the self; at the same time, however, Heidegger wants us to shy away from traditional *metaphysical* interpretations of the content of this expression, including that involved in Husserl's transcendental phenomenology (SZ 115/150 f.). Aside from the fact that these traditional interpretations might be simply wrong, Heidegger is also suspicious of the seeming "self-evidence" of what it means to say "I." This is precisely due to his acute awareness of our usual tendency to hide from ourselves in a public identity:

> Perhaps, in the closest way in which Dasein addresses itself it always says "I am it," and in the end says this loudest, when it is "not" this entity. What if the constitution [*Verfassung*] of Dasein, the fact that it is in each case mine, should be the reason that it proximally and for the most part *is not itself*? (SZ 115f./151)

The suggestion here is that some suspicion of the "givenness" of the I is warranted by Dasein's tendency to *avoid being itself*. If, in saying "I," we do so in the midst of our attempts to "barricade [*abriegeln*]" ourselves off from ourselves, then we have good reason to inquire more deeply into the "givenness" of the I. In a roundabout way, this justifies Heidegger's turn away from Husserl's purely descriptive "eidetic analysis" of pure consciousness toward a *hermeneutical* method. Perhaps, Heidegger suggests, human life is more like a richly layered novel or poem than a technical manual that "wears its meaning on its sleeve," as it were. Perhaps philosophy cannot content itself with givens and self-evident truths, but must do violence to the way things present themselves. Indeed, earlier on in *Being and Time*, Heidegger has told us that the phenomena of phenomenology are precisely those things that usually *do not reveal themselves* (SZ 30/53). The disturbing thought is that philosophy starts from an entrenched tendency to conceal or cover over what is really at issue [*was es kommt darauf an*], rather than in a *confrontation* with this tendency.

Who are we, then, when we say "I"? Heidegger's answer is calculated for maximum rhetorical effect:

> Everyone is the other, and no one is himself. The *one*, with which the question about the *who* of everyday Dasein answers itself, is the *nobody* to whom every Dasein has indeed already surrendered itself in being among one another [*Untereinanderseins*]. (SZ 128/165 f.)

What does it mean to say that we are not ourselves? Does this mean that there is some "true self," some human nature that we fail to realize? Not at all. A self is precisely *not* a thing, whether this is thought of as something that is "given" entire in every act of consciousness, or as some primordial human nature. Heidegger is comfortable with having "vaporized" such notions (SZ 117/153). Moreover, it is abundantly clear that everyday, fallen existence is in no way "less real" than authentic existence (SZ 128/166). The distinction is not one of "what," but one of "how." To say that we are not ourselves, for Heidegger, is to say that we are on the run from our lives. Because life is *in each case mine*, it is something that I *must* live. "The question of existence is always only cleared up through existing itself" (SZ 12/33). When we are not ourselves, it is because we have abandoned responsibility for living and have sought refuge in the complacency of public life.

At this point, a comparison with Heidegger's earlier discussion of the primitive Christian community is instructive. Heidegger maintains that Christian life somehow "lives" factical life-experience itself in its temporality. When we turn to the actual working out of this assumption in a close reading of Paul's epistles, there is no trace of "true self" being lived up to or of "human nature" being realized. Instead, we find a community that anxiously awaits the dawn of a new aeon, resisting the superficiality and complacency of those who cry "peace and security!" Instead of fleeing from life, hiding from its "affliction" and "distress," the Christian community confronts it head-on. Thus, those outside the community are not guilty of some metaphysical failure, but simply of dishonesty.

For Heidegger, not being ourselves means being enslaved by the public world, being victims of "the dictatorship of the 'one'" (SZ 126/164). The irreducible individuality of human life, expressed by the formal designation "in each case mine," vanishes behind a timid façade of pale conformity. "The one, which is nothing definite, and which all are, though not in the manner of sum, prescribes the kind of being of everydayness" (SZ 127/164). This prescription is characterized by "averageness," by a drive to mute the challenge of the exceptional (SZ 127/164f.). It is a basic fact of public life that "it is insensitive to every difference of level and of genuineness" (SZ 127/165).

It is important to note here that the "one" is not the same as *society*. Rather, it is a way of existing in society that we have a tendency to fall into. Recall here that the "one" answers the question of the "who" of Dasein, a question that ultimately leads us back to the irreducible particularity of human life. The "one" is a general term for those ways of living that attempt to mute this particularity and its attendant difficulty. Furthermore, the "one" is not something that can be located in the way physical objects can be. It is an "existential," i.e., a categorial structure, of Dasein. The "one" is also the kind of phenomenon that conceals itself, i.e., it is so close to us in our ordinary everyday experience that it is often overlooked. This was shown earlier by Heidegger's discussion in SS 1923 of the way it passes itself off as the "height of living."

In *Being and Time*, Heidegger writes of the "one" that "[i]f it is not accessible in the same way as a stone that is objectively present, that is not decisive in the least with regard to its way of being" (SZ 128/166). Similarly, one cannot simply explain this away as an epiphenomenon that results from the spatial proximity of several subjects. Moreover, "[t]he one is also not something like a 'universal subject' that floats above several things" (SZ 128/166). The warnings continue with the remark that "[t]he one is not the species to which temporally particular Dasein belongs, nor can one come across it as an enduring characteristic of this entity" (SZ 129/166).

All these remarks are designed to distance Heidegger's account from traditional metaphysics. The "one" is not a sociological fact, objectively present like a stone, nor is it "really nothing," nor can it be understood by means of Aristotelian or Hegelian categories. The "one" is an *ontological* category. For Heidegger, *ontology* is not concerned with what exists, but with the *being* of what exists, with the pre-conceptual meaningfulness of things we encounter in concrete life-experience. By situating the "one" in the context of ontology, Heidegger is telling us that this is the *de facto* starting point of our understanding of ourselves and of the world. The "one" is part of the "horizon" or "background" against which, according to Heidegger, our daily practices are intelligible. Thus, to say that, as the "one," we are not ourselves, is not to make a *metaphysical* claim at all, if such claims are taken to be assertions about things and their properties.

The "ontological" (rather than "metaphysical") meaning of the "one" becomes clear at the end of Heidegger's initial discussion of this phenomenon. Heidegger's comments are worth quoting in order to fully dispense with tempting sociological or metaphysical interpretations:

> If Dasein is familiar with itself as the "one"-self, then that means, at the same time, that the one sketches out in advance the closest interpretation of the world and of being-in-the-world. The "one"-self, for the sake of which Dasein is in an everyday way, articulates the referential context of significance. [. . .] From out of this, and as this, I am first of all "given" to "myself." (SZ 129/167)

The "one" is an integral part of the "horizon" of our daily activities, of the context of meaningful relations through which we make sense of the world on a practical level. Furthermore, it is always against this horizon that an "authentic" disclosure of oneself and of a context of meaningful relations takes place.

The final feature of fallen life that is clearly linked with this mode of fugitive self-concealment, in which a person relinquishes her life to the anonymous averageness of the "one," can be located in Heidegger's discussion of the movement of "falling" in §38 of *Being and Time*. I have already had occasion to discuss the "tranquilizing" nature of this tendency of life in detail. After briefly describing this once again, Heidegger is quick to point out that this tranquillity does not amount to complete inaction. To the contrary, it is most evident in our uninhibited surrender to the "hustle and bustle [*Betrieb*]" of life (SZ 177/222). Despite its overall complacency, fallen life is not at a standstill, but is constantly *aggravated*. This appears, for Heidegger, in his contemporaries' view that "the understanding of the most foreign cultures, and the 'synthesis' of these with one's own, leads to a complete and, for the first time, genuine enlightenment [*Aufklärung*] of Dasein about itself" (SZ 178/222). One never asks, says Heidegger, *what it is* we are trying to understand. In our constant comparison with everything, we drift toward "alienation [*Entfremdung*]" from our own "ability to be [*Seinkönnen*]," i.e., from the particular life and the particular possibilities that have been delivered over to us (SZ 178/222). Alienation "closes off" the possibility of taking over one's life. Facile "self-dissection" takes the place of genuine worry about oneself (SZ 178/222).

A considerable amount of material has been discussed so far in this chapter; hence, it is useful to briefly recount the main points of the discussion up to this point. The aim of this chapter as a whole is to provide a clear understanding of what Heidegger means by "inauthenticity." This term (and its cognates) is used in the context of a kind of perfectionist moral theory. According to Heidegger, there are two general ways that one can live one's life, one of which is clearly more valuable than the other, at least by his lights. The less valuable of the two is called "inauthenticity" in *Being and Time*, and is referred to earlier as "ruinance" or "falling."

"Inauthenticity" (like its cognates) is not a name for a *concept*. Instead, it is a "formal indication" that is intended by Heidegger to intimate a complex pattern that is found *in* life as it is lived. That is, the term "inauthenticity" is used to mark off, in a general way, the boundaries of a certain way of being a human being. The term itself, *Un-eigentlichkeit*, gives one a clue as to the most basic feature of this way of life. '*Eigentlichkeit*,' rendered literally, means something like "being owned" or "being proper to one." Heidegger uses the root, '*eigen*,' to refer to the irreducible singularity of human life. *Un-eigentlichkeit*, then, hints at a way of life that has somehow or other *relinquished* its singularity by failing to "own" up to it.

Heidegger describes several distinct but overlapping features of what he calls "inauthenticity." Again, it is important to realize that these features are not constitutive of the *definition* of a *concept*. Instead, they are best understood as revisable ways of pointing to or indicating features of a concrete way of life that Heidegger thinks it worthwhile to care about. I have described five such features in this chapter. (1) Heidegger often discusses the prevalent (and perhaps inescapable) *inclination* that people have toward an inauthentic life. He tries to express this with terms like "propensity," "conative inclination," and "temptation." The claim is that one often finds oneself caught up in or entangled by a certain way of life. (2) Heidegger also suggests that this inclination is motivated by a desire for *security*, an urge to "take it easy" and flee from the difficulty of living one's own individual life in one's own way. An inauthentic life thus tends to be "tranquilized." That is, one feels oneself to be "at home" in the world. (3) This powerful pull toward a "satisfying" life leads to a fragmentation of identity. A life that always follows the path of least resistance is one that lacks focus. (4) At the same time, the urge to have life as a secure position generates *hyperbolic* excesses. Boundaries are transgressed, challenges are avoided, and differences are smoothed over. In place of a genuine concern with living one's own life, one is absorbed by an "anxious worry" about where one stands vis-à-vis others. Social differences tend to be disquieting, and a life that is impelled by a drive for tranquillity tends to be preoccupied with them.

(5) On Heidegger's view, all this ultimately issues in an almost complete *abdication* of self-responsibility. Rather than living one's own life, in one's own way, one's life is itself *lived* by an anonymous public identity. One takes on "disguises" or "masks," i.e., common ways of thinking and acting, that provide a safe refuge from the "danger" of being a self.

It is important to note here that each of these five features of an inauthentic life can be traced back to Heidegger's study of primitive Christianity during WS 1920–1921 and later. The basic life-experience of the early Christian community throws the more common "way of the world" into relief. For example, the "anxious worry" of Christian life, suspended in the eschatological drama of history, contrasts with the prevailing *modus operandi* of those who are "asleep" in worldly concern. Or again, Augustine contrasts his distracted or "dispersed" life prior to conversion with a life totally focused on God. As I will show later (chapters 5–6), Heidegger takes this Christian alternative as a paradigm for a way of life that is "authentic" and which he clearly regards as the ideal.

The Language of Inauthenticity

See to it that no one takes you captive through philosophy and empty deceit, according to human tradition [. . .].

(Col. 2:7–9)

The situation is all the more difficult today, now that everyone says everything, now that philosophy is so shrewd, so deep, and so comprehensive that everyone can take comfort and be assured of his own superiority in having already said this or that, which can be found in some book or other.

(G61 194/145)

In the previous chapter, I explicated the meaning of "inauthenticity" in Heidegger's work from 1919 to 1927. I argued that "inauthenticity" (and its cognate terms) is a "formal indication" of a typical pattern of human life characterized by a number of fluid, overlapping features. One of the crucial, and most discussed, of these features is the abdication of individual identity in favor of an anonymous public identity that Heidegger calls "the one [*das Man*]." The discussion of "inauthentic" life is, however, incomplete as it now stands. A vital element of Heidegger's view concerns the role of *tradition* and *public discourse* in inauthentic life. For Heidegger, to live as a human being means to be engaged in an ongoing activity of *interpretation*—interpretation of self, of social relations, and of non-human realities. Interpretation is guided ahead of time by tradition, and is articulated, shared, and developed in public discourse.

These phenomenological "facts" about human life are, on their own, quite innocuous. The ubiquity of interpretation does not pose any obvious problem. However, as Heidegger is at pains to articulate, tradition tends to slide into "common sense" and to exercise a hidden tyranny over the ways individuals in a particular community think and act. Moreover, public discourse, as "idle talk [*Gerede*]," tends to only entrench this tyranny. This is the case not only in daily conversation, the media, or political discourse, but also, and from Heidegger's point of view more damningly, in the *intellectual* discourse of the time.

In this respect, Heidegger's position shares a great deal with those of religious thinkers like Paul, Luther, and Kierkegaard.[1] On Paul's view, the so-called "wisdom" of the "world" actually reduces to prideful self-congratulation by a sinful humanity. Heidegger refers to several passages in which Paul attacks this pseudo-wisdom: (1) "though they knew God, they did not honor him as God or give thanks to him [. . .]. Claiming to be wise, they became fools" (Rom. 1:21 f., cited at G60 281 f.); and (2) "Where is the one who is wise? Where is the scribe? Where is the debater of this age? Has not God made foolish the wisdom of the world?" (1 Cor. 1:20, cited at G60 136 f.). As Heidegger points out a lecture from 1928, the biblical term "world" refers not to the planet Earth or to the totality of what exists, but to a way of existing that is cut off from God and enslaved to sin (G26 222 f./173 f.). For Paul, there is clearly an intimate connection between the way of existing and the pseudo-wisdom of those who are wise in their own estimation. And, as I have shown in chapter 2, these ideas also play an important role in Luther's *destructio* of theology. His opponents are not neo-platonists, sophists, and Gnostics, but nominalist theologians who claim to be expounding and preserving the true faith. Figures like Paul, Luther, and Kierkegaard provided Heidegger with a vocabulary for adding a critical edge to his more general understanding of tradition and public discourse.

The aim of the present chapter, then, is to examine Heidegger's conception of the role of discourse, as tradition, as "idle talk," and as educated consciousness, in inauthentic life. The discussion will begin with a detailed discussion of the development of Heidegger's understanding of the "tradition" in the early 1920s, followed by an analysis of his pessimistic conception of tradition as "decline" and his surveys of Western intellectual history. After this, I will turn to "idle talk," the "how" of the operation of tradition at a particular time. Here I will focus on Heidegger's discussions of this notion in the lecture course from SS 1925 and from *Being and Time*. Finally, I will take up Heidegger's bitter critiques of public discourse and educated consciousness, found in texts from the "early Freiburg" period of his work (1919–1923). Heidegger singles out contemporary university philosophy, historical science, and religious discourse in particular. It is here that we find Heidegger's struggle [*Kampf*] against the complicity of the academic and ecclesiastical establishment in rootless modern life.

Tradition and Discourse

At the beginning of 1919, Heidegger wrote a now-well-known letter to his fatherly friend, Father Engelbert Krebs, in which he formally renounced his allegiance to the Catholic Church. He tells Father Krebs that "[e]pistemological insights extending to a theory of historical knowledge have made the *system* of Catholicism problematic and unacceptable to me [. . .]" (S 69). Certainly, Heidegger's passionate interest in Luther, and his commitment to a kind of "free Christianity," can account for at least part of this separation.[2] But the mention of "theory of historical knowledge" points toward the man who represents *the* philosopher of history for Heidegger, i.e., Wilhelm Dilthey. Dilthey's name shows up in a curriculum vitae from 1915, as well as in a later résumé that details some of Heidegger's teaching activities at Freiburg (G16 37, 44). It was in studying his works that Heidegger began to engage philosophically with the debates regarding historical consciousness that captivated so many philosophers and historians of the time, and from him that Heidegger learned to appreciate the relationship between history and life.[3]

By SS 1920, Heidegger has worked out his own position on the relation between history and life. One "has" a history here not in the sense of historical science, but in the sense of *tradition*. Heidegger illustrates: "The Middle Ages, for example, had no historical science, but they clearly had a rich tradition in their life, e.g. in the central direction of their life, in the religious" (G59 52). "Having" a tradition in this sense clearly has nothing to do with objectively cataloguing the facts about past forms of life. Instead, tradition is determinative, in a practical sense, of the identity of a community. According to Heidegger, "having" a tradition means:

> [P]reserving as true [*Bewahren*], in one's own Dasein that has come to be, what already is [*Gewordene*], *as* what already is *in one's own becoming* (to participate [*Mithaben*] in the becoming and to constantly have it anew).— Preserving as true in one's own Dasein *in its being carried out* [*Leistungen*]: culture (not so much as *that* wherein one has come to be); in preserving as true there *is* the rhythm of one's own Dasein, it *is* with the preserving as true that belongs to it.—The relationship referred to here belongs together with one's innermost Dasein itself [. . .]. (G59 53)

These remarks are a version of the more familiar Heideggerian claim that we *are* history (see chapter 8). Having a tradition, as pointed out previously, is not something that depends upon the level a community's historiographical capacities have reached. Instead, it means participating in the handing down of what already is [*Gewordene*] as the decisive element in one's own identity. Having a tradition means actively identifying with a context of practices and concepts, thereby perpetuating them, "preserving" them "as true." A tradition is not a complete totality that lies in the past, open for our inspection, but is instead the crucial factor in who we are and who we are becoming. Each community, and each individual in a community, is, quite simply, the "happening [*Geschehen*]" of a tradition.

Tradition fills in the "content" of identity. Moreover, it opens up the possibilities of meaning that are available at any given time. In this respect, it plays a crucial role in philosophical investigations, which always begin *in media tradi-*

tionis. In a sense, there is nothing new in philosophy. It is, Heidegger asserts, "naïve to think that one could today, or ever, begin from scratch in philosophy, or that one can be so radical as to dispose of so-called tradition" (G59 29). Appeals to ahistorical "common sense" are simply retreats into one's own "contingent spiritual horizon," and are therefore to be mistrusted (G59 30). Having arrived at this basic conviction regarding the interlocking connections of tradition, life, and philosophy, Heidegger goes on to articulate his philosophical program of *Destruktion* (chapter 8). But before this can be understood in detail, it is necessary to understand what it is about the tradition that calls for a philosophical response like the one Heidegger outlines.

Tradition and Interpretation

One of the most important texts from Heidegger's early period is the "Natorp Report," written during 1922. By way of clarifying the "hermeneutical situation" for an interpretation of Aristotle, Heidegger outlines some of the key features of factical life-experience in a way that points forward to the better known "analytic of Dasein" in *Being and Time.* As in the roughly contemporaneous lectures from WS 1921–1922, Heidegger defines the fundamental sense of life as "caring" (NB 6f./115). In our dealings with the world, things are encountered not as inert objects, but as things that have *significance.* Part of what accounts for the significance that things have is that human beings grow up into inherited contexts of meaning. For us, reality has always already been interpreted.

Heidegger writes that "[f]actical life moves at any time within a certain state of *having-been-interpreted* [*Ausgelegtheit*] that has been handed down to it, and it has reworked or worked out anew" (NB 6/116). This interpretation lays out the "paths" or "directions" on which life can go about its day-to-day activities. In addition, this interpretation harbors a definite point of view about life itself. Thus, "what is also established in it is the particular sense the Dasein of life has, i.e., the 'as-what' and the 'how' in which human beings maintain themselves within their own forehaving" (NB 6/116). Inherited interpretations provide the undiscussed background for the way we think about ourselves and about the world with which we are concerned.

Heidegger makes the same point again during SS 1923, where he asserts of factical life that "to be in some state of having-been-interpreted belongs to its being" (G63 15/11). A more specific instance of this relates to how we come to "see" objects, both in our practical affairs and in scientific investigations. Our seeing is oriented ahead of time by an antecedent familiarity with objects (G63 74/58f.). "Being familiar with them is for the most part the sedimented result of having heard about them and having learned something about them" (G63 75/59). Presuppositions about the sense of life and of other things are the conditions for our ability to make sense of things at all. But one might still wonder about what it is to have an "interpretation" built in to life in this way. What, after all, does Heidegger mean by "interpretation"?

The *locus classicus* of Heidegger's view is §32 of *Being and Time*. Interpretation [*Auslegung*] is the development of understanding, i.e., the "laying out [*aus-legen*]" or making explicit the possibilities of sense that form the horizon of human activity (SZ 148f./188f.). Interpretation is the "working out" of possibilities of sense that have been already projected in understanding. The largely implicit involvements and meaningful relations that form the "world," or background context for human activity, are "set over against one another [*auseinandergelegt*]," made explicit (SZ 149/189). On the most primitive level, this takes place when we make use of something for some purpose or other. That is, we "articulate" the reference or involvement of the thing by singling it out for a particular practice. A further possibility, however, is the *expression* in language [*Ausdruck*] of the sense that we have uncovered. Thus, Heidegger says that:

> For the most part, discourse [*Rede*] is expressed by being spoken out, and has always been so expressed; it is language [*Sprache*]. But, in that case understanding and interpretation already lie in what has thus been expressed. In language, as a way things have been expressed or spoken out [*Ausgesprochenheit*], there is hidden a way in which the understanding of Dasein has been interpreted. [. . .] The understanding which has thus already been "deposited" in the way things have been expressed, pertains just as much to any traditional discoveredness of entities which may have been reached, as it does to one's current understanding of being and to whatever possibilities and horizons for fresh interpretation and conceptual articulation may be available. (SZ 167f./211)

Earlier, during SS 1925, Heidegger provided another, more succinct explanation of this phenomenon. The function of discourse is, ultimately, *communication*: "it lays out or interprets, that is, it brings the referential relations of meaningfulness into relief in communication. [. . .] In being articulated, in the articulated word, the meaning highlighted in interpretation becomes available for being-with-one-another. The word is articulated in public. This articulated discourse preserves interpretation within itself" (G20 370/268). The claim is that once the interpretation has been expressly articulated in the spoken (or written) word, it becomes the shared property of a linguistic community. The interpretation has been made *available* to the speakers of a language. As one is acculturated to the use of language, one is thereby "delivered over [*überantwortet*]" to the interpretation that has been thus articulated. Through communication, the interpretation is handed down through the generations. Thus we come to inhabit (in a largely unconscious way) a definite tradition, a definite way of thinking about the world that is structured by our shared linguistic practices.

On this account, then, the tradition is integral to who we are as self-interpreting beings. Tradition is the previously articulated realm of possibilities that form the starting point of our particular self-interpretations. This is true not only of our conceptions of ourselves *qua* selves, but also of our practical activities. As I have already pointed out, on Heidegger's view practical activity is the most basic level of interpretation. Tradition presents the "paths" on which we can realize our projects. None of this can be understood as our autonomous creation. At the same time, individuals at any particular time are not simply passive channels for the inertia of tradition. As beings that are fundamentally *futural*, the tradition structures our identity in terms of *possibilities* of acting and of conceiving of things. Thus, in being selves, i.e., in being human beings that form practical conceptions of themselves, we participate in the handing down of the tradition. As I discussed above, in SS 1920, Heidegger conceives of preservation [*Bewahren*] not as a task for antiquarians, but as a fundamental part of the formation of human identity. In carrying out the projects we have taken over from our inheritance, we participate in the historical development of this complex of possibilities. Thus, over time, some possibilities simply fade in significance. For example, while we certainly understand the notion of a divinely ordained monarch, this is not a "live option" for most people in the Western world today. As tradition evolves, carried on by the choices of individuals, certain possibilities simply cease to be available.

While Heidegger clearly recognizes the *developmental* nature of tradition and does not conceive of it (at least in the 1920s) as a static, monolithic block of possibilities of sense, he nevertheless places the emphasis on the way tradition functions "behind the scenes" in our daily understanding of ourselves. Selfhood, or practical identity, is not to be conceived of in Cartesian-Kantian terms as the pure transcendental "I think." As self-interpreting beings, we are always caught within the circle of interpretation (SZ 152f./195f.). As such, there is always the undiscussed assumption of a definite horizon of intelligibility or "meaning [*Sinn*]."[4] Within certain limits, of course, we can make of ourselves and of the world what we will. But the fundamental "fact" about us is that we have the structure of a "thrown possibility," that we have always already been "delivered over" to a range of possibilities (SZ 144/183). These possibilities are available to us because they have been expressed, talked about, written down, etc. As we grow into membership in a linguistic community, this expressed interpretation becomes the background against which we understand ourselves and the world.

Decline

Heidegger's account of tradition is, however, by no means exhausted by the conception, sketched out above, of the general role it plays in human beings' interpretive activities. Heidegger is also interested in the particular effects that tradition has on our ways of thinking and acting. Here one can find two interlocking theses: (1) tradition tends to "decline" to a level of self-evidence that blocks the possibility of genuine appropriation, and (2) it perpetuates *particular* interpretations at the expense of other possibilities. The combination of these two tendencies results in a *leveling* of meaning and a consequent foreclosure of some possibilities of meaning which themselves reveal things about the deep structures of human life. This truncated, impoverished interpretation of human life masquerades as common sense, effectively *obstructing* the path to an appropriation of other possibilities.

John Van Buren has argued that during the early 1920s, much of Heidegger's work was devoted to revalidating lost possibilities of meaning. More specifically, Heidegger criticized the foundations of modern philosophy, viewing the normative ideals of "method" and "scientific knowledge" as attempts to "master the unruly abousiological and heterological character of life by turning it into a presence that can be calculated according to rules."[5] In his early lecture courses at Freiburg, Heidegger tried to challenge the hegemony of the "theoretical attitude" not only by critically examining its foundations in life, but also by exploring the philosophical potential of marginal or neglected traditions: medieval mysticism, Luther's *theologia crucis*, life-philosophy, art and literature.

The dominance of certain strands over others in Western intellectual history, and the consequent foreclosure of meaning, ultimately results, on Heidegger's account, from a "decline" into self-evidence. The ideas involved in this claim first began to take definite shape during the early 1920s. In SS 1920, Heidegger argues that his conception of philosophy as destruction [*Destruktion*] is mandated by the nature of life itself. This means that a particular feature of life is what calls for philosophical examination: the *"fading of significance* [*Verblassen der Bedeutsamkeit*]" (G59 37). Heidegger explains that this means a "progress in the states and modes of non-originality [*Nicht-ursprunglichkeit*], where the genuineness of enactment, especially of the renewal of enactment, goes astray, where the relations are worn down and the self is actually no longer 'interested' in the content that is possessed" (G59 37). What has thus faded is not, though, simply forgotten; instead, it floats around in a kind of "availability [*Verfügbarkeit*]," and can further decline into mere "usability [*Verwendbarkeit*]" (G59 37).

The notion of "fading of significance" has much in common with elements of Heidegger's later account of the genesis of "idle talk," which will be the subject of a later discussion. The above account is a story about the way the meaning of the words we use can ultimately be completely uprooted from the original life-contexts from which they have sprung. The full complexity of referential relations of meaning has been clipped down to the point where words are simply "there," available for our use. Heidegger's example in this course is the word "history." He goes on to distinguish at least six common usages of this word, which he further analyzes into three primary senses. The point of all this is that we use words without knowing what we are saying at the deepest level. Concealed in the seeming self-evidence of ordinary discourse are a variety of relations, patterns, and usages of which we are, for the most part, simply unaware. Having become available, the meaning of words is now something "self-evident," such that we can speak of "our concept of" something or "what we mean" by something without irony.

Heidegger begins to describe the results of this "fading of significance," when viewed as part of the historical transmission of meaning, in the early 1920s. This account that is developed in his lecture courses and other writings is also clearly present in *Being and Time* (see §6), as well as in lecture courses and other works following it. By the mid-1930s, however, Heidegger had worked out a different conception of the tradition that received its first public articulation in the *Letter on Humanism* of 1946. In the latter, we learn of something called the "history of being." It is this conception of the nature of the Western intellectual tradition that dominates Heidegger's readings of Nietzsche in the 1930s and 1940s, his diagnoses of nihilism in the 1950s and 1960s, as well as his interpretive efforts with respect to early Greek philosophy. On this conception, Western intellectual and cultural history is encapsulated in a series of epochal transitions of different "sendings" of being, culminating in the modern, subjectivistic, technical understanding of being.

In the 1920s, Heidegger's conception of history lacks these elements, while he nevertheless certainly perceives a continuity in the tradition. More-over, the pessimistic narrative of cultural decline that one finds in the "later" Heidegger is certainly presaged in much of his work from the 1920s.[6] A more detailed discussion of the *content* of the tradition, as Heidegger conceives it, will have to wait until the next section. My concern here is more with the *nature* of tradition and its influence on the present. Most of Heidegger's remarks concerning this are, quite naturally, focused upon the role of tradition in philosophy and in intellectual endeavor more generally. However, as I have pointed out above, tradition is not at all restricted to the environs of academic debate and scholarship. Instead, it forms the essential content of who we are, both individually and communally. Confronting the intellectual tradition then becomes something far more relevant than simple historiography, as I will show in greater detail in chapter 8.

Much of Heidegger's discussion in WS 1921–1922 is devoted to the problem of "defining" philosophy. This topic leads Heidegger to discuss not only various rival attempts to reach a definition, but also the nature of definitions themselves. The "situation" of the "enactment" of philosophy, i.e., the university, becomes relevant to the discussion (G61 62/47 ff.). During his discussion of one particular tendency in the search for a concept of philosophy, Heidegger introduces the topic of the tradition. He describes the tendency in question as the "overestimation" of the task of determining the nature of philosophy. One assumes here a normative idea of "definitions" and "principles" as what is most general or universal (G61 21 f./18). Heidegger precisely describes what one is looking for here: "The definition of philosophy must be one of principle, and that which it determines must be determined as a principle, as the most general, such that the determination applies to every individual domain of philosophy, i.e., to every individual philosophical discipline [. . .]" (G61 22/18).

Lurking behind the seeming self-evident correctness of this quest is a hidden assumption about what one ought to do in philosophy. This hidden assumption betrays what Heidegger takes to be the slavish dependence of contemporary philosophy on the tradition. Not only is this idea of "definition" taken for granted, so too is the conception of what such a definition must accomplish. The definition must "make sense of the variegated manifold handed down in the history of philosophy [. . .]" (G61 22/18). Heidegger expresses his worry in the following remarks:

> The endeavor to resolve the (supposedly urgent) task of definition is driven by a care which demands . . . that . . . everything "accord" with what has been handed down in the tradition, precisely as it has been handed down, with no manifest contradictions or vicious circles. The fact that, perhaps, the tradition [*Überlieferung*] to which one should adhere and to which the definition should conform—again, in a basically genuine tendency—might be under consideration here in an interpretation that is just as superficial as is the business of definitions—that is never troubling to anyone. This concern is passed down from generation to generation in the philosophical literature, as we take it as purely unscientific to suspect that it might be erroneous. Certainly we are not simply to define philosophy *privatim*, arbitrarily brushing aside its entire rich history! (G61 22/18f.)

Not only does one uncritically pass on the "business of definitions [*Definitionsgeschäft*]" as a worthwhile philosophical project, but one demands that conceptions of philosophy must conform to the tradition. That is, philosophy must in the end be seen as the most universal, principled "science." Any attempt to shake off the hegemony of the past is simply to be cast aside as "arbitrary." Similarly, one assumes that, in the usual understanding of philosophy, one has gotten hold of something *essential*. Heidegger's suggestion is that, beyond the inertia of particular interpretations, there is no reason to think that this is the case. The tradition itself, to which one hopes philosophy will always conform, might be completely misunderstood. Ultimately, philosophy is reduced to just another cultural object, to be studied by "typifying" historical science (G61 1/3). This, of course, takes itself to be "strict factual research," while everything else counts as mere "prattle [*Geschwätz*], even the attempt to bring itself to understanding in its conditioned status and standpoint" (G61 1/3). For Heidegger, then, it all comes down to a fundamental choice: "either we live, work, and do research relative to unexamined needs and artificially induced dispositions, or we are prepared to grasp concretely a radical idea and to achieve our existence in it" (G61 70/53).

Philosophy is always situated within a certain familiarity [*Bekanntsein*] with itself and with its subject matter. This is, for Heidegger, best understood as the effect of tradition (G63 75/59). Yet the tradition we find ourselves situated in is one in which the subject matter is ultimately covered over or concealed. A particular way things show themselves can be rigidly "fixed through *tradition*," such that one no longer is even able to recognize that something is missing (G63 75/59). For example, on Heidegger's view, the original articulation of philosophical thought in ancient Greece has slipped into moribund self-evidence; to use Heidegger's language, the tradition as "fallen away" from its originality (G63 76/59). Contemporary philosophy is situated within this long history of decline, in which the interpretations of basic concepts have become fixed and passed off as self-evident.

This situation is characteristic not only of philosophical research, but of life itself. Indeed, the situatedness of life within an "inauthentic" tradition is part of the explanation for the state of philosophy. This situation is articulated by Heidegger in the Natorp Report from 1922:

> Life is always stuck fast in, and pushed around by, inauthentic traditions and customs of one sort or another. Out of them develop certain yearnings, and in them the paths along which such yearnings are to be satisfied has been mapped out for one's concern. Life conceals itself from itself in the world in which it is absorbed and in the averageness in which it goes about its dealings. (NB 11/118)

The idea that tradition "falls" or "declines" into a kind of leveled-down, superficial self-evidence is described a bit later in this text as follows:

> Due to its tendency toward falling, factical life lives for the most part in what is inauthentic, in what has been handed down to it, in what has been transmitted and reported to it from the past, in what it has appropriated and learned in an average way. Even what has been worked out in an original manner as an authentic possession falls into averageness and publicness. [. . .] This falling touches all of the dealings of factical life, all of its circumspection, and not least of all its own actualization of its interpretation [. . .]. (NB 18f./122f.)

It is not simply philosophy, then, that finds itself caught within the web of tradition. Our ordinary ways of thinking and acting are, on Heidegger's view, profoundly and subtly shaped by our cultural inheritance. The problem with this is not that we have a cultural inheritance *per se*, but rather the problem is the way this inheritance operates for the most part. It is something "self-evident," something that needs no further explanation or investigation. "This is," one says, "simply how we do things." Instead of self-consciously and critically engaging with our unavoidable inheritance, we tend to simply slip into prearranged tracks of thinking and acting. Thus the tradition is complicit in our inauthentic longing for presence and security and in our fugitive self-abdication.

Elements of our cultural inheritance tend, says Heidegger, to live a "shadowy life," one that "has hardened into a long, degenerate, and spurious tradition, and that has never been appropriated in an original manner" (G9 3/3). Here, Heidegger has in mind epistemic norms in particular, but it is clear from what has gone before that this assessment applies more globally. Certain concepts take on a veneer of self-evidence such that we inevitably come to conceive of ourselves in a certain way, missing out on other, richer possibilities. Heidegger maintains that "the self quickly becomes experienced as having an objective kind of significance (personality, ideal type of humanity), and within this experiential orientation comes to be understood theoretically and takes on meaning in philosophy" (G9 34/29). Factical life is, accordingly, "loaded down [*Belastung*]" with tradition, particularly with respect to its conception of itself (G9 34/29 f.). Again, tradition does its work not only within philosophy, but within the larger whole of "factical life" itself, of which philosophy is only a part.

Particularly notable, however, in these passages (from the review of Jaspers's *Psychology of Worldviews*) is the connection that Heidegger draws between tradition and the *self*. "Loaded down" with tradition, we conceive of ourselves as "objective." That is, we think of ourselves as the kinds of things that can be disposed of through everyday activities (*zuhanden* in *Being and Time*), or as objects of aesthetic contemplation (*vorhanden* in *Being and Time*). In either case we have lost a sense for what it means to be a human being, i.e., to be a radically finite, temporally incomplete project. A human being is never "finished" like a chest of drawers or a research project, nor is a human being there all at once for disinterested contemplation. We are, as Heidegger liked to say, always on the way to ourselves, never completely at our own disposal. It is the deeply unsettling nature of human nature that impels us on our quest for quiescent security. Thus it comes as no surprise that the tradition perpetuates an understanding of human life that only serves to coddle our disquiet.

The dictatorship of the tradition also forms part of Heidegger's reflections in his 1924 lectures on Dilthey at Kassel. Here, the power of tradition is polemically contrasted with the battle cry of phenomenology, i.e., "to the things themselves!" (S 160). The promise of phenomenology, then, rests upon the cogency of a general view that "returning to self-evident things concealed from the consciousness of everyday life is always the genuine path to great discoveries" (S 160). Thus, despite its seeming triviality, the motto of phenomenology is actually a challenge to philosophy. For Heidegger, philosophy has a remarkable tendency to become lost in artificial constructions, pseudo-problems, and conceptual dead-ends. Attending to the "things themselves [*die Sache selbst*]" is not quite as straightforward as it might seem. Instead, philosophy inhabits the superficial shadow-world of received opinion. Heidegger explains:

> Research and life have the strange tendency to leap over what is simple, originary, and genuine and to get hung up on what is complicated, derivative, and non-genuine. That is true not only today but for the whole history of philosophy. Contemporary philosophy is traditional; its newness lies in its renewal of previous philosophy, not in any new way of formulating questions about things. Traditional philosophy begins with opinions about things, i.e., with concepts that are not examined regarding their original appropriateness in the past. (S 160)

The tradition is the repository of what is "self-evident," what is a "matter of course," both for everyday life and for scientific research (S 164). Thus the past, as Heidegger puts it in *Being and Time*, is not something that simply "follows along after" human existence, but rather "is something that already goes ahead of it in each case [*geht ihm je schon vorweg*]" (SZ 20/41). Dasein "falls into [*verfällt in eins*]" tradition, which "relieves it of its own proper leading role in questioning and choosing" (SZ 21/42f.). When the tradition takes on this kind of "hegemony [*Herrschaft*]," it tends to actually occlude our understanding of things (SZ 21/43). What is received is delivered over to self-evidence in a way that conceals its origins. This even extends to the point that one no longer thinks it worthwhile to inquire after these origins, and instead occupies one's time with the classification and typology of alien cultural possibilities (SZ 21/43).[7]

Historical Sketches

The conclusion to be drawn from the preceding discussion is that, for Heidegger, the tradition not only serves as the background of possibilities of interpretation, but also that the tradition obstructs or occludes fundamental possibilities of sense by covering them over with a veneer of self-evidence. This both precludes critical appropriation of our intellectual heritage and forces contemporary philosophy and science into a rigid, unquestioned *Fragestellung*.[8] Moreover, the veneer of self-evidence taken on by certain concepts and possibilities of sense is such that alternatives never even come into consideration. Similarly, entrenched interpretations of certain possibilities block the way to a renewed appreciation of them. Heidegger tries to illustrate these claims by means of more focused discussions of the intellectual heritage of Western culture. The meanings of certain ideas, such as "man" or "life," are worked out in predetermined ways, due in part to the dominance of a particular way of conceiving of philosophical or scientific knowledge that one might call "Greek aestheticism" or the "theoretical attitude." The result is not only that a richer understanding of human life is foreclosed by this tradition, but also that a particular context of sense comes to be misinterpreted.

To make sense of Heidegger's story about the tradition, it is important to get at least some grasp of his complicated views about the fundamental assumptions of European intellectual heritage. Heidegger's unflattering picture of this heritage has its roots in KNS 1919, and his first attempts to describe the "environmental experience" of pre-theoretical life. Heidegger takes the cardinal feature of this experience to be the immediate *meaningfulness* or *significance* of things (G56/57 72f./61).[9] It is from this primal experience, the experience of the world that is in fact closest to us, that the "theoretical attitude" comes to be generated by means of a process of "de-vivification [*Ent-leben*]."

Things lose their specifically "worldly" or meaningful character, becoming now mere "objects" before the disinterested gaze of the "de-historicized" self (G56/57 73f./61). In and of itself, this is not problematic and may in a certain way be unavoidable. The philosophically objectionable part of this is that the derivative (i.e., a totality of objects that can be conceptually determined by a theoretical subject) is taken for the *real* (G56/57 85/71f.). Consequently, a philosophical "obsession" with "explanation through dismemberment" blocks one's way back to the lived experience of things in their "worldly" character (G56/57 88/74). The origins of theory in "life" fade from view, and along with them any sense for the "ultimate problems" (G56/57 91/76). Instead, philosophers spend their time trying to reconstruct the primal lived experience of the world "objectively" and, according to Heidegger, land themselves in the kinds of *aporias* that are distinctive of pseudo-problems.

On Heidegger's view, the *de facto* assumption of Western philosophy is that what is real is what is simply "present," and that the proper mode of access to it is "sheer awareness of something objectively present in its objective presence" (SZ 25 f./48). Elsewhere, Heidegger refers to this as the "fundamental aesthetic attitude," which ultimately underwrites the entire tradition since Parmenides (G9 23 f./20; G63 91 f./70). Heidegger traces out the development of another assumption, side by side with this basic position, regarding the nature of human beings as "rational animals," i.e., as beings whose primary relation to reality is to be understood in terms of knowing or representing (G63 21 ff./17 ff.; S 165; SZ 59/86 ff.).[10] This position was used by Aristotle to ground the claim that the ultimate form of life for human beings is a life of disinterested contemplation. What really matters about human beings, then, is their ability to have objective cognitive access to reality. On Heidegger's view, once this idea becomes a self-evident part of our cultural inheritance, the way back toward a deeper appreciation of the pre-theoretical richness of human life is blocked.

During the first half of the 1920s, the story that one most often finds in Heidegger's works concerning the nature of the tradition is the story of the foreclosure of "primitive Christianity" by "Greek aestheticism." Having abandoned the neo-scholasticism of his younger years, Heidegger reaches a decidedly *Protestant* view about the intermingling of Hellenistic philosophy and Christianity.[11] Luther's hostility to Aristotelianism, rooted in his commitment to an evangelical soteriology, has already been discussed at some length (chapter 2). Texts from the early 1920s indicate that Heidegger shared this assessment.

In a transcript of his WS 1919–1920 lectures, one finds the view that the original Christian proclamation came to be gradually obscured through a process of "Hellenization" (G58 205). This process is again discussed during the "religion course" of WS 1920–1921 (G60 27 f.). The following semester, in his lecture on "Augustine and Neo-platonism," Heidegger focuses these considerations on Augustine's *Confessions*. Heidegger asserts that, in regard to some phenomena, such as the "seeking God" that is inherent in the Christian life, Augustine is dominated by a "Greek" or "theoretical" relational stance (G60 194). This is obliquely referred to again later in the lecture (G60 215). Augustine's axiological categories, such as the "divine light," "enjoyment of God," and the "highest good" are all basically Greek, and hence unbiblical (G60 257).

The "anxious worry [*Bekümmerung*]" that lies at the heart of Christian facticity is "perverted" into a kind of "calculation [*Berechnung*]" (G60 262). Romans 1:20 is seen as the decisive entry point for Hellenizing tendencies in Christianity (G60 264). This account appears again, in a more general form, during WS 1921–1922 (G61 6/6 f.). Throughout Western history, the compromise between primitive Christianity and Greek life and thought was challenged in various eruptions of the former, particularly in the medieval mystics, in Luther, and in Kierkegaard (G61 6/6 f.). In the case of Luther, however, the *status quo* soon returned in the form of Melanchthon's Protestant scholasticism (G61 7/7; G17 118).

This process has, in Heidegger's view, inevitably shaped the way the Christian proclamation is understood today. In reality, this understanding has foreclosed the basic possibilities opened up in the apostolic *kerygma*. This is illustrated particularly clearly in the case of primitive Christian eschatology. Heidegger's discussion of the earliest Pauline epistles is aimed at challenging the "self-evident" picture of primitive Christianity that dominates both theology and the study of religion (G60 80, 88, 97, etc.). This is aimed not simply at *understanding* the primitive proclamation, but also at freeing up the possibility for an *appropriation* of it.

The way of thinking about the world embodied in these aspects of the tradition foreclose the ability of philosophers to understand life in its full historical richness. In Heidegger's view, these combined epistemological and ontological commitments motivate the entire history of Western thought, both philosophical and theological, right up to the present. These basic ideas have become so hidden beneath a veil of self-evidence that the business of philosophy is carried out unconsciously within the framework constituted by them. Throughout his career, Heidegger attempts to appropriate alternative or marginal elements of the tradition, like primitive Christianity or Hölderlin's poetry, to overcome the dominance of this moribund tradition. In a manner analogous to Wittgenstein or Rosenzweig, Heidegger hopes to help us "get over" our bondage to metaphysics, understood as the confluence of these two epistemological and ontological assumptions.

Idle Talk: The "How" of Tradition

Understanding Heidegger's conception of the tradition is vital to understanding the *linguistic* element of inauthenticity. As historical beings, humans are essentially the loci of the transmission of tradition at a particular time. This tends to occur, however, in an uncritical, matter-of-course fashion. Rather than seizing our own unique historical destiny, we tend to simply perpetuate the superficial interpretations and hackneyed modes of life that have been handed on to us. All this is, of course, quite congruent with Heidegger's more general picture of inauthentic human life. On this picture, our lives are predominantly motivated by a powerful urge to seek security and tranquillity and to ultimately abdicate responsibility for ourselves. It is only natural, then, that we tend to slip into uncritical ways of thinking and acting. At the same time,

Heidegger makes it clear that our heritage or tradition is the repository of all the possibilities that are available to us at a particular time. Thus what inauthenticity comes down to is our manner of inhabiting our own particular historical world.

An important part of Heidegger's account of how we tend to be inauthentically historical is the idea of "idle talk [*Gerede*]." This idea receives its most detailed expositions during the lecture course of SS 1925 and in *Being and Time*. Put briefly, "idle talk" is Heidegger's term for the "inauthentic" way we inhabit the social and linguistic world. As has already been alluded to, Heidegger understands the purpose of spoken language as bringing "the referential relations of meaningfulness into relief in communication" (G20 370/268). That is, talking to one another is the primary way we inhabit our distinctively human world. The articulated word makes meaning available to other people. Moreover, it makes possible our acculturation to a particular range of possibilities or "referential relations of meaningfulness," which provides the necessary background for our concrete dealings with things. In uttering words, we make the "discoveredness" of things itself into something "worldly," i.e., something that can be talked over, discussed, modified, taught, etc. At any particular time, meaning has always already been made available in a certain way. Heidegger puts the point this way in SS 1925: "Every Dasein moves in such an interpretation, which for the most part coincides with the way the generation of a particular time has been interpreted and which is modified with the time" (G20 372/270).

When meaning is made available in this way through communication, there belongs to it a certain "public understanding" or "average intelligibility" (G20 370/268; SZ 168/212). This allows for a certain modicum of understanding between communicators, one which does not require any kind of deep appropriation or "primordial understanding" (SZ 168/212). This is possible because the actual focus is not on the *subject matter* of the discourse, but on "what is said in the talk [*das Geredete als solches*]" (SZ 168/212). On the other hand, what the talk is about [*das Worüber*] is only understood superficially. "In other words, articulated discourse can be understood without an original being-with involved in what the discourse is about" (G20 370/268). The tendency that follows up on this is for the matter to fade from view more and more as communication progresses. Heidegger writes:

> This means that in hearing and subsequent understanding, the understanding relation of being to that about which the discourse is can be left undetermined, uninvolved, even emptied to the point of a merely formal belief in what the original understanding had intended. The matter being spoken of thus slips away with the absence of the understanding relation of being. But while the matter being talked about slips away, what is said as such—the word, the sentence, the dictum—continues to be available in a worldly way, along with a certain understanding and interpretation of the matter. (G20 370/268f.)

Thus, while what is said has been "uprooted" from the "native soil" of the subject matter, it still retains a certain level of intelligibility (G20 371/269). "Hearing" no longer involves participation in a shared context of meaning so much as it means preoccupation with talking as such. "Hearing is now hearing *mere talk as talk* and understanding is understanding based on mere hearsay" (G20 371/269). Things that have been thus understood can, in turn, be quite easily passed along, since the lack of a genuine understanding does not function as a deterrent to this mode of communication. For Heidegger, this signifies a process of increasing groundlessness. "Discourse undergoes an increase in groundlessness in repetitive talk to the extent that a hardening of a specific opinion being expressed in discourse corresponds to such groundlessness" (G20 371/269). That is, an opinion rooted not in what the talk is about, but in a kind of average intelligibility, comes to have a certain normative weight in public discourse. When this happens, the way to the "ground" or "root" of what is at issue comes to be increasingly obstructed. The resulting kind of discourse, which amounts to simply passing this opinion along, is what Heidegger calls "idle talk" (G20 371/269). What is said takes on an authoritative character and gets spread around (SZ 168/212). "Idle talk is constituted by just such gossiping and passing the word along—a process by which its initial lack of grounds to stand on [*Bodenständigkeit*] becomes aggravated to complete groundlessness [*Bodenlosigkeit*]" (SZ 168f./212).

Idle talk promulgates a kind of universal availability, a superficial level of intelligibility that everyone can appropriate. In this regard, discourse once again feeds quite nicely into our inauthentic tendency to make things easy for ourselves. There is no need for deeper understanding, for soul-searching, or for dialogic struggle. Instead, "everyone knows" what it is all about. Here, discourse exercises a function of "closing" off what is to be understood (SZ 169/213). The result is a kind of detached, uprooted mode of existence (SZ 170/214).

Heidegger illustrates this idea in several different ways. In both SS 1925 and in *Being and Time*, Heidegger focuses on the peculiarly modern manifestation of idle talk, i.e., the "reading public" and the business of writing that serves it. Idle talk is not restricted to spoken communication: "much more idle talk today comes from what is written" (G20 371/269). Not only do writers simply pass off opinions as self-evident, but the reading public is satisfied with this kind of superficial, average intelligibility. Heidegger tells us that "[s]uch reading takes place characteristically without understanding the subject matter, but in such a way that the reader [. . .] acquires the possibility of dealing with the matters with great skill without ever having seen them. Something being said here to some extent acquires an intrinsic authoritative character" (G20 371/269). This is not confined to the world of dime-store fiction or popular journalism, but, Heidegger laments, it pervades even academic discourse. He continues, "They pass along what they have read and heard about the matter without any sensitivity for the distinction of whether or not that opinion or their own is actually relevant to the matter. [. . .] For idle talk is just the possibility of interpreting something without first making the matter one's own" (G20 372/270). In *Being and Time*, Heidegger succinctly labels this whole phenomenon "scribbling [*Geschreibe*]" (SZ 168f./212).

Another example comes from SS 1925 and concerns aesthetic appreciation. One might well wonder what Heidegger's opinion would be today about the profusion of desk calendars depicting masterpieces of world art. He writes:

> For example, nowadays one says, and everyone hears it and has heard it, that Rembrandt is esteemed. *One* says that. The manner of preoccupation and seeing is thereby prescribed, so that for that very reason one is excited by a Rembrandt without experiencing why, perhaps even against the insight that one finds nothing in it oneself. But *one* says it, and therefore it is so for *one*. (G20 373/270)

Heidegger offers similar thoughts on the business of academic philosophy a bit later in this lecture course:

> Nowadays, one decides about metaphysics or even higher matters at congresses. For everything which must be done nowadays, there is first a conference. One meets and meets, and everyone waits for someone else to tell him, and it doesn't really matter if it isn't said, for one has now indeed spoken one's mind. [. . .] There are people nowadays who travel from one conference to another and are convinced in so doing that something is really happening and that they have accomplished something; whereas in reality they have shirked the labor and now seek refuge in idle talk for their helplessness, which they of course do not understand. (376/272f.)

It is not merely popular opinion that perpetuates its mediocrity and superficiality in idle talk; so too, the alleged "experts" on things that are "deep" are often all too willing to be complicit in the promulgation of rootless opinion. As Heidegger sees it, human life is more or less continually enmeshed in a cycle of self-abdication and slavish conformity, only too happy to relinquish self-responsibility to the mindless circulation of what "one" says about a particular matter. The real disaster is that one takes all this for "really living," for the fulfillment of what it is to be a human being. Like many others of his generation, Heidegger is keenly aware of this as the core of modern bourgeois existence, and just as deeply senses its ultimate bankruptcy. His views on this matter, though definitely framed within a unique overall philosophical position, are quite congruent not only with those of the "Conservative Revolutionaries" of post–World War I Germany, but also with Christian eschatological thought embodied in the neo-orthodoxy of Barth, Kierkegaard's attack on the "present age," Luther's polemic against the "pig-theologians" of late scholasticism, and the primitive Christian rejection of the "world."

Public Intellectual Discourse and Inauthentic Life

Philosophy

In chapter 2, I showed that, for Luther, the dominant modes of theological discourse tend toward complicity in a life of sin, itself largely understood in terms of *superbia* [pride]. Luther's well-known aversion to scholastic theology, and his vitriolic rantings about reason and about Aristotle, have earned him the suspicion of philosophers ever since. Upon closer examination, however, it becomes clear that Luther, despite his rhetoric, has no objection to reason or to philosophy *per se*. Instead, Luther objects to the soteriological doctrines formulated by medieval theologians on the basis of, among other things, Aristotle's *Nicomachean Ethics*. The scholastic teaching of *facere quod in se est* is, on Luther's view, simply not Christian. Thus, rather than taking a stand on the struggle against sin through preaching the "foolishness" of the cross, learned discourse tends to subtly reinforce our complacency and willful rejection of the Gospel.

Like Luther, and through Luther's inspiration, Heidegger was also critical of learned discourse and what he viewed as its complicity in an inauthentic mode of life. Certainly Heidegger learned the art of critical unmasking not just from Luther; Nietzsche, Kierkegaard, Spengler, Van Gogh, and Dostoyevsky all find their way into Heidegger's rare acknowledgments of sources. At the same time, however, two considerations point to the importance of Luther in Heidegger's philosophical development. First of all, in his explicit acknowledgments of sources during two different semesters, Heidegger singles out Luther. In a loose page found in Heidegger's notes for the WS 1921–1922 course, one finds Luther, along with Kierkegaard, in a "motto, along with a grateful indication of the source" (G61 182/137). The editors point out that elsewhere in his notes, Heidegger tells us that he presents this motto to "characterize the intention of the interpretation."

A much more complete indication of Luther's influence is to be found in Heidegger's notes for the lecture of SS 1923. Here he writes that "companions in my searching were the young Luther and the paragon Aristotle, whom Luther hated" (G63 4/4). Before presenting this revealing assertion, however, Heidegger takes an opportunity to rail against the "corruption" of philosophy:

> [Q]uestioning has today fallen out of fashion in the great industry of "problems." Here one is in fact secretly working at abolishing questioning altogether and is intent on cultivating the modesty of blind faith. One declares the *sacrum* [sacred] to be an essential law and is thereby taken seriously by one's age, which in its frailty and impotence has need for such a thing. One stands up for nothing more than the trouble-free running of the "industry"! Having become ripe for the organization of mendacity. Philosophy interprets its corruption as the "resurrection of metaphysics." (G63 4/4)

The manifest tendency of this passage is a critique of the complicity of philosophy in the numbing complacency of contemporary life. The "Aristotle" whom Luther hated was the "Aristotle" put to use by scholastic "pig theologians" in their insidious drive to conceal the "foolishness of the cross" beneath pagan "glory." Heidegger, too, has nothing but contempt for the stultifying "industry" of philosophy, with its pseudo-questions and blind dependence on tradition. Moreover, the nature of Luther's attack on scholasticism also reveals its importance for Heidegger's critical assault on academic philosophy. For Luther, the failure of theology to heed the hiddenness of God in the cross amounts to a failure to recognize that Christian life is not grounded in theory, but in repentance and struggle. Benumbed by a vision of eternal glory, theology has forgotten the *molestia* ["distress"] and *angustia* ["anxiety"] of facticity. This forgetfulness, which often takes the form of presumption and pride, lies at the heart of sin. For Heidegger, the same can be said of inauthenticity. Philosophy thus finds itself complicit in our drive to conceal the difficulty of life.

In the following pages, I will examine in detail Heidegger's early critiques of what he regards as the soporific banality of contemporary intellectual life. Not only does philosophy find itself under the gun, but so too do other forms of public "educated" discourse. An abiding feature of Heidegger's thought is his chastisement of intellectuals for their mindless conformity and for their contributions to the "idle talk" of an age. During the early 1920s, he singles out philosophy, historical science, and religion as the primary culprits.

A crucial grounding for Heidegger's attacks on contemporary culture and intellectual life can be found in the lecture course of SS 1923. Here Heidegger expounds on a phenomenon called "the today [*das Heute*]," which provides a way of conceiving of the public discourse of a time. Among the features of "facticity," or human life, that Heidegger singles out for particular consideration in this lecture is the idea of "temporal particularity [*Jeweiligkeit*]" (G63 5/5). "The being-there of our own Dasein is what it is precisely and only in its *temporally particular* 'there,' its being 'there' for a while" (G63 29/24). Human life is not an abstract generality, but is always something that occupies a finite span of time. Heidegger continues: "A defining feature of the awhileness of temporal particularity is the *today*—in each case whiling, tarrying for a while, in the present, in each case our own present. (Dasein as historical Dasein, its present. Being 'in' the world, being lived 'from out of' the world—the present-everyday)" (G63 29/24). Our "everyday" life, which forms the starting point for Heidegger's hermeneutics of facticity right up through *Being and Time*, is always the everyday life of a particular time, a particular historical situation. It is here we find the "givens" that are closest to us, and hence most easy to overlook (G63 30/24).

The "today" calls for a deep hermeneutical explication, not simply a report on the culture of a particular time (G63 30/25). That is, the philosopher's job is to articulate or "bring to light [*zu Tage*]" the concealed assumptions about human life buried beneath the obviousness of what "one" says and how "one" behaves. This is because the "today" is a mode of discourse, a way human life articulates or expresses itself (G63 31/25). The characteristic features of the "today" need to be "lifted up," or brought into relief. In the modern world, this public discourse includes "educated consciousness." Heidegger elaborates:

> An example of an exponent of being-interpreted in the today is the *educated consciousness* of a time, *the talk heard in the public realm from the average educated mind*—today: the modern "mind." It lives off definite modes of interpreting. In the following what will be brought into relief as two such modes are: (1) historical consciousness (cultural consciousness), (2) philosophical consciousness. (G63 33/27)

As has already been discussed, Heidegger proposes that the proper way to go about gaining a philosophical understanding of human life is *hermeneutical*. This is because human life is, at bottom, an act of interpretation. Life has, accordingly, always already expressed itself in some way or other in the public discourse of a linguistic community. As Heidegger puts it later, "[i]n history and philosophy, Dasein is speaking about itself directly or indirectly [. . .]—it is there in these modes as having been interpreted in such and such a manner" (G63 48/38). Further on, the same point is made again quite clearly: "History and philosophy are modes of interpretation, something which Dasein itself is, in which it lives [. . .]" (G63 49/39). The philosophical project, then, is to bring into relief the basic structures of life that are concealed within this discourse.

Heidegger wants his readers to think of life as a palimpsest, as a variegated text with multiple layers of meaning, not all of which are explicit. The hermeneutics of facticity, then, aims at making all this explicit. During SS 1923, Heidegger suggests that the "educated" consciousness of a particular time (namely, the time of the hermeneutician herself) be interrogated as part of this general hermeneutical project. One of the conclusions Heidegger reaches on the basis of this interpretation is that educated consciousness tends to have, in each case, already understood human life as *objective presence*. By and large, the educated consciousness of a time represents one of the many ways human life seeks to make itself certain and secure about itself (G63 65/51). For Heidegger, when we read the palimpsest of human life, as it is expressed in public discourse, we tend to find nothing but cowardly, irresponsible inauthenticity.

As Heidegger's discussion in SS 1923 shows, the primary forms of educated consciousness that merit investigation are (1) philosophy and (2) historical consciousness. Heidegger takes the latter to be a culture's own awareness of itself as part of a developmental historical tradition, its sense of where it has come from and where it is heading. On the other hand, Heidegger's interest in interrogating the public role of philosophy stems not only from his own situation within that discipline, but also from the kinds of claims that philosophy makes for itself in the public sphere. Traditionally, philosophy takes itself to be the arbiter of the highest things, the ultimate expression of rational human nature, and the guardian of values like objectivity and rationality. Certainly, a glance at the dominant modes of philosophy in Heidegger's Germany bears out this impression. Between the 1870s and the 1940s, neo-Kantianism of one form or another dominated academic philosophy. Neo-Kantians tended to think of themselves as the ultimate arbiters of validity in all the other sciences, as the pathbreakers and codifiers of scientific methodology, and as the custodians of timeless values. The phenomenological school, anchored on Husserl, also shared a sense of the "kingly vocation" of philosophy as a "rigorous science," as the ultimate court of appeal for any and all claims to knowledge. Husserl himself, beginning in the 1911 *Logos* essay, expanded the competence of phenomenology to the preservation and grounding of culture. Dilthey, too, defended the privileged place of philosophy in the intellectual world. Given this intellectual climate, Heidegger's suggestion that philosophical discourse in the public sphere be interrogated seems eminently reasonable.

I will confine the present discussion to Heidegger's general characterizations of contemporary philosophy during the first half of the 1920s. In limiting the discussion this way, I hope to draw attention to a specific aspect of Heidegger's critique of philosophy, namely philosophy's complicity in timid inauthenticity. Throughout his career, Heidegger also engages in more specific reflections on *particular* philosophical positions, both historical (e.g. Plato, Leibniz) and contemporary. My aim, however, is simply to give an account of one aspect of a *general* critique of philosophical discourse that is common in Heidegger's lectures and other writings during the 1920s. More specifically, I want to focus upon the lectures from WS 1921–1922 and SS 1923, and on the 1922 Natorp Report and the critical review of Jaspers's *Psychology of Worldviews*. While it is certainly true that other writings from this period contain similar views about the sorry state of academic philosophy, and that Heidegger continues to develop similar ideas throughout his career, this more circumscribed body of material is more than sufficient for the present purposes.[12]

A considerable portion of Heidegger's lecture for WS 1921–1922 is devoted to working out the proper idea of philosophy itself. Not surprisingly, Heidegger has some things to say during the course of these reflections regarding other ways of doing philosophy. It goes without saying that Heidegger's notion of philosophy as the "hermeneutics of facticity" (an idea that emerges publicly around 1922–1923) is critically opposed to the dominant strands of academic philosophy at the time. This emerges, in the first instance, in Heidegger's characterization of vulgar life-philosophy as "fanaticism [*Schwärmerei*]" (G61 35/28).[13] At least part of what Heidegger seems to have in mind here is the tendency to valorize "great" philosophies without hazarding any kind of critical engagement (G61 36/28). This is a "fanaticism for so-called 'depths.'" One talks romantically about philosophy as "lived experience," of the "genius" of past thinkers, much in the way that Romantic aesthetics understood the artist.[14] Philosophy is reduced either to a private affair, or, if it is communicated, one takes care that it is dressed up as nicely as possible for public consumption (G61 36/28f.). Heidegger alludes also to the "fanatical" inclination to seek a "what philosophy is supposed to 'give,' as a perverse historical salvation" (G61 36/29).

Related to this "fanaticism" is the idea that philosophy is essentially world-view formation. This is an issue Heidegger devoted considerable attention to throughout the 1920s. At every point, he hoped to critically unmask this conception of philosophy as a plea for "making things easy" for the business of culture. During WS 1921–1922, he focuses on its totalizing impulses. "What is decisive for philosophizing," so it is alleged, "is the formation of a '*world-view*,' one that should be as comprehensive [*umfassende*] and as certain as possible" (G61 43/34). He defines the object of this quest as follows: "a system as the synoptic order and ordering characterization of the various domains and values of life, along with a designation of their context, together with the 'subordinate' thought that certainty and determinateness are thereby provided for the proper orientation of one's own practical life" (G61 43f./34). A world-view is a comprehensive ordering of values, a kind of ready-made recipe for certainty in moral and practical affairs. Worrying about these things, and having the requisite encyclopedic knowledge of various aspects of human culture, is what one takes for philosophy. Heidegger leaves us with little doubt regarding his position on this:

> In the word [i.e. world-view]—fully understood—the disaster of our contemporary spiritual circumstances basically comes to expression. Philosophy participates in this disaster and aggravates it precisely by orienting its problematic towards world-view, whether this means that we philosophize "in a world-view [*auf Weltanschauung*]," just as we might travel "in rough cloth or Belgian lace," whether one strives for a scientific (founded and developed) world-view, or opposes a scientific philosophy against world-view philosophy. (G61 44/34)

The entire situation of contemporary philosophy, in which one argues back and forth about the problem of world-views and about the countervailing "scientific [*wissenschaftlich*]" tendency in philosophy, amounts to a failure to penetrate to the genuine matter for thinking, i.e., "philosophy as philosophizing," "*the* task" of passionately appropriating philosophy as a science (G61 43/33). The quest for a world-view, with its "fanaticism, superficiality, and literary pretensions" must give way before scientific philosophy as "task, a problem (indication!)" (G61 44/35f.).

With ironic understatement, Heidegger also suggests that the prevailing notion of "scientific" philosophy, e.g., that of the Marburg School, Rickert, or Husserl, "needs supplementation" (G61 46/35). This notion is burdened by an orientation to the "sciences," in the sense of the natural sciences that developed during the nineteenth century. For Heidegger, "science" has a "formal" sense, signifying "passion" (G61 46/35). The "scientific" nature of philosophy is not something that can simply be read off from other disciplines; instead, it must be worked out in its own way through a radical commitment to critical inquiry. The whole debate is ultimately of little substance, since both "world-view" and the prevailing academic notion of "philosophy as a rigorous science" fail to seize on the special sense of philosophy as a task. Instead of questing after *the* philosophy as the timeless "guarantee of the future periods of culture and destinies of mankind," one ought instead to take up the task of philosophy in passion and uncertainty (G61 66/50).

Later in this lecture, after thematizing the "easy" as a basic category of factical life-experience, Heidegger turns to denouncing the common stock of philosophical opinions at the time. In particular, he is critical of what he takes to be the facile distinction between the "historical" and "systematic" aspects of philosophical research (G61 110/82). Here again, it is a confused orientation of philosophy to the "sciences" that results in a failure to radically conceive of its tasks. For Heidegger, a "knowledge of principles," i.e., a philosophical grasp of the *Sache selbst* of factical life, transcends this distinction. Moreover, it also transcends the common ideals of "exactitude" that are borrowed from the sciences. "Philosophy, as knowledge of principles, must thereby learn to renounce the swindle of an aesthetical befogging of itself and of its confederates" (G61 111/83).

In cultural life, and in philosophy in particular, the "tendency toward security" can be elevated into a task in its own right. As such, one loses sight of its "inauthentic" roots, and it becomes even more entrenched (G61 120/89). The result is that the possibility of a "vital encounter" with the intrinsic "insecurity" of life is lost. It is in this tendency that traditional philosophy, with its focus on the "objective," takes shape. "From there, the philosophical interpretation is one step away from determining life itself, in its entirety, encompassing its worlds, as something objective, and, in that sense, the fundamental reality" (G61 120/89). This corresponds to a valorization of the "theoretical attitude" as the "highest value in the form of objectivity, scientificity, free intellectual honesty and impartiality, and as the tribunal of a theoretical reason whose demonstrations are ever correct" (G61 122/91). Over against this, the sphere of the "irrational" is carved out. This, too, can then assume the character of something "absolute," as it tended to do in the life-philosophy of Heidegger's day. Ultimately, this kind of "anti-intellectualism" is no closer to life than its erstwhile opposite.

Heidegger's pessimistic evaluation of the complacency and ultimate morbidity of contemporary philosophy is even more pronounced in a loose page that he later inserted into the text of the notes for this lecture course.[15] For Heidegger, the task of philosophy is not to say something new or novel, but to "understand what is old (the historical) in the proper sense" (G61 193/145). Yet precisely the task of carrying out radical research in philosophy is impeded by the prevailing attitudes. Today "everyone says everything" and "everyone can take comfort" in having said something or other about philosophy (G61 194/145). Heidegger bitterly quips that any literate person can publish anything in philosophy. One simply dashes off treatises on the basis of the relevant "literature" and the "circulating gossip" (G61 194/146). One simply talks about philosophical issues, without any real direction.

Heidegger's pessimistic ruminations are carried over into other writings from this period. As in WS 1921–1922, everything points to Heidegger's condemnation of the complicity of philosophy in inauthenticity. A remark from the Natorp Report suffices to make this clear:

> All making it easy, all the seductive compromising of needs, all the metaphysical tranquilizers prescribed for problems having been for the most part derived from mere book learning—the basic intention of all this is from the start to give up with regard to the task that must in each case be carried out, namely, bringing the object of philosophy into view, grasping it, and indeed preserving it. (NB 4/113)

The "object of philosophy," during the early 1920s, is "factical life" or (simply) "facticity." In avoiding this subject matter through its constructions and pseudo-problems, philosophy is clearly of a piece with life's inauthentic tendency to avoid itself, to cover itself up. One distracts oneself in philosophy with "hustle and bustle" about preserving culture, about "prophetic pageantry that promises the salvation of the world" (G9 5/5 f.). Ideals of "perfection" or of a return to "paradisiacal naturality" are simply illusions concocted to divert philosophy from a confrontation with life (NB 10/117).

At the outset of SS 1923, in a course entitled "Ontology: Hermeneutics of Facticity," Heidegger presents a cautionary note regarding the title of his course. The term "ontology" should not be taken to signify Heidegger's allegiance to the "anti-Kantian" reaction that attempted to resurrect pre-critical metaphysics. All this, Heidegger asserts, is a "slave revolt against philosophy as such" (G63 1/1). Here one simply takes up ancient metaphysics again uncritically in a kind of superficial antiquarianism (G63 3/2 f.). Equally reprehensible in Heidegger's eyes is the false modernism that constantly demands something "new" and "interesting" from philosophy. "Everything modern is recognizable in the fact that it artfully steals away from its time and is capable of creating an 'effect' only in this fashion (industry, propaganda, proselytizing, cliquish monopolies, intellectual racketeering)" (G63 19/15). Philosophy gives into the public craving for "solutions" and "useful information," fed by an inauthentic drive to make everything easy and available:

> We have today become so pithless and weak-kneed that we are no longer able to hold our own in the asking of a question. When the one philosophical medicine man cannot answer it, then one runs to the next. The demand increases the supply. In popular terms, this is called: an increased interest in philosophy. (G63 20/16)

Contemporary philosophy (especially neo-Kantian "value philosophy") strives for the articulation of a timelessly valid classificatory order that can be "applied" to the irrational manifold of sensible reality (G63 41/33). This can be either characterized in neo-Kantian fashion as something "free floating" and "valid" in itself, or in neo-Hegelian terms as "what is thought by an Absolute Spirit *and* its thinking" (G63 41/33). Thus, whether one views the classificatory order as something static or something that realizes itself dialectically, one is still always directed toward what is ultimately beyond experience. Heidegger quotes a recent essay in *Logos* by Eduard Spranger as evidence for the pervasiveness of this way of thinking:

> All of us—Rickert, the phenomenologists, the movement associated with Dilthey—meet up with one another in the great struggle for *the timeless in the historical* or *beyond the historical*, for the *realm of meaning* and its historical expression in a concrete developed culture, for a *theory of values* which leads beyond the merely subjective toward the objective and the valid. (G63 42/33)

Heidegger, as a phenomenologist, respectfully asks to be exempted from the catalogue of adherents to what he calls the "Platonism of barbarians" (G63 42/34). Heidegger goes on to devote more attention to "dialectic," i.e., to Hegelianism, in light of its alleged tendency to synthesize the historical with the timeless validity of the Idea (G63 43/34ff.). "One ought," Heidegger suggests, "to have a close look at the sophistry being pursued today with schemata like form-content, rational-irrational, finite-infinite, mediated-unmediated, subject-object" (G63 46/37). The value of phenomenology lies in its demand that one strive for the "things themselves," rather than simply passing on uncritically accepted distinctions as the starting points of philosophical inquiry. And yet phenomenology, too, falls victim to the "tendency toward security" in its inordinate trust in the veracity of "intuition." "Perhaps called once to be the conscience of philosophy, it has wound up as a pimp for the public whoring of the mind, *fornicatio spiritus* [fornication of the spirit] (Luther)" (G63 46/37).

In what sense, then, does Heidegger take philosophy to be complicit in inauthenticity? In WS 1921–1922, he suggests that the twin pillars of traditional philosophy, i.e., the primacy of the objective and of the theoretical, emerge from life's "prestructive" attempt to secure itself against its own inherent restlessness. Thus, it is the "tendency toward security" that is most consistently manifest in Heidegger's general critiques of philosophy. One strives to secure "culture," either through a world-view or through the alleged rigor of "scientific philosophy." Alternatively, one muddles through, relying on the uncritical acceptance of traditional concepts and ways of posing questions, all the while becoming progressively blind to the subject matter, i.e., life. In Heidegger's day, philosophers were greatly concerned by the implications of historicism in particular for the age-old quest for "timeless validities." Beneath all this, Heidegger detects the disquiet of life about itself, and its attempts to secure itself (cf. G60 33 ff.). As for the actual conduct of academic philosophy, Heidegger seems to have nothing but contempt for what he regards as superficial "scribbling" and even more superficial "understanding."

Cultural and Historical Consciousness

As previously mentioned, in SS 1923, Heidegger labels the public consciousness of a time the "today." One important element of this public consciousness is philosophy. The other, which receives extended treatment by Heidegger, is "historical consciousness." There is no doubt that this is an element of public discourse that Heidegger paid particular attention to during the 1920s. The significance of historical consciousness here is that it represents the explicit relation that a time has to its past. Given what I have already shown about Heidegger's conception of the "historicality" of human life, i.e., the way identity is shaped by the past, it should come as no surprise that he discusses this feature of public discourse in detail.

Indeed, Heidegger makes his motivation clear at the outset of the discussion. He writes:

> The manner in which a time (the today which is in each case for a while at the particular time) sees and addresses the past (either its own past Dasein or some other past Dasein), holding on to it and preserving it or abandoning it, is a sign of how a present stands regarding itself, how it as a being-there *is* in its "there." (G63 35 f./28)

Here Heidegger is claiming that the view of the past at a particular time can tell the attentive hermeneutician a great deal about that particular time itself. Heidegger takes human life to *be* the unfinished process of the handing down of a tradition. The "projects" that ground particular self-interpretations are inherited. Thus, since the past ultimately constitutes the self-interpretation of the present, the view of the past that prevails at a particular time offers a clue as to the nature of this self-interpretation.

As Heidegger was well aware, the nineteenth century had witnessed the birth of an explicit "historical consciousness" amongst the European intellectual elite. Never before had the "past," and the position of the present within the progress of history, been such an explicit matter of concern. As Heidegger sees it, historical consciousness has become irrevocably bound up with the notion of "culture." "In going back to the driving forces that bring about the concept of culture as a conscious interpretive element of life, we are led to the idea of historical consciousness, the idea of historicality—and to the question of its genesis within intellectual history" (G56/57 130/111). This genesis, according to Heidegger, lay in the Romantic reaction of Herder and Schlegel against the Enlightenment (G56/57 133f./114). The resulting idealistic synthesis is summarized in the view that "[h]istorical development pertains to consciousness and spirit" (G56/57 134/115). That is, the multiplicity of historical cultures is viewed as the product of the development of the human spirit.

With the eventual collapse of the Hegelian synthesis, philosophers strove to secure "culture" and "value" against possible dissolution in the face of historicist skepticism.

Also characteristic of the nineteenth century, and of Heidegger's own "today," is the development of the "historical human sciences" as autonomous disciplines (G63 36/28). These disciplines are now taken as the definitive authority on the past; "they give leading directives for the manner in which what is past is to be objectified in scientific theory" (G63 36/28f.) More specifically, the "past" that gets discussed by public consciousness is one that has been "handed over" to it by these disciplines. This totality of material is synthesized ahead of time in a definite way. Heidegger explains:

> Art, literature, religion, morals, society, science, and economy stand within an anticipatory characterization which runs in advance of, prepares a path for, and guides all particular instances of concretely interrogating and defining them: they are being encountered as "expression," as objectifications of the subjective, of the life of a culture (*the soul of a culture*) which presses forth into form in these objectifications. (G63 36/29)

This overarching understanding of the past is itself the result of a complex process of development in which the Romantic aesthetics of genius came to be fused with a kind of historicism that valued the irreducible uniqueness of every past culture. This aesthetic pedigree appears in the notion of a "style," or the "pervasive uniformity" that holds in a particular culture for a particular time (G63 36/29). This legacy has been realized most fully, according to Heidegger, in the work of Spengler, though "Nietzsche, Dilthey, Bergson, the Vienna school of the history of art (Karl Lamprecht)" are all part of this trend (G63 37/29).[16] On this approach, each particular culture, as "a closed organism with its own life," is viewed as being on a par with all the others (G63 37/30). As a result, there can be no good reason for limiting our theoretical gaze to one particular culture. Instead, according to Spengler, the "becoming of *all* humanity" must be swept up into our field of vision. Having taken this stand, Spengler proceeded to catalogue the different "styles" of culture through a kind of "*morphology*" (G63 38/30). When employing this method of comparing forms, history "becomes graspable in charts and under rubrics in which the paths on which comparisons can be made have been laid down and fixed in an orderly manner" (G63 39/31).

It is in terms of this "style" that one gets an initial grasp on the complex body of source material. This is the principle whereby sources are selected and sifted out (G63 52f./41). For Heidegger, what is particularly notable about this kind of methodology is the *temporality* of the *relation* that it takes with respect to these cultural forms. A parenthetical note in the text indicates that this is the case: "Classifying as sojourn, abode, holding out, a how of temporal being, the present. Form—look—being-an-expression of—distinguishing feature" (G63 53/42). With this remark, we see that the same basic relational attitude that characterizes the "Platonism of barbarians" is also characteristic of historical-cultural consciousness. Like detached philosophical contemplation, this method is supposed to secure "objectivity." At the same time, this attitude gets "pulled along" by its subject matter. In its universal survey of human history, nothing remains in view for long. Thus, according to Heidegger, historical consciousness is a kind of *curiosity* (G63 54/43). Here the past is "[c]ircuitously reported and talked about without having a relation to it" (G63 39/31).

As a mode of public discourse, historical consciousness of this variety "brings to language what it thinks it is all about and comes to" (G63 55/43). Given Heidegger's initial principle for investigating such public discourse, it follows that "its self-interpretation in the public realm will accordingly express what Dasein itself thinks *it* is all about and comes to" (G63 55/43). The dominant theme in this public discourse, if Spengler is a good model, is the task of securing *objectivity*. This means that historical knowledge must be "freed" from the biased standpoint of the observer. "In this self-interpretation [i.e., Spengler's work], historical consciousness accordingly places itself before the task of gaining an overview of 'the total fact of man,' i.e. bringing human Dasein into view in an absolutely objective manner" (G63 56/44). For the historian's objective, unbiased gaze, the totality of human life is present all at once. Thus some of the more bizarre elements of Spengler's work are quite consistent with his basic approach. Heidegger elaborates:

> The prediction and advance calculation of the future, the "decline of the West," is not a whim on Spengler's part or a cheap witticism of the masses, but rather the consequential expression of the fact that regarding its own-most possibilities which have been prescribed for it, inauthentic historical consciousness has thought itself through to the end. (The not-yet, actually the present when it is *calculated*—reading it off and anticipating it by way of comparison). (G63 56/44)

The ultimate motivation behind this kind of historical consciousness should be clear enough, i.e., the desire to have human life as a whole and throughout history *objectively* present and secure for one. The unrest of life is quieted by the soporific fog of Spengler's comforting prognostications about the rise and fall of civilizations. This has, of course, long been a temptation for people faced with the uncertainties of history. Right up until today, for example, people expend great effort trying to "calculate" the precise date and time for the Parousia of Christ by reading off "patterns" from history. Like the "Platonism of barbarians," historical consciousness seeks to quiet the essential unrest of life, to calculate the "not-yet" of the future with "certainty" and "objectivity." As such, both represent primary expressions of inauthentic life. Against this kind of morphological hermeneutics, Heidegger hints at the possibility of a radical alternative, one that I will explore in due course:

> Religion is misunderstood in the very core of its being-there when history of religion today buys into the cheap game of sketching out types, i.e., stylistic forms, of religiosity in entertaining illustrated charts. Analogous points need

to be made about economic history, history of philosophy, and legal history. In their genuine character at particular times [*jeweilig*], these possibilities concretely come into being and are there not by having a cleverly thought-out philosophical system of cultural systems laid before them as a plan of operation, but rather only through the fact that at the particular time and respectively [*jeweils*] in "this" discipline the right man at the right place and at the right time steps in and takes hold of it in a decisive manner. (What philosophy should contribute to this—that is not something which needs to be "talked" about.) (G63 57/45)

Religion and Theology

The final instantiation of public discourse in Heidegger's early philosophy is *religion*. As I argued in chapter 1, religion is both personally and *philosophically* central to Heidegger's project. It comes as no surprise, then, that he has something to say about state of public religious discourse in his time. Religion had played a central role in Heidegger's first forays into academe. During his "student years," prior to 1914, Heidegger published a number of articles in the ultraconservative Catholic periodical *Der Akademiker*. Here he rails against the superficiality and relativism of the modern age and proposes a radical appropriation of the lost grandeur of medieval Catholicism.[17] During the war years, however, Heidegger rejects the reactionary attitude of the anti-modernists. He comes to hold that religion has been impoverished and that it, too, only serves to coddle the inauthentic urges of the everyday man.

Heidegger's correspondence and lectures from 1917 to 1924 are filled with critical attacks on the timid dogmatism of his contemporaries' religion. As early as 1914, Heidegger has begun to react strongly against the anti-modernist pronouncements of Pope Pius X, as one of his letters to Father Krebs indicates. He comments on a recently issued papal pronouncement in which the teaching activities of Italian university professors are strictly curtailed: "We [in Germany] still don't have the *motu proprio* on philosophy [. . .] all who succumb to having independent thoughts could have their brains taken out and replaced with spaghetti. Philosophical demand could be met by setting up vending machines in the train stations (free of charge for the poor)."[18] Heidegger's worries about the attitudes of the *magisterium* come to a head in a later letter to Father Krebs, already discussed briefly above. He tells his fatherly friend that he "would not be able to hold and teach freely, were I bound to a position outside of philosophy" (S 69). This letter, written in 1919, is taken by most to be Heidegger's public rejection of Catholicism. However, this move is one that has been building for a while in the young philosopher, as other correspondence indicates. Writing to Rickert on February 27, 1917, Heidegger tells his advisor that:

> I have never stood on the *narrow* Catholic standpoint, i.e., that I would or had to somehow orient the problems, the conceptions, and the solution to a traditional, extrascientific point of view. I will seek for, and teach, the truth

> according to a more free personal conviction. I have also never regretted
> dedicating my book to you, and so defining my position and appraisal of
> modern philosophy. With an actual, living, and free conception of Chris-
> tianity, in the sense of Troeltsch, it is naturally quite difficult for me to make
> a "career" on both sides. But, scientific accomplishment is what is ul-
> timately decisive. (HR 42)

It is against the background of his commitment to some kind of "free
Christianity," i.e., Christianity that is not confessionally determined, that Heidegger undertook the philosophical investigation of religious life during 1920
and 1921. Many factors contributed to Heidegger's shift of standpoint and to
his critiques of contemporary religious discourse. One that has been particularly emphasized by Theodore Kisiel is the influence of Franz Overbeck.[19]
Kisiel documents Heidegger's forceful invocation of Overbeck during a talk by
the Barthian theologian Heitmüller. Overbeck's name appears elsewhere, for
example, in a letter from Karl Jaspers, dated November 24, 1922, in which
Jaspers thanks Heidegger for sending him Overbeck's posthumous *Christentum und Kultur* (HJ 37). Overbeck also appears in Heidegger's introductory
remarks, written in 1970, to his 1927 address "Phenomenology and Theology."
He writes:

> Almost one hundred years ago there appeared simultaneously (1873) two
> writings of two friends: the "first piece" of the "Unfashionable Observa-
> tions" of Friedrich Nietzsche, wherein the "glorious Hölderlin" is men-
> tioned; and the "little book" *On the Christianness of Today's Theology* of
> Franz Overbeck, who established the world-denying expectation of the end
> as the basic characteristic of what is primordially Christian. (G9 45 f./39)

The former work is "David Strauss the Confessor and the Writer," Nietzsche's vitriolic attack on contemporary culture. Hölderlin's name appears in
the midst of Nietzsche's famous denunciation of the "cultured philistines" of
his day.[20] As Heidegger rightly notes in these remarks, Overbeck located the
essence of Christianity in its eschatology. Christianity, he maintains, "came
into this world announcing its imminent doom."[21] On Overbeck's view, the
uncompromising radicality of the original Christian proclamation had been
negated by millennia of compromise with "culture." This was, he felt, particularly true of the liberal theology of his own day.[22] More specifically, it was
the modern era's faith in progress that simply blocked it from really appropriating the core of primitive Christianity. Overbeck consequently became profoundly skeptical about the possibility of reinvigorating Christianity and of the
whole enterprise of theological reflection:

> Calm reflection sees plainly that Christianity outfitted itself with a theology
> only when it wanted to render itself possible in a world which it was actually
> negating. [. . .] For precisely in the beginnings of theology, i.e., in the oldest
> Christian Alexandrian theology, it becomes as clear as it possibly can be
> [. . .] that Christianity wanted to use its theology to recommend itself to the

wise men of the world and to make itself acceptable to them. Viewed in this way, however, theology is nothing more than part of the secularization of Christianity, a luxury it allowed itself which, like every other luxury, is not to be had without a price.[23]

Overbeck, along with Luther, Kierkegaard, and many others, only served to fuel Heidegger's deep misgivings about the comforting prognostications of liberal theology. It would, however, be a mistake to hold that Heidegger adopted Overbeck's skepticism wholeheartedly. While he recognized that liberal modernism and primitive Christian eschatology were fundamentally opposed, there is nothing to suggest that he doubted the possibility that the latter could be appropriated anew. To the contrary, laying the groundwork for such an appropriation seems to have been one of Heidegger's primary philosophical preoccupations in the 1920s. There can be no doubt, however, that Heidegger wholeheartedly rejected dogmatic orthodoxy and that he shared his contemporaries' interest in reviving the eschatology of the early Church.

Some of the other catalysts for this move can be seen in a *curriculum vitae* from 1922. Heidegger describes how the "critical work of Albert Schweitzer came into my field of vision" during his studies (G16 41). Schweitzer, of course, is still much discussed as the rediscoverer of the "apocalyptic Jesus" and the strong critic of the liberal "quest for the historical Jesus." Schweitzer's Jesus, by all accounts, would be ill at ease amongst the bourgeois moderns of the *fin de siècle*. Such a radical picture would certainly have appealed to the young Heidegger. Along with Schweitzer, Heidegger mentions Hermann Gunkel (1862–1932), Wilhelm Bousset (1865–1920), Johannes Wendland (1871–1947), and Richard Reitzenstein (1861–1931), all scholars of the so-called "History of Religions School," whose research into the development of Judeo-Christian ideas called into question their "eternal validity."

All these influences, along with Heidegger's already demonstrated aversion to faith by papal *fiat*, transformed "Heidegger the ultra-conservative Catholic" into Heidegger the radical critic of timid dogmatism. His writings are peppered with critical remarks about contemporary religious discourse. During WS 1919–1920, Heidegger diagnoses the cause of the "fundamentally perverted" tendencies of "philosophy of religion," "theology and apologetics," as a failure to attend to the basic phenomena of life (G58 158). Genuine "devotion [*Hingabe*]" to the matters themselves precludes "talking about the world" as well as "rhetorical construction of the world and of religion" (G58 168). A similar point is made in the critical review of Jaspers's *Psychology of Worldviews*:

> If we have appropriated the basic sense of the phenomenological attitude in a genuine way, to what extent would we sooner have it misused in any other type of intellectual and literary nonsense than have it misused to supply a forced orthodox dogmatics with its apologetic principles, a "perversion" for which a desire has recently begun to stir in phenomenology (and be this dogmatics, in its tenets, ever so praiseworthy and today still ever so misun-

> derstood as the dogmatics of the Middle Ages, which was, according to *its*
> *own* sense, a genuine type of dogmatics). (G9 36/31 f.)

One text that contains a particular preponderance of these sorts of remarks is that of the lecture course of WS 1921–1922. Heidegger sets forth several possible alternative responses to the alleged "foundering" of culture in the contemporary era. His contempt for one is quite undisguised: "degeneration in the embellishment of mythical and theosophical metaphysics and mysticism and in the trance of a preoccupation with piety, which goes by the name of religiosity" (G61 70/53). Here, Heidegger seems to be particularly targeting "religiosity" as a kind of escape from the demands of the present. Later, he once again argues that phenomenology must avoid "idle talk about religion and world-views" (G61 193/145). Philosophy must carry out its tasks in a way that divorces it from "religious ideology and fantasy" (G61 197/148).

During SS 1923, Heidegger links his worries about a kind of timid religiosity with the already discussed notion of the "resurrection of metaphysics":

> That such minor matters are lost sight of today should not be surprising,
> given the great industry of philosophy where everything is geared merely to
> ensuring that one will not come too late for the "resurrection of meta-
> physics" which—so one has heard—is now beginning, where one knows
> only the single care of helping oneself and others to a friendship with the
> loving God which is as cheap as possible, as convenient as possible, and as
> profitably directly as possible into the bargain inasmuch as it is transacted
> through an intuition of essence. (G63 20/16)

By all accounts, educated religious discourse, e.g., in theology, is, like philosophy and historical consciousness, all too complicit in a fugitive, inauthentic mode of life. During the 1920s, Heidegger often challenged theologians to live up to their true vocation, to "preserve" genuine faith rather than to coddle. Here Heidegger finds himself altogether in agreement with Luther, who centuries before had made similar requests of his own contemporaries. Indeed, Heidegger's critique of these three forms of public consciousness bears a good deal of affinity with Luther.

The aim of chapters 3 and 4 has been to examine and clarify the meaning of "inauthenticity" in Heidegger's work during the early 1920s. My purpose in doing so is to provide an understanding of what philosophy, as *Destruktion*, is supposed to struggle against. A discussion of authenticity, on behalf of which philosophy carries out this struggle, will come in the following chapters. My contention in all this is that one has an incomplete understanding of Heidegger's conception of philosophy should these *practical* issues not be taken into consideration. While it is true that Heidegger's "hermeneutics of facticity" is not supposed to be "edifying discourse" or moral homiletics, it is also assuredly not purely theoretical. As Heidegger puts it at one point: "The theme of this hermeneutical investigation is the Dasein which is in each case our own and indeed as hermeneutically interrogated with respect to and on the basis of the character of its being and with a view toward developing in it a *radical wakefulness* for itself" (G63 16/12, emphasis added).

While there is no single "definition" of inauthenticity, I have argued that a number of important features of it can be easily identified. Taking in all of these features at a glance, we have a picture of a way of life that is profoundly *alienated* from itself. An inauthentic life is one dominated by a drive for security, absorbed in everyday concerns, and in flight from the intrinsic unrest of life. Along with these features, inauthentic life is characterized by a specific mode of public discourse called "idle talk." In the superficial passing on of information, the tradition comes to exercise a tyranny over human life. Uncritically accepted, traditional interpretations of the sense and purpose of life are left entirely unquestioned. Public discourse tends to entrench and rigidify inauthentic habits. Heidegger finds this particularly true of "educated discourse." Here the alleged "experts," the custodians of truth, simply pass along uncritical opinions and concoct theoretical interpretations of historical reality designed to comfort the unease of humanity.

The Roots of Authenticity

Only the individual is interesting.[1]

My central claim is that Heidegger's conception of philosophy as *Destruktion* is best understood as an attempt to realign the practice of philosophical inquiry toward a specific moral idea. To put it in a slightly different way, philosophy is viewed not as something narrowly *theoretical*, but rather as something eminently *practical*. I have argued that Heidegger's theological provenance, and particularly his interest in the "young Luther" during the early 1920s, can help to explicate the sense of this claim (chapters 1–2). Luther is Heidegger's paradigm of an intellectual who, out of a passionate personal interest, critically unmasks the complicity of the dominant trends in educated discourse in a kind of superficial, self-congratulatory way of life. In this respect, it is no surprise that Heidegger's work represents a unique and radical alternative to both neo-Kantianism and to life-philosophy.[2] Heidegger rejected the detached irrelevance of the former as well as the anti-intellectualism of the latter. Like Luther, he conceived of intellectual activity as directed at a certain way of life, rather than as a factory of self-congratulatory rationalizations. Even phenomenology does not escape this opprobrium; in SS 1923, Heidegger approvingly borrows a typically bombastic phrase from Luther to denounce phenomenology as "a pimp for the public whoring of the mind, *fornicatio spiritus* (Luther)" (G63 46/37).

Philosophy, for Heidegger, begins and ends with the "genuineness of personal life," and it does so by "hunting down the alienation from itself" that afflicts human life (G56/57 220/188; G63 15/11). The actual practice of philosophy is, in Heidegger's mind, inextricably linked to a certain way of life. The crucial question then becomes, what exactly does Heidegger mean by the "genuineness of personal life"? What is it to live "genuinely," and in what sense is this "personal"? Answering these questions clearly is crucial to my overall argument. Another equally important question, particularly for Heidegger, is how to articulate this ideal without lapsing into moralistic pedantry or ethereal abstractions?

The aim of this chapter is to begin to answer these difficult questions. Each of these questions is concerned with a particular subject matter, i.e., the way of life Heidegger calls "authenticity" in *Being and Time*. In order to substantiate my general claim about Heidegger's conception of philosophy as *Destruktion*, it is necessary to achieve as much clarity as possible about what Heidegger means by "authenticity" and about how this idea fits with his other philosophical commitments. This task is faced with the immediate difficulty posed both by Heidegger's reticence on this issue and by the obvious difficulty of his language; Heidegger does not speak the language of contemporary moral theory. While the ideal is unmistakably present in his lectures, essays, and correspondence, one looks in vain for anything like a rigorous conceptual definition. I have already suggested that this is due not to any uncertainty on Heidegger's part, but to a deliberate rhetorical strategy captured by the notion of "formal indication." I suggest the following as a good way of explicating the meaning of authenticity while at the same time heeding these difficulties. The procedure I will employ in this and in the succeeding chapter is to combine textual analysis with a more general *historical* reflection on Heidegger's place within the tradition that is most clearly linked with an ideal of authenticity.

With respect to the latter issue, my contention is that "authenticity" can best be understood as a creative reappropriation of the Christian origins of what I call the "Romantic personalist" tradition. Especially important in this regard is Heidegger's understanding of *Christian eschatology*. This point should come as no surprise, for, as I have already discussed at length, Heidegger clearly held that "primitive Christianity" provides a window onto the pre-theoretical immediacy of life by means of a special modality of experience.

This chapter will be devoted first of all to exploring Heidegger's affinity for the tradition of Romantic personalism, particularly as articulated in the works of Wilhelm Dilthey (1833–1911). Second, I will show how Heidegger followed Dilthey's lead in tracing the origins of personalism back to primitive Christianity. It is against this background that I propose to examine in depth Heidegger's exploration of primitive Christianity in WS 1920–1921. The result of this investigation will be a schematic view of what it means, for Heidegger, to live an *authentic* life. With this basic outline in place, I will go on, in the next chapter, to examine his more detailed treatments of authenticity during the period up to and including the publication of *Being and Time*.

Heidegger's Place in Tradition

Romantic Personalism

In chapter 3, I argued that one plausible way of making sense of Heidegger's talk of authenticity and inauthenticity is to understand it in terms of moral theory. The claim is that Heidegger maintains a species of *perfectionism*; that is, he holds that it is possible for people to lead a worthwhile way of life, called "authenticity," which is not to be identified with pleasure, happiness, or desire satisfaction. On some accounts of moral theory, though, such an ideal would probably not get to count as a *moral* ideal at all. Morality, intuitively, has to do with human interaction, whereas, at least at first glance, *authenticity* is an ideal that is mostly concerned with an individual's relation to herself. However, at least *one* thing that moral theories sometimes do is to articulate a *way of life* or a particular *character* that is importantly *better* than some alternatives. It cannot be denied that Heidegger does just that.[3] I appeal here to the classical *virtue* tradition (Aristotle, Stoicism) to support the idea that, at least some of the time, moral theorists have focused their reflections on one's relation to oneself.

I am quite aware, however, that Heidegger's discussions of the ideal of authenticity do not fit neatly within any familiar type of moral theory. This is mostly due to both Heidegger's language and to the overall philosophical project that provides the context for the articulations of this ideal. Heidegger himself seems to have publicly acknowledged as much in his 1947 "Letter on Humanism" (G9 353 ff./268 ff.). The impression one gets from his discussion there is that while he is certainly aware of the moral predicament of modern humanity, he nevertheless is more interested in the much more basic question of the "truth of being," as he called it during these years.

In his earlier work, moreover, the most Heidegger ever provides us with concerning authenticity is a series of highly suggestive "formal indications." As I have argued elsewhere, these are not philosophical concepts in the standard sense, but rather are pointers to a uniquely individual way of existing that, on Heidegger's view, cannot be properly captured by standard concepts and propositions. A further important difference between his version of perfectionism and others is that there is no indication of a more general theory of values or of moral life that grounds any claim about the value of authenticity. For example, Heidegger does not provide the usual naturalist-Aristotelian kind of argument for self-realization, e.g., that authenticity is somehow the fulfillment of the essence of humanity.

While all of this renders it extremely difficult to read Heidegger as a moral theorist, it nevertheless seems to be the case that the only way to make good sense of his talk about inauthenticity and authenticity is to employ the language of moral theory. It is quite evident that Heidegger is *recommending* something to us, that he thinks it is *a* human good, if not *the* human good, and that he thinks it is manifestly better than an alternative. This seems to be, at least some of the time, the sort of thing that moral theorists do. Furthermore, it is much closer to moral theory than to other ways of thinking about value, e.g., aesthetics, since it concerns a whole way of life.

The ideal of authenticity is not by any means new with Heidegger. Rather, it has its roots a century or more before he articulated his version of it. While it is surely the case that the idea had been in the air for some time, it was at the end of the eighteenth century that it was first clearly expressed. In order to better understand Heidegger, it is useful to briefly discuss the contours of this idea as well as the major figures associated with its development.

Authenticity is difficult to accurately characterize. This is due, I think, to the multiplicity of sources from which it is drawn, two of the most important being early modern political thought and Protestantism. The basic idea, however, is something that is quite familiar to us today. Authenticity means something like "being true to oneself." It is an ideal grounded on a commitment to the value of the unique individual. Another closely related way to understand the idea is through the notion of self-fulfillment or the realization of one's own unique potential as an individual. One could capture something of the basic idea by appeal to the Nietzschean dictum, "become what you are."

Charles Taylor has examined this ideal and its historical origins in *The Ethics of Authenticity*. I think his characterization of it is substantially correct:

> There is a certain way of being human that is *my* way. I am called upon to live my life in this way, and not in imitation of anyone else's. But this gives a new importance to being true to myself. If I am not, I miss the point of my life, I miss what being human is for *me*.[4]

As Taylor points out, this is an essentially *Romantic* ideal, which has its proximate roots in the eighteenth-century notion of a "moral sense," of Rousseau's *"sentiment de l'existence,"* and similar ideas.[5] J. G. Herder, for example, defends the idea that each person has an original, unique way of being a human being and that this is something that ought to be fully realized through personal cultivation. With the Romantics, this ideal is raised to a new level of importance. It comes to be particularly identified with the aesthetic value of self-expression. For someone like Schleiermacher, the idea seems to be that of constructing one's individual life as a coherent whole through a process of self-cultivation.[6]

Given the historical provenance of this ideal, I have elected to call it "Romantic personalism." It is most certainly the nineteenth-century tradition with which Heidegger's thought on the subject bears the most affinity. I have chosen the designation "personalism" mostly to avoid the egoist connotations of "individualism." While the unique individual is the core value category of this line of thought, I think it is a mistake to assimilate it to modern egoist moral philosophy. In addition, John Van Buren has convincingly articulated what he calls a "personalist" strand in Heidegger's early thought.[7] Given that I find Van Buren's analysis both illuminating and accurate, I have chosen to employ his terminology.

Heidegger and Romantic Personalism

None of this would be particularly salient here were it not for the fact that a number of sources indicate Heidegger's deep affinity for this line of thought about the value of "being true to oneself." These indications can be mostly drawn from Heidegger's explicit comments in his earliest lecture courses from 1919, as well as from some of his contemporaneous correspondence. Heidegger clearly endorses *something* about the Romantic personalist tradition, employs its language, studies its figures, particularly Schleiermacher and Dilthey, and professes his affinity for the neo-Romantic German youth movements of the 1910s and 1920s.

Before looking at Heidegger's explicit or implicit avowals of allegiance to this particular line of thought, I want to point to some more *systematic* endorsements of it from his work in the 1920s. A few examples will, I think, be quite sufficient for this purpose. The relevant points here are Heidegger's use of two terms, *'Jeweiligkeit'* and *'Jemeinigkeit.'* These terms signal a systematic commitment to the irreducible individuality of personal life, something that was also strongly emphasized by thinkers in the Romantic tradition. More importantly, the way Heidegger employs these terms generally points to a normative commitment of some sort to the value of living an authentic life.

The lecture course for SS 1923 is entitled "Ontology: The Hermeneutics of *Facticity.*" At this point, Heidegger is still employing a variety of terms to refer to the topic of philosophy, i.e., human life in a world of sense. I have drawn attention to this variety of usage earlier; terms like "facticity," "factical life-experience," "lived experience," and "Dasein" all function in roughly the same way. Here, in 1923, this plurivocity is also evident, though Heidegger does give us some help by way of a "definition":

> *'Facticity'* is the designation we will use for the character of the being of "our" "own" Dasein. More precisely, this expression means: *in each case* "this" Dasein in its being-there *for a while at the particular time* [. . .]. (G63 7/5)

Heidegger attempts to lend some more terminological precision to his discussion by deploying the term *'Jeweiligkeit,'* which Van Buren carefully renders as "the 'awhileness' of temporal particularity" (G63 7/5). The sense of this idea can be clarified if we jump to an earlier text, the "Natorp Report" from October 1922, where Heidegger tells us that "Factical Dasein always is what it is only as one's own Dasein and never as the Dasein in general of some universal humanity" (NB 4/114). Heidegger's comments here clearly echo Schleiermacher's dissatisfaction with the Enlightenment conception of universal humanity, grounded in reason: "I was not satisfied to view humanity in rough unshapen masses, inwardly altogether alike, and taking transient shape externally only by reason of mutual contact and friction."[8] There is also a clear affinity here with Kierkegaard's impassioned protests against Hegelian Absolute Idealism on behalf the "single individual." Indeed, Heidegger acknowledges Kierkegaard as an important source of his ideas in these lectures (G63 5/4).

Importantly, in 1923, Heidegger is quick to point out that none of this denotes "an isolating relativization into individuals," but rather "a how of being, an indication which points to a possible path of being-wakeful" (G63 7/5). The claim that each person has his or her own unique way of being human does not entail a commitment to solipsism. As I have already argued at some length, on Heidegger's view, one is only oneself in any substantive way by virtue of membership in a linguistic community that hands down a definite tradition. More importantly, however, Heidegger singles out "being-wakeful" as a possibility that is grounded in the temporal particularity of the individual. These connections show up again in other texts from the early 1920s, such as the lecture course of SS 1925:

> Dasein is the entity which I myself am in each instance, in whose being I as an entity "have an interest" or share, an entity which is in each instance to be it in my own way. (G20 205/153)

Dasein is, he tells us, a "being-possible [Möglichsein]," not in a logical sense, but in a personal one: in each case, Dasein is my possibility to be. This grounds an ability to modify this possibility: either I can sincerely take it up as my possibility, or I can relinquish it into the anonymous homogeneity of the "one" (G20 206/153f.). It is here, Heidegger says, that we can begin to make sense of "authenticity" and "inauthenticity." A similar story gets told in Being and Time. What is once again definitive of Dasein is a feature he calls its "being in each case my own [Jemeinigkeit]" (SZ 42/68). As in SS 1925, this means that "in each case Dasein is mine to be in one way or another" (SZ 42/68). This is what grounds the possibility of authenticity (SZ 43/68).

Turning now to Heidegger's professions of allegiance to the Romantic-historicist tradition, consider his comments during SS 1919 on the historical roots of contemporary philosophy. He begins by briefly characterizing the idea of Enlightenment, the condemnation of the backward "peoples of nature" and their "barbarism," and the universalistic conception of persons as rational animals. The thought of the Enlightenment "regards the individual as but an instance of the species, as an historical atom so to speak (thus the poets were valued not as figures within a genuine world of life-experience, but as perfecters of language who with their refinement and polish brought public and social life to an elevated level)" (G56/57 133/113). Herder, among others, reacted against these trends. "With Herder, however, historical consciousness arrived at a decisive insight. [. . .] he saw historical reality in its manifold irrational fullness, especially because he recognized the autonomous and unique value of each nation and age, each historical manifestation" (133/113 f.). It is difficult not to detect the sympathetic tone of Heidegger's discussion here; he speaks as though, on his view, Herder and his successors really did "recognize" something that is in fact the case. Herder and his heirs, at least according to Heidegger, succeeded in challenging Enlightenment philosophy of history and in promoting the value of individuality. As a result of this, "[r]egard for individual, qualitatively original centers and contexts of action [comes about]. The category of 'ownness' [*Eigenheit*] becomes meaningful and is related to all formations of life [. . .]" (G56/57 134/114). With Schlegel, one begins to study the past without first rejecting it as barbarous. In addition, "Schleiermacher saw for the first time the integrity and legitimacy of community life and the specificity of Christian consciousness of community. He discovered primal Christianity [. . .]" (G56/57 134/114).

As Heidegger tells the tale, this line of thought culminates in Dilthey (G56/57 163/138). For Heidegger, Dilthey advances beyond earlier work in this tradition by seeing the need for an understanding of life in its historical concreteness (165 f./139 f.). "Dilthey already saw clearly (1883) the meaning of the singular and unique in historical reality [. . .]" (G56/57 165/140).

At the same time Heidegger was trying to find his own way within the tradition of Romantic personalism and historicism, he was also articulating, in the classroom, ideas of "life-intensification" and of "genuine personal life" that have clear Romantic overtones. Of the pre-theoretical "something" of life, so often missed by his predecessors and contemporaries, Heidegger says, "It is a basic phenomenon that can be experienced in understanding, e.g., in the living situation of gliding from one world of experience to another genuine life-world, or in moments of especially intensive life; not at all or seldom in those types of experience that are firmly anchored in a world *without* reaching, precisely within this world a much greater life-intensity" (G56/57 115/97). One can clearly see here that Heidegger is contrasting what he eventually comes to call an *inauthentic* life, one that is depersonalized and absorbed in its concerns, with an alternative mode of life that is *intensified*. The following semester (SS 1919), Heidegger returns to these ideas:

> Moreover, there are genuine life-experiences, which grow out of a genuine life-world (artist, religious person). Depending upon the genuine motivational possibilities, there arises the phenomenon of life-intensification (in the opposite case, minimizing of life). This phenomenon is not determined by a feeling of experienced content. There are people who have experienced much in various "worlds" (artistically, etc.) and yet are "inwardly empty." They have reached only a "superficial" experience of life. Today the forms of life-intensification are becoming ever more pregnant, fraught with meaning. "Activism" is in motive genuine, in form misguided. The "free German youth movement" is in form genuine, but without fertility in its setting of goals. (G56/57 208/175 f.)

This passage has all the hallmarks of the Romantic personalist tradition: the paradigmatic status of the artist, the contrast between a vehement, intense life and one that is "minimized" and "superficial." Importantly, the "religious person" is also taken to be paradigmatic. I have already discussed the general significance of religion in Heidegger's "hermeneutics of facticity" (chapter 1). Religious life, on Heidegger's view, is a paradigmatic instance of a more general type of experience that allows one to gain a familiarity with human life in its immediacy. Here, in 1919, Heidegger draws an explicit connection between "genuine life-experiences" of this kind and the life of the "religious person." As I will show in more detail, this link is the key to understanding what Heidegger means by authenticity.

Heidegger's guarded appreciation for the Free German Youth is also telling. The Free German Youth, coming on the scene around 1913, were the successor to the earlier Wandervogel, who had, in the words of one commentator, previously rebelled against the "depersonalized ethics of mass society [. . .]."[9] The Free German Youth were more activist than their predecessors, seeking the development of alternative lifestyles. Left-wing elements were briefly united here with more *völkisch* groups in a neo-Romantic rejection of mass society, industrialization, and the rigid class hierarchy of the *Kaiserreich*. While Heidegger is clearly reserved toward this group, he retained a lifelong affinity with its idealization of rural life and an abiding concern for the renewal of life through contemporary youth (cf. G16 45). It is also worth pointing out here that Heidegger's enthusiasm for the *Jugendbewegung* also casts a shadow on his thought because the Nazis were able to make ample use of the sentiments of these groups in fomenting their own "blood and soil" ideology. Moreover, even in the relatively innocuous form of the pre-war Wandervogel, the youth movement often had more than a whiff of militant nationalism. The "heroes of Langemarcke," much idealized by the radical right in the Weimar Republic, were greenhorn infantrymen largely drawn from the idealistic ranks of the youth movement. Moreover, many members of the right-wing *Tat-Kreis* from the early 1930s were former members of youth groups. It would, however, be a major error to call the Free German Youth either "fascist" or even "proto-fascist." The Hitler Youth was, after all, a completely separate organization, coming onto the scene much later as part of a blatantly cynical drive for indoctrination. Ultimately, it was the *Kampfbünde* of the radical right and various associated *Freikorps* units that can be located much more plausibly in the pedigree of National Socialism than any element of the youth movement. At most, Heidegger's enthusiasm for the youth movement (which is, as I noted earlier, guarded) locates him within a widespread rejection of adult, bourgeois society that was quite common amongst the so-called "Front Generation." While this radical attitude certainly did nothing to assist in the task of consolidating democracy and liberalism in the Weimar era, it would be too extreme to suggest that it contributed in any direct way to the rise of Nazism.

Heidegger's personalistic proclivities are even more pronounced in his correspondence with Elisabeth Blochmann. Spiritual (i.e., cultural) life can only be renewed, he contends, through "an impulse born out of the personal [. . .]" (HB 7). Cultural goods achieve their real value to the extent they are appropriated by the "ownmost existence" of individuals who possess an "inner wakefulness." Difficult demands are placed upon the "existence of ownmost personality and value," in faith in one's own "self-worth" (HB 7). "Every accomplishment gains the character of final validity in the sense of genuineness, i.e., of an inner belonging to a central I and its god-directed steadfastness of purpose" (HB 7). In several letters, Heidegger clearly espouses an ideal of "inner truthfulness" (HB 7, 9). Arid theory must be replaced by "the most personal experience" in approaching theological and philosophical problems. The personalist trend in these letters comes to a head in a long passage, in which one finds Heidegger outlining his early, neo-Romantic ideal of authenticity for his friend Blochmann:

> It is a rationalistic misjudgment of the essence of the personal stream of life, if one intends and demands that it vibrate in the same broad and sonorous amplitudes that well up in graced moments. Such claims grow out of a defect in inner humility before the mystery and grace-character of all life. We must be able to wait for the tautly strung intensities of meaningful life—and we must remain in continuity with these moments—not so much to enjoy them as to mold them into [*eingestalten*] life—in the continuing course of life, they are taken along and incorporated into the rhythm of all future life. [. . .] having oneself with understanding is only genuine when it is truly lived, i.e. when it is at the same time a be-ing. By this I do not intend the triviality that one must now also adhere to what is known—but rather a vehement life, a turning inwards [*Innewerden*] to one's own unique (though not theoretical) total spiritual direction. (HB 14)

Here again one can see the idea of moments of intensity of life, along with a notion of personal self-cultivation and vocational commitment. All these are central features of the ideals articulated in the Romantic personalist tradition. Heidegger's endorsement of this ideal is unhesitant. We find here almost all the core elements of Heidegger's own ideal of authenticity as it develops in the years following this important letter. Heidegger rejects the calculative manipulation of life, a hallmark of the *ambitio saeculi* or "hyperbolic" sense of inauthentic life that I have previously discussed (chapter 3), in the name of humble reverence and devotion. Moreover, in contrast to the dispersion and restless curiosity of an inauthentic life, Heidegger advocates an *integrated* self, one that has its own unique personal "rhythm," guided by a steadfast, vehement commitment to a vocation. Heidegger's endorsement of this ideal of an authentic life is also quite clear in his contemporaneous letter to Father Krebs:

> It is difficult to live as a philosopher—inner truthfulness regarding oneself and in relation to those for whom one is supposed to be a teacher demands sacrifices, renunciation, and struggles which ever remain unknown to the academic technician. I believe that I have the inner calling to philosophy

and, through my research and teaching, to do what stands in my power for the sake of the eternal vocation of the inner man, and *to do it for this alone*, and so justify my existence [*Dasein*] and work ultimately before God. (S 70)

Notable in this passage is Heidegger's repeated invocation of the "inner" as a special domain of value. Thinkers of the post-Enlightenment age, like Schleiermacher and Kierkegaard, also deployed this language of "inwardness" to express their unreserved esteem for the depths of personal experience and the unique value of individuality. Taylor has pointed out how the eighteenth-century doctrine of the "moral sense," a kind of inner voice that guides a person's actions, played a crucial role in the modern development of the concept of authenticity.[10] Also important to the development of the category of inwardness is Lutheran Pietism, with its emphasis on the lived experience of conversion over against more orthodox notions of "forensic" justification.[11] The Pietists regarded themselves, with some justification, as the true heirs of Luther's Reformation. In many of his early works, most notably the 1520 work "The Freedom of a Christian," Luther also tries to locate the event of salvation within the "inner man." Clearly, the *religious* side of Romantic personalism was deeply compelling to the young Heidegger.

Schleiermacher, Dilthey, and Primal Christianity

Amongst the thinkers who can be placed within the Romantic personalist tradition, the two who were most important to the young Heidegger were Friedrich Schleiermacher and Wilhelm Dilthey. Both appear in Heidegger's brief but approving discussion of this tradition during SS 1919. The work of both Schleiermacher and Dilthey formed independent subjects of study during Heidegger's early years. Thus Heidegger's appropriation of Romantic personalism is crucially mediated through the work of these two thinkers. The most important lesson the young Heidegger learned from these men lay in their identification of the personal experience of primal Christianity as the historical root of Romantic personalism. Heidegger took this idea as a clue to his own project of developing a "hermeneutics of facticity," and, during the 1920s, sought to creatively reappropriate the religious roots of Romantic personalism.

John Van Buren has focused on Heidegger's debt to Schleiermacher in this regard. On Van Buren's reading, Heidegger was deeply impressed by Schleiermacher's view that one ought to cultivate one's unique identity in conjunction with a particular form of communal life.[12] Van Buren correctly argues that Heidegger aligns himself self-consciously with the likes of Herder and Schleiermacher.[13] He also accurately characterizes the elements of Schleiermacher's views that were most influential on Heidegger's intellectual development.[14] On this reading, Heidegger developed some of Schleiermacher's insights into a more robust ontological view of the person as the unique site for the temporal disclosure of being.

The other figure that is crucially important to Heidegger at this stage is Wilhelm Dilthey. Dilthey's importance for Heidegger's creative reappropriation of Romantic personalism has yet to be explored and articulated.[15] Since Van Buren has already done much to illuminate the importance of Schleiermacher, the present discussion will be limited to Dilthey. This does not, however, imply that Dilthey was somehow less important to Heidegger than was Schleiermacher. To the contrary, judging by the actual volume of Heidegger's discussions of Dilthey, the opposite seems to be the case. In Dilthey's work, Heidegger saw a clue he would follow up in his own attempt to radically transform the Romantic-historicist tradition of German philosophy into his own powerful critique of metaphysics and of naturalism.[16] Heidegger himself directly attests to Dilthey's significance in *Being and Time*: "The researches of Dilthey were, for their part, pioneering work; but today's generation has not as yet made them its own. In the following analysis the issue is solely one of furthering their adoption" (SZ 377/429).

Dilthey comes onto the radar quite early, most extensively during SS 1920, when his work, along with that of Paul Natorp, become the objects of critical investigations by young Professor Heidegger.[17] While Heidegger is certainly reticent about accepting some parts of Dilthey's work, such as his adoption of the method of "inner reflection," he nevertheless rejects the common stock of dismissive opinions (G59 163 ff., 152 f.). Heidegger urges his hearers to shed their fears about "historicism" and "relativism" and instead to try to appropriate what is positive about Dilthey's work (G59 154). The positive trend is toward the reconception of philosophy as the attempt to understand life (G59 156). This is anchored in Dilthey's basic conception of "life-experience" as the interaction between a unitary, individuated center of life and its milieu (G59 157). On Heidegger's reading, unlike some of his Romantic and historicist predecessors, Dilthey actually attempted a detailed exposition of the basic categories of life.

Dilthey is once again the object of explicit concern in the spring of 1924, when Heidegger delivers his recently translated lecture at Kassel. Importantly, one finds Heidegger pointing to the *theological* origins of Dilthey's work during these talks.

> Dilthey was a theologian in the beginning and was thus provided with specific horizons and an openness for Dasein that remained effective later on. For him, theology had a relation to philosophy and to history, namely, the history of Christianity and its fundamental fact, the life of Jesus. Dilthey planned a history of Western Christianity, but this plan and his whole program of theological studies fell apart during his study of the Middle Ages. (S 151)

The Romantics were, of course, also decisive influences on Dilthey. This is quite obvious in the case of Schleiermacher, whose thought Dilthey did much to preserve and to advance, largely through his monumental *Leben Schleiermachers* (GS14). Other Romantics, like Novalis and Hölderlin, were also, according to Heidegger, vitally important to Dilthey (S 153).[18] His work on these poets involves an attempt "to understand concrete historical individuals from their intellectual core ('from the center,' as one says in the George circle)" (S 153). From Dilthey himself, however, we can learn to pursue a "vital questioning after the sense of history and human being" (S 154).

According to Heidegger, "Dilthey's central problem was how to see historical reality in its own reality. He sought to salvage the unique character not of science but of reality" (S 155). His topic was "the human being as a spiritual being [. . .], the primal vital unity of life itself" (S 156). On Heidegger's view, then, Dilthey is important not primarily as a theorist of the "human sciences [*Geisteswissenschaften*]," but as a theorist of the concrete historical reality of personal life itself. With Dilthey, *the* topic of philosophy, as far as Heidegger is concerned, has come into view. The Romantic personalist tradition, with its emphasis on the unique, irreducible value of individual life, thus gains its most significant articulation in the work of Dilthey.

A look at Dilthey's own work certainly lends Heidegger's assessment a good bit of plausibility. It is evident that Dilthey belongs wholeheartedly to the Romantic-historicist tradition. In *Introduction to the Human Sciences* (1883), Dilthey asserts that an individual is a "psychophysical whole" that is irreducibly unique (GS1 29/80). Like Herder, Dilthey also thinks of "peoples" or "nations" as unique individuals (GS1 41/92). He shares the historicists' rejection of *metaphysical* interpretations of the meaning of history. The concepts employed by this kind of history are "abstract essences which condense the historical course of the world into colorless abstractions" (GS1 104/154).[19] The subject matter of the human sciences is a single "unit" that can be known "from within" (GS1 109/153). The real core of history is not to be sought in metaphysics, but rather in the "vital nexus" in which the will of the individual intermeshes with a larger purposive system (GS1 127/177).

Dilthey's interest in the individual as a category in the human sciences is also apparent in his well-known view of biography and autobiography as tools for understanding. In *Introduction to the Human Sciences*, he writes that "[h]uman memory has found a great many individuals worthy of interest and preservation" (GS1 33/85). That which is unique, he argues, is always more interesting than "any other object or any generalization." Dilthey goes on to link biography specifically with the moral tradition of individualism: "The progress and destiny of the human will is here apprehended in its dignity as an end in itself."

In his later *Aufbau* studies, from the first decade of the twentieth century, Dilthey presents similar convictions. He writes:

> Each life has its own sense. It consists in a meaning-context in which every remembered present possesses an intrinsic value, and yet, through the nexus of memory, it is also related to the sense of the whole. This sense of individual human existence is unique and cannot be fathomed by concep-

tual cognition; yet, in its way, like a Leibnizian monad, it represents the historical universe. (GS7 199/221)

Here again, Dilthey's considered position is that autobiography is an invaluable tool for the historian (GS7 200/222). Using these sources, the goal is to grasp the individual, who is "an intrinsic value in the world of human spirit," not to reduce the individual to some larger whole, but rather to see the individual as a whole in itself (GS7 212/233). "The mystery of the person," Dilthey writes, "lures us for its own sake into ever new and deeper attempts at understanding."

Dilthey's final writings on the "doctrine of world-views" also testify to his deep kinship with the Romantic tradition originating with thinkers like Herder and Schleiermacher. Life, he says, presents itself to us in "uncounted forms" (GS8 78). From out of a complex web of relations, each individual life "creates" its own world (GS8 79). Each individual context of "life-experience" is irreducibly unique. From this context there arises a unique "life-attitude [*Lebenstimmung*]," a certain "coloration [*Färbung*]" or "interpretation [*Auslegung*]" attached to life (GS8 81). These attitudes change and shift about, but "certain life-attitudes [*Lebenstimmungen*]," such as optimism or pessimism, "predominate in different individuals according to their personal nature."

Dilthey's affinity for this way of thinking, the one I have been calling Romantic personalism, is also pronounced in his later work *Das Wesen der Philosophie* (1907):

> Every moment, every epoch of our life has a self-establishing value in itself to the extent that its special conditions make possible a determinate manner of the satisfaction and fulfillment of our existence [*Dasein*]; at the same time, every stage of life is bound together in a historical development in which we strive to achieve, in the course of time, an ever richer development of life-values, an ever stronger and more highly cultivated configuration of psychic life. (GS5 374)

In his *Introduction to the Human Sciences*, one finds Dilthey appropriating the Romantic valuation of personal life for the wider purpose of grounding the "human sciences." The problem up to this point, as he sees it, has been the constant obfuscation of personal life and its "ownmost value" by metaphysics. Dilthey urges that we "observe without prejudice the reality of our inner life and, proceeding from there [. . .] establish the meaning of nature and history for this inner life" (GS1 408/240). Metaphysics, however, blocks our progress in this direction. Dilthey expresses his vitalistic protest against metaphysics in terms that Heidegger would, no doubt, have heartily commended:

> A metaphysics is consistent only when it is, as its form dictates, a rational science, i.e., when it seeks a logical world-system. Rational science was thus the backbone, as it were, of European metaphysics. But the feeling of life of a genuine and vigorous individual and the richness of the world given him cannot be exhausted in the logical system of a universally valid science. (GS1 395/228)

Naturalism, though it purports to be a revolt against metaphysics, is ultimately just as guilty of obscuring the reality of personal life. On Dilthey's view, the original "life-nexus" is detached from, or only partially accounted for, by science. Poetry, on the other hand, brings this more fully to expression (GS1 371 f./205 f.). More significant for my argument, however, is that Dilthey regards *religious experience* as a vital link to the original richness of historical personal life. This claim most often takes the form of reflection on the vicissitudes of European intellectual history. In *Introduction to the Human Sciences*, Dilthey tells the story of modernity as the emancipation of the "powers of the individual"(GS1 352/186). While medieval humanity certainly possessed the "independent power of religious life," this had ultimately been constrained by the coercive power of the institutionalized Church. Dilthey characterizes the situation so:

> The mixture of Christianity with ancient science affected the purity of religious experience. The institutional and authoritative constraint placed upon individuals hindered people from free intercourse with one another in spheres of activity like science and religion, which draw their lifeblood from freedom. [. . .] The goals of society which most seem to require freedom were supported and controlled by authoritarian and corporate [structures]. (GS1 353/186f.)

All the same, it was religion which, according to Dilthey, harbored a hidden protest against the authoritarian control of the individual and the metaphysical occlusion of personal life, a protest that finally came to fruition in European modernity. The irreducible element of "personal experience" is, at one point, identified by Dilthey with "moral-religious truth" (GS1 384f./218). This personal dimension cannot be captured by metaphysical concepts. This is clear from the historical fact that "each metaphysics has had to contend with the protest of religious experience, which is clearly rooted in the will, from the first Christian mystics who opposed medieval metaphysics—and were no poorer Christians on that account—to Tauler and Luther" (GS1 385/218). Dilthey's idea seems to be that the intense personal experience of religious devotion captures the irreducible uniqueness of personal life. "The expression of this state of affairs is the liberation of religious belief from its metaphysical bondage through the Reformation, in which religious life attained its autonomy" (GS1 385/218). The idea that religious experience is uniquely disclosive of personal life is also articulated later in the so-called "Breslau Draft" for Part II of the *Introduction*. Here, Dilthey explicitly links his own methods of investigation into life with what he sees as its historical provenance in Christian mysticism.[20]

Dilthey singles out the importance of the Reformation with regard to the reassertion of personal life in an essay from the 1890s entitled "Auffasung und Analyse des Menschen im 15. und 16. Jahrhundert." Dilthey's assessment of the Reformation is made clear at the outset: "through the shift of the justification of dogmas to religious-ethical inwardness, the development of a critical theology was enabled, and in its progress the moral and religious autonomy of the person was made to be the foundation of our spiritual life" (GS2 39). Dilthey's discussion covers many figures, but the most significant one for my overall argument is, of course, Luther. Dilthey views Luther's work on a kind of continuum between the intensely personal "practical mysticism" of the Middle Ages and the philosophy of subjectivity in German Idealism (GS2 41, 55). With Luther, there comes about a new kind of theology, rooted not in "scholastic speculations," but rather on "what is experienced, on the lived religious process and Christian literature" (GS2 42). Dogmas are now to be grounded in the personal experience of the election of grace, not on their conformity to Aristotelian philosophy. Dilthey focuses in particular on Luther's works from 1520, such as "On the Freedom of a Christian," to support this reading. "Life for [Luther] is the primary thing [*das Erste*]. For him, it is from out of life, of our ethico-religious experiences that are given in it, that all knowledge about our relation to the invisible derives, and remains bound to it. And so, the intellectual bond of the cosmos, that binds the rational animal to world-reason, recedes behind the moral context" (GS2 58).

These ideas reappear in Dilthey's later *Aufbau* studies. Here he draws attention to a certain kinship between the Enlightenment and Pietism in their common distrust of superficial conformity (GS7 183/204). "Thus we see," he writes, "how Pietism belongs to the great movement of individualism, because it goes beyond [orthodox] Lutheranism by excluding the Church from the inner life of the person" (GS7 184/204). This was an age in which people discovered "the archetype of a more free religiosity [. . .] in primitive Christianity" and valued "the individuality of creativity and genius" (GS7 184f./205). On Dilthey's view, Pietism represents an attempt to "liberate" the individual through a radical "individualism" and concomitant move toward toleration (GS7 342ff./362ff.).

In other works, such as *Das Wesen der Philosophie*, Dilthey also discusses the importance of religious inwardness for the emancipation of the individual. The mystic or religious person experiences a kind of inner liberation from the irrational, dark forces of nature, an intensification of self-consciousness (GS5 385). These ideas appear again in a late essay called "The Problem of Religion" (1911). The "problem" in question is the conflict between religion and other forms of worldly life (GS6 288f.). What Dilthey finds important about religion is, as always, its disclosure of the sphere of personal existence. Here he is particularly concerned with the post-Reformation personalist impulse in Western Christianity, typified by Jansenism, various Anglo-American sects, and German Pietism. All, on Dilthey's reading, are animated by "an impulse to experience personally the inwardness of religion." Emphasis is placed here on the individual soul and its ownmost value (GS6 292). Dilthey is, not surprisingly, most concerned with German Pietism. He traces a direct historical link between this religious revival and the thought of Schleiermacher, Fries, and Novalis (GS6 294). Here religion is the inner, non-objectifiable participation of the individual in the mysterious universal. Dogmatics is only a secondary product of this primary thing, i.e., personal life-experience. Dilthey summarizes these ideas in a comment on Schleiermacher:

> Religious experience lays hold of a context that transcends the sensible context that is graspable by the understanding; the content of this experience is inaccessible to the understanding, and cannot be presented in concepts: a real effect on the present conscious condition of the soul is experienced in a condition of passive surrender [Hingabe], which, according to the type of experience, is interpreted as something that is derived from an invisible context. (GS6 301)

What one can conclude from this brief survey of Dilthey's thought is that he, himself a member of the Romantic personalist tradition, found the roots of this tradition in the experiential religiosity of medieval mysticism, Luther, and the religious revivals of the seventeenth and eighteenth centuries. Religion (though not necessarily *theology*) contained an experiential demonstration of the uniqueness and irreducible value of individual life. Dilthey's project, at least on Heidegger's reading of it, was to articulate the structures of this personal life as it had been initially disclosed in religious experience. Studying Dilthey, Heidegger began to see that the heart of the modern "ethics of authenticity" really lay in "primal Christianity." By returning to these sources, Heidegger hoped to give a fresh face to the ideals of the Romantic personalist tradition.

This claim is substantiated by a look at some of Heidegger's work from the early 1920s. What one finds is Heidegger actively appropriating Dilthey's thesis about primal Christianity and tracing out the intellectual connections involved in it. As I have already discussed, Heidegger situates Dilthey himself within this tradition and draws attention to the latter's theological roots. On Heidegger's account, this theological ground lies beneath the entire Romantic personalist tradition, of which Dilthey is one of the most important members.

Dilthey's thesis about Christianity and personal life, i.e., that the former discloses the latter and perseveres against the totalization and depersonalization of Greek metaphysics, appears quite explicitly during Heidegger's lectures from WS 1919–1920. In his early work, Heidegger distinguishes three interpenetrating contexts of meaning in factical life-experience: the surrounding world [*Umwelt*], the with-world [*Mitwelt*], and the self-world [*Selbstwelt*]. He begins to investigate the last of these through a consideration of its disclosure in autobiography, or, borrowing Dilthey's term, "self-reflection [*Selbstbesinnung*]" (G58 56). This is, he tells us, a phenomenon as old as literate humanity itself, which has a special manifestation in "religious reminiscence about fate, the effective powers of life that hinder or assist, punish or bless" (G58 56f.). In such works, the "inner experience" of the self presents itself or expresses itself (G58 57). What is noteworthy about this is that "factical life 'is able' to be centered in an emphatic way on the self-world" (G58 57).

Heidegger's example of religious "meditation on the self" is Augustine's *Confessions* (G58 58). Such a "confession" manifests the "development and formation of an inner self-experience of one's own life" (G58 58). What is expressed is the "continuous, living, ownmost attitude towards its particular inherited lifeworld" (G58 58). The particular "direction" or "special disposition [*besonderen Verfassung*]" of the self imparts a uniqueness to that lifeworld. What we find here is Heidegger more or less taking over some of the key ideas of Romantic personalists like Dilthey. Like Dilthey, Heidegger is interested in autobiography and in confessional literature because it presents the individual as an irreducibly unique source of meaning. This type of literature testifies directly to what Heidegger calls the "in each case my ownness [*Je-meinigkeit*]" of life in a way that theoretical treatises cannot. Moreover, it also testifies to the possibility that an individual might be "centered" on herself. That is, confessional literature testifies to the possibility that an individual can struggle with the meaning of her own life *as* her own life. It reveals the ways one's commitments give shape and cohesiveness to a life that is irreducibly unique.

As I have already discussed in a previous chapter (chapter 1), Heidegger fixes these ideas through the term '*Zugespitztheit*,' meaning something like "intensifying concentration." John Van Buren reads this as Heidegger's appropriation of the mystic doctrine of the *Seelengrund*, of the individual soul as the unique site of the inward birth of the divine Logos, found, most notably, in the work of Rhineland mystics like Eckhart, Tauler, and the anonymous author of the *Theologia Germanica*.[21] Van Buren thus takes the term '*Zugespitztheit*' to refer to a more or less non-optional feature of human life, rather than a rare achievement or an ideal. Van Buren's idea is that the incalculable "event [*Ereignis*]" of meaning is played out at the most personal, individual level in the lives of particular men and women. While the young Heidegger (and the old Heidegger too) certainly held this view, the context in which the term '*Zugespitztheit*' gets used does not clearly justify Van Buren's reading. Admittedly, however, Heidegger's usage in this lecture course is ambiguous. On the one hand, '*Zugespitztheit*' is something that is particularly manifested only in *certain lives*, as typified by religious autobiography. Yet Heidegger added a later note in which he observes that the "whole page is not clearly articulated" (G58 60). What it ought to say is "(1) Factical life *can* concentrate itself in a special way towards the self-world; (2) This functional accentuation is not something that arises from some special continual attention but is rather a factically actual world-directed [*weltwärts*] enactment of life" (G58 60). At the same time, in the original notes, to which this remark was later added, Heidegger designates this whole phenomenon in more general terms as "the indexing of the tendencies and world-characteristics" from the self, and he says that "intensifying concentration toward the self-world is always there [*immer da*] in factical life" (G58 60).

In this whole passage, Heidegger is shifting between two distinct phenomena: (1) the phenomenological fact that life is always *my* life, and (2) the comparatively rare achievement of some kind of "accentuation" of the uniqueness and individuality of life. Both are clearly attested to by confessional literature and autobiography. Matters are complicated by the fact that the title of the very next section dispenses with the term *'Zugespitztheit'* altogether and instead talks of "Christianity as the historical paradigm for the shift of emphasis of factical life to the self-world [*die Verlegung des Schwerpunktes des faktischen Lebens in die Selbstwelt*]" (G58 61). What this title seems to indicate is that there is something that *sometimes* happens in life, but which is by no means a necessary feature of life. Were it not so, it would seem odd to claim that a particular historical phenomenon offers something paradigmatic of it. In the section after this, Heidegger again reverts to the term *'Zugespitztheit.'*

Later supplementary remarks, however, tend to multiply the confusion. Here one reads that "[t]he self-world does not only have this special functional tendency in significant personalities, rather, *every* psychic life lives in some way or other centered on a self—even if in an implicit way" (G58 206). He goes on to designate this more *general* feature of life by the term *'Zugespitztheit'* (G58 206). The point here is that *'Zugespitztheit'* is not an event confined to the few, but is, in principle, a possibility open to all. That is, "significant personalities" are simply more visible instances of a general ability to "own up" to one's life.

The term *'Zugespitztheit'* is thus employed equivocally in two distinct senses by Heidegger. I think these senses can be clearly distinguished from one another, as I have indicated above. One sense is supposed to designate a general feature of life, a feature that Heidegger later comes to call *Jemeinigkeit* or "in each case my own-ness." This refers to the *personal* nature of human existence, to the fact that it is indexed in each case to a unique individual who has a unique life history. This is true regardless of whether or not anyone realizes it about herself. The other sense indicates, albeit vaguely, a *kind* of life that conforms to some kind of ideal of individuality. *'Zugespitztheit'* indicates what happens in a life that is *one's own* in some richer sense than in the general indexicality of life. I do not think there is a principled way of settling which thing this term should refer to, but the fact that it seems to be used in the second sense, at least when it is introduced, lends warrant to restricting it to this.

It is Heidegger's appropriation of Dilthey's thesis on the *religious* origins of the personalist tradition and its importance for grounding an "original science [*Ursprungswissenschaft*]" of historical life that is of most interest to me. Heidegger's own take on these ideas at this stage is quite clear from his explicit remarks. What is most important to him is the "radical inversion of the direction of the tendency of life—one has in mind particularly world-denial and asceticism" that one finds in the earliest Christianity (G58 61). At the same time, he notes that, over time, "the inner experiences and new attitudes towards life" are constricted or obscured by "ancient science" (G58 61). This by now should be a familiar Heideggerian trope: the "Greekification" of Christianity. Like Dilthey, however, Heidegger is aware of the continual protest on behalf of religious life against metaphysical obfuscation, citing figures such as Augustine, Bernard of Clairvaux, Bonaventura, Eckhart, Tauler, and Luther (G58 61).

In this lecture course, Augustine's *Confessions* seems to be particularly important to Heidegger, due not only to its place in intellectual history, but also to "a new attitude toward the self-world" that "erupted" within this classic work (G58 62). In a later supplementary remark, Heidegger again characterizes this religious protest as a "violent eruption" and singles out Augustine, Luther, and Kierkegaard as paradigmatic instances (G58 205). On Heidegger's view, it is in the works of these thinkers, rather than in Descartes's *Meditations*, that the uniqueness and autonomy of the individual have received decisive expression (G58 205).

As Heidegger's thoughts on these issues develop, he comes to express the idea that Christian religious experience is uniquely disclosive of personal life in slightly different ways. None of these differences, however, seem to indicate any lessening of a commitment to the fundamental idea. During WS 1921–1922, as I have already discussed at several points, Heidegger tells the story of the "Greekification" of "Christian life-consciousness" once again (G61 6/6). What is new about the way the story gets told here is that *Luther* replaces Augustine as the most important figure. At the same time, the story is extended to include post-Reformation Protestant theology, which Heidegger regards as the "root soil of German Idealism" (G61 6/6). The philosophy of subjectivity *par excellence* is thus linked to the reassertion of personal life in Christian mysticism and the young Luther. Heidegger puts the claim quite strongly: "Fichte, Schelling, and Hegel were theologians, and Kant can be understood only in terms of theology, unless we would make of him the mere rattling skeleton of a so-called epistemologist" (G61 7/7). Moreover, he attributes this insight directly to *Dilthey*. Roughly the same story is told in the contemporaneous Natorp Report from October 1922:

> The idea of man and of human Dasein taken as the starting point in this Graeco-Christian interpretation determined the philosophical anthropology of Kant and that of German Idealism. Fichte, Schelling, and Hegel came out of *theology* and received from it the basic impulses of their speculative thought. This theology is rooted in the theology of the Reformation, which succeeded, only in very small measure, in providing a genuine explication of Luther's new fundamental religious position and its immanent possibilities. (NB 21 f./125)

Luther, in turn, was himself shaped by the tradition as it had been up to him, a tradition Heidegger traces back to the earliest works of Christian theology, i.e., Paul's epistles and the Gospel of John (NB 23/126). This passage also seems to suggest, albeit indirectly, that something has been overlooked in this tradition and that it would be worthwhile to go back and work out just what the "fundamental religious position" articulated by Luther involves. That Heidegger had such a reappropriation in mind is, as a matter of fact, demonstrated by the historical facts: he lectured on Paul during WS 1920–1921, on Augustine during SS 1921, and on Luther in 1924. What Heidegger maintains is that something went somehow awry during the period between Luther and the German Idealists. It is not too difficult to see what this is: the reassertion of Greek metaphysics, particularly the category of the *subject*, culminates in the reflective philosophy of the idealists.

In SS 1923, Heidegger again takes up the traditional concept of humanity and distinguishes two alternative elements in it: (1) a human being as a rational animal, and (2) a human being as a *person*. According to Heidegger, "[t]he second concept arose in the Christian explication of the original endowments of man as a creature of God, an explication which was guided by revelation in the Old Testament" (G63 21/16). He traces out the peregrinations of this idea through the New Testament, patristic theology, medieval theology, and the Reformation. "From here the interpretation of personhood proceeds via German Idealism to Scheler" (G63 24/20).

The importance of these reflections for Heidegger is made clear by his remark that "[i]t is only from out of and on the basis of this situation that the meaning of ideas of humanity, personhood, being-a-person can be understood, i.e., as certain formalizing detheologizations [*Enttheologisierungen*]. Cf. Kant, *Religion Within the Limits of Reason Alone* (1793)" (G63 26/21 f.). What Heidegger is particularly interested in is Kant's notion of a "person" as something worthy of *respect*, as well as Max Scheler's development of this idea in the context of a philosophy of life. Heidegger's worry is that through being mixed with the Greek idea of the "rational animal," the original Christian concept of person became universalized and thereby watered down to the point that what is valuable about persons is not that they are unique creations of God, but that they have the capacity for knowledge.

In all of this, the original theological anthropology has been trivialized and obscured almost beyond recognition. Heidegger approvingly quotes Kierkegaard, who also worried that personhood had been reduced by modern philosophy to being a specimen of a species with special cognitive endowments (G63 108/83). Genuine theological anthropology, according to Heidegger, is motivated not by general definitions but by the specific *experience* of the individual in her situation before God. As Heidegger puts it here:

> The formation of the state of the believer is now in itself motivated out of the respective [*jeweiligen*] primordial experience of being-sinful at the particular time, and for its part this experience is motivated from out of the respective primordiality or, alternatively, nonprimordiality of the relation to God at the particular time. (G63 28/23)

The advantage of this sort of anthropology, as Heidegger (following Dilthey) sees it, is that rather than originating in some *a priori* metaphysical system, it *emerges* from the concrete, living situation of the actual person in her life with or without God; at its best, it expresses the full richness of historical reality. In a later seminar discussion, Heidegger explicitly identifies this sort of anthropology with Luther's "Heidelberg Disputation" of 1518 (S 108). By way of contrast, "[i]n the modern philosophical idea of being-a-person, the God-relation constitutive for the being of man is neutralized into a consciousness of norms and values as such" (G63 28f./23). A person becomes simply the "ego-pole" of general intentional relations.

All these texts from the early 1920s show that Heidegger is, beyond a doubt, committed to something very much like Dilthey's thesis about the assertion of unique individuality and personal life against metaphysics. In the preceding chapter, I showed how Heidegger conceives of metaphysics as an extension of life's everyday tendencies toward self-avoidance and depersonal-ization. Throughout the same period, Heidegger speaks favorably of, and uses the language of, Romantic personalism. Not only does he appropriate the *ontological* view that life is radically individuated, in contrast to Enlighten-ment ideas about "universal humanity," he also clearly endorses some ideal of "wakefulness," "inner truthfulness," or "life-intensification."[22] Both the on-tological point and the moral point belong together in the tradition that flows from Herder to Dilthey. What Heidegger maintains, following Dilthey, is that the roots of this tradition lie not in the Greek notion of the "rational animal" but in the biblical and primitive Christian experience of the individual's re-demption from sin. It is, moreover, quite uncontroversial that, at least during the early 1920s, Heidegger was intensely interested in arriving at an original understanding of this primitive Christian experience. Similarly, it has long been recognized that the notion of *authenticity*, at least as this appears in *Being and Time*, owes a great deal to the insights Heidegger had gained while carry-ing out this project. What has not been seen is that "authenticity" itself repre-sents the fruit of Heidegger's attempt to reinvigorate the core ideal of Romantic personalism by returning to its religious roots.

Primitive Christianity as Paradigm

I have already presented what I regard as conclusive evidence that Heideg-ger himself regarded primitive (i.e., New Testament–era) Christianity to be a historical paradigm for an authentic way of life (chapter 1). By itself, this would be an interesting claim, but it would also be one that ultimately does little to shed light upon Heidegger's discussions of authenticity. However, the task of interpretation is greatly facilitated by the fact that, during WS 1920–1921, Heidegger spends about half a semester lecturing on the "factical life-experi-ence" of the primitive Christian community. If one takes seriously the paradig-matic status of primitive Christianity for Heidegger, as I have argued one ought to do, then one has a rich body of primary source material at one's disposal which can, I am confident, do much to help us understand Heidegger's ideal of authenticity.

The classic treatment of this lecture course comes from Thomas Sheehan's well-known essay. Sheehan performed an invaluable service for scholars by providing a detailed account of Heidegger's early lectures on primitive Christianity a decade before the text of the lectures was made available to a general audience.[23] Sheehan's reading is guided by the idea that Heidegger's discussion during WS 1920–1921 anticipates the key ideas of *Being and Time*, particularly temporality [*Zeitlichkeit*]. On this reading, the core "existential categories" of Heidegger's treatise, e.g., understanding [*Verstehen*], affect [*Befindlichkeit*], ability to be [*Seinkönnen*], and facticity can all be located within Heidegger's discussion of primitive Christianity. However, Sheehan's reading of this crucial text largely neglects its importance with respect to authenticity. I hope to correct this lack in the following discussion.

The basic feature of primitive Christian life-experience, as Heidegger sees it, can be stated succinctly as follows: Christian life is defined by uncanny uncertainty that is suspended between the incalculable eruption of the "proclamation" and the incalculable arrival of the Parousia. Taking this formulation, which is admittedly abstract, I want to expound Heidegger's understanding of Christian life-experience as paradigmatically *authentic*. I begin with the importance of the "proclamation [*Verkündigung*]," or, as New Testament scholars are wont to call it, the *kerygma*. Heidegger is quite clear about the decisive role this plays in Christian life. "The factical life-experience of the Christian is historically defined to the extent that it always begins with the proclamation" (G60 116). This idea is spelled out in more detail a bit further on: "Christian factical life-experience is historically defined in that it originates with the proclamation, which comes to a human being in a moment, and is continually co-actual in the enactment of life" (G60 117).

The point that the proclamation is "continually co-actual in the enactment of life" is especially important to Heidegger's account. What it indicates is that the relation between proclamation and life is much deeper than a commonsense theory-practice model would seem to suggest. In other words, that which is proclaimed is not a neutral theory about the objective nature of reality, but something more akin to a personal *address*. One way to help understand what Heidegger is getting at here in 1920–1921 is to look to his brief account of "Christianness" in 1927. Here he notes that revelation is not a matter of imparting information about "present, past, and imminent happenings; rather, this imparting lets one 'part-take' of the event of revelation [. . .]" (G9 53/44). Response to the proclamation amounts to participation in the special "history" or "destiny" that is grounded in it. In other words, the proclamation is integral to one's identity.

What is it that is "proclaimed"? Heidegger formulates this in different ways during his discussion. While absolute precision would be helpful here,

we have to keep in mind that Heidegger is giving a lecture course on phenomenology, not writing an essay in New Testament scholarship or in dogmatics.
At times, he takes up the Pauline-Lutheran message of "preaching the cross,"
the "scandal of the cross" (e.g., G60 144). At another point, the subject matter
of the proclamation is Jesus himself, the Messiah who has *already* come
(G60 117). With respect to this formulation, it is worth observing that Heidegger notes earlier on that the expression "word of God" must be taken both
objectively and subjectively. That is, the proclamation belongs to God, while
at the same time God himself comes to language in the preaching of the cross.
All these formulations point to the idea, familiar from recent theology, that
God himself somehow "comes to language" in the proclamation.

The "how" of such a proclamation is particularly important for Heidegger: it "breaks in [*einschlägt*]" (G60 143). As the word *of* God, it is not like
worldly speech, not like a historical report. Instead, it radically *interrupts* the
normal flow of events. The proclamation delivers a "shock [*Anstoß*]," something that should not be concealed by assimilating it to other ways of speaking
(G60 144). This is evident from the manner of Paul's delivery: "not in wise
discourse [*Weisheitsrede*], not in much chatter, through which the cross would
be emptied of meaning, but rather simply through his fittingly unpretentious
talk" (G60 144). A proclamation such as this does not provide one with a new
theory about life, but rather reorients one's whole existence. As Heidegger puts
it, commenting on 1 Corinthians, "the Gospel is power and it has the basic
enactment of faith" (G60 136). One is called upon not to file it away as useful
information, but to persevere in "anxious worry [*Bekümmerung*]," to "authentically appropriate [the proclamation] in factical life-experience [. . .]"
(G60 137). The "proof" or "demonstration" of what is proclaimed is thus not a
matter of apodictic deduction; rather, it lies in the proclamation itself, in its
ability to radically interrupt life and reorient it, or, as Paul puts it, in "spirit"
and in "power" (G60 137).

Both Paul and the community at Thessalonica share the common "condition" of those whose lives have been forever interrupted (G60 93). Heidegger
calls this their common "having already become," or "being-already [*Gewordensein*]" (G60 93).[24] As Heidegger puts it, "their being-already is also the
being-already of Paul" (G60 93). Paul, as the one who has been called to
proclaim the message of the cross, is one who has already entered into their
lives in a decisive way (G60 94). "Their being-already is bound together with
his entrance into their life" (G60 94). What does Heidegger mean by their
"being-already"? He characterizes this as "a reception of the proclamation
[. . .] in great tribulation [*Trübsal*]" (G60 94). Here again, we can see that the
proclamation is not just neutral information, but is something that radically
disrupts the course of their lives. "Being-already is understood in such a way
that, with the reception, that which is received pushes the one who receives
into an effective connection with God" (G60 94f.). That which has been
received determines the "how" of factical life (G60 95). Paul's language is

quite unequivocal on this point: "We also constantly give thanks to God for this, that when you received the word of God that you heard from us, you accepted it not as a human word but as what it really is, God's word, *which is also at work in you believers*" (1 Thess. 2:13, emphasis added).

By characterizing the reception of the proclamation in terms of "being-already" or "having already become," Heidegger is trying to drive home this point about the nature of this radical interruption. Hearing the word of God, which comes in "spirit and power," is not like listening to a philosophy paper. Its interruption irrevocably changes the way one lives. From 1 Thessalonians, Heidegger learns that this amounts to an "*absolute reversal* [*Umwendung*]," a "turning *toward* God and *away* from idols" (G60 95). Or, more explicitly, "[t]he absolute turn towards God is explicated within the enactment sense of factical life in two directions: *douleuein* and *anamnein*, running the course of one's life before God [*Wandeln vor Gott*] and waiting upon him in service [*Erharren*]" (G60 95). The reception of the proclamation is the "achievement of a living, effective connection with God. God's being present has a fundamental relation to the journey of life [*Lebenswandel*] (*peripatein*). The reception is itself a living before God" (G60 95).

So far, it is safe to say that Heidegger's analysis anticipates a good deal of the "word-event" or "New Hermeneutic" theology that developed during the 1960s. The Pauline proclamation of the one who is crucified, but who is also the Coming One, is *eschatological*. It is the incalculable word *of* God. It breaks in upon life, utterly transforming it and reversing its course. Among contemporary theologians, Jürgen Moltmann has placed eschatology at the very center of his thought. In his most recent work on eschatology, we find the following discussion, which, I think, Heidegger would largely concur with:

> The prophets "interrupt," but not just for a moment; they call the people to the conversion of the courses of time. Conversion and the rebirth to a new life change time and the experience of time, for they make-present the ultimate in the penultimate, and the future of time in the midst of time.[25]

Or, consider what Moltmann says a bit later:

> Entering into God's coming future makes possible a new human becoming: "Arise, *become* light, for your light is *coming*, and the glory of the Lord is rising upon you" (Isa. 60:1). The proclamation of the near—the coming—the arriving kingdom of God makes human conversion to this future possible. 'Be converted, for the kingdom of heaven is at hand' (Matt. 4:17).[26]

With the latter point, we come to the core of the uniquely Christian experience of time. The Christ of God has *already* come to the world, but redemption is *not yet* fulfilled. Thus the proclamation that interrupts the flow of events is not simply the announcement of a past event, but the anticipation of a new era. Through the proclamation, the Christian is lifted out of the world, as it were, and suspended in a kind of uncanny position that Heidegger tries to express with words like "tribulation [*Trübsal*]," "affliction [*Bedräng-nis*]," "distress [*Not*]," and "anxious worry [*Bekümmerung*]."[27] The recurring feature of Christian life is that it has been *interrupted* or *broken up*: "Christian life is not continuous and linear, but is broken up: all the relations to the surrounding world must pass through the context of enactment of the being-already [. . .]" (G60 120). This "brokenness" is the root of the tribulation and distress of life (G60 121). Consider his introductory remarks regarding the expectation of the Parousia:

> The expectation of the *Parousia* of the Lord is decisive. The Thessalonians hope for it not in a human sense, but rather in the sense of the experience of the *Parousia*. This experience is an absolute affliction [*Bedrängnis*] (*thlip-sis*) which itself belongs to the life of the Christian. The reception (*de-chesthai*) is a placing of oneself into distress. This affliction is a fundamental characteristic, an absolute anxious worry in the horizon of the *Parousia*, of the end-time return. (G60 97f.)

The "natural idleness" of the Thessalonians, however, quickly asserts it-self, and they wonder aloud *when* the eschatological event will be consum-mated. For Paul, however, what matters is "how I comport myself to it in an authentic [*eigentlich*] life" (G60 99f.). The proper relation, quite evidently, is not simply the idle expectation of a future event, but rather the transformation of life, which Heidegger expresses as "placing oneself into distress" (G60 102). Here it is helpful to recall Heidegger's discussion of confessional literature from WS 1919–1920, where *both* Augustine and the primitive Christian com-munity were paradigms. For Augustine, the reception of the proclamation puts one into question: "*mihi quaestio factus sum.*"[28] By interrupting one's life, such an event throws one's life as a whole into relief. It makes possible a renewed struggle for the *meaning* of one's life, such as is clearly attested in confessional literature.

Paul gives the Thessalonians an answer which forces them back upon themselves. He does not give them a date and time, nor does he say that he does not know the answer. Rather, he tells them that they *already* know (G60 102f.). Then he presents them with two alternatives: a life of complacent "darkness" or one of sober "wakefulness." The first is the way of those who cry, "Peace and security!" They find no motive for disquiet [*Beunruhigung*], ori-ented as they are to the daily concerns of life. They "cling on to the world," since it provides them with the peace and security of the everyday routine of life (G60 103). "Sudden destruction" is their fate: "They are overwhelmed by it, they do not expect it. [. . .] their expectation is absorbed in what lies present before them" (G60 103). Heidegger's gloss continues: "They cannot rescue themselves because they do not have themselves, they have forgotten the ownmost self [*das eigene Selbst*], because they do not have themselves with the clarity of authentic [*eigentliche*] knowing" (G60 103).

What this suggests is that the partisans of "peace and security" have somehow or other alienated themselves from their own lives as affairs that they themselves are called upon to define. The unnerving reality of being radically individuated seems to have escaped them on account of their preoccupation with worldly affairs. To avoid "distress" in this context is to fail to "become an enigma to oneself," to fail to make an attempt to work out the meaning of one's life for oneself. Hence, this is ultimately a failure to recognize one's own life *as* one's own. This is why Heidegger describes it as a failure of self-knowledge.

Paul characterizes the alternative in 1 Thess. 5:4: "But you, brothers, are not in darkness, so that the day might overwhelm you like a thief." "Day," in this passage, on Heidegger's reading, has a double signification: (1) the "light" of self-knowledge, and (2) the actual "day of the Lord" (G60 104). Paul urges the believers to "be wakeful." Such a life is one for which there is no security, unlike those who say "peace and security," and who "submit themselves to what life offers them, occupy themselves with some of the tasks of life" (G60 105). Instead of feeding worldly curiosity about when the day will come, Paul admonishes them to be "wakeful" and "sober" (G60 105). Those who have heard the call "must be in despair, because the distress is intensified and *each one stands alone before God*" (G60 112, emphasis added). Being "wakeful" and "sober" are metaphorical ways of describing the process of owning up to one's life, of taking oneself seriously as an "enigma," to borrow Augustine's formulation. In a Christian context, one might conceive of this as a matter of having to given an *account* of one's life. One *wakes up* to the fact that one must *account* for one's own life. Again, confessional literature illustrates what Heidegger has in mind here. In undertaking to author such a work, one has taken on the burden of having to account for one's life as one's own.

Thus the reception of the proclamation, on Heidegger's plausible reading, involves one in a self-decision (G60 113). In other words, the reception of the proclamation bears on one's identity. This is the real point, according to Heidegger, of Paul's proclamation of the Anti-Christ. What Paul urges upon them is that they must cling fast to what they *already* are in the face of the possibility of deception: "So then, brothers and sisters, stand firm and hold fast to the traditions that you were taught by us, either by word of mouth or by our letter" (2 Thess. 2:15). The point of Paul's second letter is to intensify the "distress" of the community, for he has learned that some have become idle. One cannot simply remain unconcerned; a continual reappropriation of the proclamation, a continual "placing oneself into distress" is required. Heidegger cites Romans 12:2: "Do not be conformed to this world, but be transformed by the renewing of your minds [. . .]," as well as 1 Cor. 4:11, "Become my imitators!"

The call to be "awake" and "sober" is an admonition not to slide back into complacent self-satisfaction. Faith, on Heidegger's interpretation, is not some once-and-for-all achievement, but rather "an anxiously worried arrival into the future," characterized most fully in terms of "struggle" and eschatological "running after the goal" (G60 127f.). Paul admonishes the early church to anxiously reappropriate the calling again and again, so that they might not become cut off from God (G60 140). Paul tries to "constantly thrust open" their "urgency" (G60 141). Accordingly, Heidegger contends that "[t]he *hope* that the Christians have is not simply belief in immortality, but is rather a faithful *perseverance* [*Durchhalten*] grounded in Christian factical life" (G60 151). The point of these remarks is clearly that owning up to one's life is not a once-and-for-all achievement. Having chosen to ground the meaning and overall cohesiveness of one's life on a particular possibility, in this case a life of conformity to Christ, one must continually return to this root commitment. Focus is achieved not simply by making an initial decision, but requires constant vigilance about the way that this decision plays itself out in one's life.

If Heidegger's readings of primitive Christianity were indeed of decisive importance for the development of the ideal of authenticity in his work, then it would be a good idea to take some time to pick out the guiding features of the account just discussed in order to see how they reappear in later discussions. I think close scrutiny of Heidegger's lectures from 1920–1921 shows that all the important features of what he calls "authenticity" are clearly present there. What, then, are these features?

One of the recurring themes in Heidegger's discussion is that of *interruption*. For the primitive Christian community, the normal course of life has somehow or other been radically disrupted. For Heidegger, this disruption is grounded in the proclamation of the incalculable arrival of the Messiah. The life that was being lived, which Paul polemically characterizes as idolatry and sexual promiscuity, has been decisively shaken up. So too has the converts' attitudes toward the future. All eyes are focused not on the fulfillment of particular practical projects, but on the incalculable arrival of God.

One important result of this interruption is that the converts have gained in self-knowledge. This self-knowledge does not seem to have the form of cognition of the metaphysical facts about human nature. It is something much more subtle than that, and is, I think, quite difficult to adequately express. This is a point at which we cannot hope for much more than metaphor from Heidegger. It is as if the converts are *aware* of their lives as *their own lives* for the first time. They have been shocked, awoken somehow from their somnolent existence up until that point. At the same time, they have a definite sense of who they are, "the ones who are called." This is why Heidegger lays so much stress on what he calls the "being-already [*Gewordensein*]." They are "awake" to the fact that their lives are their own. They understand themselves within the framework of the eschatological drama of world history.

A third element of this discussion that is important to bring out more explicitly rests upon this "being-already," the Christians' sense of identity. Paul urges on them that they continually reappropriate it anew, that they not slip back into idleness and complacency. His martial language of "struggle" and his quite evident attempts to increase the distress of the community both testify to the significance of this aspect of Christian life. As I have argued earlier, this is also an important part of Luther's protest against scholastic theology and the medieval penitential system. He taught that "the cross continues until death [. . .]."[29] The Christians have received a call, a call that radically interrupts their lives. But they are admonished to remain true to the call, to reappropriate its disturbing shock again and again, not to get lost in idleness, enthusiasm, or empty speculation about the end of history.

These, then, are the key features of Christian life on Heidegger's reading: interruptedness, self-knowledge, and commitment.[30] These features circumscribe the parameters of what might be called an *eschatological* conception of authenticity. I think this designation is apt in light of Heidegger's emphasis on the notion of a life that has been *interrupted* and consequently placed into "distress [*Not*]" and "anxious worry [*Bekümmerung*]." On one reading, this reflects one of the more important features of eschatology, i.e., the radical interruption of the normal course of events. Significantly, this reading gained a great deal of currency precisely during the earliest period of Heidegger's work. It is not too much of a stretch to maintain that Heidegger was part of the overall revival of eschatology witnessed during the first quarter of the twentieth century. Most important for this development was the neo-orthodox revolt of theologians like Barth and Gogarten against the optimistic, secularized eschatology of historical progress that had dominated the liberal theology of the nineteenth century. Side by side with these systematic developments, interest in the apocalyptic eschatology that informed the earliest Christian thought grew among scholars and historians. The more recent work of theologians like Pannenberg, Jüngel, and, especially, Moltmann has carried on this tradition.

As he searched for a way to reappropriate the historical roots of Romantic personalism, Heidegger embarked upon a decisive intellectual encounter with primitive Christianity. Along with this, he absorbed the spirit of the early twentieth-century "Luther Renaissance" and looked to the early works of the Reformer as an instance of just the kind of reassertion of primitive Christianity that he himself hoped to accomplish. It was during these fruitful years that he located the paradigm for the idea of a life that has been radically interrupted and permanently reoriented. With the parameters of this idea in place, I think we are now in a much better position to understand the rough indications of authenticity in Heidegger's work from the 1920s.

Authenticity

In the preceding chapter, I have presented what I regard as the most fruitful context in which to understand Heidegger's ideal of authenticity, i.e., the Romantic personalist tradition, particularly as represented in the work of Wilhelm Dilthey. This tradition combines a commitment to the unique value of each individual with a normative claim on behalf of an ideal of "being true to oneself." I have shown how Heidegger appropriates these ideas in his own way during the earliest period of his work. He does so by tracing the roots of this tradition back to primitive Christianity in order, through a close examination of the relevant sources, to bring these basic ideas to life once more. The result is a moral ideal heavily influenced by primitive Christian eschatology and its reassertion in the theology of the young Luther. An authentic life, on this view, is one that has been shocked out of its complacency, consequently achieving a new level of self-knowledge and vocational commitment.

During the early 1920s, up to and including the publication of *Being and Time*, Heidegger employs a variety of terms, metaphors, and analogies to capture the ideal of authenticity. Each of these gives voice to slightly different aspects of the ideal in question, and there is no obvious reason to privilege one over the other. Certainly, the most well-known terminology is that of *Being and Time*, with its talk of "conscience," "resolve," "authenticity," and "repetition." There is, however, no suggestion from Heidegger that this vocabulary is final or definitive. To the contrary, everything we know about Heidegger points to the opposite conclusion. Witness his own chosen motto for the "Collected Edition [*Gesamtausgabe*]" of his life's work: "Ways, not works." The conclusion of *Being and Time* itself makes a similar point: "One must seek a *way* of casting light on the fundamental question of ontology, and this is the way one must go. Whether this is the *only* way or even the right one at all, can be decided, only *after one has gone along it*" (SZ 437/487). The titles of two collections of essays by Heidegger also reveal his own recognition of the incompleteness and provisionality of his vocabularies: *Wegmarken*, "pathmarks" or "signposts," and *Holzwege*, "paths that lead nowhere."

With this point in mind, the aim of the present chapter is to explore Heidegger's formulations of the ideal of authenticity in the decade leading up to and including the publication of *Being and Time*. I will argue that, despite the divergent vocabularies, Heidegger remains committed throughout this period to his own version of the Romantic personalist ideal. I will show how the elements clearly articulated in his WS 1920–1921 investigation of primitive Christianity appear again and again throughout his work. I do not, however, maintain that Heidegger employs a univocal *concept* for which he has several different names. To the contrary, Heidegger eschews the traditional philosophical language of concepts as much as he is able, opting instead for his own idiosyncratic vocabulary of "formal indications," which are more like suggestive intimations and metaphors than they are like concepts with necessary and sufficient conditions.

Heidegger's interest in the German youth movements of the 1910s and 1920s, in university reform, and in the communal life of the primitive Church indicate that there is a clear *social* aspect of the ideal of authenticity. Discussion of this aspect is relatively rare in the secondary literature on Heidegger and is usually confined to *Being and Time* or to his more controversial work from the 1930s. This is largely due to the sparseness of Heidegger's own discussions of the issue. All the same, this is something that warrants careful examination. This is particularly the case in the present study, the ultimate aim of which is to grasp Heidegger's understanding of philosophy as *Destruktion*, i.e., as a discipline of critical questioning intimately linked with social, political, and cultural concerns.

The present discussion will begin with a review of some of the most plausible readings of authenticity that have been offered by commentators. I will argue that while each of these succeeds in illuminating certain aspects of Heidegger's thinking, each is incomplete by itself. Following this discussion, I will explore the vocabularies of authenticity that Heidegger employs prior to *Being and Time* (1927). Turning next to the account in *Being and Time*, I will focus on the two elements of this discussion that are less pronounced in earlier accounts, i.e., the "voice of conscience" and the role of history in authentic individuality. Finally, my discussion will conclude with an examination of Heidegger's conception of a community of authentic individuals, a generational "community of struggle [*Kampfgemeinschaft*]."

Reading Heidegger on Authenticity

It is an uncontroversial claim that "authenticity" is one of the central terms in Heidegger's work, particularly during the 1920s. The truth of this claim is reflected in the amount of commentary this theme has received in anglophone Heidegger scholarship. But it is also the case that during the 1990s, the discussion shifted to other aspects of Heidegger's work, particularly those that have come to light through the publication of his earliest lectures at Freiburg and his unpublished treatise *Beiträge zur Philosophie*, written in the latter half of the 1930s. Another contributing factor to this shift is, I think, the renewed controversy over Heidegger's involvement in National Socialism. The suggestion, mostly implicit but occasionally explicit, is that Heidegger's ideal is somehow tainted by his unfortunate political entanglements.[1]

The past twenty-five years have seen a variety of attempts to explicate "authenticity." I would like to single out three of these readings for consideration here. While there are certainly others, I think these interpretations, each in its own way, illuminate important features of Heidegger's thought in a way that many other discussions fail to do. Nonetheless, I also think that as they stand, each one of these interpretations is incomplete. At the same time, I hope I can incorporate the valuable elements of these other accounts, supplement them with what I take to be missing elements, and articulate the whole as a more accurate rendering of Heidegger's position.

The three accounts I have in mind each focus on a particular aspect of Heidegger's notion of authenticity. For the sake of clarity, I have chosen particular designations for each of these accounts. The accounts are: [1] the "ontological" account, [2] the "narrativist" account, and [3] the "emancipatory" account. In what follows, I will briefly discuss each one.

Three Interpretations of Authenticity

The best feature of what I am calling the "ontological" account is that it integrates Heidegger's conception of authenticity into a more general account of his philosophical project as a whole. The project, of course, is *ontology*, meaning Heidegger's lifelong quest after the meaning of *being*. The two commentators who have most clearly articulated this reading are Michael E. Zimmerman and Thomas Sheehan. Zimmerman offers the following by way of a definition of the idea: "To be inauthentic means to objectify oneself as a continuing ego-subject, thereby concealing the fact that one is really openness or emptiness. To be authentic means resolving to accept the openness which, paradoxically, one already is."[2] On Zimmerman's reading, authenticity involves an *ontological* transformation of the temporality of an individual life.[3] What is crucial to this account, however, is that an authentic individual has gained a more "appropriate" understanding of herself.[4] Key elements of Heidegger's overall conception, e.g., *Angst* and the call of conscience, serve to disclose the "truth" about what it is to be a human being.[5] Sheehan gives a parallel reading. Consider the following: "Resolve and authenticity (*Eigentlichkeit*) mean simply waking up to and 'allowing' one's appropriation-unto-beingness (*Ereignis*)."[6] This point is made again later in the same essay, with more detail:

> The excess/recess-dimension is man's *proper* dimension, he is *appropriated* unto it. In order properly to be what he already is, man must re-appropriate his excessive appropriation unto recess, not in the sense of overcoming and controlling it, but in the sense of accepting it as ever recessive. Only because he is *already* appropriated unto this excess/recess-dimension [...] can man acquiesce in and *become* this condition and thus re-appropriate what he properly is, i.e., achieve "authenticity" (*Eigentlichkeit*: "properness").[7]

The attraction of this view, besides its fit with a more general interpretation of Heidegger's *opus*, is that it brings to the fore the *alienated* nature of inauthentic life. As I have already discussed (chapter 3), one of the most important features of an "inauthentic" life is that it entails a *flight* from the finitude of "factical life," along with a concomitant tendency to abdicate self-responsibility and to generally dim down the challenge of having a self. The "ontological" reading of authenticity clearly brings this "alienation," and the overcoming of it in authenticity, to the forefront of the discussion. However, this account also faces some difficulties.

According to what I am calling the "ontological" account, authenticity is best understood as a kind of cognitive achievement. There is a way human beings are, which Zimmerman calls "temporal openness" and Sheehan calls "excessive appropriation unto recess," a way of being that people generally conceal, ignore, or misunderstand. Being authentic is thus a matter of gaining some insight into and then identifying with the way human beings *really* are. On this view, "authenticity" is a term that has its meaning within a more general *theory* about human nature.

The difficulties with this view stem from its abstractness and "theoretical" flavor. The impression one gets is that, on this picture, authenticity is like having the proper *theory* about human nature. Zimmerman seems to be aware of this tension, and he makes it clear that "understanding" in Heidegger does not mean simple cognition of neutral facts.[8] At the same time, however, at points during his discussion, he makes authenticity out to be something like Aristotelian *theoria* or self-contemplation.[9] Inauthenticity is consistently read as some kind of cognitive error, a sort of failure to regard ourselves as we *truly* are. The "theoretical" nature of conception of authenticity gives rise to at least three specific problems.

The first is that it is difficult to pinpoint any link between the cognition of what we are and some kind of transformation of how we behave. By themselves, metaphysical theories about human nature seem to lack motivating power. Some sort of *bridge principle*, either a claim about value or about duty, is needed to translate such a pure theory into action. Imagine, for example, a person who completes a standard measure of intelligence. The results of the measure unambiguously indicate that she has an aptitude for mathematics. By itself, this realization is unlikely to prompt her to undertake any significant change in lifestyle. What she needs is some further claim about how mathematics is *good*, or even *interesting*. Alternatively, she could be introduced to a claim that one has a *duty* to exercise one's intellectual abilities as far as possible. With such claims in place, one can see how a realization about human nature (e.g., having an aptitude for mathematics) could motivate someone to act differently than she had done previously, e.g., by enrolling in a Ph.D. program in mathematics. The "ontological" reading of Heidegger, however, seems to simply assume that the proper theory of human nature, *qua* theory of human nature, provides sufficient impetus for a significant change of lifestyle.

A second difficulty is grounded in Heidegger's assertions to the effect that no explicit reflection at all needs to be involved in authenticity. He carefully and intentionally avoids the language of "theory" and "truth," particularly during the early 1920s. For example, in the review of Karl Jaspers's book, he writes that the enactment of this special possibility has nothing to do with an "attitude of observation" (G9 33/28). In the contemporaneous "Natorp Report," Heidegger stipulates that this "is not a matter of brooding over oneself in egocentric reflection" (NB 14/120).[10] In *Being and Time*, the claim that authenticity is about getting the right theory of human nature is explicitly denied. As I will describe in more detail below, a phenomenon called the "voice of conscience" is the centerpiece of Heidegger's account of authenticity in *Being and Time*. "Voice of conscience" is a kind of catchall designation for the occasional moments in which our own lives are set into relief in such a way that we have the opportunity to take *responsibility* for them. Heidegger makes it clear, however, that the "voice of conscience" does not provide one with any *information* (SZ 273/318). Rather, it "attests" or "bears witness [*bezeugt*]" to something, and the proper response to it is *not* the cognitive achievement of the right theory about human nature, but a *resolve* to live one's own life in one's own way (SZ 300f./346f.). He wants to stress that such a resolve is *not* predicated on "cognitively [*kenntnisnehmend*]" representing our universal nature to ourselves.

Closely linked with this orientation toward theory is the implicit idea, present in this sort of account, that there is something like an "essence" or "true self" that underlies the mere appearances of ordinary life. It is clear, of course, that neither Zimmerman or Sheehan conceives of this basic core of human existence as being a *substance* in the traditional sense. Both are keen to emphasize Heidegger's conception of Dasein as "temporal openness." All the same, I think there is a danger here of sliding into what Heidegger was wont to call the "language of metaphysics." Thus I want to avoid reifying Heidegger's categories as far as possible, and I do not think that the "ontological" account goes far enough in doing so. Heidegger stresses that unlike other accounts of "conscience," his has no recourse to positing explanatory "natures" or other occurrent entities (SZ 275/320). To hold that Heidegger *has* a theory of human nature at all is to overlook the meaning of his repudiation of the metaphysical tradition (see G61 186/139f.; G63 1ff./1ff.; SZ 27/49). Heidegger is not interested in "telling a story," i.e., in "defining a being as being by tracing it back to another being in its origin [. . .]" (SZ 6/25).

The second reading of authenticity I want to consider is what I call the "narrativist" reading. This view has been most fully developed by Charles Guignon, though I think there are elements of Zimmerman's position that come very close to this reading in some respects. The key merit of this account, as I see it, is the recognition that authenticity involves a subtle change in the "how" of our lives, rather than in the specific possibilities that we choose to actualize as authentic individuals. It is, as Guignon puts it, a "matter of style rather than content."[11] This is important because it integrates an understanding of authenticity with Heidegger's conception of the self as a process of identification with a cultural inheritance. Guignon's work is also significant in the challenge it presents to the classic "existentialist" reading of authenticity, as a virtue of the lonely individual who creates her own values.[12] The "narrativist" reading is sensitive to the important role tradition and community play in Heidegger's more general account of selfhood and in his account of authenticity. As such, this view represents a significant contribution to our understanding of Heidegger's work.

According to Guignon, the shift in "style" is best captured on this view through a notion of "coherence" of a person's "life story," or "personal integrity." On this view, authenticity involves somehow projecting a "coherent and unified configuration of meaning for [one's] life as a whole."[13] Guignon clearly conceives of this "configuration" as a kind of narrative structure. Inauthenticity is a failure to be "coherent" or "integrated," while authenticity, characterized by a new "self-focus," results in "coherence, cohesiveness, and integrity."[14]

Despite the obvious strengths of this reading, the notions of inauthenticity and authenticity are much richer than Guignon's account would indicate. As I have argued in chapter 4, "incoherence," or "fragmentation," is indeed an important feature of an inauthentic life. The opposite feature, not surprisingly, is importantly characteristic of an authentic life. Other features of inauthenticity, however, should not be minimized, e.g. complacency, hyperbolic excess, alienation, and self-abdication. By placing "coherence" or "integration" at the center of his account, Guignon overlooks other aspects of authenticity, such as vocational commitment and the need for a special kind of disclosive experience. Guignon's view also makes it difficult to see how all these features fit together. This may, of course, be because there is no single defining sense of "inauthenticity," or of "authenticity" either. But this gives us even more reason to resist casting it in the light of only *one* of its key features.

In addition, I find Guignon's talk of "coherence" as an element of authenticity to be potentially misleading. First of all, the notion of "coherence" is not clearly defined. Guignon offers what appear to be synonymous notions, such as "integrity," "cohesiveness," and "focus." However, none of these are defined, so it is difficult to judge their application to Heidegger's work. Further, it is not apparent that "coherence" is really a term that belongs in company with these others. This is because "coherence" has *epistemic* connotations that these others manifestly lack. It is this epistemic tinge that presents this account with the real danger of heading down the wrong track. In the absence of any further clarification, "coherence" calls to mind something like the Kantian view about the moral value of rational consistency. On such a view, being a moral person turns on the consistency of one's behavior with certain requirements rooted in the way one has to think of oneself in order to be an agent, i.e., as a free rational being. Given Heidegger's well-documented suspicions about the conception of persons as "rational animals," as well as his explicit critiques of Kantian moral theory in *Being and Time* and elsewhere, it is clear that such a notion of "coherence" is deeply incompatible with Heidegger's thinking.

The final account I want to consider is more a hint or an indication of an account than a fully developed view on authenticity. Nonetheless, there are definite features of Heidegger's talk that are clearly articulated in this nascent reading. This third account emerges from the work of John Van Buren on Heidegger's earliest period. Given its emphasis, I have chosen to call it the "emancipatory" reading. Van Buren's interpretation is evidently influenced by his own readings of figures like Levinas and Derrida. Indeed, Van Buren unhesitantly asserts that the young Heidegger comes very close to Levinas.[15] On this view, the real problem with inauthenticity is that it *depersonalizes* life. What Heidegger urges against this is that "[t]he self is not a thing, an assemblage of thingly parts, or an instance of a universal, but rather a nonobjectified, unique, unitary, personal, self-caring, and ultimately temporal site of the historical worlding of being."[16] Young Heidegger attacked the totalizing, homogenizing effects of metaphysics and ideology in the name of the emancipation of the unique individual, protesting all along against the "dictatorship" of the "one" and its calculative mastery over the individual.[17] Heidegger's ideal, which owes a great deal to Schleiermacher, is on this view a free community of individuals, each of whom realizes his or her own personal vocation.[18]

There are several interesting points about this account. First of all, it does justice to the Romantic personalist origins of Heidegger's notion of authenticity in a way the others do not. Moreover, it suggests that the authentic person has broken out of the dictatorship of the "one" and its various ideological manifestations and so no longer remains complicit in these. The only problem with Van Buren's view, as I see it, is that Heidegger's position is not sufficiently distinguished from other emancipatory critiques, such as that of Levinas or

Derrida. On the whole, however, I find that Van Buren has provided a valuable reading that I hope to develop and to supplement in what follows.

Authenticity before *Being and Time*

It is a fact about anglophone Heidegger scholarship that, with a few relatively recent exceptions, almost all the literature on authenticity has focused on Heidegger's 1927 treatise *Being and Time*, whereas his work *prior to* this publication has not received as much attention. For example, the debate sparked by H. Dreyfus's account in *Being-in-the-World* has looked only to *Being and Time* for resolution. The only monograph exclusively devoted to the subject, Michael E. Zimmerman's *Eclipse of the Self* (1981), while it treats Heidegger's intellectual development before *Being and Time*, devotes the bulk of the account to this work and to Heidegger's later thought. All of Charles B. Guignon's discussions of authenticity, beginning with *Heidegger and the Problem of Knowledge* (1983), appeal only to *Being and Time*. Much of this is simply because Heidegger's pre-1927 work only became available for the general community of scholars during the 1990s. Moreover, *Being and Time* contains Heidegger's most detailed and sustained treatments of the idea.

In what follows, I will depart from these trends and focus on Heidegger's brief but highly suggestive discussions of authenticity prior to *Being and Time*. On one level, it is not strictly correct to call these discussions of "authenticity" at all, since the term itself only starts to be used frequently by Heidegger around 1924, becoming standard usage by the time of *Being and Time*. All the same, an idea that recognizably conforms to the contours of both the "eschatological" conception sketched out in the preceding chapter (chapter 5) and much of Heidegger's more detailed treatment in *Being and Time* can be easily discerned in many of his works from the period immediately following the First World War.

Earliest Indications: 1919–1920

In my discussion of Heidegger's evident affinity for the ideals of Romantic personalism, I called attention to several indications of a practical ideal in his earliest work, particularly from his lecture courses of 1919–1920 and his early correspondence with the pedagogical theorist Elisabeth Blochmann. Most of these discussions, while showing Heidegger's Romantic personalist leanings, are not particularly full of content. In his lectures, he speaks formally and succinctly about "life-intensification" and "intensifying concentration [*Zugespitztheit*] toward the self-world." Two of his more detailed discussions from this period can, however, be singled out to provide a basic working idea.

I have pointed out both of these passages in my previous discussion (chapter 1, chapter 5), but they are worth reprising to provide a clear point of reference for discussion. The first comes from the lecture course for the SS 1919:

> Moreover, there are genuine life-experiences, which grow out of a genuine life-world (artist, religious person). Depending upon the genuine motivational possibilities, there arises the phenomenon of life-intensification (in the opposite case, minimizing of life). This phenomenon is not determined by a feeling of experienced content. There are people who have experienced much in various "worlds" (artistically, etc.) and yet are "inwardly empty." They have reached only a "superficial" experience of life. Today, the forms of life-intensification are becoming ever more pregnant, fraught with meaning. "Activism" is in motive genuine, in form misguided. The "free German youth movement" is in form genuine, but without fertility in its setting of goals. (G56/57 208/175 f.)

Heidegger's remarks here are certainly suggestive of some substantive ideal, but he ultimately gives us little to go on. Two phenomena seem to be linked: "genuine life-experiences" and "life-intensification." They are contrasted with a "minimizing of life [*Lebensminderung*]" or "superficial [*flächigen*]" experience of life. Following Guignon's terminology, drawn from a consideration of other sources, we can see that this ideal is more a matter of the "style" of life than of its content. Its opposite numbers are "inwardly empty," though perhaps rich in content. It is difficult to make out from this passage exactly what Heidegger means by this. He gives the example of someone who has "experienced" much in art. The impression one gets is of a person who has seen a good bit of art, has a good deal to say about it, and yet is somehow missing something that would make her artistic experience "genuine."

Matters might be slightly clearer if we look at Heidegger's other example, the "free German youth movement." The German youth movements were part of a general attack on industrial modernity, typified in other lands by figures like D. H. Lawrence and Fyodor Dostoyevsky (both of whom Heidegger read). These groups rejected what they took to be the depersonalization of modern mass society and sought to re-establish the primacy of the human bond over what they viewed as its destruction through machines and urban civilization.[19] The challenges of post–First World War reconstruction, and the collapse of the Bismarckian state, lent new life to these sorts of organizations. "Genuineness" was something of a slogan amongst the youth movement's adherents and was employed in their valorization of rural communal life against anonymous urban life and of personal charisma and commitment against conformism and pedantry. Heidegger seems to certainly be appealing to these sorts of values in the brief passage quoted above. The passage also clearly shows that he has some reservations regarding these popular movements. This suggests that he has his own definite views on just what an "intensified" or "genuine" life really amounts to. As I have already pointed out (chapter 5), the German *Jugendbewegung* was an incredibly diverse historical and cultural phenomenon. On the one hand, the neo-Romanticism characteristic of some elements in the movement is consonant with some of the basic ideological commitments of the Conservative Revolutionaries. At the same time, Jewish, Protestant, and Roman Catholic tendencies were also strong, as were Marxist and neo-socialist ideas. Thus, an affinity for the youth movement tells one little, by itself, about a person's political inclinations.

One has to look elsewhere to find Heidegger expounding his own version of Romantic personalism. A lengthy passage from one of his early letters to Elisabeth Blochmann presents the most detailed articulation of Heidegger's thinking at this stage in his career:

> It is a rationalistic misjudgment of the essence of the personal stream of life, if one intends and demands that it vibrate in the same broad and sonorous amplitudes that well up in graced moments. Such claims grow out of a defect in inner humility before the mystery and grace-character of all life. We must be able to wait for the tautly strung intensities of meaningful life—and we must remain in continuity with these moments—not so much to enjoy them as to mold them into [*eingestalten*] life—in the continuing course of life, they are taken along and incorporated into the rhythm of all future life. (HB 14)

While this passage is certainly not without its obscurities, it nevertheless gives a much better idea of the kind of thing Heidegger is after in the remarks from SS 1919 discussed earlier. Notable in this passage is the notion of "moments" of intensity in life; moments that one cannot create or will, but which one must instead wait upon in "inner humility before the mystery and grace-character of all life." Unfortunately, Heidegger does not give us any examples of these sorts of moments, but I think we can get a good idea of their main feature. These "graced moments" *interrupt* the regular flow of life, they are qualitatively different in some way. Heidegger tells his friend Blochmann that these moments are analogous to the "tautly strung" moments of special intensity in a musical composition. Heidegger is concerned that we not let them slip away, beneath the ordinary flow of our workaday existence. Moreover, he cautions against enjoying them for their own sake, like so many aesthetic adornments appended to an otherwise trivial and boring existence. These moments somehow provide life with a new orientation, which Heidegger later characterizes as a "vehement life," one committed to "one's own unique [. . .] spiritual direction" (HB 14). The interruption is supposed to make it possible to "have" oneself with genuine understanding. They disclose the "direction" of one's life as something that is not "there" like an object, but is rather something that must be "truly lived" (HB 14).

This passage shows that even before his explicit intellectual encounter with primitive Christianity during WS 1920–1921, the basic contours of Heidegger's ideal of authenticity were in place. During WS 1920–1921, he finds what he already suspected, namely, that primitive Christianity is the historical paradigm for a "vehement" life that is "truly lived." In the letter to Blochmann, the key features of authenticity are evident: interruption of the normal flow of life, self-understanding, and vocational commitment. Heidegger no doubt found the ideology of the German youth movement attractive to the extent it articulated similar values. In particular, the value of "genuineness" as opposed to "superficiality" seems to have ranked highly in Heidegger's thinking at this time.

Existenz: 1921–1922

The basic contours of the ideal of authenticity, formulated in neo-Romantic language during 1919–1920, more or less remain unaltered throughout Heidegger's work during the 1920s. What does change is that he begins to articulate this ideal more explicitly in his lectures and other courses than he had done previously. During the lecture course for WS 1921–1922, as well as in the Natorp Report from October 1922, Heidegger deploys new terminology in his discussions of authenticity. This vocabulary reflects his engagement with Karl Jaspers and with Kierkegaard, both regarded as exponents of *Existenzphilosophie*.

The notion of *Existenz* receives its most detailed discussion in the Natorp Report, though it was introduced slightly earlier, in the lecture course for WS 1921–1922. Here, while discussing the contemporary crisis of culture, Heidegger presents his readers with a choice between "theosophical metaphysics and mysticism," the "dream-state" of piety, and another possibility that he only just intimates:

> an actual transformation of facticity in genuine distress, facticity's letting itself be wrested away, which, if defended, constitutes *Existenz* (which is a radical, existentiell *anxious worry* [*Bekümmerung*]). (G61 70/53)

This brief remark encapsulates the ideal that Heidegger tried to express to his friend Blochmann in more neo-Romantic language several years earlier and which he had found decisively instantiated by primitive Christianity. "Facticity," i.e., human life, is "wrested away," placed into "distress," or disrupted in some sense. The ideal that Heidegger is gesturing toward involves "defending" this disruption. Only when the "distress" is fully taken on board by a person, fully integrated into life, can that person be said to have realized the ideal in question, which Heidegger here calls 'Existenz.' He glosses this term with another that emerges in his WS 1920–1921 lectures on primitive Christianity, as well as his SS 1921 explorations of Augustinian *molestia*, i.e., "anxious worry [*Bekümmerung*]." This was used earlier to describe the uncanny, disrupted quality of Christian life, balanced between the irruption of the proclamation and the incalculable arrival of the Coming One. Obviously, "distress" and "anxious worry" are meant to contrast with complacency, which, as I have already discussed (chapter 3), is the dominant attitude of an inauthentic life. Here Heidegger is clearly counseling that this sort of complacency, and the ideologies that foster it, be utterly repudiated.

This brief indication receives a much more detailed elaboration in the Natorp Report of October 1922. The ideal of authenticity is also referred to with the term 'Existenz' in this text. However, Heidegger introduces the idea by drawing a distinction between the "circumstances [*Lage*]" of fallenness and the "situation [*Situation*]" of an authentic existence. The former is meant to capture the totality of the fallen, complacent mode of life, characterized by "unworried security" and the optimism of "business as usual" (NB 10f./117f.). In contrast, Heidegger explains the term "situation" in this way:

> In contrast to *circumstances*, the *situation* of factical life means the stand taken by life in which it has made itself transparent [*durchsichtig*] to itself in its falling and has, in concrete anxious worry at the particular time, *seized upon* the possible counter-movement to the falling of its care. (NB 10/118)

The "wakeful sobriety" that characterized primitive Christian life shows up in this passage as "transparency." The image one gets from these indications is that life has become *aware* of itself somehow, has suddenly recognized that it has been living in the mode of falling. One has "seen through [*durchsehen*]" one's life as it has been lived. This presents a person with an opportunity to take hold of one's life *as one's own*, to *make oneself accountable*. Over against this tranquillity and complacency, one now "takes a stand" by appropriating or committing oneself to a "possible counter-movement." Heidegger does not tell us what this "movement" amounts to here; it is defined purely negatively vis-à-vis the everyday movement of falling. He does employ the familiar language of "anxious worry" as a way of indicating that in taking a stand, life breaks out of the complacency and security of fallenness. Presumably, the idea here is that one can enter into a *struggle* against the somnolent reality of everyday life and against the values and ideologies that uphold it. In a note, he tries to clarify the direction of this indication a bit further:

> "Anxious worry [*Bekümmerung*]" refers not to a mood in which one wears a woebegone expression, but rather to a factical being-resolved [*Entschiedensein*], that is, the seizing [*Ergreifen*] of *Existenz* (cf. p. 13) as something to be concerned about. If we take "care" to be *vox media* [middle voice] (which in itself, as a category of meaning, has its origin in the speech of facticity), then anxious worry is the care of existence (*gen. ob.* [objective genitive]). (NB 193, note 5)

This passage clearly looks ahead to Heidegger's later discussions of "resoluteness [*Entschlossenheit*]" in *Being and Time*. At the same time, one can see how Heidegger's earlier Romantic formulation has been recast in the language of *Existenzphilosophie*, i.e., the language of "resolve," "decision," and "seizing" hold of one's existence. Heidegger also wants to caution his readers against any sort of merely psychological reading of "anxious worry." In fact, he says, this is not a "mood" at all, but rather a shift in the whole "style" of a life. The remark about "care" and the "objective genitive" are meant to indicate the idea that "anxious worry" involves making life into an *explicit* object of concern. This does not, however, mean that life is a project that can be dealt with instrumentally. To the contrary, the instrumental orientation toward life is the hallmark feature of a *fallen* life. Heidegger also wants to stress, in this regard, that any sort of "idealistic" easing of the burdens of life is also a characteristic of falling. This implies that "anxious worry" is not served by decision procedures, practical algorithms, or a normative moral code. What is at issue is owning up to and taking over life as *one's own*.

Later in this text, Heidegger again turns to indicating the ideal of life that he places over against falling. Here he employs the image of a "detour [*Umwege*]" around the ordinary trajectory of life toward self-alienated absorption in the practical world (NB 13/119). This "detour" is "anxious worry about not becoming lost [*Nichtinverlustgeraten*]" in the anonymous complacency of everyday existence. Heidegger again calls this possibility '*Existenz*' (NB 13/120). "As anxiously worried about *Existenz*, factical life is *on a detour* [*umwegig*]" (NB 13/120). This possibility, Heidegger stresses, is not a matter of course, but is very much something that one can fail to achieve.

Moreover, and more importantly, this is a possibility that always belongs only to a "concrete facticity" at the particular time. Thus there is no general truth about what *Existenz* is like, only indications of a "detour" away from everyday modes of living. "The question of what will show up in such *Existenz* cannot in any sense be asked in direct and universal terms" (NB 14/120). A list of propositions that spell out exactly what it is to actualize this possibility will not be forthcoming. Several years later, Heidegger tries to drive this point home again in his address at Marburg on the "Concept of Time." We cannot, he says, simply "cross" out the specificity and irreducible uniqueness of each individual, nor ought we settle for some kind of general "information" about others as a substitute. "I never have the Dasein of the other in the original way, the sole appropriate way of having Dasein: I never *am* the other" (BZ 11). This is not surprising since, as Heidegger makes clear, the very notion at play here is that of a person realizing or taking hold of her own unique individual life. Generalities only serve to mask the radically individual character of this way of life, reducing the authentic person to an instance of an ideal, or, even worse, presenting her with some new tranquilizing formula for self-actualization. The most Heidegger is willing to give us is a series of suggestive indications, along with some more definite articulations of what *Existenz* is not.

Existenz is emphatically *not* a "flight from the world [*Weltflucht*]" (NB 14/120). "What is typical of all such flight from the world," Heidegger says, "is that it does not intend life in terms of its existentiell character. That is, it does not seize upon and stir it up in its fundamental questionability, but rather imaginatively inserts it into a new *world* of tranquility" (NB 14/120). Flight from the world is simply another mask that everyday self-alienation wears in an attempt to escape the "existentiell" character of life, i.e., the inescapable fact that life is in each case my own to be it in my own way. Heidegger's remarks here are close to his earlier reading of Paul's letters to the Thessalonians. Recall his focus on Paul's refusal to spell out the "when" of the Parousia, his chastisement of those who have slipped into idleness, and his admonishment to remain "awake" and "sober." Also parallel is Luther's critique of nominalist theology and the penitential system it served to underwrite; instead of tranquilizing oneself through the remittance of punishment, Luther urges a lifelong path of repentance and self-denial.

Heidegger goes on to spell out *Existenz* a bit further:

> The factical circumstances of life at the particular time are not changed at all by anxious worry about *Existenz*. What is changed is the how of the movement of one's life, and this how can as such never become a matter of publicness and the "one." The concern in one's dealings is [at the same time] a being anxiously worried about the self. And when in factical life one is anxiously worried about *Existenz* in this way, this is not a matter of brooding over oneself in egocentric reflection. Rather, such anxious worry is what it is only as a motion running counter to the tendency of life toward falling [. . .]. Here the *"counter to"* as a *"not"* attests to a primordial achievement that is constitutive on the level of being. (NB 14/120)

At the beginning of this passage, Heidegger is clearly making use of some notion of "inwardness," as he had done earlier in his correspondence with Blochmann and in his famous letter to Father Krebs from 1919. This is an idea one can find in Protestant writers like Schleiermacher and Kierkegaard, who often employ it to describe the uniquely *individual* aspects of life. What is "inward" is "private" and, hence, belongs to one's self alone. Heidegger is making a similar point here by contrasting the "style" of a life with its "factical circumstances." Here, however, he tries to lend some more precision to the idea by using the language of "movement" and the "how" of the movement of life.

Existenz is not some fantastical possibility utterly removed from everyday life in a social environment, but rather a subtle, invisible shift in the "how" or "style" of a life. It is as if everything remains the same on the "outside," while a person is radically altered "within." Here again, reference to Paul and Luther provides more details regarding Heidegger's indications. In his discussion of 1 and 2 Thessalonians, Heidegger focuses in on the *hōs mē*, "as if not," ethos of Paul's letters. The idea is captured by the familiar talk of being "in" the world but not "of" the world. The early Christians live outwardly worldly lives, but their relations to the cares and concerns of everyday life have passed through the radical "brokenness" that characterizes their existence.

Also significant in this passage is Heidegger's stipulation that "anxious worry" does not mean narcissistic or egocentric brooding over oneself. Again, the idea is that *Existenz* is a new "style" or "how" of existing in the same social environment that one has always inhabited. Heidegger wants to avoid conveying the impression that this is a matter of self-contemplation or of getting the right "theory" about human life. Much closer to Heidegger's idea is some notion of *vocational commitment*. This was an important feature of the ideal as it was initially formulated in Heidegger's letter to Blochmann, discussed above. "Having oneself" in an anxiously worried way is not like "representing" oneself to oneself as an object, but is a modification of the *practical identity* that is characteristic of human selfhood more generally. What Heidegger recommends is thus best understood as clear-sighted commitment to one's own unique "spiritual direction," an ideal of taking a stand on oneself as identified with a certain vocational possibility. In one of the letters to Bloch-mann, Heidegger illustrates what he has in mind through his praise of her "commitment [*Verhaftetsein*] to scientific work—out of the total genuineness of your personal being [. . .]" (HB 14).

Another important element of this passage comes right at the end, when Heidegger draws attention to the *negative* definition of this ideal possibility. Heidegger is clearly trying to intimate the *disrupted* quality of a life that "has" itself in "anxious worry." The dominant tendency of life, which by this time Heidegger referred to as "falling," is somehow *negated* or reversed. There is little suggestion as to what effects this abrupt reversal, though Heidegger does briefly discuss mortality and its individuating potential. However this interruption occurs, it is obvious that such an interruption is crucial to Heidegger's account of authenticity. Heidegger's deployment of the language of *negation* places him in the company of the young dialectical theologians of the post–First World War era, such as Karl Barth. Barth's *Römerbrief* is full of highly charged, almost expressionistic depictions of the "crisis" of divine judgment on human vanity, on the divine "No!" to sin and the to the "righteousness of man." This is very much in line with the soteriological conception of the young Luther, who, as I have previously discussed, also employs the language of divine judgment disrupting and breaking down the edifice of human self-satisfaction. This idea of interruption remains a key factor in all of Heidegger's more detailed formulations of the ideal of authenticity, right through to *Being and Time* and his discussion in that work of the intrusive "call" of conscience.

SS 1923: The "Wakefulness" of Factical Life

As the 1920s wore on, Heidegger continued to experiment with other ways of intimating an authentic life. By the summer of 1923, he begins to employ some of the general terminology that shows up later in *Being and Time*. However, in the case of authenticity, he employs language that is unique to this lecture course, i.e., the manifestly Pauline language of "wakefulness." It is worthwhile to briefly examine some of the more interesting points of Heidegger's discussion in this lecture course.

I have already noted that in SS 1923, Heidegger first explicitly draws some systematic link between the temporally particular individuality of life [*Jeweiligkeit*] and the possibility of an authentic existence. At the beginning of this lecture course, he tells his audience that " '[o]wnness [*Eigenheit*]' is, rather, a how of being, an indication which points to a possible path of being-wakeful [*Wachseins*]" (G63 7/5). Note the terminology here: back in SS 1919 Heidegger employs the term "ownness" to describe the value of individuality so highly esteemed by J. G. Herder and his Romantic successors (G56/57 134/114). Just like his predecessors in the Romantic personalist tradition, who rejected Enlightenment conceptions of the "natural man" and stable human nature, Heidegger sees a link between the irreducible particularity and plurality of life and the possibility of individual self-creation or self-ownership as a moral ideal. True to form, though, Heidegger's use of the term "wakefulness" or "being-wakeful" to intimate this ideal is particularly characteristic of his own approach to these matters. As I have argued at length (chapter 5), this approach is best understood as an attempt to reappropriate the primitive Christian roots of Romantic personalism. The Romantic personalist ideal of self-creation, self-expression, or "individuality [*Eigentümlichkeit*]" is expressed now in Heidegger with the Pauline language of "wakefulness."

Heidegger picks up the idea of wakefulness once again a bit later in the lecture. There he characterizes it abstractly as "a possibility of its [facticity's] becoming and being for itself in the matter of an *understanding* of itself" (G63 15/11). The link between individuality, wakefulness, and self-knowledge is not new in SS 1923 but has been a key feature of authenticity all along. This formal characterization nonetheless points back to the Pauline image of the "day" of self-knowledge, while at the same time pointing forward to the notion of "transparency [*Durchsichtigkeit*]," which forms one of the themes in the discussion of *understanding* in §31 of *Being and Time*.

As Heidegger's dense discussion unfolds at this early stage in the lecture, he starts deploying a whole medley of terms, each of which is familiar from other contexts and clearly aimed at intimating the ideal of authenticity. First, he once again gestures toward the possibility of life having a "radical wakefulness for itself" (G63 16/12). Then he reverts back to the language of *Existenz*, but not before introducing once again the language of "ownness" or "one's own":

> The being of factical life is distinctive in that it *is* in the how of the being of its *being-possible*. The *ownmost* possibility of be-ing itself which Dasein (facticity) is, and indeed without this possibility being "there" for it, may be designated as *Existenz*. (G63 16/12)

Heidegger rounds out this medley of terms with the remark that the possibility under consideration here is the possibility of "authentic be-ing itself [. . .]" (G63 16/12). In just a single paragraph, all the designations for authenticity that Heidegger employs during the 1920s are clearly present: "wakefulness," "*Existenz*," and "authenticity" itself. That Heidegger found this approach acceptable adds more warrant to the claim that "authenticity" is not the name of a *concept* at all, but rather of an *experience* that Heidegger is perfectly content to intimate with a variety of open-ended and highly metaphorical phrases.

Another important feature of the discussions of authenticity in SS 1923 is that both the *artist* and the *religious person* play the role of exemplars. This has also been a feature of Heidegger's thought since the very beginning, in SS 1919, when he intimates the phenomenon of "life-intensification." The religious paradigm appears in later notes that were included in the edited text of the lecture course. The first clear reference to it comes in a brief note entitled "*Ontology* Natura hominis." Making an obscure reference to Pascal, Heidegger tries to capture the idea thus: "Holding back from a ruinous movement, i.e. being in earnest about the difficulty involved, actualizing the *wakeful* intensification of the difficulty which goes with this, bringing it into true safekeeping" (G63 109/85).

Two later notes, both sketchy, also point to the often-demonstrated paradigmatic status of religion for Heidegger. The first is entitled "Homo iustus," the "righteous man," a key theme in Pauline and Lutheran theology (G63 111/86). The sketchiness of this note renders any clear sense problematic, but Heidegger seems to be drawing some link between theological anthropology and the existential experience of redemption. The note closes with these dark but suggestive intimations: "See especially Paul: glory of *Christos* [Christ] as the Redeemer—the exile of humanity into distress and death! The *death* of Christ—the problem! Experience of death in any sense, death—life—Dasein (Kierkegaard)" (G63 111/86). The following note, "On Paul," is equally sketchy, but the subject of the remarks is easier to make out. "Flesh-*spirit* [. . .]: to be in them, a 'how' as a 'what' [. . .]. Explication of facticity: of the unredeemed and being-redeemed: *huioi theou* [sons of God] (Rom. 8.14)" (G63 111/86). The passage referred to here reads, "For all who are led by the Spirit of God are children of God," and is set within the context of the most eschatological passage in the entire epistle.

Earlier, in the main text of the lecture, it is the artist who becomes the paradigm of "wakefulness" and *Existenz*. Heidegger writes:

> An example: At a critical time when he was searching for his own Dasein, Vincent van Gogh wrote to his brother: "I would rather die a natural death than be prepared for it at the university. . . ." This is not said here so as to give greater sanction to the moaning heard everywhere about the inadequacy of academic disciplines today. Rather, we want to ask: And what happened? He worked, drew the pictures in his paintings from the depths of his heart and soul, and went mad in the course of this intense confrontation with his own Dasein. (G63 32/26f.)

Van Gogh, on Heidegger's reading, clearly staked his very life on the pursuit of his artistic vocation, which he was determined to realize in his own unique way, rather than along the tracks of the sterile academic art of the day. Van Gogh was "searching" for "his *own* Dasein," rather than some instantiation of universal humanity or some predetermined vocational path. Rather than let himself be formed by the shallow whims of the public, Van Gogh "confronted" his "*own*" Dasein. This whole discussion clearly resonates with the Romantic cult of the artist, as well as with Wilhelm Dilthey's interest in autobiography as a window into personal life. The Romantic roots of Heidegger's ideal of authenticity could not be more clearly demonstrated than in these remarks.[20]

Authenticity in *Being and Time*

Up to this point, I have shown that Heidegger's vocabularies change during the course of the 1920s, but his basic commitments remain essentially the same. Throughout the period in question, Heidegger upheld a moral ideal of authenticity rooted in his own appropriation of the Romantic personalist tradition, mediated by Dilthey and nourished by his readings of primitive Christianity. Terms like "inner truthfulness," "wakefulness," and "*Existenz*" are formal indications employed by Heidegger in an attempt to present this ideal without transforming it into a rigid concept or universal moral imperative. By the time *Being and Time* was published in 1927, Heidegger had once again begun to employ a new vocabulary. The central term during this period is "authenticity," which due to its familiarity I have been using to designate Heidegger's ideal in general terms.

In this treatise, Heidegger emphasizes certain elements of his thought on the matter that had received little or no treatment previously. The first, which is not entirely new to *Being and Time*, is the use of the term "conscience" to indicate a part of the total experience of authenticity. While the term "conscience" appears from time to time in writings and lectures before *Being and Time*, it receives by far its most complete treatment in §§54–60 of that work. The second element Heidegger brings into greater relief in *Being and Time* is history, the "history that we are," and its constitutive role in the vocational commitment that forms such an important part of authentic life. Finally, in *Being and Time*, Heidegger articulates more clearly the relation between an authentic individual and the community or group of communities of which that individual is a part. Authenticity, by its very nature, is a style of life that is restricted to an individual. There is no suggestion in any of Heidegger's work from the 1920s that there can be an authentic community as such, as opposed to a community *of* authentic individuals. All the same, he has definite ideas about what the latter would look like and about the social aspects of authenticity. Some of these ideas were also discussed prior to *Being and Time*, particularly in Heidegger's correspondences; however, it is in *Being and Time* that they receive a clear treatment for the first time.

The "Voice of Conscience"

A careful reader of *Being and Time* cannot fail to notice that "conscience" occupies an absolutely central place in Heidegger's account of authenticity in that work. In §54, he tells us that it is the "conscience" that provides the much needed "testimony [*Bezeugung*]" to the possibility of an authentic way of life. In other words, "conscience" provides the crucial "evidence" that authenticity is a real possibility rather than a free-floating abstraction. Earlier in *Being and Time*, Heidegger had expressed the worry that his discussion of authenticity "still hangs in mid-air" (SZ 267/311). Accordingly, following the phenomenological dictum "to the things themselves!" Heidegger is forced to present a detailed explication of the kind of "testimony" that "conscience" provides. Thus it is fair to say that §§54–60, in which this account is given, contain the very core of Heidegger's thought on this issue.

The term "conscience," however, is not new to Heidegger's work in *Being and Time*. To the contrary, it appears in a number of writings prior to the publication of this treatise. More specifically, the term appears in Heidegger's review of Karl Jaspers's *Psychology of Worldviews*, written between 1919 and 1922, in his "Concept of Time" lecture at Marburg in 1924, and in his lectures at Kassel on Dilthey from the same year. The last of these discussions does not differ in any substantial respect from the usage in *Being and Time*. The former two uses are, however, subtly different, and so warrant further discussion. In the Jaspers review and in the Concept of Time lecture, "conscience" is used as a catchall term for what comes to be called "authenticity" in *Being and Time*. As I have already discussed, authenticity involves three components: (1) an interrupting experience, (2) self-knowledge, and (3) vocational commitment. Moreover, as I described in a previous chapter, Heidegger is committed to the idea that tradition, history, and public discourse constitute the content of an individual's identity. All these elements are telescoped into a single point in the notion of "conscience" as it shows up in these texts prior to *Being and Time*.

In the Jaspers review, Heidegger describes a way of "having oneself" in "anxious worry [*Bekümmerung*]," an experience that is not "extraordinary and removed," but can be easily located within "our factical experience of life" (G9 33/28). Heidegger gives the name "conscience" to this "historical experience" (G9 33f./28f.). This is a way of "having" a self that is enacted constantly anew "in a constant renewal of anxious worry that is of necessity motivated by a concern for the self as such, and is moreover oriented in a historical manner" (G9 33/28). This remark should remind one immediately of what Heidegger says in an earlier letter to Elisabeth Blochmann, in which he counsels "molding" the "tautly strung intensities of meaningful life" into the "continuing course of life," such that "they are taken along and incorporated into the rhythm of all future life" (HB 14). At the same time, it harks back to his exploration of primitive Christianity during WS 1920–1921. As I showed at some length in the previous chapter, the issue for Paul, according to Heidegger, is to spur the community at Thessalonica to constantly renew their appropriation of the Gospel by committing themselves again and again to the way of life that accords with it. This renewal of commitment is "historical" in the sense that it requires the *remembrance* of a past experience or message as a future *possibility*.

This whole experience of being "authentically historical" is summed up for Heidegger by the term "conscience," as the following remark indicates:

> In accord with its fundamental sense, "conscience" is understood here as
> the enactment of conscience, and not merely in the sense of occasionally

having a conscience about something (*conscientia*). Conscience is a historically defined "how" of experiencing the self (the history of this "concept" needs to be examined in connection with the problem of existence, and this is not just an academic problem, even if it is already a pressing problem when approached in such a way). (G9 33/28f.)

Heidegger immediately goes on to focus on the "historical" aspect of "conscience" in more detail, admitting that at least on the usual understanding, "history" seems to have little to do with "conscience," since the former is regarded "almost exclusively as something objective, i.e., an object of knowledge and curiosity [. . .]" (G9 33/29). Heidegger's aim is to allow us to experience once more "the meaning of conscience and responsibility that lies in the historical itself," reminding his reader that "the historical is not merely something of which we have knowledge and about which we write books; rather, we ourselves are it, and have it as a task" (G9 33f./29).

In this dense passage, amounting to less than a single paragraph of the text, Heidegger more or less articulates his ideal of authenticity *in toto*. Authenticity is a style or way of life that involves "anxious worry" about the self, as opposed to the usual abdication of responsibility. This "anxious worry" is something that must be renewed again and again, in the form of taking responsibility for the "history that we are." Just what this kind of responsibility entails is not clear from this passage. It is only, as I will show, in *Being and Time* that Heidegger explains it as the choice of a possibility of existence derived from one's shared culture. This element of authenticity, and its connection with conscience, are perhaps more explicit in the 1924 Concept of Time lectures:

The past remains closed off from any present so long as such a present, Dasein, is not historical. Dasein, however, is in itself historical in so far as it is its possibility. In being futural Dasein is its past; it comes back to it in the "how." The manner of its coming back is, among other things, conscience. (BZ 19)

Here again Heidegger contrasts the objectifying view of the past in historical consciousness with an earnest appropriation of one's past as a possibility for the future. One way to understand the latter is as "conscience." Thus in these works preceding *Being and Time*, the term "conscience" is employed by Heidegger as a way of referring to an individual's transformation of some aspect of her own cultural inheritance into a possibility for the future. "Conscience" amounts to giving the past a *new* and *unique* future in the life of a particular individual. "Conscience" is Heidegger's term for being authentically historical.

Later, in *Being and Time*, Heidegger draws the boundaries around "conscience" more tightly, distinguishing this phenomenon from a person's response to it, which he characterizes variously as "wanting to have a conscience," "resoluteness," and "repetition." At this stage in his thought, Heidegger uses the term "conscience" much more narrowly to refer only to the moments of "life-intensification" that interrupt the downward trajectory of inauthentic life.

"This haphazard [*wahllose*] being carried along by the nobody, through which Dasein is ensnared in inauthenticity, can only be rescinded if Dasein is, on its own, brought back to itself from lostness in the 'one'" (SZ 268/312). This requires, he says, that one first of all be "shown" the possibility of being authentic. This is the role that is played by the phenomenon called the "voice of conscience" (SZ 268/312).

It is important to realize that, in this context, "conscience" is a formal indication that is meant to capture something about the structure of a particular concrete experience. In everyday discourse, on the other hand, "conscience" has both moral and quasi-epistemic connotations. The former usage is the more familiar one. Here "conscience" is the "little voice" inside a person's head that supposedly rebukes her for some past action (the "pangs of conscience"), or perhaps gives a warning about embarking on a future course of action. In its epistemic usage, "conscience" connotes something like "judgment," as in phrases like "freedom of conscience." Clearly, Heidegger is using the term "conscience" in a different sense. His choice of terminology, however, is not arbitrary. To the contrary, "moral" and "epistemic" conscience can be regarded as *instances* of the more general experience that Heidegger is trying to indicate.

Heidegger tells us next that inauthenticity is characterized by a failure to "listen" to oneself due to an occupation with "listening" to the "idle talk" of the "one." Dasein, Heidegger says, "pricks up its ears" or "listens in on [*hinhören*]" the "one," a metaphor that calls up images of idle gossip and intrusive curiosity. Rather than taking hold of her own life as something that she must live in her own way, a person might flee away from this by passively "listening in on" the lives of others. This "listening in" is a kind of risk-free contemplation rather than a deeply personal confrontation. This whole image calls to mind the motto that Heidegger chose for his SS 1921 course on Augustine: "A curious lot they are, eager to pry into the lives of others, but tardy when it comes to correcting their own" (G60 158).[21] As a result, Heidegger says:

> This listening in must be *broken*, i.e., a possibility of hearing that in each case interrupts must be given to it from Dasein itself. The possibility of such a break lies in its becoming immediately appealed to. (SZ 271/316)

In order for this kind of interruption to effect the necessary conversion to a new way of life, the "call" must "call noiselessly and without any ambiguity, without a foothold for curiosity" (SZ 271/316). There is little here for one to "listen in on," for Heidegger is describing a kind of direct, and disturbing, disclosure of one's own individual situation. In characterizing this phenomenon as a "call," Heidegger does not mean to imply, he says, that actual vocal utterance is required. He has in mind the simple fact that there are moments in life in which a new understanding of our situation is opened up, often unexpectedly. These moments have a certain degree of obtrusiveness about them. "In the tendency to disclosure which belongs to the call," Heidegger writes, "lies the momentum of a push [*des Stoßes*]—of an abrupt [*abgesetzen*] shake up" (SZ 271/316).[22] This point certainly bears a large degree of similarity with Heidegger's earlier characterization of the Christian proclamation as something that "breaks in [*einschlägt*]," delivering a "shock [*Anstoß*]" that makes possible a reorientation of one's entire way of life (G60 143f.).

Other parts of Heidegger's discussion of the "call of conscience" also highlight the disruptive quality of this experience. The "voice of conscience" is an "appeal [*Anruf*]" to an individual to be herself, a "call up [*Aufruf*]" or a "summons" (SZ 269/314). The term '*Anruf*' connotes, in a military context, a challenge issued by a sentry, whereas '*Aufruf*' or "call up" is used in such contexts to refer to a conscription order. The "voice of conscience" calls a person to join the "battle [*Kampf*]" against an inauthentic way of life.[23] Later Heidegger wants to capture the power of the "voice of conscience" by accentuating its unpredictability. He writes:

> The call is indeed not, and can never be, planned, prepared for, or voluntarily enacted *from ourselves*. "It" calls, against expectation and against will. (SZ 275/320)

This observation harks back to both Heidegger's letters to Elisabeth Blochmann and to his investigation of primitive Christianity. In the former, he is critical of those who "demand" these moments, who fail to "wait upon" them in inner humility before the "mystery" and "grace" of life. In the lectures from WS 1920–1921, it is the "Day of the Lord," which comes "like a thief in the night" which cannot be subjected to rational control procedures. Just as Paul chastised the Thessalonians for their attempt to calculate the date of the Parousia, and Luther attacked the "pig-theologians" who treat God like a cobbler treats his leather, so too Heidegger wants to resist any attempt to rationalize or *explain* the "voice of conscience."

On Heidegger's view, the "voice of conscience" testifies to the power of the unexpected to alter the course of one's life in a profound way, making a new *future* possible for an individual by throwing one's life into relief. Clearly, Heidegger regarded religious experiences as paradigmatic of such "graced moments." I have repeatedly shown how this is the case in the earliest period of his work. The same is true even in 1929, as a letter to Elisabeth Blochmann regarding their mutual experience at the Benedictine cloister at Beuron shows. "Inner truthfulness," he says, "requires those days and hours in which we have Dasein as a whole. Then we experience that our heart must hold itself open in all that is essential to it for grace. God—or whatever you call it—calls each person with a different voice" (HB 31f.). Heidegger takes the ancient service of Compline as an exemplar of this sort of "gift of the moment" (HB 32).

At the same time, Heidegger certainly does not exclude other, non-religious, examples of "graced moments." In 1919, he employs the example of the Theban elders witnessing the sunrise in Sophocles' *Antigone*, citing the German translation by Friedrich Hölderlin (G56/57 74/62f.). In his notes for

WS 1919–1920, Heidegger remarks that these moments can be located in the lives of "artists, scientists, saints, and also in the conduct [*Benehmen*] of every individual in the experienceable life-world, in history, in literary and artistic presentation (Shakespeare's dramas, Dostoyevsky)" (G58 85). In the same semester he also refers to other experiences, like being "on a hike in an autumnal forest," hearing the distant clock-tower of an ancient church strike the hour, being caught outdoors in a thunderstorm, or feeling guilty about something one has said (G58 96 f.). These are all unexpected occasions when one can be "there for oneself." As I have already discussed, it is worth noting that many Conservative Revolutionaries experienced the war as such a life-altering moment, which it no doubt was. While Heidegger occasionally refers to the much-discussed *Fronterlebnis* (e.g., HB 9–12), it is crucial to understand that the preponderance of examples are drawn from other sources, and that *religious* experience is paradigmatic.

The "voice of conscience" in *Being and Time* is a sort of catchall designation for these types of experiences. Heidegger is not suggesting that anyone has ever or will ever experience the "voice of conscience" as such, for the phrase does not refer to a *specific* experience at all. Heidegger is simply using the suggestive term "conscience" to gesture toward the meaning of a particular *type* of experience. It is not immediately obvious why he settled on this terminology. The most plausible explanation is that "conscience" is a term that plays a large role in the tradition of moral and religious thought, from Socrates's *daimon*, to Pauline Christianity, to the "inner spark" of the Godhead in Rhineland mysticism, and to eighteenth- and nineteenth-century moral philosophy.

In his discussions prior to *Being and Time*, Heidegger had more or less left the content of these moments of "life-intensification" indefinite. This is no doubt due to his deep commitment to their radically *individualistic* character and to his concomitant resistance to any attempt to generalize. All the same, in *Being and Time*, he presents a much more complete view of what "life-intensification" involves. One of the most important characteristics he singles out for discussion is the nature of the "voice of conscience" as a "summons" or "call up [*Aufruf*]." The "call of conscience" is a summons to take hold of "one's own self [*Auf das eigene Selbst*]" (SZ 273/317). This does not mean, however, that it provides "information about worldly events" (SZ 273/318). At the same time, one cannot mistake the "direction of impact [*Einschlagsrichtung*]" of the "call" (SZ 274/319).[24] This "direction" points toward taking responsibility for oneself as a person who finds herself in a situation not of her own making, yet forced to make a radical decision to be a certain sort of person. It is emphatically not an occasion for detached "reflection" on the nature of human existence. The "self" that one is summoned to is a *practical task*, not an *object*. Heidegger writes:

> But at the same time this is not the self that can become an "object [*Gegenstand*]" of judgment, nor the self of flustered, curious, and baseless dissection

of its "inner life," not the self of an "analytic" gaping at psychic states and what lies behind them. The appeal to the self does not force it inwards upon itself, so that it can close itself off from the "external world." (SZ 273/318)[25]

Following this description of the way the "voice of conscience" disrupts the complacency and blindness of an inauthentic life, Heidegger tells us that a more complete *ontological* understanding requires that we make it clear "who" does the "calling" (SZ 274/319). An "ontological" account, on Heidegger's view, does not involve the provision of concepts that capture the nature of things, nor of concepts the determine the necessary *a priori* forms of consciousness under which all experiences are to be conceptualized. Nonetheless, Heidegger's curious insistence on finding out "who" it is that "calls" has led many commentators into the trap of reading Heidegger's account as *metaphysical*, i.e., as concerned with providing a *ground* for the "call of conscience." For example, William J. Richardson argues that the source of the "call of conscience" is "[t]here-being in its sheer thrownness as disclosed by the disposition of anxiety."[26] A similar view is offered by Jacques Taminiaux, who tells us that "it is from the Self that the call emanates, it calls Dasein to face its own Self [. . .]."[27] Mark Blitz asserts unequivocally that "Dasein himself [*sic*] is the caller. For it is the man authentically revealed in anxiety, the man who finds himself in uncanniness, who calls."[28] Indeed, most commentators on these pages from *Being and Time* have offered just this sort of a reading.[29]

Heidegger's explicit remarks, both in *Being and Time* and elsewhere, indicate clearly that this sort of *metaphysical* reading is off the mark. Right in the midst of his discussion of the "call of conscience," Heidegger tells us that he wants to reject both "theological" and "biological" accounts that seek to explain the "voice of conscience" in terms of something that is "objectively present [*vorhandene*]" (SZ 275/320). Previously, during WS 1921–1922, Heidegger explicitly separates his own project from any attempt to acquire "new concepts" or a "fantasized representation of new categories" (G61 186/139f.). Indeed, he is comfortable with the assertion that his "hermeneutics of facticity" is "not philosophy at all" (G63 20/15f.). The project Heidegger had undertaken has nothing whatsoever to do with giving "a narrative account of a being" (G20 203/151). Having recourse to *natures* or to *transcendental concepts* here robs Heidegger's account of its idiosyncratic character and belies his own explicit warnings about such readings.

A careful reading of Heidegger's explicit comments about his own project, as well as of the relevant sections of *Being and Time* that deal with the "voice of conscience," simply rules out the usual "metaphysical" way of understanding the question of "who" does the calling. Indeed, it is immediately after raising this mysterious question that Heidegger disavows both "theological" and "biological" accounts. The answer to the question lies, instead, in the observation that "[e]ach Dasein always exists factically" (SZ 276/321). Heidegger unpacks the meaning of this "facticity" as follows:

> It is no free-floating projection of itself, but, by virtue of thrownness as a fact of the being that it is, it has always already been delivered over to existence, and constantly remains so. The facticity of Dasein is essentially distinct from the factuality [*Tatsäschlichkeit*] of something that is objectively present. Existing Dasein does not encounter itself as something objectively present within the world. But neither does thrownness belong to Dasein as a characteristic that is inaccessible and unimportant for its existence. As thrown, it is thrown *into existence*. It exists as a being that has to be how it is and can be. (SZ 276/321)

Being "thrown into existence" is, simply put, the human condition. "Thrownness" indicates our basic experience of finding ourselves already embedded in a "world" of meaningful relationships as soon as we are able to become conscious of it. We find ourselves already speaking a certain language, belonging to a particular social group and family. In any situation in which we find ourselves, we also find ourselves having already made certain choices, undertaken certain courses of action, thereby further implicating ourselves in a web of relations. At the same time, we are "thrown into *existence*." The life we find ourselves already implicated within "is an issue [*es geht um . . .*]" for me, it is "in each case mine [*je meines*]" for me "to be [*zu sein*]" (SZ 42/68 f.). Heidegger's view is that we are always under way in a life, there is always something still outstanding, and our life is something we must ultimately live in our own way. The web of relations into which we have been "thrown" defines the range of possibilities we have and guides our day-to-day activities.

What Heidegger is saying about the "voice of conscience" here is not that there is some "true self" that reaches up from the depths of our inner "being" through some kind of private illumination. Instead, the "voice of conscience" is simply a formal indication for those moments in life in which one's situation discloses itself. This is the situation of finding oneself already under way in a life, with still more life outstanding in the future. The "voice" does not "belong" to anyone or anything. That is why Heidegger tries to capture it through the impersonal locution "it calls me" (SZ 277/322). Heidegger often employs these kinds of locutions as a way of formally indicating the pre-conceptual meaningfulness of human life without resorting to the neo-Kantian view that all meaning rests upon the synthetic activity of a subject.[30] The interesting thing about these expressions, such as '*es regnet*' ("it is raining"), for Heidegger is that they have neither subject nor object. There is nothing that is *doing* the "raining," raining is just *happening*. But in using this kind of expression, Heidegger is simply struggling to find a way of articulating the meaning of life without appeal to concepts or to "natures." In the "it calls me," there is no one and no thing that is doing the calling.

Another way Heidegger tries to capture the meaning of these disrupting experiences is by using the term "guilt" and by claiming that the "voice of conscience" reveals our "guilt" to us. Again, "guilt" is a formal indication rather than some general concept that is supposed to represent the content of a kind of experience. Heidegger is explicit that some "general" sort of guilt is never revealed to us, but always only our own unique, individual version of the human condition (SZ 278/323). "The call gives no ideal, general ability to be to understand; it discloses it as the ability to be of temporally particular Dasein, individuated at the particular time" (280/326).

"Guilt," then, is another formal indication for the human condition, part of which involves being in each case a unique individual. At the most formal level, Heidegger describes "guilt" as "[b]eing the basis for nullity" (SZ 283/329). He explains what he has in mind by first of all referring the reader once more to *facticity*. The human situation, we will recall, is one of being "thrown" into the world, of finding oneself already in a world not of one's own choosing (SZ 284/329f.). One is constantly "delivered over" to oneself, to the painful truth *that* one exists and that one *has to* exist. To "exist," it will be recalled, does not mean simply being there, but rather means being oneself in the "projection" or practical identification with possibilities that one has inherited (SZ 284/330). Hence, "[t]he self, which as such has to lay the basis for itself, can *never* get that basis into its power; and yet, as existing, it must take over being a basis" (SZ 284/330). "Taking over" one's life simply means choosing to live in terms of particular possibility, e.g., a particular career. The tragedy of human life is, of course, that living one possibility means enduring *not* having chosen another. This is the "nullity" or "negativity" of freedom: "Freedom, however, *is* only in the choice of *one* possibility—that is, in tolerating one's not having chosen the others and one's not being able to chose them" (SZ 285/331).

To sum up, the "voice of conscience" is Heidegger's formal indication of those moments in life when our situation is revealed to us in all its forceful "uncanniness [*Unheimlichkeit*]." These moments disclose the painful reality of having to make tragic choices in situations that are not of our own choosing. The "voice of conscience" is a way of capturing the power of the unexpected to make possible a new future for an individual, a future that has been set free for the possibility of living one's own life in one's own unique way. Heidegger, as I have previously shown, often describes the way we spend a good deal of our time trying to ignore this basic human reality. As he puts it here, "Dasein flees before this into the relief of the supposed freedom of the one-self" (SZ 276/321). In other words, we too often abdicate our responsibility for living our own lives in our own way, instead handing matters off to an anonymous public that has already made all of our difficult choices for us.

Resoluteness and Repetition

I have already drawn attention to Heidegger's view of the "voice of conscience" as a "summons [*Aufruf*]" or an "appeal [*Anruf*]." Clearly this phenomenon shares a good deal with the early Christian proclamation, at least as Heidegger understands it. Both the "voice of conscience" and the proclamation are not to be understood as, in the words of *Being and Time*, an "indifferent making known" (SZ 295/341). In other words, one has not understood the "voice of conscience" if it is taken to be the provision of some information about the self, about human existence, or about anything else for that matter. Instead, the "voice of conscience" is like a "challenge [*Anruf*]" issued by another, which calls not for detached observation but for a response of one's whole person.

Hearing the "call" correctly is, says Heidegger, a matter of "projecting oneself" onto one's own being "guilty" (SZ 287/333). As I have already shown, "guilt" is a formal indication of the human predicament, i.e., the situation of finding oneself already in a world, yet called upon to live one's own life in one's own way. Hearing the "call of conscience" means committing oneself anew to living one's own life in one's own way. As Heidegger puts it in *Being and Time*, "[i]n understanding the call, Dasein is *in thrall to its ownmost possibility of existence*. It has chosen itself" (287/334).

Hearing the "call" properly means choosing one's own way of life. Together with this goes an attitude that Heidegger calls "becoming free" for the "call," i.e., a wakeful openness toward the possibility of a "graced moment" that will present a further possibility for self-knowledge and renewed commitment (SZ 287/334). Heidegger calls this "wanting to have a conscience [*Gewissenshabenwollen*]" (288/334). He quickly notes that "wanting to have a conscience" does not mean that one voluntarily brings about or seeks to bring about these "graced moments." Indeed, this is precisely the "rationalistic misunderstanding" of the "mystery" of life about which Heidegger had warned Blochmann in 1919. Instead, "it means solely that one is ready to be appealed to" (288/334). "And what I say to you I say to all: keep awake" (Mark 13:37).

In §60, Heidegger goes a bit further in characterizing our response to the "voice of conscience" as "resoluteness [*Entschlossenheit*]" (SZ 296f./343). This, he tells us, amounts to "one's letting oneself be summoned out of one's lostness in the 'one' " (SZ 299/345). While there can be no doubt that resoluteness is a style of life that is radically different from that which characterizes inauthenticity, Heidegger is strongly committed here, as in his discussions from the early 1920s, to the claim that an authentic individual is not somehow withdrawn from or detached from the world. "The 'world,' " he says, "[. . .] is not 'contentfully' different, the circle of others is not exchanged for a new one, but [. . .] are now given a definite character in terms of the ownmost ability to be oneself" (SZ 297f./344f.). There is no suggestion that one has withdrawn from "actuality" (SZ 299/346). To the contrary, a proper response to the "voice of conscience" involves seizing upon definite possibilities that have been made available to us by the web of relationships in which we find ourselves "always already" involved (SZ 299/346).

The best way to understand "resoluteness" is as a kind of *vocational commitment*. As I have pointed out numerous times, Heidegger was particularly interested in religious life as an exemplification of a proper response to the "voice of conscience." In WS 1920–1921, Heidegger glossed the reception of the Pauline proclamation as "itself a living before God" (G60 95). The Christian community is called upon to remain steadfast, "wakeful," and "sober," to continue the struggle of "running after the goal" (G60 127f.). What Heidegger is recommending here in *Being and Time* is best understood as this sort of clear-sighted commitment to one's own unique "spiritual direction," an ideal of taking a stand for oneself as a certain kind of person. In one of his letters to Blochmann, Heidegger praises her "commitment [*Verhaftetsein*] to scientific work from out of the total genuineness of your personal being [. . .]" (HB 14).

This way of understanding "resoluteness" is vindicated by a later section of *Being and Time*, namely §74, "The Basic Constitution of Historicality." Here Heidegger notes that the boundaries of his own commitments prevent him from delineating that which might be "resolved" by any particular person in some particular situation. Indeed, as remarks scattered throughout his works in the 1920s show, authenticity is not something that can be spelled out in general terms. As Heidegger likes to say, it is not a matter for the "public." This is because being authentic means living one's own individual life in one's own unique way. Heidegger is, however, confident in his own ability to intimate the meaning of this style of life in a formal way.

In this context, he proposes that this be done by investigating *whence* the possibilities upon which a person "resolves" can be drawn (SZ 383/434). Here he has recourse to a structure that I have already described, i.e., "thrownness [*Geworfenheit*]." Part of having been "thrown" into the world is finding oneself already implicated within a particular linguistic community, whereby one conceives of oneself in the terms set by the prevailing public discourse of the time. The lesson to be learned here is that "[a]uthentic existentiell understanding is so far from extricating itself from this received interpretation that it is in each case from out of it, against it, and yet again for it that the chosen possibility is grasped in resolve" (SZ 383/435). More concretely, Heidegger tells us that these possibilities are drawn from "out of the heritage [*aus dem Erbe*]" into which each one of us has been "thrown" (SZ 383/435). He makes this point in a more straightforward fashion in the 1924 lectures at Kassel, where he tells us that "[w]e are history, i.e. our own past. Our future is lived from out of the past. We carry the past with us" (S 174).

At the most concrete level, then, resoluteness is to be understood as the "freeing up for oneself [*Sichüberliefern*]" of an inherited possibility (SZ 384/435). In responding to the "voice of conscience," a person "frees up [*überliefert*]" a possibility that is at once "inherited [*ererbten*]" and "chosen [*gewählten*]" (SZ 384/435). Here it is worth noting the subtle resonance between "resoluteness [*Entschlossenheit*]" and "freeing up for oneself [*Sichüberliefern*]." In translating '*überliefern*' as "free up," I am making use of a suggestion offered in a recent article by Sheehan and Painter.[31] They refer to several passages from Heidegger's works in the 1950s and 1960s in which he draws the correct etymological link between the root verb '*liefern*' and the Latin '*liberare*,' "to set free."[32] '*Liefern*' was a verb adopted by German merchants from the French '*livrer*,' meaning something like "to remit." The latter is itself derived from the

Latin '*liberare*.'[33] A similar idea can be found by looking at the root of '*Entschlossenheit*,' i.e., '*entschließen*.' Originally, this verb had the same sense as the modern German '*aufschließen*,' meaning "to unlock," from '*schließen*.'[34] The latter is cognate with Latin '*claudere*,' "to close," and '*clavis*,' a "bolt."[35] Hence, '*entschließen*' means to "remove a bolt," "to open," or "to unlock."

The sense one gets from this whole vocabulary of "setting free" and "unlocking" is that an authentic way of life opens up a new possibility, a new future, for a past that has become stale or moribund. One "unlocks" one's heritage, opening up the possibility that it might take a new form in one's own unique life. This is clearly a departure from the "leveling down of possibilities" to "the attainable" and "the respectable" that Heidegger had discussed earlier in the book (SZ 194/239). There he tells us how the possible is "dimmed" so that the "average everydayness of concern becomes blind to its possibilities, and tranquillizes itself with that which is merely 'actual' " (SZ 194f./239). An authentic life is one that realizes one of Heidegger's favorite mottos: "Higher than actuality stands possibility" (SZ 38/63). An authentic person is someone who, having been shaken out of her complacency, is no longer satisfied with what "one" says is appropriate, realistic, or meritorious, and instead "liberates [*liefern*]" some element of her heritage from its obviousness and banality, "unlocking [*entschließen*]" it as an object of vocational commitment.

Charles Guignon argues that this kind of commitment requires the recognition of one's "heritage" as such, suggesting that Heidegger uses the term "heritage [*Erbe*]" to describe a special meaning which the past has for an authentic individual.[36] This reading is, however, grounded on a mistranslation of the relevant passage from *Being and Time*. In Guignon's version, the passage runs "Dasein's resoluteness 'discloses current factical possibilities as *from the heritage* which resoluteness, as thrown, *takes over*.' "[37] The crucial misstep lies in the "as" which is inexplicably inserted into the sentence prior to the phrase "from the heritage." The original simply runs "*erschließt die jeweiligen faktischen Möglichkeiten eigentlichen Existierens* aus dem Erbe [. . .]" (SZ 383).[38] The sentence simply says "from the heritage," not "*as* from the heritage," nor "in terms of the heritage," as Macquarrie and Robinson render it in their interpretation. Moreover, Heidegger explicitly says there is no need for the possibilities that one has "freed up" to be recognized "as" being inherited (SZ 383/435; cf. 385/437). Guignon's reading suggests that *historical consciousness* is somehow required for authenticity, something Heidegger clearly rejects. Regardless of whether or not one is *aware* of it, one's choices always occur within a largely inherited framework.

Heidegger uses the term "fate [*Schicksal*]" as a formal indication of this "authentic occurring [*Geschehen*]" of human existence (SZ 384/435). In other words, "fate" intimates the full phenomenon of freeing up for oneself a possibility that one has chosen. He picks out "singleness [*Einfachheit*]" as an important feature of this phenomenon. This "singleness" is set in opposition to various ways of "shirking" or "taking things lightly," which, as I have already discussed in chapter 3, represent some of the hallmark features of an inauthentic lifestyle. "Fate" is something that is irreducibly and unavoidably one's own; it is an indication of a life that has been chosen on its own terms. Heidegger no doubt chooses the term "fate [*Schicksal*]" here due to its etymological connections with "occurrence [*Geschehen*]" and "history [*Geschichte*]," both terms that play an important role in this portion of *Being and Time*.

Heidegger clearly does *not* have in mind the deterministic connotations that the word usually possesses. As he says, "[f]ate does not first arise from the clashing together of events and circumstances" (SZ 384/436). Fritsche, however, seems to offer this kind of deterministic reading in his recent analysis of §74 of *Being and Time*.[39] As I have already shown, Heidegger does not use ordinary terms like "conscience" or "guilt" in anything approaching their everyday uses, but instead as "formal indications" for something which he thinks is not even adequately captured by such terms. Furthermore, Heidegger's well-documented insistence on the primacy of possibility and of freedom simply rule out any deterministic reading of the term "fate." Hence, the fact that Heidegger is completely silent about causal determinism gives us reason to infer that he did not hold this particular view.

Section 74 of *Being and Time* is not, however, without its peculiar obscurities. Foremost among these is the page-long discussion of "repetition [*Wiederholung*]." As I have already pointed out, Heidegger clearly rejects the idea that authenticity *requires* historical consciousness. Indeed, he makes this very point forcefully at the outset of his discussion of "repetition": "It is not necessary that resoluteness know *explicitly* [*ausdrücklich*] about the provenance [*Herkunft*] of the possibilities upon which it projects itself" (SZ 385/437). However, it is possible for this kind of explicit knowledge to occur. In "repetition," he tells us, "Dasein first has its own history made manifest" (SZ 386/438). And yet this explicit knowledge does not require the services of *historical science* [*Historie*] (SZ 386/438). The difference between resoluteness *simpliciter* and "repetition" seems to rest on the fact that in the latter, "Dasein chooses its hero for itself" (SZ 385/437). Or, in slightly more detail, Heidegger tells us that one makes a choice that "liberates one for struggling imitation [*kämpfende Nachfolge*] and loyalty to the repeatable" (SZ 385/437). In other words, over and above the personal dedication to being a sort of person which is sufficient for authenticity, there is also the possibility that one might *model* oneself on an exemplary person, or perhaps an exemplary *type* of person, that one has access to in virtue of one's cultural heritage. This is what Heidegger seems to have in mind with his talk of "repetition" and "choosing one's hero."

This ideal of "struggling imitation" had previously appeared in Heidegger's WS 1920–1921 lectures on primitive Christianity.[40] Here he cites Paul's injunction at 1 Cor. 4:11: "Become my imitators [*Nachfahren*]!" (G60 121). Earlier he had briefly alluded to 1 Thess. 1:6f.: "And you became imitators of us and of the Lord, for in spite of persecution you received the word with joy inspired by the Holy Spirit, so that you became an example to all the believers in Macedonia and in Achaia." The idea one gathers from these passages is that part of a fully Christian way of life consists in the emulation of Jesus and of other exemplary members of the community. This is a notion that has persisted throughout the Christian tradition, as evidenced by the continuing popularity of various hagiographies.

A text from the following semester provides some clue as to how one ought to understand this talk of "imitation." During SS 1921, Heidegger makes reference to Luther's works of 1518, contrasting the "axiological abstraction" of timeless values with "existentiell anxious worry" or the "enactment of existence" (G60 259). In this cryptic note, Heidegger is concerned with "destroying" the aesthetic, "Greek" elements of Augustine's work in the name of resurrecting an ideal of constant seeking, struggling, and suffering in tribulation. This concern for timeless values is, on his own view, "doing business [*Geschäftigkeit*] with God, which makes it easy" (G60 265). We must instead confront the "factical" rather than flee from it. Heidegger's suggestion here is that the Platonic language of "values" tends to distort an authentic way of life into something purely cognitive or contemplative. Like Luther, he endorses the view that valuable ways of life require the personal dedication of concrete individuals.

Indeed, Luther's early works are filled with references to "conformity" to Christ, to "bearing the image of Christ," and to "partaking" of his "substance."[41] His attacks against scholastic "theology of glory" are aimed at replacing idle contemplation of divine truths with active, passionate conformity to the "image" of Christ. At the same time, as I discussed in chapter 2, Luther's commitment to the corruption of human nature, and his very real eschatological sensibilities, require that this "conformity" not be a matter of attainable perfection, but of constant hope, struggle, and identification with the "invisible" future. To have faith, on Luther's view, is to identify with, be transformed by, and participate in the ongoing history of salvation by continually re-enacting the movements of repentance and conversion. Not surprisingly, this same conception makes its way into Heidegger's own articulation of Christian faith in 1927:

> [F]aith is an appropriation of revelation that co-constitutes the Christian occurrence, that is, the mode of existence that specifies a factical Dasein's Christianness as a particular form of destiny. *Faith is the believing-understanding mode of existing in the history revealed, i.e., occurring, with the Crucified.* (G9 53f./45)

Faith, as "history," gives us a better idea of what Heidegger means by "repetition" as "explicit freeing up for oneself" of some inherited possibility. With the revelation (or "proclamation," to use Heidegger's favored term from WS 1920–1921) of the "Crucified God," a new *possibility* for human existence has been opened up. Faith can be understood as a kind of active recollection of this revelation, aimed not at "objective" knowledge or aesthetic enjoyment, but rather at the continual re-enactment of a radically alternative way of life, which can itself be understood as a *participation* in the ongoing history of salvation. Jürgen Moltmann has given a clear expression of these ideas: "Belief in resurrection is not summed up by assent to a dogma and the registering of a historical fact. It means participating in this creative act of God. A faith of this kind is the beginning of freedom."[42] Similarly, "repetition" involves the active participation in the unfolding history of one's own tradition, consisting in one's own personal and individual commitment to some exemplar that one finds particularly valuable. Hans Sluga, in an essay on Heidegger's 1935 lecture course *Introduction to Metaphysics*, captures this element of Heidegger's thought quite well. Sluga argues that Heidegger wants to hold up great works of art, philosophical ideas, and the like as "paradigms for other creations" that present us with new "possibilities of living."[43] "Repetition" of some possibility involves explicitly modeling one's *future* on it.

Heidegger makes it clear that the goal here is not simply to "re-actualize" some past state of affairs. "The repetition of the possible is neither a bringing back of the 'past,' nor a binding of the 'present' back to something that is 'outmoded [*Überholt*]'" (SZ 385f./437). The key term here, after all, is *possibility*. The past is not some rigid actuality that needs to be preserved at all costs or slavishly imitated. As Sluga rightly points out, the whole point is that the past becomes an exemplar for something radically *new*, for an individual's own unique and unrepeatable act of self-creation.

For an authentic life, i.e., one that has been liberated from the soporific banality of the everyday in order to be lived in its own way, the past can only be meaningful as a possibility, not as some "golden era" that needs to be actualized again, nor as the "good old days" as a repressive measure of the present. The past is never simply brought back *for its own sake*, but rather always for the sake of the *future* (SZ 386/437f.). "Repetition" is an activity that "responds [*erwidert*]" to the past as a possibility, i.e., an activity that takes the past as a challenge for the future rather than something intrinsically valuable as such. It is thus simultaneously a "disavowal [*Widerruf*]" of "that which is effective in the today as the 'past'" (SZ 386/438). That is, repetition of a past possibility for the sake of a new future is a *protest* against hegemony of the obvious, of the self-evident, of how "one" says things ought to be, and it is the realization of the promise of something radically *new* hidden in what is *old*.

Over the years, a variety of worries have been raised about Heidegger's views on these issues. Giving some consideration to them will aid in the task of explicating Heidegger's position. Lawrence Vogel has recently summarized the principal charge against Heidegger as "evaluative nihilism."[44] As Vogel correctly observes, the repeatable possibilities of existence envisioned by Heidegger are not eternal moral truths. The problem, then, as Vogel and others see it, is that if this is indeed the case, then there seems to be no basis for the kind of *critical* appropriation of one's tradition that Heidegger clearly appreciates. Is Heidegger not guilty of "relativism," "historicism," "nationalism," or "irrationalism"? Are not these the sorts of pernicious views that are entailed by a rejection of transhistorical values? How can one criticize one's own cultural inheritance without making reference to something that transcends the confines of one's culture?

Whatever one might ultimately think about the plausibility of Heidegger's views, it is not clear that any of these charges really hold. The most pressing charge, of course, is that of "nationalism," a claim that is bolstered by Heidegger's bombastic rhetoric about a special German destiny [*Sonderweg*] from the 1930s.[45] In *Being and Time*, however, there is no suggestion that any one tradition or culture is more valuable than another, nor does there seem to be any claim that tradition is simply valuable in itself. The charge of "irrationalism" is less well-grounded, and, I think, founders for the same reason, i.e., a lack of evidence. While it is certainly the case that Heidegger offers no decision procedures or moral algorithms, there is no suggestion in any of his writings from the 1920s that he is an advocate of blind leaps or arbitrary acts of will. There is nothing about the ideal of individual vocational commitment that precludes one's thinking the matter through beforehand. Further, in a number of his early lectures and letters Heidegger clearly denounces the various irrationalist pseudo-prophets and theosophists who proliferated during the tumultuous years of the Weimar Republic (G61 70/53). In SS 1923, for example, he attacks the "noise of the day," the "George circle, Keyserling, anthroposophy, Steiner" and a little-known work on the phenomenology of mysticism, warning his students to "[b]eware of all this!" (G63 78f./58). In a January 22, 1921, letter to Karl Jaspers, Heidegger also attacks "fanatical spirits [*Schwarmgeister*]" and "followers of George" (HJ 19). Whatever Heidegger's philosophical shortcomings might be, it is far from clear that "irrationalism" is one of them.[46]

A related worry, one Vogel articulates well, is that Heidegger is somehow a "relativist." The claim here is that Heidegger's apparent denial of transhistorical values and his insistence of the perspectival or "hermeneutical" quality of judgment together render any kind of self-criticism virtually impossible. Vogel captures the worry thus: "there is no perspective independent of the heritage in which one stands—and the 'prejudices' that govern it—to judge whether one set of idols or ideals is better than others."[47] The textual evidence certainly gives the strong impression that this is indeed Heidegger's position. In SS 1923, for example, he labels the "demand for observation which is free of standpoints" as a "disastrous" prejudice (G63 82/63). Whatever "objectivity" one might achieve in any particular case is "itself something historical [. . .] and not a chimerical in-itself outside of time" (G63 83/64). On its own, this strikes one as a sober depiction of the human condition rather than as a wild-eyed endorsement of some vicious relativism. It is far from clear how the conditioned character of any standpoint renders that standpoint incapable of providing critical analysis. Criticism requires that people be able to revise their basic judgments in light of further facts, alternative principles, and so forth.

This implies no commitment to some moral version of the "view from nowhere."

An example from American history, i.e., the abolition movement in the first half of the nineteenth century, illustrates that Heidegger's views do not entail vicious relativism that undermines the possibility of criticism. Looking back, it seems clear that the abolitionists drew upon a shared tradition of humanism and of Judeo-Christian morality to support their arguments. It is notable that this is the *very same* tradition which the advocates of slavery called upon in making their ill-fated case. That the abolition movement obviously drew upon a stock of historically transmitted ideas peculiar to European culture certainly did not preclude their ability to effectively criticize perceived social injustices. One need not be a Platonist to have good reasons for rejecting certain elements of one's own culture.

Authenticity and Community

Up to this point, my discussion has been focused exclusively on the explication of authenticity as an ideal of *individual* vocational commitment and personal integrity in Heidegger's writings from the 1920s. In the preceding chapter, I showed how the ideal of authenticity has its roots in Heidegger's attempt to appropriate the primitive Christian origins of Romantic personalism. Romantic personalism can itself be captured by the single word '*Eigentümlichkeit*,' or "individuality." Heidegger's own distinctive version of this line of thought can also be captured by the term '*Jemeinigkeit*,' the quality of life such that it is "in each case my own." An authentic life is one that "owns up [*eigen*]" to itself as a finite, individual process of self-identification.

Heidegger's emphasis on life's being "in each case my own" does not come at the expense of a realistic recognition of the social aspects of human life. The meaning each individual life has is always contingent on the social "world," the context of meaningful relations, which a person inhabits. As early as WS 1919–1920, Heidegger is at pains to articulate the way some social sphere always puts a claim on an individual (G58 32). It is only within a shared context of language, custom, and social practices that one is able to make sense of one's own experiences (G58 34). Beginning early, Heidegger analyzes the total phenomenon of "factical life-experience" into three interlocking contexts: the "environing world [*Umwelt*]," the "with-world [*Mitwelt*]," and the "self-world [*Selbstwelt*]." In *Being and Time*, the "with-world" has become "being-with [*Mitsein*]," something to which Heidegger devotes considerable attention (SZ 117 ff./153 ff.). Here he points out how part of the meaning of the things we encounter in our daily lives lies in their reference to other people: "the book we have used was bought at So-and-so's shop and given by such-and-such a person [. . .]" (SZ 118/153 f.). Even objects that are unfamiliar to us are referred to an unknown other. The broken skis in the corner call to mind our trip with someone, the table speaks to us of family dinners (G63 90 f./69 f.). Heidegger rejects the Husserlian problematic of "constitution," i.e., the issue of "other minds," as a totally artificial problem.[48] We do not first find ourselves cut off from our shared world. The "others" are actually those from whom, Heidegger says, we do not distinguish ourselves. That is, the "others" are those amongst whom we ourselves belong; our world is a "shared" world (SZ 118/154f.).

Given these commitments, it is no surprise that Heidegger finds himself compelled to give some account of how an authentic individual stands with respect to these inalienable social relations. Nonetheless, the account offered is not only brief, but is also scattered throughout Heidegger's lectures, essays, and correspondences from this period. Hence, this requires a good bit of reconstruction. A good place to start is §74 of *Being and Time*, where Heidegger cryptically intimates the total phenomenon that he has in mind:

> But if fateful Dasein, as being-in-the-world, exists essentially as being-with others, its occurring is a co-occuring and is determinative for it as *destiny* [*Geschick*]. This is how we designate the occurring of the community [*Gemeinschaft*], of a people [*Volk*]. [. . .] Our fates have already been guided in advance, in our being with one another in the same world and in our resoluteness for definite possibilities. Only in communicating and struggling does the power of destiny become free. Dasein's fateful destiny in and with its "generation" goes to make up the full authentic occurring of Dasein. (SZ 384f./436)

A good place to begin trying to understand what Heidegger is saying in this dense passage is with the term "generation." This term appears a handful of times in Heidegger's writings preceding *Being and Time*, with little elaboration of its sense (G59 157; G61 161/122; G63 106/82). At several points, including here in *Being and Time*, Heidegger attributes the term to Dilthey. The most detailed explication of the idea that Heidegger gives us occurs not in *Being and Time*, but in his earlier lectures at Kassel on Dilthey. "Generation" is a term used to articulate something about the way the self-understanding of individuals is decisively shaped by membership in a cultural tradition. Heidegger explains:

> We carry the past with us. That clearly can be seen in being-with-one-another within a generation. Dilthey discovered that this concept of generation was important for the phenomenon of historicality. Each of us is not only his own self but also belongs to a generation. The generation precedes the individual, is there before the individual, and defines the Dasein of the individual. The individual lives in terms of that which has been in the past, drags himself or herself through the present, and finally is overtaken by a new generation. (S 174)

Both here and in *Being and Time*, Heidegger does not indicate that he is using "generation" in a sense that differs from that found in Dilthey's work. Hence it is worthwhile to explore Dilthey's notion of a "generation" a bit more closely. The idea first appears in an 1865 essay on Novalis, later included in the volume *Das Erlebnis und die Dichtung*.[49] Here Dilthey proposes to investigate Novalis's life and work in order to gain a window onto the "general motives" of his "generation," i.e., the generation of Romanticism.[50] A "generation" is a group of individuals sharing a common "intellectual culture," itself shaped by the preceding age and by innumerable conditions of a more contemporary nature.[51] For the purposes of historical understanding, a researcher can delimit a definite generation. The one that interests Dilthey here (and elsewhere) is that of A. W. and Friedrich Schlegel, Schleiermacher, Alexander von Humboldt, Hegel, Novalis, Hölderlin, Wackenroder, Tieck, Fries, and Schelling.[52]

The idea of a "generation" is mentioned again in the work cited by Heidegger in *Being and Time*, viz. the 1875 essay "Über das Studium der Geschichte der Wissenschaften vom Menschen, der Gesellschaft, und den Staat." Here Dilthey tells us that this is a concept that can be used for conceiving of the unifying sense of an age (GS5 36). It is a determinate "period [*Zeitraum*]" usually lasting about thirty years (GS5 37). It can be more closely "defined" as "a designation for a relation of contemporaneity between individuals." He explains this "contemporaneity" in a bit more detail later:

> Those who experienced the same guiding influences during their receptive years together comprise a generation. Taken in this way, a generation forms a close circle of individuals who are bound into a homogeneous whole through dependence on the same great facts and vicissitudes that occurred in their receptive period, despite the differences with respect to other supervening factors. (GS5 37)

On Dilthey's view, a generation is clearly not an accidental assemblage of persons who simply happen to have been born at roughly the same time. Instead, a generation is a "close circle" of individuals, the identity of each of whom has been shaped by common experiences and a shared cultural and intellectual milieu. As in the Novalis essay, Dilthey regards the generation of "1800" as paradigmatic (GS5 37). The decisive events for this generation were the French Revolution and the Napoleonic Wars, both of which profoundly affected the likes of Novalis, Hölderlin, Schelling, and Hegel. Dilthey's final discussion of this idea occurs in his later *Aufbau* studies. Here he professes an interest in grasping the influence of commonalities on the "life-experience" of individuals (GS7 133/155). Making a point that Heidegger will echo a little over a decade later, Dilthey claims that self-understanding *and* the possibility of understanding others both depend upon these commonalities (GS7 147/168; 208f./229). They can take more determinate forms in what Dilthey calls "objective spirit," i.e., more precisely delineated "purposive systems" like religions or economic systems. These kinds of "continuous wholes" are "separable into temporal phases." Dilthey elaborates:

> What primarily characterizes generations, ages, and epochs is that they are general, dominant, and permeating tendencies. They involve the *con-*

centration of the whole culture of such a temporal span within itself, so that the values, purposes, and life-rules of the time can provide the norm for judging, evaluating, and assessing the persons and the tendencies or directions that give a specific time its character. An individual, a tendency, and a community derive their *meaning* with this whole through their inner relation to the spirit of the age. (GS7 177/198)

Following Dilthey, Heidegger is also committed to the notion that individuals always belong to a generation that has been shaped by a common heritage and by other decisive events. Heidegger's own generation had inherited the legacy of nineteenth-century philosophy and had been deeply shaped by the First World War, the collapse of the Wilhelmine state, and the Russian Revolution. A generation forms the unique *context* or *situation* within which individuals find themselves faced with the universally human predicament of having to live their own lives in their own way. This context comprises not only the specific possibilities that are available to a person at the time, but also defines the range of tasks, problems, and conflicts that face a particular member of the generation. To take Heidegger's generation as an example, one could say that each individual found himself or herself charged with the recreation of German culture and civil society in the open-ended and tumultuous environment of the Weimar Republic. Heidegger's view is clearly that part of what it means to be an authentic individual is to take hold of these sorts of challenges as part of one's overall commitment to living a certain kind of life. Earlier on in *Being and Time*, he had described this as each individual's "staking oneself [*Sicheinsetzen*]" on "the same issue [*Sache*]," a kind of commitment to a common goal that "is determined by one's own Dasein that has been grasped in each case in one's own way [*je eigens ergriffenen Dasein bestimmt*]" (SZ 122/159).

It is clear, then, given Heidegger's emphasis on the role of the "generation," that part of being an authentic person requires the incorporation of some shared task or group of tasks into one's overall pattern of vocational commitment. It is also clear, however, that this does not entail the subordination or sacrifice of the individual to the collective.[53] Whatever common goals there might be, an individual is always more than simply a part of a generation. What really matters to Heidegger is the "inner truthfulness of a worthwhile, self-cultivating life" (G56/57 5/4). This is something that is never a "matter for universal humanity or for a public" (G63 19/15). As he suggests in a letter to Karl Löwith, the best kind of interpersonal solidarity is one that is committed to the authenticity of each individual:

It is only important that we agree that what really matters for each of us is to go to the radical, uttermost limit for what and how each of us understands the "one thing necessary." Perhaps we are far apart with respect to "system," "doctrine," and "position," but we are *together* as human beings alone can be together: in existence [*Existenz*]. (HL 32)

The question is, then, how does Heidegger envision the relation between authentic individuals each committed to a common project or task? The answer is only just intimated by the passage from §74 of *Being and Time* quoted above: "In *communicating* [*Mitteilung*] and *struggling* [*Kampf*] the power of destiny first becomes free" (SZ 384/436). What this suggests is that individuals form a bond not through submission to some collective will, but rather through a polemical dialogue aimed at challenging the other person to uphold her own way of being true to herself. Indeed, if we look at where the term "struggle [*Kampf*]" first shows up in Heidegger's vocabulary, this is precisely the idea we get. "Struggle" is a term used to characterize the *Sitz im Leben*, the concrete context, of Paul's epistles to the Galatians and to the Thessalonians. In the former, the "struggle" in question is between two ways of life indicated by the opposition between "law" and "faith" (G60 68). Paul's "struggle" is aimed at the assertion of a Christian mode of life against the surrounding world (G60 72; cf. 138).

Heidegger provides considerably more detail about Paul's "struggle" in his discussion of 1 and 2 Thessalonians. Here Paul's various admonitions are rooted in the "being-already [*Gewordensein*]" that he shares with the community at Thessalonica. Paul has partaken of their own condition, not only through having undergone his own conversion, but also as the person who first proclaimed the Gospel to them, thus making their conversion possible. Paul's concern is clearly that the community there remains faithful to this new, post-conversion way of life (G60 98). Paul's own identity is deeply bound up with this concern with their faithfulness: "For we now live, if you continue to stand firm in the Lord" (1 Thess. 3:8). Accordingly, he tries to answer the community's questions about the Parousia, or, as Heidegger puts it, "Paul's proclamation is formally characterized by an influencing of the knowing of the Thessalonians at a decisive moment" (G60 101). He does so, of course, by directing the question back upon the members of the community themselves, exhorting them not to get lost in idle speculation or complacency, but to remain steadfast in their struggle to remain true to their own callings. "Paul's answer to the question of the when of the *parousia* is thus the admonition to be awake and sober" (G60 105).

The term '*Kampf*' appears around this same period in Heidegger's correspondence with Karl Jaspers. In a letter of June 27, 1922, Heidegger presents Jaspers with a condensed prospectus of his philosophical project, i.e., with an investigation of "life" or "the historical" combined with a radical critique of the metaphysical tradition (HJ 27). Heidegger clearly views this project not as an idle academic business, but as a matter of deep personal commitment. The choice here involves one's "wagering his whole 'outer' and 'inner' existence" (HJ 28). Heidegger feels that Jaspers is someone who shares similar commitments: "Your work has made it clear to me that your investigations into the critique of the psychology of world-views are positioned within the proper,

positive tendency towards the problem. That strengthens in me the consciousness of an exceptional and independent community of struggle [*Kampfgemeinschaft*] that I find all too rare these days" (HJ 29). In a later letter from
November 22, 1922, Heidegger characterizes his friendship with Jaspers once
more as a "community of struggle [*Kampfgemeinschaft*]" (HJ 33). In a letter of
July 14, 1923, following Heidegger's appointment to Marburg, he tells Jaspers
how he plans to "give [Nicolai Hartmann] hell," assisted in this by a "shock
detachment [*Stoßtrupp*]" of students from Freiburg (HJ 41). Heidegger's pro-
posed "revolution [*Umsturz*]" in university and cultural life requires an "invisible community," one that is not bound together by a common ideology or
some party line like a political "association [*Bund*]" (HJ 42). This point is
particularly significant in judging the political character of Heidegger's convictions in this domain. Associations, fighting organizations [*Kampfbünde*],
and political groupings were all-pervasive during the Weimar era. Political
parties, even the Social Democrats, had their own gangs of toughs who
heckled people at rival party rallies and engaged in frequent street brawls.
Heidegger's motley "shock detachment" of philosophy students presents an
entirely different picture.

If the discussions of primitive Christianity from WS 1920–1921 and the
correspondence with Jaspers and Löwith are taken together, a clearer picture of
Heidegger's ideas about authenticity and community begins to emerge. Paul's
"struggle" is aimed single-heartedly at encouraging the individual members of
the community to remain true to their calling, to avoid the tempting slide into
idleness and enthusiasm. As Heidegger conceives his friendship with both
Jaspers and Löwith, this kind of concern for another person is not necessarily
dependent on common beliefs. This is perhaps most obvious in the case of
Jaspers; one of Heidegger's early essays was a review of Jaspers's first philosophical offering, *Psychology of Worldviews*. In this review, Heidegger is
sharply critical of some of the basic tendencies of Jaspers's work at this stage. All
the same, Heidegger praises his *Kampfgemeinschaft* with Jaspers, rooted in their
common dedication to the renewal of philosophy through deeper appreciation
of concrete human life. In the above-quoted letter to Karl Löwith, Heidegger
makes it clear that a real bond between people does not require conformity or
homogeneity, but instead a commitment to the *Existenz* of each individual. It
will be recalled that '*Existenz*' is one of Heidegger's early terms, employed
between 1921 and 1923, for what *Being and Time* calls "authenticity."[54]

In *Being and Time*, Heidegger describes this mutual commitment to the
authenticity of the other person as being the "conscience" of the other
(SZ 298/344). To be the "conscience" of another person is to practice the
"solicitude that leaps forth and liberates" (SZ 298/344). Heidegger makes it
clear, both here in *Being and Time* and elsewhere, that being the "conscience"
of another person has nothing to do with being a "leader [*Führer*]," with
making another person's decisions for her or propounding some rigid rule of
life. If one recalls Heidegger's own peculiar usage of the term "conscience,"

then it is immediately obvious that he is not interested in paternalism of any sort.[55] "Conscience" is his formal indication in *Being and Time* of those moments in a person's life that interrupt the normal course of things, disclosing the individual's own unique situation and throwing that person's life into relief. These moments have the function of *liberating* a person from her bondage to invisible dictatorship of the "one," thereby making possible an *authentic* life. Clearly, being the "conscience" of another person cannot perpetuate this subtle dictatorship.

It is earlier in *Being and Time* that Heidegger actually clarifies this relation in more detail. Here, in §26, he formally indicates the most immediate way people relate to one another in a concrete world of practical concerns as "solicitude [*Fürsorge*]" (SZ 121/157). In ordinary German, this word connotes social welfare work, as in the phrases '*öffentliche Fürsorge*,' meaning "public relief," or '*soziale Fürsorge*,' "social welfare," or, in a nominative form, '*Fürsorger*,' a "social worker." Heidegger himself draws attention to this connection: "The 'concern [*Besorgen*]' for food and clothing, the nursing of a sick body, are solicitude" (SZ 121/158). Any particular activity of this sort is clearly only intelligible in light of the fact that individuals always inhabit a *social* world. These more extreme modes of caring for other people are, says Heidegger, "motivated in the fact that Dasein immediately and for the most part maintains itself in deficient modes of solicitude" (SZ 121/158). One cannot avoid detecting the polemical flavor of these remarks, captured by the claim that welfare work is necessary because most people are "deficient" when it comes to caring for one another.

Besides ignoring other people and their manifest plight, there are other, more "positive" modes of solicitude. Heidegger characterizes the first of these as follows:

> It can, as it were, take "care" away from the other and put itself in his position of concern: it can *stand in* [*einspringen*] for him. This solicitude takes over what is of concern for the other. He is thrown out of his place; he steps back so that afterwards, when the matter has been attended to, he can either take it over as something finished and at his disposal, or disburden himself of it completely. In such solicitude the other can become one who is dominated and dependent, even if this domination is implicit and remains hidden to the one who is dominated. (SZ 122/158)

"Standing in" for another person clearly contributes to her natural tendency to abdicate self-responsibility, i.e., to be inauthentic. Heidegger makes this clear by using the language of "disburdening," which he uses later to characterize the dictatorship of the "one" in everyday life (SZ 127f./165). "Standing in" for someone simply multiplies the possibilities for that person *not* to take possession of her own unique individual life. Moreover, as Heidegger tells us, this kind of relationship, though it appears to be an activity aimed at the welfare of another person, is a more or less subtle form of paternalistic domination. The other is literally treated as a child, as one who cannot take "care" of things for herself and who thus needs to be relieved of the burden of having to live her own life in her own way. According to Heidegger, this tends to create a dominance-dependence relation, in which the individual concerned becomes more and more alienated from the possibility of living authentically.

The alternative to this, which Heidegger later characterizes as being the "conscience" of another person, is described as follows:

> a solicitude which does not stand in for the other so much as *leap ahead* [*vorausspringt*] of him in his existentiell ability to be, not in order to take "care" away from him, but rather to give it back to him in the first place authentically and as such. This solicitude is essential to authentic care—i.e., it concerns the existence [*Existenz*] of the other and not some *what* with which he is concerned; it helps the other to become transparent for himself in his care and to become *free for* it. (SZ 122/158f.)

The contrast here is clear: on the one hand, we have the guiding hand of paternalism; on the other, we have a mode of exemplifying an authentic life aimed at inspiring and challenging another person to take hold of her own life in her own way. The object of concern here is not what another person is good for, but instead the sheer possibility that she might be an authentic person, committed to her own personal vocation. Vogel contends that this non-paternalistic, emancipatory mode of solicitude signifies the kind of transhistorical principle that is needed to dodge the danger of historical relativism that lurks in Heidegger's view.[56] However, Vogel does not offer a particularly clear formulation of this principle, describing it instead as "an *interpersonal* orientation [...]." More problematic for this claim is that Heidegger makes no suggestion that emancipatory solicitude is an imperative or principle of any kind. At most, one might be able to assert that an individual who values authenticity would be inconsistent were she to fail in promoting this value both in her own life and in that of other people. However, this, too, is a claim that one cannot find in Heidegger.

Just as the "voice of conscience" gives no "practical injunctions" or "univocally calculable maxims," so too the authentic individual does not tell another person how to run her own life, but instead silently exemplifies a life that has been taken hold of on its own terms and in its own way (cf. SZ 294/340). This ideal of *exemplification* can be clearly found in Heidegger's writings outside of *Being and Time*. I have already drawn attention to his invocation of Paul's injunction to "[b]ecome my imitators [*Nachfahren*]!" Heidegger presents the idea in his own words in a letter to Elisabeth Blochmann from June 15, 1918:

> Spiritual life can only be *lived in advance in an exemplary way* [*vorgelebt*] and shaped so that those who ought to partake of it are immediately seized by it in their existence [*Existenz*]. The value of spiritual realities, insight

into duty, and the will to fulfillment is only stirred up and liberated [*lösen sich . . . aus*] as the fruit of a vigorous and enduring awakening that is inwardly nourished without theoretical and didactic assistance and bridges. (HB 7)

In this passage, Heidegger uses the term '*vorleben*' to capture an idea that is clearly parallel to what he calls "leaping ahead [*vorausspringen*]" in *Being and Time*. Less than a year after this letter to Blochmann, Heidegger finds himself in front of a classroom of recently returned veterans of the First World War. He begins the "War Emergency Semester" with a brief discussion of "Science and University Reform," which reaches its climax in the claim that the "awakening and heightening of the life-context of scientific consciousness" requires not theories or programmatic pronouncements, but simply "exemplary pre-*living* [*Vorleben*]" (G56/57 5/5). On June 27, 1922, still concerned with university reform and the life of the youth in Germany, Heidegger describes his own vision of the role of intellectuals in the same terms. Instead of engaging in "idle talk [*Gerede*]" about the crisis of the sciences, we "must live such issues in advance in an exemplary way for the youth," otherwise "we have no right to live in scientific research" (HJ 28).

What, then, is Heidegger's considered view on the *social* aspect of authenticity? I have pointed to several interrelated ideas in the preceding discussion; it will prove useful later (chapters 7 and 8) to have a clear picture of all these ideas. Hence, some words of summary are in order. First of all, it is clear that, on this view, an authentic individual inevitably incorporates shared ideals and projects into her overall pattern of vocational commitment, simply in virtue of belonging to a "generation." In addition, given that authenticity involves sensitivity to the demands of the present situation, authentic individuals participate in one way or another in the resolution of common problems or in the realization of common goals. On a deeper level, however, we find Heidegger elaborating the idea of a generational "community of struggle [*Kampfgemeinschaft*]." Here individuals are united not only through a common culture or a shared historical situation, but also through a commitment on the part of each person to the value of an authentic way of life. This commitment seems to entail the rejection of paternalistic relationships of a sort that ultimately subjugate other people by encouraging the innate drive to self-abdication. In place of this, Heidegger envisions the possibility of a community in which each individual *exemplifies* what it means to be authentic in his or her own unique way.

PART THREE. HEIDEGGER'S "METHOD"

Heidegger on the "How" of Philosophy

It is entirely correct and completely in order to say, "You can't do anything with philosophy." The only mistake is to believe that with this, the judgment concerning philosophy is at an end. For a little epilogue arises in the form of a counterquestion: even if we can't do anything with it, may not philosophy in the end do something with us, provided that we engage ourselves with it?

(G40 9f./13)

Two points have become clear during the course of my discussion: (1) that Heidegger had an abiding concern with the value of an authentic life is beyond dispute; and (2) it is equally clear that Heidegger was sharply critical of the ways public discourse, particularly among the educated classes, tended to be complicit in timid inauthenticity and thus to foreclose the possibility of authenticity. In chapter 4, I showed how philosophy was, at least in Heidegger's eyes, especially guilty. In his letters, lectures, and essays from the 1920s, Heidegger takes up the *prophetic* style of religious critics like Paul, Luther, and Kierkegaard, railing against the superficiality of contemporary thought and culture.

Beginning around 1929, Heidegger sharpened his critical focus on particular aspects of modern technological civilization. This move shaped his thought in decisive ways. In the 1930s, he was led to embrace the myth of a special German destiny (*Sonderweg*) as the only way out of the cultural cul-de-sac of technological modernity. In the 1950s and 1960s, this concern with technological civilization continued to be a powerful element in Heidegger's thought. During the early period of his work, however, this critique is much less pronounced. In the 1920s, Heidegger appears to have worried more about the comforting platitudes of "world-view" philosophy and the abstractions of neo-Kantianism than about technology.

It was during the course of a confrontation with the latter two trends in philosophy, as well as with the religious and theological heritage of the West, that Heidegger articulated his earliest vision of the social, cultural, and intellectual role of philosophy. Over time, his thoughts on this matter crystallized around the term "destruction [*Destruktion*]." The practice that this term refers to forms the vital heart of Heidegger's conception of the nature and role of philosophy. Before delving into the meaning of "destruction," however, I want to examine Heidegger's more *general* views about what philosophy is supposed to be. The aim of this chapter is to provide such a *general* account.

My discussion will begin with an examination of Heidegger's dissatisfaction with the prevailing accounts (ca. 1920) of the nature and tasks of philosophy. Rejecting the aridity of "scientific" philosophy and the pedantry of "world-view" philosophy, Heidegger attempts to articulate a conception of philosophy that is ultimately motivated by a concern with the value of an authentic life. This motivation shapes the conception in such a way that the latter is meant to cohere with the commitments involved in the former. One example of this is the notion of "formal indication," a method that employs provisional intimations to direct individuals toward the matter of thinking and toward certain values without prescribing the details of one's life. More important for my present discussion, however, is Heidegger's claim that philosophy is supposed to *struggle* against the tempting complacency of everyday life. The "duty" of the philosopher, according to Heidegger, is to "make things hard." As I will show in the succeeding chapter, this struggle eventually takes form in a practice Heidegger's calls "destruction [*Destruktion*]."

"Science (*Wissenschaft*)" or "World-view (*Weltanschauung*)"?

The conception of philosophy that Heidegger articulated during the 1920s did not emerge in a vacuum. In accord with his settled conviction that all intellectual labor is bounded by the horizon of one's generation, this conception represents a considered response to the philosophical situation of the day. Heidegger's response is, however, a radical one, for it involves the rejection of the prevailing tendencies of the time in favor of something totally distinctive.

With respect to intellectual culture, Heidegger's "generation" was deeply shaped by the course of German philosophy in the nineteenth century. In concrete terms, philosophers of the time were faced with what has been called a "legitimation crisis."[1] Following the collapse of German idealism and the spectacular advances of the specialized sciences, the question that philosophers faced was this: what legitimate role, if any, can philosophy play in modern European intellectual life? There were basically two responses to this question. The first revolved around the idea of "science [*Wissenschaft*]" in one way or another.[2] One trend in this direction included varieties of naturalism and positivism, all of which basically held that the specialized sciences now fulfilled the intellectual role once played by philosophy. For those unwilling to completely reject the prerogatives of philosophy in this way, the legitimacy of philosophy was secured by conceiving of its main project as *epistemology*, as the "science of science." The dominant representatives of this view were the neo-Kantians, though Husserl's conception of "philosophy as a rigorous science" shares some of the same intuitions that guided the former.

The second major response to the "legitimation crisis" is known as "world-view philosophy." Bambach has captured the basic tendency as an attempt "to overcome the demands of science by synthesizing knowledge into a personalized system of wisdom, relating all experience of the world to the subjective life-conditions of the individual."[3] This movement, too, took on a variety of different forms. At one extreme, some of the neo-Kantians regarded their attempts at a "critical science of value" as steps toward providing a "scientifically" valid world-view or philosophy of culture.[4] On the opposite side were those who totally rejected the allegedly "lifeless" demands of science for one or another form of *Lebensphilosophie*. Some opted for a Nietzschean voluntarism, others for vaguely religious or theosophical positions, all of which were popular among the educated classes of the day.

In his own way, Heidegger too attempted to respond to this "legitimation crisis." In WS 1920–1921 he tells the students that "[t]he problem of the self-understanding of philosophy is always taken too lightly" (G60 8). His response, however, dispensed with both "science," as it was widely understood, and with "world-view." Much of his polemic in this regard was directed against the neo-Kantians and against Husserl. The more vulgar forms of *Lebensphilosophie*, however, also came under attack. In place of all these alternatives, Heidegger erected a vision of philosophy ultimately motivated by his commitment to the value of an authentic life.

Philosophy as "Science"?

In the era immediately preceding and during Heidegger's earliest period, the majority of philosophers in German universities held that the legitimacy of philosophy depended upon its being "scientific." By this they meant that philosophy ought to be objective and rigorous, and that all philosophical claims must ultimately rest on indubitable foundations. Only in this way, it was thought, could philosophy have a legitimate place in the polity of the sciences. While Heidegger certainly appreciated the need for rigor, he nonetheless held that the prevailing notion of "science" had no rightful place in philosophy. Right at the beginning of his mature philosophy, in KNS 1919, Heidegger rejects the idea that philosophy must be bound by the uncritical notion of "science" inherited from the ancient Greeks (G56/57 21/18). More specifically, he makes it clear that what he is ultimately concerned with is the "groundless naturalism and historicism of the nineteenth century" that has perverted the whole notion of "science" (G56/57 27/23).[5]

Heidegger's worry about this talk of "science" is that by "absolutizing" the "theoretical attitude," it effectively blocks any connection with the immediacy of life. He suggests that all this can be left behind in the name of something radically new and so radically uncertain: "We have gone into the aridity of the desert, hoping, instead of always *knowing* [*erkennen*] things, to intuit under-standingly and to *understand intuitively* [*zuschauend zu verstehen und ver-stehend zu schauen*]" (G56/57 65/55). By starting with the "theoretical atti-tude," scientific philosophy "wants to explain something [i.e., life] which one no longer has as such, which one cannot and will not recognize in its validity" (G56/57 86/73). Scientific philosophy has effectively severed its link to con-crete human existence by starting from the assumption that the immediacy of life is mute and irrational. Scientific philosophy transports one to a realm that is "absolutely worldless, world-foreign; it is the sphere which takes one's breath away and where no one can live" (G56/57 112/95).

Two semesters later (WS 1919–1920), Heidegger again announces his rejection of nineteenth-century "scientism." Here, however, he singles out the views of his erstwhile mentor, Edmund Husserl, for particular opprobrium. Heidegger sees no reason why philosophy must feel itself beholden to the mathematical natural sciences as paradigms of genuine intellectual inquiry. The nature and tasks of phenomenology, his own "primordial science [*Ur-wissenschaft*]," need not be borrowed from something foreign to it, particularly not from one or more of the "special sciences" (G58 2 f.). Heidegger wants to steer clear of the "cozy conventionality and allure of scientific day-laborers" (G58 5). In other words, the fact that the special sciences produce "results" is no reason to elevate them into models for all intellectual disciplines. "There is," Heidegger maintains, "no *iurare in verba magistri* [swearing by the word of a master] in scientific research [. . .]" (G58 6). This means that one ought to avoid importing ideals of "science," not to mention particular research prob-lems, from the special sciences. As an example of failure to heed this principle, Heidegger mentions Husserl's well-known talk about "philosophy as a rigorous science." The problem is this idea takes its cue from the successes of the mathematical natural sciences.

Here as well, the problem with "scientific" philosophy is that it has lost any connection with life, especially with "practical" or "intensified" experi-ences like *religious* experiences (G58 68). Heidegger describes how one priv-ileges the standpoint of botany over the sight of a meadow in bloom, of essays in art history over the appreciation of a Rembrandt, or of theological tracts over the experience of a choral mass (G58 76). The rich, personal relations of immediate life-experience have thus been "petrified," translated into a "do-main of objects" that completely lacks the "rhythm and contextual character of life as it is lived" (G58 78). Heidegger aspires to replace this sort of approach with something he calls a "primordial science [*Urwissenschaft*]," which treats of the "original meaning of existence" expressed in the concrete experiences of "grace, vocation, fate" (G58 167).

Heidegger's critique of "scientific" philosophy continues unabated in the following semester (SS 1920). Here Heidegger attempts to raise a question mark over the pervasive understanding of philosophy as nothing but "rational cognition" (G59 24 ff.). Instead, Heidegger suggests the possibility of arriving at a radically new understanding of the nature and problems of philosophy. Ultimately, "scientific" philosophy is to be cast aside because it replaces genuine motives with empty theoretical tasks (G59 170). All philosophizing, he maintains, has a motive, and the question that needs to be asked concerns the origins of this motive. Is philosophy to be motivated by theoretical pseudo-questions, or by something altogether more urgent, more "original [*ürsprunglich*]"?

In his lectures on Paul's epistles, Heidegger expresses similar worries about the real motivations behind talk of "scientific" philosophy. The problem, once again, is that prevailing conceptions of philosophy are motivated by empty, "theoretical" concerns derived from an uncritical acceptance of a tradition that ignores or denies the immediate meaningfulness of practical life. Heidegger urges that philosophy must be motivated by the concrete situation of "factical life-experience" itself. He writes:

> One should not define philosophy in the common manner, should not characterize it by means of a classification [*Einordnung*] in a material context, as when one says: "chemistry is a science" and "painting is an art." One has also attempted to classify philosophy in a system of concepts, such that it is said that philosophy deals with a definite object in a definite way. But here, the scientific conception of philosophy has already been put into play. (G60 8)

Heidegger's suggestion here is that, *prima facie*, there is no clear reason to hold philosophy to the dictates of an unexamined tradition. He even goes so far as to urge that the "idea of science" be kept as far away from the project of understanding the nature of philosophy as possible (G60 9). Heidegger recognizes that this move certainly flies in the face of tradition and is particularly problematic from the standpoint of the late-nineteenth-century concerns about philosophy as "science [*Wissenschaft*]" that I have outlined above. The received view, which Heidegger is challenging here, is that all "great" philosophies seek to elevate themselves to the status of a "rigorous science" (G60 9 f.). Heidegger contends, however, that "[p]hilosophy must be liberated from the 'secularization' with respect to science [. . .]" (G60 10). Just as a philosophy that is simply "secularized" theology would be objectionably dependent on traditional ideas from another discipline, so too the demand that philosophy be a "rigorous science" strips philosophers of the need to sort out their own tasks and self-conceptions.

Several years later, in SS 1923, Heidegger makes a remark that clearly suggests that his willingness to forgo the project of "scientific" philosophy is still intact:

> It is not a matter of obtaining and delivering a series of propositions and dogmas about this Dasein, generating a philosophy around it, about it, and with it, or, as is the main concern for most today, staging a new direction in phenomenology and increasing still more the noise and industry of philosophy which already looks suspicious enough. (G63 47/38)

In case this rejection of traditional philosophical projects is not clear enough, one needs only to look at a remark from earlier in the lecture course. "Hermeneutics," which is his name for his own unique project, "is itself not philosophy. It wishes only to place an object which has hitherto fallen into forgetfulness before today's philosophers for their 'well-disposed consideration'" (G63 20/16). The following semester, Heidegger's first at Marburg (WS 1923–1924), he delivers similar renunciations at the outset of the course. "[N]o foundation, no program or system will be given here: a philosophy is not to be expected. It is my conviction that it is all over for philosophy. We stand before completely new tasks, which have nothing to do with traditional philosophy" (G17 1).

Throughout the early 1920s, the point that Heidegger makes again and again is that the detached irrelevance of "scientific" philosophy must be replaced by a way of doing philosophy that is both sensitive to and motivated by life itself. During WS 1923–1924, he castigates Husserl's "neglect" of "historical life" in the name of a "worry about known knowledge" (G17 89ff.). Heidegger's explicit concern is to challenge, and to ultimately refute, all those conceptions of philosophy that turn it into "an artificial occupation that merely accompanies life and deals with 'universals' of one sort or another and with arbitrarily posited principles" (S 15/121). Such an approach "de-lives" life, cutting it off from personal anxious worry about one's "grace, vocation, [and] fate." "Scientific" philosophy is depersonalized to such a degree that it is rendered incapable of really *addressing* life as it is lived.

"World-view (*Weltanschauung*)?"

Heidegger clearly rejects the demand for "scientific" philosophy. His primary motivation for this was the worry that the very idea of "scientific" philosophy grounded philosophy in artificial problems taken over from an uncritically accepted tradition, rather than in the concrete, urgent demands of "factical life-experience" itself. This aspect of his critique shares much with the polemics of "world-view" philosophers against naturalism, positivism, and neo-Kantianism. Like Heidegger, these thinkers regarded life itself as that which provided the proper sphere of problems and concepts for philosophical research. Heidegger, however, did not go over to the camp of the "life-philosophers." Instead, he subjected them to a critique even more vitriolic than the one he directed against the "scientific" camp.[6]

From the outset of his philosophical maturity, Heidegger unequivocally rejected the construction of a "world-view" as a legitimate task for philosophy.

In the highly charged atmosphere of early 1919, Heidegger addresses the claim that the creation of a world-view is the proper role of philosophy. "Today," he writes, "world-view is a spiritual concern of everyone [. . .]" (G56/57 7/6). A "philosophical" world-view is one that pronounces on the "final sense or origin" of the world, on "nature as a cosmos of the ultimate lawfulness of simple movements or energies" (G56/57 7f./6). What is the purpose of all this frenetic philosophizing? "Within and by means of such fundamental conceptions of the world, man acquires the 'explanations' and interpretations of his individual and social life. The meaning and purpose of human existence, and of human creation as culture, are discovered" (G56/57 8/7). Heidegger has no doubt that historically, philosophical research has often had a connection to world-view. He wants to suggest, however, that there is an alternative, one predicated on a "radical separation" between philosophy and world-view and which implies "an entirely new concept of philosophy which would be totally unrelated to all the ultimate questions of humankind" (G56/57 11/9f.). But one might protest that "[p]hilosophy would thus be deprived of its most traditional entitlements as a regal, superior occupation. What value at all could it have if it should lose this role?" (G56/57 11/9f.). Indeed.

The main text of the lecture course leaves Heidegger's final position on this issue ambiguous. While there is some suggestion that he sees no essential connection between philosophy and world-view, this is by no means explicit (see G56/57 17/14f.). However, in Brecht's transcript of the course, which has recently been published, Heidegger's repudiation of "world-view" philosophy is absolutely clear: "Apparent suitability of this philosophy [i.e., Heidegger's] for world-view. The opposite is the case" (G56/57 220/187). Or, in case there is confusion about Heidegger's position, he asserts that "[p]henomenological philosophy and world-view are opposed to one another" (G56/57 220/187). What is the reasoning behind this claim? Brecht's notes relate one basic worry:

> World-view: this is bringing to a standstill (Natorp maintains this against phenomenology). Life, as the history of the spirit in its transcendental expression, is objectified and frozen in a definite moment. Religious, aesthetic, natural-scientific attitudes are absolutized. All philosophy of culture is world-view philosophy. It freezes definite situations in the history of the spirit and wants to *interpret culture*. World-view is freezing, finality, end, system. (G56/57 220/187f.)

Heidegger presents his worry as being analogous to a common objection to philosophical research of any sort, i.e., that it "stills the stream" of life by fixing it in some conceptual framework, and thus inevitably distorts its concrete richness. This concern is parallel to his other worries about the "theoretical attitude" that derails "scientific" philosophy into artificial problems. What Heidegger means by "the history of the spirit in its transcendental expression" is not immediately clear, though it is likely that Dilthey's later notions of "expression" and "objective spirit" are at work here. Whatever the case may be, the latter portion of this passage clarifies the objection. The problem is with the "absolutizing" of particular contingent values or periods in the development of a culture. In other words, the problem with a "world-view" is the claims to universal validity that are made on its behalf. Such claims restrict the creative possibilities of life, as expressed in the "history of the spirit." This worry is certainly reminiscent of Heidegger's problem with the "system" of Catholicism, expressed in his contemporaneous letter to Father Engelbert Krebs. In that letter, he appears to distinguish between the "life-world" of the Catholic faith and the "system" of Catholicism. Indeed, the Church in this anti-modernist period seems to exemplify the whole problem with "world-views," for it invests historically contingent interpretations of the world and of life with the semi-divine authority of the *magesterium*.

In the following semester, WS 1919–1920, Heidegger once again presents his convictions regarding the illegitimacy of "world-view" philosophy. This time, however, the objection is slightly different from the one presented above. While he no doubt remained suspicious of "absolutizing," in WS 1919–1920 he is more concerned with a kind of moralistic pedantry involved in proclaiming universally valid "world-views." Philosophy, he remarks, is not world-view, but is instead an "understanding that leads into the forms of life itself," though not by trumpeting some "directives and regulations" (G58 150). He then takes the opportunity to clearly reject *both* "scientific" philosophy and "world-view" philosophy: "Philosophy—neither mere investigation of subject matter and objects (validity of propositions); nor sermonizing, practical direction or regulation; rather, a leading [*Führung*] that understands; not the practical usefulness of norms, but rather genuine possibilities of leading and of cultivation [*Bildung*]" (G58 113 f.). What is significant here is not only the rejection of "world-view" and its "sermonizing" proclivities, but also that Heidegger seems to still maintain the possibility that philosophy ought to have some sort of concrete, practical role to play in human life.

During SS 1920, Heidegger's target is those who proclaim grandiose "cultural missions" for philosophy.[7] On the one hand, he repudiates bourgeois ideologues who emulate the grand era of German idealism with its ideals of "humanity" and "culture." On the other hand, he also takes a stab at more socialist tendencies of the sort which proliferated in Germany in the wake of World War I and the Russian Revolution:

> Philosophy, insofar as it remains loyal to itself, is not to be defined in such a way that it must rescue or save the age, the world, etc., or must alleviate the misery of the masses, or must make human beings happy, or cultivate or enhance culture. All of this signifies the direction of an anxious worry in which what it all comes down to simply vanishes. All world-view philosophy corrupts the original motive of philosophizing. (G59 170)

Philosophy, Heidegger contends, is "corrupted" when it becomes ideology. It seems, however, that this conviction had faded by 1933, when Heidegger publicly enlisted his thought in the service of the National Socialist "revolution." While it is true that Heidegger never became a crude ideologue, spouting Nazi doctrine as if it were philosophical truth, it is still undeniable that much of his work from the 1930s is congruent in a general way with the "blood and soil" ideology of the NSDAP. His earlier work, while certainly motivated by particular values, lacks the explicitly political or ideological character that one can easily detect in his lectures and other addresses, particularly from 1933 to 1936.[8] However one might evaluate Heidegger's political commitments from the 1930s, the nature of his position in 1920 is quite clear. While philosophy ought to be motivated by life and not by lifeless pseudo-problems, a concern for "life" should not translate into ideology.

This point is made again clearly during WS 1921–1922. Here Heidegger explicitly comments that the demand that philosophy receive its orientation from "life" is not at all tantamount to the demand that it also offer some "perverted historical salvation" (G61 36/29). He rejects the idea that one can "make proclamations about philosophy from some sort of high, yet, at bottom, unfixable place" (G61 66/50). He is even more strongly opposed to the idea that philosophy should "stand security for the coming period of culture and the fate of humanity." Who, he wonders, has conferred this "cultural mission" onto philosophy? As in KNS 1919, Heidegger is here critical of the way traditional ideas about the nature and tasks of philosophy simply get passed along without further ado. "The philosophy," he suggests, "in this general, soothing timelessness [. . .] does not exist" (G61 66/50). Philosophy ought not to make any claims about what is ultimately "valid and objective for humanity" (G61 165/125). As he puts it in SS 1923, "philosophy has no mission to take care of universal humanity and culture, to release future generations once and for all from care about questioning, or to interfere with them simply through wrongheaded claims to validity" (G63 18/14). "Not every time," Heidegger remarks, "needs to have a grand philosophical system" (G63 75/59).

Heidegger's contemporaneous essays contain similar denunciations of the dubious program of the "world-view" philosophers. For example, in a review of Karl Jaspers's work, Heidegger rejects the prevalent "hustle and bustle" about the "preservation of culture" (G9 5/5). "Thinking phenomenologically," he observes, "is neither mere sport nor prophetic pageantry that promises the salvation of the world" (G9 6/5). Heidegger has no interest in compelling philosophy to "curry favor with the hustle and bustle of an avant-garde culture that is at bottom really hungry for other things, even if it does display wonderful religious antics" (G9 28/25).

Heidegger's primary objection to "world-view" philosophy is that it presumes to pronounce about the "meaning" of life and to construct systematic guidelines for the conduct of life. I have already described Heidegger's general objection to much intellectual discourse, namely, that it is complicit in a fugitive, inauthentic way of life. The "fanaticism" of "world-view" philosophers also comes under the scope of this more global critique (see G61 36/28f.). The whole business of "world-views" is, in Heidegger's mind, nothing less than a "disaster" (G61 44/34). By claiming to offer people "meaning" and "historical salvation," such views give in to a deep urge for ready-made solutions to life's perennial questions, to a "pithless and weak-kneed" avoidance of all radical questioning (G63 20/16). "We do not philosophize," says Heidegger, "in order to fashion for ourselves and others a salutary world-view that could be procured like a coat and hat. The goal of philosophy is not a system of interesting things, nor a sentimental edification for faltering souls" (G26 22/17).

The Motive of Philosophy

This brief overview of Heidegger's positions regarding the various trends in philosophy that were current in his generation makes it clear that he intends to reconceive of the nature of philosophy in a radical way. Just what this conception amounts to is yet to be seen. Before this can be clarified, it is absolutely essential to understand what *motivates* Heidegger's new conception of philosophy. What state of affairs justifies doing philosophy in the way Heidegger recommends? Another, deeper, question also presses itself: Why should one think that philosophy is the proper way to achieve anything at all? Why not let life fend for itself, or pass the buck to some other discipline? The first of these questions, fortunately, is relatively easy to answer. While it is abundantly clear that Heidegger rejected the "cultural mission" of "world-view" philosophy, it is, as I will presently show, also clear that he nonetheless viewed philosophy as an enterprise motivated by life itself. The second question, however, has no obvious answer. Heidegger offers no definitive argument designed to justify the necessity of doing philosophy.

With respect to the first question, recall that one of Heidegger's principal worries about "scientific" philosophy is that it is motivated *not* by concrete life, but by theoretical pseudo-problems rooted in an uncritically accepted tradition. Thus while he certainly rejects the pretensions of the "world-view" camp, Heidegger does not retreat into the detached irrelevance of the "scientific day-laborers" whom he had criticized in WS 1919–1920. Heidegger shares the "world-view" philosopher's concerns with the concrete lives of individuals. The problem, on Heidegger's view, is that the construction of grand systems that encapsulate the "meaning of life" into neat formulas, and the proffering of normative pronouncements of dubious provenance, ultimately fail to really do justice to the issues faced by living men and women. More specifically, this magisterial style of philosophizing is guilty of unburdening individuals of responsibility for their own lives by offering "metaphysical tranquilizers" (NB 3 f./113). As I have already shown (chapter 5), one of Heidegger's abiding worries about intellectual discourse is that it tends to promote a complacent, self-congratulatory way of life.

If philosophy is supposed to be motivated by life, yet must avoid the trap of relieving individuals of self-responsibility, then, given what I have already shown about Heidegger's most basic values, it seems that the primary value that motivates philosophy is the value of an *authentic way of life*. This concern for authenticity is what helps philosophy steer a path between the twin dangers of arid "science" and moralistic "world-view." Most commentators, however, have failed to appreciate the values that motivate Heidegger's whole approach to philosophy. Typical of this trend is Charles R. Bambach, who contends that the "genuine meaning" of Heidegger's work has nothing to do with "sociological anomie or cultural disenchantment," but rather has the more rarefied aim of "rethinking 'crisis' in its phenomenological or originary meaning."[9] There is certainly no reason to think that "sociological anomie" represented a significant concern on Heidegger's part. Nonetheless, it is a mistake to overlook the concrete values that ultimately motivated his idiosyncratic way of doing philosophy.

Heidegger begins to articulate his conception of a kind of philosophy motivated by life itself early in his career. In a letter to Heinrich Rickert from January 17, 1917, Heidegger comments on the obituary of Münsterberg that Rickert had sent to him. He notes the similarities between the deceased and the phenomenologist Emil Lask, who was killed in World War I, singling out "the living unity of personal life and of philosophically creative work" as particularly praiseworthy (HR 37). With respect to any systematic philosophical position, Heidegger's contention is that "personal spirituality and openness" are required to make it effective in an individual's life. For Heidegger, then, "pure logic" ought not to be the ultimate arbiter of worthwhile philosophy, for it does violence to the "living spirit" and "blocks philosophy from a connection with the basic streams of personal life and the fullness of culture and spirit" (HR 38).

Heidegger's correspondence with Elisabeth Blochmann during this period is filled with expressions of a similar sort. His letter of June 18, 1918, for example, is primarily occupied with expressing Heidegger's real concerns about the future of cultural life in Germany (HB 7). Genuine progress requires "unpretentious simplicity [*Schlichtheit*]," rather than "blasé attitudes, decadence, or affectation" (HB 7). Several days before the formal armistice that ended World War I, Heidegger again writes to Blochmann expressing his worries and hopes about the future of Germany. At the close of the letter, he expresses his conviction that intellectuals have concrete obligations with respect to their own people. He writes:

> How it will shape up after the end—which must come, and which is our only salvation—is uncertain. What is certain and unshakeable is the demand on truly spiritual people not to become weak now, but rather to take decisive leadership in hand, and to instruct the people for truthfulness, and for a genuine appreciation of the genuine goods of Dasein. (HB 12)

These remarks no doubt express a sentiment shared by many "truly spiritual people" at the time. Certainly, the "world-view" philosophers and neo-Kantian "philosophers of culture" shared Heidegger's concern with defining the role of the intellectual in public life. Heidegger, however, expresses his own particular values here, calling for something he names "truthfulness." As I showed earlier (chapter 6), Heidegger uses terms like "truthfulness," "inner truthfulness," and "genuineness" in the immediate post-war period as ways of intimating an authentic way of life. However, while this ideal is unmistakably present in this passage, there is little indication of what the "genuine goods of Dasein" might be, or of how "truly spiritual people" are supposed to foster appreciation of them.

The motivations for philosophizing appear again in Heidegger's well-known letter to Father Engelbert Krebs, in which he renounces his Catholic faith and intimates his new beginning in philosophy. He contrasts the "philosopher," who is called upon to face "sacrifices, renunciation, and struggles," with the shallow "academic technician" (S 70). Here again, this sentiment animated many in Heidegger's generation, and in the one preceding. It certainly calls to mind Nietzsche's attacks on the pedestrian "laborers" of the academy in the name of the creative "philosopher of the future." Such critiques, as well as Kierkegaard's mocking assault on the self-importance of "assistant professors," resonated with many people who lived through the devastations wrought by World War I, an event that had been rationalized by many intellectuals. For Heidegger, the "business" of philosophy is of no importance. What matters to him is that he wants to commit himself to philosophy as a vocation. He ends his letter to Krebs thus: "I believe that I have the inner calling to philosophy and, through my research and teaching, to do what stands in my power for the sake of the eternal vocation of the inner man, and *to do it for this alone*, and so justify my existence [*Dasein*] and work ultimately before God" (S 70).

These letters reveal that Heidegger's philosophizing was motivated by a concern for "life" and for valuable ways of life. A famous letter to Karl Löwith, written a few years after these, expresses similar convictions. He argues, "One can only show what philosophy in the university is through his own life" (HL 29). For him, there is ultimately no real separation between "the scientific, theoretical, conceptual, researching life and the one's own [*eigene*] life" (HL 30). He continues, "Thus, for me, the motive and purpose of philosophizing is never to add to the stock of objective truths, because the objectivity of philosophy—so far as I understand it, and in terms of which I carry out [my research]—is something peculiar to oneself [*eigenes*]" (HL 30). These statements candidly reveal Heidegger's motivation for rejecting "scientific" philosophy and its demands for "objectivity." His aim in teaching at the university (in this case, Freiburg) is "*to seize hold of* [*zugreifen*] human beings" (HL 31).

Heidegger's later correspondence with Jaspers is also revealing. For Heidegger, philosophy should not remain a detached academic exercise, but instead must be understood as a personal vocation. He writes to Jaspers that a decision to "deal seriously with philosophy and its possibilities as principled, scientific research" requires staking one's entire life on this project (HJ 28).

Carrying out philosophical research is not some private affair, but has clear implications for the wider community. "These are things that one does not talk about, and which one can only indicate in a certain manner of expression. If one does not succeed in awakening such consciousness in the youth in a positive and concrete way, then all talk [*Gerede*] about the crisis of the sciences is just that, idle talk [*Gerede*]" (HJ 28). A quiet vocational commitment to philosophy, or to science more generally, is worth much more in Heidegger's eyes than "chatter" about university reform and intellectual crises. In the end, talk is always cheap. He writes to Jaspers that if "we are not clear with ourselves that we must exemplify [*vorleben*] such matters for the youth [. . .]," then "we have no right to live within scientific research" (HJ 28). Genuine philosophy is a matter of entering into a "fundamental struggle" rather than choosing the easy path of "business" and "indifference" (HJ 29).

A year later, on July 14, 1923, Heidegger gives voice to similar ideas. Reforming philosophy in the university "will never be attained through merely writing books. Whoever has not yet realized that today, and who leads a pseudo-existence in the humdrum routine of today's hustle and bustle, does not know where he stands" (HJ 42). The "fearful, miserable handiwork" of the "medicine-men" of philosophy must be exposed for what it is (HJ 42). For Heidegger, genuine "upheaval" or "revolution [*Umsturz*]" takes place "inconspicuously," not with loud announcements about the decline of civilization or the promulgation of ideological programs. In all the letters I have cited here, Heidegger makes it abundantly clear that the practice of philosophy is supposed to be motivated by a concrete concern with the "genuineness" of human life. What is ultimately at stake for him is not whether or not he makes some contribution to the "academic business," but rather that he remains loyal to his own vocation as a philosopher. Philosophy, on Heidegger's view, is not only motivated by life, but is itself a total way of life.

These ideas are also unmistakably present in Heidegger's lecture courses from this period. One of his earliest and most detailed discussions of the practical role of philosophy comes in KNS 1919. University and cultural reform are real issues for him, though the usual approaches to these issues are totally unsatisfactory to Heidegger, not surprising given what I have already discussed. Carrying out work in the university is not a private affair, for the "scientific man [. . .] does not stand in isolation. He is connected to a community of similarly striving researchers with its rich relations to students" (G56/57 4/4). While clearly recognizing the importance of the issue of university reform and expressing a willingness to contribute to it, Heidegger nonetheless finds most discussions of it to be "totally misguided," occupied not with "genuine revolutionizing of the spirit" but rather with "appeals, protest meetings, programs, orders and alliances" (G56/57 4/4). Heidegger's view is that "life-relations renew themselves only by returning [*im Rückgang*] to the genuine origins of the spirit" (G56/57 5/4). What is required is the "truthfulness of a worthwhile [*wertvolle*] and self-cultivated [*sich aufbauenden*] life" (G56/57

5/4). Or, as he puts it a bit later, "[o]nly life, not the noise of frenetic cultural programs, is 'epoch-making'" (G56/57 5/4).

While he rejected the "chatter" about university reform current at the time, Heidegger nevertheless was struggling to articulate some conception of the broader cultural and social role of philosophy. This conception appears to be based upon Heidegger's well-documented commitment to an authentic way of life, or, as he calls it here, the "truthfulness of a worthwhile and self-cultivated life." This guiding value dictates the nature of the philosophical program that was then taking shape in Heidegger's mind. He writes that "[t]he awakening and heightening of the life-context of scientific consciousness is not the object of theoretical representation, but of exemplary pre-living [*Vorleben*] —not the object of practical provision of rules, but the effect of primordially motivated personal and nonpersonal *being*" (G56/57 5/5). This suggests that the role of the philosopher in the renewal of the university (i.e., the "life-context of scientific consciousness") is not to add to the stock of programmatic prescriptions for pedagogical reform. The philosopher's place in the revolution of society is a quiet one, even a silent one. The actual *life* of "scientific research," not theoretical pronouncements about it, is the only thing that is capable of achieving a "genuine revolutionizing of the spirit."

As I have already shown (chapter 5), Heidegger's notion of an "authentic life" represents his own particular version of the Romantic personalist ideal of individuality [*Eigentümlichkeit*]. One of the key features of the latter is the assertion of the artist as a paradigmatic figure. In Heidegger's own version of Romantic personalism, derived from his readings of Schleiermacher and Dilthey, the religious person plays a similar role. Here, in KNS 1919, as he tries to articulate his vision of the role of the philosopher in the community, Heidegger calls upon these models from the Romantic personalist tradition to express the sort of "personal *being*" that is required for genuine reform: "But just as the awe of the religious man makes him silent in the face of the ultimate mystery, just as the genuine artist lives only in his work and detests all art-chatter, so the scientific man is effective only by way of the vitality of genuine research" (G56/57 5/4). Life, it seems, speaks louder than theory. As with the artist or the religious person, Heidegger is convinced that "scientific," i.e., philosophical, research is only practically efficacious when it grows out of an "inner calling" (G56/57 5/5). Brecht records how Heidegger concluded his course with a similar observation: "The genuine insights [. . .] can only be arrived at through honest and uncompromising sinking into the genuineness of life as such, in the final event, only through the genuineness of *personal* life as such" (G56/57 220/187 f.).

While Heidegger's thoughts on the nature of philosophy are still sketchy during the early months of 1919, it is abundantly clear that he is attempting to articulate a view of a philosophy not motivated by theory but by the concrete value of an authentic life. Almost a year later (WS 1919–1920), Heidegger is still struggling to articulate these ideas without compromising them. Here he once again alludes to the "innermost living vocation" of philosophy without, however, spelling this out in much detail (G58 2). He does, however, discuss what he calls the "radicalism" of philosophy:

> a consciousness of problems that is genuine, original, living, continually ploughing up the ground anew, never resting—genuine science, which our age, and the nineteenth century, have lost, and which one cannot define ahead of time for the newly dawning age, but which has to be lived anew. A living concern, personal *being and creating* (→ radicalism). (G58 5)

In this passage, Heidegger enumerates some of the principal features of what he calls the "radicalism" of philosophy. One can imagine that he probably elaborated on these ideas for his audience. Even though these remarks are sketchy, their basic intention is more or less clear. For Heidegger, the "radicalism" of philosophy consists in making "science" into a *personal vocation*. He has no interest in adumbrating some universal project for future generations, but only in struggling to find his own way, in his own particular time, of doing philosophy. Philosophy, for Heidegger, is motivated not by theory, but by "living concern," by "personal being."

This does not mean, however, that philosophy is the private affair of a particular individual. Remarks from a later section of this lecture course reveal that the opposite is the case: the philosopher *qua* philosopher must have some role to play in the social and cultural life of her particular generation. Philosophy, Heidegger contends, is an enterprise that is ultimately concerned with "a genuine motivation for the fates (tasks) that fall to it, to its generation, and to humanity" (G58 150). Philosophy is a "leading that understands," a project that is focused upon the development of "genuine possibilities of leading and of cultivation" (G58 150). Philosophy ought to be motivated by a concern for the concrete problems and possibilities that face one's generation as a whole, of which one is inevitably a part. Heidegger concludes these reflections by clearly articulating his conception of the real motive for philosophical research:

> Understanding is itself a leading, so long as understanding is always an understanding of life, and hence a cultivation [*Bildung*], preservation, unlocking of motivations, and of the genuineness of life that understands. Every genuine philosophy is born of the *lack* of fullness of life, not from some epistemological pseudo-problem or fundamental ethical question. (G58 150)

As I have shown above, in KNS 1919 all signs point to "authenticity" as the primary value that motivates the actual practice of philosophy as a "living" vocation. This is suggested as well by remarks Heidegger makes toward the end of his SS 1920 lecture. Having examined the work of Paul Natorp and Wilhelm Dilthey in some detail, Heidegger takes the opportunity to clarify his own conception of the nature of philosophy and of its peculiar motives and tasks.

> Philosophy has the task of preserving and strengthening the facticity of life. Philosophy, as factical life-experience, requires a motive, where the anxious worry about factical life-experience persists. [. . .] This is not some special illumination, but is possible for every concrete Dasein, where anxious worry brings itself back to actual Dasein. In this reversal [*Umkehr*], the renewal [of anxious worry] is directed towards the self-world, and the conceptuality of philosophy must be understood, and defined, in terms of this. (G59 174)

Philosophy, according to Heidegger, is a kind of extension or articulation of a tendency that can be found in concrete life itself, i.e., "anxious worry" about the "self-world." As I have discussed previously (chapter 6), terms like "anxious worry [*Bekümmerung*]," "intensifying concentration [*Zugespitzt-heit*]," and the like are used during this period (ca. 1920) by Heidegger as formal indications of an authentic way of life. It will be recalled that the crucial feature of an authentic way of life is that it overcomes or clears away the "masks," provided by its own culture and by public discourse, that alienate a person from her own life. An authentic life is one of profound self-honesty, something Heidegger later calls "wakefulness." As Heidegger makes clear in this passage, an "authentic life" is not some "special illumination" only available to the spiritual or cultural elite. Indeed, all signs point to the fact that, on his view, this elite and its "idle talk" are largely complicit in foreclosing the possibility of an authentic life. In a way analogous to Aristotle's grounding of philosophy on the universal desire of human beings for knowledge, Heidegger here grounds philosophy on the universal possibility that human beings can gain knowledge of themselves of a particular sort. It is on the basis of this possibility, and in the interests of preserving it and cultivating it, that philosophy ought to be undertaken.

I have discussed in detail (chapter 1) that, for Heidegger, philosophy must be rooted in a "basic experience" so as not to float free of "factical life." An authentic way of life, of which Christian faith is a paradigmatic instance, represents just the sort of "basic experience" that Heidegger is after (see also chapter 5). As I suggested in chapter 1, the proper way to understand Heidegger's lifelong project of "saving" primitive Christianity is to recognize it as an attempt to preserve, articulate, and cultivate the radical spirit of individuality, personal vocation, and self-knowledge that he found in Paul, Luther, and others. As the passage quoted above from SS 1920 clearly indicates, this project was by no means a peripheral concern for Heidegger, but cut right to the heart of his conception of the nature of philosophy.

Indeed, during WS 1920–1921, the famous "religion lectures," Heidegger makes some general statements about the real motives and aims of philosophical research. It is worth noting that these remarks are found in contiguity with his most detailed analysis of primitive Christian life-experience. Near the beginning of the course, Heidegger takes time to consider the problem of the "self-understanding" of philosophy. He claims that "[s]hould one happen to take up this problem in a radical way, one would find that philosophy springs from [*entspringt*] factical life-experience, and then it leaps back into factical life-experience itself" (G60 8). The term Heidegger uses here for the "factical" genesis of philosophy, '*entspringen*,' has a number of connotations. First, it connotes the origination of a river or stream from its source. To take this metaphor a bit further than Heidegger does here, one might say that, on his conception, philosophy remains in organic connection to its sources in "factical life-experience." At the same time, '*entspringen*' also connotes "leaping away" from something, an act of rejection or repudiation. Insofar as the "spring" from which philosophy flows is "anxious worry" (SS 1920), it can be concluded that philosophy involves the repudiation of an inauthentic, complacent way of life. This much is suggested by Heidegger's talk, a bit later on, of the "inversion [*Umwendung*]" of life that leads to philosophy, which he glosses as an "authentic *transformation* [*Umwandlung*]" (G60 10).[10]

As a practice that emerges from life, philosophy is something that must be *motivated* by life. During SS 1923, Heidegger expresses this motivation in the Pauline language of "wakefulness." The first passage relevant to the present discussion, however, sounds more "Left Hegelian" than Christian, a fact which has led Jean Grondin to draw an analogy between Heidegger's work and that of Hegelian social critics such as Marx and Lukács. Heidegger writes:

> Hermeneutics has the task of making the Dasein which is in each case our own accessible to this Dasein itself with regard to the character of its being, communicating Dasein to itself in this regard, hunting down the alienation with which it is smitten. (G63 15/11)

Particularly striking in this passage is that Heidegger explicitly assigns the overcoming of alienation as a "task" for his "hermeneutics." This claim indicates once again that some sort of concrete, practical project lies at the very heart of Heidegger's philosophical work. Heidegger uses the language of "alienation" here to describe the concrete situation that calls for philosophy in the first place. As I have shown previously (chapter 3), "alienation" is one of the principal features of an "inauthentic" way of life. Having relinquished self-responsibility, an inauthentic person lives at the beck and call of the anonymous public (see SZ 178/222). During SS 1923, Heidegger dubs his own idiosyncratic approach to philosophy the "hermeneutics of facticity." He makes it clear that hermeneutics not only takes "facticity" (i.e., human life) as its object, but also that it *belongs* to facticity itself. Hermeneutics, then, attempts to overcome "alienation" by engaging with life at the most immediate, concrete level. Hence hermeneutics is supposed to be a way of doing philosophy that overcomes the aridity and abstractness of the usual "scientific" approaches.

In place of this vaguely defined "alienation," Heidegger's hermeneutics attempts to cultivate a kind of clear-sighted self-understanding that he calls "wakefulness." Heidegger emphasizes this point a number of times in this lecture (G63 15f./12). The term "wakefulness [*Wachsein*]" derives from Heidegger's reading of 1 Thessalonians during WS 1920–1921 (see G60 104f.). Paul contrasts the "wakefulness" of the primitive Christians with the "darkness" of those who live in the "world," who do not know themselves, and who will consequently be overwhelmed by the sudden "day of the Lord." Paul's letter aims to foster this brand of self-knowledge and personal commitment by warning the Thessalonians against the danger of getting "lost" or "alienated" from themselves in everyday life or in eschatological enthusiasm. He writes: "So let us not fall asleep as others do, but let us keep awake and be sober [. . .]" (1 Thess. 5:6). He calls on the community to arm themselves for a struggle to remain loyal to the proclamation that led to their conversion in the first place (1 Thess. 5:8f.).

As in his private correspondences, Heidegger takes many opportunities during his lectures to intimate the concrete motivations for his philosophical project. In a number of passages from his lectures, we can see that there is an explicit connection between the practice of philosophy and the value of an authentic way of life, itself referred to variously as "wakefulness," "anxious worry," or "truthfulness." The situation is much the same with regard to an unpublished essay that Heidegger composed in late 1922. This text, the much-discussed "Natorp Report," is a particularly rich source of Heidegger's views on the nature of philosophical inquiry. This is particularly true with respect to the term "destruction [*Destruktion*]," which appears a number of times in this essay. I will have occasion to examine "destruction" in more detail below. At this point I will simply draw attention to a number of passages from this essay which clearly articulate Heidegger's commitment to the concrete or, as he would say, "factical," dimension of philosophical research.

This text not only corroborates my contention that on Heidegger's view, philosophy is motivated by a concern with authenticity, but it also suggests an answer to one of the questions I raised at the beginning of this discussion. Granted that philosophy for Heidegger is indeed motivated by a concern with authenticity, why should one think it has any essential role to play in human life in the first place? In the Natorp Report, Heidegger contends that philosophy is not some adventitious appendage to life. "Rather," he asserts, "it needs to be understood as an explicit taking up of a basic movement of factical life. In this movement, life is in such a way that in the concrete temporalizing of its being, it is anxiously worried about its being, even when it goes out of its way to avoid itself" (NB 3/113). This passage bears a clear affinity to the remarks, quoted previously, from SS 1920, in which Heidegger also links the motive for philosophy with "anxious worry [*Bekümmerung*]." As in WS 1920–1921, Heidegger here presents the idea that philosophy is an organic outgrowth of a concrete possibility that can be found in human life as such. The claim that philosophy is an articulation of the natural capacity of human beings for critical self-awareness is restated in a slightly different way in the years after the publication of *Being and Time*. For example, in his lecture for WS 1928–1929, Heidegger asserts abruptly that "[t]o be there as a human being means to philosophize" (G27 3). This bold assertion is rooted in the view that there are different "levels of being awake" or of self-knowledge that can be found in life itself (G27 3, 11 f.). A few years later, during WS 1929–1930, Heidegger states that philosophy is simply an expression of the basic "restlessness" or "home-sickness" of human life in general (G29/30 8/5 f.). Philosophy takes place within this "essence" of humanity (G29/30 10/7). Heidegger elaborates on this claim later: "Philosophy is the opposite of all comfort and assurance. It is turbulence, the turbulence into which man is spun, so as in this way alone to comprehend Dasein without illusion" (G29/30 28 f./19). Again the idea is that philosophy is one of the ways human existence can be "awake" to itself (G29/30 33/23).

Human beings, according to Heidegger, have a native ability to understand life. In *Being and Time*, he states this in a slightly different way, pointing out that a "vague understanding" of "being" is one of the primitive "facts" about humanity (SZ 5 f./25). Philosophy attempts to "articulate" or "lay out [*aus-legen*]" this basic, ground-level understanding (SZ 37/61 f.). These remarks are meant to show that philosophy is not simply *arbitrary* or *adventitious*, but rather emerges from what Heidegger takes to be *the* basic feature of human life. Ultimately, however, Heidegger gives no deep justification for the view that philosophical research is a necessity for life. There is no suggestion, for example, that philosophy is the *only* way to combat the deleterious effects of public discourse on individuality. The most one can say here is that there is philosophy and that it has played a decisive role in the shaping of European culture. In the end, however, philosophy is always something that is questionable for Heidegger.

During the early 1920s, "anxious worry" often functioned as a way of indicating an "authentic" style of life. Heidegger is once again linking this with philosophy in a way that strongly suggests the recognition that, on his view, the ultimate motivating force behind philosophy is the ideal of authenticity. That some such motivation is at work is clear from a later remark as well. Heidegger rejects the idea that philosophy is "an artificial occupation that merely accompanies life and deals with 'universals' of one sort or another and arbitrarily posited principles" (NB 15/121). Instead, he contends that philosophy is a discipline that "has radically and clearly resolved to throw factical life back on itself as this is possible in this factical life itself and to let it fend for itself in terms of its own factical possibilities" (NB 16/121).

The Practice of Philosophy

In the previous section, I presented clear evidence that while he rejects the superficial pedantry of "world-view" philosophy, Heidegger nonetheless has more in mind for philosophy than the staid research of "science." This other element in his philosophy can be understood in two ways: (1) with respect to motive, and (2) with respect to practice. With respect to motive,

Heidegger contends that at least for him, philosophy is motivated by a concern with the value of an authentic way of life. With respect to practice, this motivation translates into a desire to do philosophy in such a way that it actually serves to foster this value. For Heidegger, this means that, above all, philosophy should be regarded as a *personal vocation*. At the same time, in order to realize the demands implicit in its motivation, philosophy is called upon to address itself to "factical life-experience," i.e., to the real, concrete situation of actual men and women united by the intellectual climate of their generation. How to do this without lapsing into the "prophetic pageantry" and "sermonizing" of the "world-view" philosophers? How can philosophy realize its practical goal without compromising its commitment to the value of individuality?

Part of the key to understanding Heidegger's answers to these questions is to recall his conception of the social side of an authentic life. As I argued in a previous chapter (chapter 6), Heidegger's view is that an authentic individual acts in such a way as to promote the authenticity of the other people with whom she finds herself inextricably linked in a generational "community of struggle." The way to do this is not through paternalistic "sermonizing," nor through demanding a uniformity of belief and practice, but rather through dialogue, "struggle [*Kampf*]," and silent exemplification of what it means to live an authentic life. I have already noted that in KNS 1919 in particular, Heidegger envisions a similar kind of practice with regard to the role of the philosopher within the academic community. Elsewhere, Heidegger candidly admits that his desire is to compel people to self-reflection (G9 42/36). Yet, he asserts, this can only really be accomplished by "traveling a stretch of the way oneself" (G9 42/36). Rather than offering up new possibilities for self-deception, new "masks" that allow individuals to hide from the challenge of "genuinely" being themselves, one ought only to "call something to the attention of others" (G9 42/36). Heidegger also says that the "claims" of his particular mode of philosophizing "must be restricted to *calling something to the attention of others*. This is," he writes, "ultimately the predicament of all philosophizing regarding its intention of having an effect in the world of others" (G9 6/5).

What does it mean to "compel" someone to "reflection" through example and through calling something to her attention? Part of the answer lies in the notion that philosophical language is "formal indication." Philosophical discourse is supposed to point to possibilities of meaning, without giving too much away. Heidegger makes this point a bit more poetically in his 1946 "Letter on 'Humanism'": "With its saying, thinking lays inconspicuous furrows in language. They are still more inconspicuous than the furrows that the farmer, slow of step, draws through the field" (G9 364/276). In addition to this, however, Heidegger's remarks during the early 1920s make it clear that there is another side of the practice of philosophy that is also relevant to realizing its concrete, practical project. A philosopher can "compel" someone to "reflection" not only by offering suggestive intimations of thoughtworthy issues, but also by violating the boundaries of the complacent self-images, the "masks," that keep individuals locked in an inauthentic way of life. Herbert Marcuse, one of Heidegger's students, described the situation of modern humanity as "one-dimensionality." This is a metaphor for the kind of leveled-down homogeneity that characterizes an inauthentic way of life. In addition to "laying inconspicuous furrows," Heidegger also wants to break up the level ground of everydayness by directly challenging the hegemony of uncritically accepted ways of thinking and acting. His ultimate purpose in doing so is to break out of superficial "one-dimensionality" and to expand the horizon of meaning available for authentic vocational commitment.

This critical practice, Heidegger notes at one point, is what really constitutes the "rigor" of philosophy, rather than any slavish imitation of the mathematical sciences. "The *rigor* of philosophy," he writes, "is more original than all scientific rigor, for it must heighten anxious worry in its constant renewal in the facticity of Dasein, and must ultimately make actual Dasein insecure" (G59 174). Philosophy is a practice that disturbs the security of an "inauthentic" life. Heidegger makes this clear in WS 1921–1922, where he asserts that the "basic sense" of philosophy is the "radical existentiell grasping" of "questionableness" (G61 35/28). "Skepticism, so understood, is the beginning, and as the genuine beginning, it is also the end of philosophy" (G61 35/28). Later in this same course, he mentions Plato's portrait of Socrates as a paradigm of the sort of thing he has in mind. Philosophy, according to Plato, is a "vocation [*Beruf*]," and a "dangerous" one at that (G61 49/38). Heidegger clearly shares this romanticized picture of the philosopher's vocation, for he ultimately argues that the only proper response that can be made to the problems of "university reform" is a critical reflection that challenges what seems "obvious" at a particular time (G61 72f./54f.).

Philosophy is to be understood, on Heidegger's view, as a "counter-motion," a "motion against [*Gegenbewegtheit*]" the "ruinance" that life inflicts upon itself (G61 132/99). It can do so only because there is the actual possibility that life can "question the insular and uncontested certainty of its immediacy and can inquire into the possible guarantee of that certainty" (G61 152/113). As a "counter-ruinant motion," philosophy does not aim at securing eternal answers to life's troubling questions (G61 153/113). Rather, the questioning must be kept alive as long as possible, a kind of questioning that must be understood as "the constant *struggle* of factical, philosophical interpretation against its own ruinance, a struggle that always accompanies the process of the actualization of philosophizing" (G61 153/114).

I have already mentioned that the Natorp Report of 1922 is a rich source for understanding Heidegger's conception of philosophy. This is true with regard to the present issue, i.e., the idea that philosophy realizes its practical goals, at least in part, through making life insecure. Here Heidegger contends that "the genuinely fitting way of gaining access to [life] and of truly safekeeping it can only consist in making itself hard for itself" (NB 3/113). Even more striking is Heidegger's assertion that this is the only real "duty" that a philosopher has:

> This [making things hard] is the only duty philosophical research can be required to fulfill, unless of course it wants to miss its object completely. All making it easy, all the seductive compromising of needs, all the metaphysical tranquilizers prescribed for problems that have been for the most part derived from mere book learning—the basic intention of all of this is from the start to give up with regard to the task that must in each case be carried out, namely, bringing the object of philosophy into view, grasping it, and, indeed, preserving it. (NB 3 f./113)

Heidegger contrasts his own vision of the nature of philosophical research with the sort of intellectual discourse that provides "masks" behind which individuals hide from the realities of life. I have previously shown (chapter 4) how, like Luther, Heidegger is critical of the way public discourse, particularly intellectual discourse, functions as an accomplice in an inauthentic way of life. While Luther was particularly exercised with the use of Aristotelian concepts in attempts to formulate the doctrine of "justification," Heidegger's opprobrium falls on historical consciousness, philosophy, and various kinds of religious discourse. Despite the greater breadth of the scope of Heidegger's critique, it nevertheless shares a great deal with Luther, as well as with Kierkegaard and the neo-orthodox "dialectical" theologians of the 1920s.[11] Hans-Georg Gadamer recalls several incidents in which Heidegger publicly criticized these "radical" theologians for not being radical enough. Theodore Kisiel also relates how Heidegger raised some critical questions on the occasion of a talk by Barth's colleague Josef Heitmüller, "On the Interpretation of the New Testament" (June 27, 1925).[12]

All this should come as no surprise, for the evidence of his lectures, essays, and correspondences clearly reveal that Heidegger's conception of philosophy as a *critical* discipline motivated by a concern with authenticity owes a great deal to his readings of Paul, Luther, Kierkegaard, and others. Heidegger's analysis of the Pauline "proclamation [*Verkündigung*]" is particularly instructive in this regard. During WS 1920–1921, Heidegger takes Galatians, as well as 1 and 2 Thessalonians, as the subject of his lecture. While his remarks on Galatians are rather sketchy, he nonetheless is able to convey a clear picture of the "how" of the "proclamation." Paul's discourse in this epistle is motivated, according to Heidegger, by a "struggle [*Kampf*]," a "religious passion" that lies at the center of Paul's "existence [*Existenz*] as an apostle" (G60 68). That is, just as philosophy, which "makes it difficult [*Schwermachen*]," is a personal vocation, so too Paul's preaching has its place not in rarefied theory but in his own personal vocation as an apostle. As Heidegger puts it a bit later, "[t]he love of God for human beings is the foundation, not theoretical cognition" (G60 71). Paul has no interest in a "theological system" (G60 73). The ultimate value that motivates Paul's "struggle" is, of course, "salvation," or, to use the parlance of the New Testament itself, "life" (G60 68f.). While Paul's concern for the community is not in question, Heidegger nevertheless maintains that his ultimate purpose is not the "rescue of the Galatians" (G60 69).

Similar things can be said about 1 and 2 Thessalonians. Rather than bringing illusory comfort, Paul's letter brings "tribulation [*Trübsal*]" (G60 94). Instead of offering material for objective contemplation, it "pushes the one who receives it into an effective connection with God" (G60 94f.). Furthermore, Paul has no interest in providing entertaining information about mystical experiences in order to ground his authority (G60 98). Heidegger refers to 2 Cor. 12:2–10, where Paul praises weakness over mystical self-glorification, thus causing a "dissociation" between the "enraptured mystic [*Entrücker*]" and the "apostle" (G60 98). Paul's response to the community's questions does not set them at ease, but instead "forces the Thessalonians back upon themselves" (G60 102f.). He has nothing to offer those bent on "enthusiasm" or "inquisitive brooding," to those who "have no authentic personal interest in it" (G60 105).

According to Heidegger, in 2 Thessalonians, Paul "only makes their distress greater" (G60 107). There is no room whatsoever for a "Christian worldview," for getting a "handle [*Halt*]" on God (G60 122). A more detailed discussion of Paul's motives can be found in an appendix to the main body of the lecture notes. There, Heidegger tells us that "[t]he motivation for writing the letter lies in Paul's actual life, in a struggle against life that has 'actual significance,' rather than in 'an accidental mood, diversion, pleasure, amiability, or personal sympathy'" (G60 143). In Paul's preaching, the Gospel "breaks in [*einschlägt*]" (G60 143). It does so "not in wise discourse [*Weisheitsrede*], not in much chatter, through which the cross would be emptied of meaning, but rather simply through his fittingly unpretentious talk" (G60 144). Paul's preaching, then, is clearly a paradigmatic instance of the sort of quiet exemplification designed to challenge people to take on the burden of their own individual lives, which, as early as KNS 1919, Heidegger had identified with philosophy.

A similarly uncompromising way of conveying the basic Christian message can be found in Luther's works. As Van Buren in particular has shown, we have every reason to think that Luther's famously vitriolic style had a great impact on Heidegger.[13] Van Buren asserts, correctly, that "[t]he young Heidegger saw himself at this time as a kind of philosophical Luther of western metaphysics."[14] I have already examined (chapter 2) Luther's radical conception of the Christian proclamation, which he often captured by the term '*destructio*' and its cognates. What Van Buren does not discuss, but which can be clearly seen through a close reading of Luther's works, is that the ultimate purpose of '*destructio*' is *soteriological*. '*Destructio*,' whether it be the painful experience of "spiritual trial [*Anfechtung*]" or the biblical exegesis of a theology professor at Wittenberg, is a way of clearing the ground to make room for the grace of God. If we take Paul and Luther as Heidegger's paradigms, as the evidence suggests we must, then it becomes clear that the ultimate motivation for the way of doing philosophy that comes to be called *'Destruktion'* is none other than *authenticity*.

Heidegger's vocabulary clearly suggests that it was Luther who ultimately taught him to reconceive of philosophy's critical function as a "destruction." His term *'Destruktion'* is a Germanization of Luther's Latin *'destructio.'* Luther uses the latter as a way of talking about the disruptive effect of the Christian message on self-satisfied sinfulness. The proximate aim of the Word of God, according to Luther, is "to pluck up and to break down, to destroy [*destruas*] and to overthrow" (LW25 136; WA56 158). The Gospel, he claims, "does nothing else than to destroy [*destruit*] those who are presumptuous concerning their own righteousness to make room for grace, that they may know that the Law is fulfilled not by their own powers but only through Christ, who pours out the Holy Spirit in their hearts" (LW25 326f.; WA56 338). The Word "destroys [*destruit*] and eradicates and scatters [*dissipate*] everything, as Jer. 23.29 says, 'Is not my Word like fire, says the Lord, and like a hammer which breaks the rocks in pieces?'" (LW25 415; WA56 423).

Like Heidegger, Luther also takes Paul to be a paradigm. The "whole task of the apostle," he comments, is "to destroy their own righteousness" (LW25 191f.; WA56 200). He opens part of his commentary on Romans by observing, in a similar vein, that "[t]he chief purpose of this letter is to break down, to pluck up, and to destroy [*destruere*] all wisdom and righteousness of the flesh" (LW25 135; WA56 159). In so doing, Paul is simply conforming to the purposes of God. Luther, of course, often complains that this is beyond the powers of his theological enemies, particularly the nominalist theologians with their doctrine of *facere quod in se est*.

While Luther certainly puts a great deal of emphasis on *'destructio'* as the proximate goal of divine activity, he also makes it clear that ultimate goal is the salvation of humanity:

> So it seems to me, and I declare: When God begins to justify a man, he first of all condemns him; him whom he wishes to raise up [*aedificare*], he destroys [*destruit*]; him whom he wishes to heal, he smites; and the one to whom he wishes to give life, he kills, as he says in 1 Kings 2 [1 Sam. 2:6], and Deut. 32 [:29], "I kill and make alive, etc." (LW31 99; WA1 540)

Given Luther's influence on Heidegger's developing conception of the nature and tasks of philosophy, it is no surprise that during WS 1919–1920, he employs the manifestly Lutheran term *'Destruktion'* to describe the critical aspect of philosophical research. As I have argued up to this point, this critical aspect that "makes things hard" for life and roots out its fugitive "masks" is Heidegger's way of conceiving the possible contribution of philosophy to an authentic way of life. Heidegger, too, aims to "destroy" these "masks" in order to "raise up" the possibility that one might take hold of one's own individual life.

Destruction

Since we are unable to see phenomena of existence today in an authentic manner, we no longer experience the meaning of conscience and responsibility that lies in the historical itself (the historical is not merely something of which we have knowledge and about which we write books; rather, we ourselves are it, and have it as a task).

(G9 33f./29)

My discussion up to this point has been driven by two primary goals: (1) to understand what Heidegger means by '*Destruktion,*' and (2) to clarify and demonstrate the pervasive influence of Christian thought and experience on this central aspect of Heidegger's project. Destruction [*Destruktion*] itself has yet to have been made an explicit theme of discussion. Instead I have focused on the task of clarifying the context in which it makes sense. This context includes these three general elements: (1) Luther's "theology of the cross," in which the term '*destructio*' and its cognates are frequently employed, (2) Heidegger's views on the role of tradition and public discourse in shaping individual identity, and (3) Heidegger's moral ideal of an *authentic* way of life. It is only against this complex background that the real meaning of "destruction" can become apparent.

The present chapter is the culmination of my study. Having articulated what I take to be the proper context, my aim here is to examine in detail the meaning of the term "destruction." While destruction has long been recognized as a vital element in Heidegger's thought, few have examined its meaning in detail. For the most part, the term is used in the literature without much significant comment. For this reason, there is a serious *deficiency* in our under-standing of Heidegger's thought. My goal in this chapter is to correct this by articulating a detailed account of the use of the term *'Destruktion'* in Heidegger's work from the 1920s.

As I will show in more detail below, the lack of comment on destruction is not the only problem that has dogged the secondary literature on Heidegger. Even in cases where it has received some comment, scholars have overlooked the vital and obvious link between this term and Heidegger's attempt to foster an *authentic* way of life. Part of the key to overcoming this more serious problem is, as I have already suggested (chapter 2), seeing that the roots of Heidegger's destruction lie in his appropriation of Luther's "theology of the cross." Luther uses the term *'destructio'* and its cognates to describe the critical efforts of theology that are aimed at preserving the purity of the Gospel against the "prudence of the flesh." Like Luther, Heidegger wants his philosophy to address the real struggle of individuals for an *authentic* life. This is what destruction is supposed to accomplish.

The practice that Heidegger eventually calls *'Destruktion'* is first discussed during SS 1919, where he calls it "phenomenological critique." The term *'Destruktion'* appears for the first time the following semester (WS 1919–1920). In this lecture course, Heidegger makes it clear that destruction is integral to his phenomenological way of doing philosophy, and he tries to explicate its meaning by drawing some analogies between it and Hegel's dialectic. In SS 1920, Heidegger attempts to give a more precise determination of the meaning of destruction as a practice that (1) strips commonly used concepts and expressions of their acquired self-evident quality and (2) uncovers once more what is "genuine" about them. Having examined this "pre-history" of destruction in Heidegger's work, I turn next to explicating his mature conception. I show that a crucial stage in the process of the development of this idea was Heidegger's confrontation with contemporary philosophical debates about historical consciousness. This confrontation issues in a conception of history and of tradition that has been freed from both historicist strictures about "objectivity" and neo-Kantian concerns about "relativism" and "validity." With this conception of history in place, Heidegger goes on to develop the practice of destruction as at once a critical liberation *from* the past and a positive liberation *of* the past as a possibility for the future.

Doing Philosophy and "Destruction"

That the term "destruction" is used by Heidegger to refer to the philosophical attempt to foster an authentic way of life has been universally over-looked by commentators. This is due in part to a failure to get clear about what Heidegger might mean by this term. With a few notable exceptions, the term "destruction" gets used as if its meaning were obvious. One of these exceptions is Robert Bernasconi's recent essay on what he calls "destructuring" in *Being and Time* and in the SS 1927 lecture course.[1] While Bernasconi certainly attempts to clarify what "destruction" means, he nonetheless fails to address the ultimate goal of this way of doing philosophy. Another recent commentator on Heidegger's early period comes closer to appreciating this. Charles R. Bambach rightly notes that "destruction" is a term Heidegger uses to encapsulate a conception of philosophy distinct from both neo-Kantianism and "modish world-view philosophies."[2] "Destruction" is, according to Bambach, an attempt to keep philosophy from wandering into the arid wilds of the "logic of the sciences" or the confusing landscape of cultural renewal programs, by bringing its attention back to the "one thing that mattered."[3] But what is the "one thing that mattered"? Bambach gives us no indication, though Heidegger's lectures, correspondences, and essays from the period under consideration are filled with references to authenticity as the motivating value behind philosophical research.

Bambach does come closer to this realization later in his discussion. He notes that "[f]or Heidegger, philosophy [. . .] provokes a *Kampf*, or 'battle,' against the routinized practices of everyday indifference."[4] More specifically, Heidegger's goal is to overcome the domination of "theory" that has rendered philosophy "artificial, cerebral, and impotent."[5] Why should Heidegger think that one ought to "battle" against "routinized practices"? What sorts of "routinized practices" are worrisome to him? Most importantly, what exactly is accomplished by joining this "battle"? Here again, Bambach gives us little in the way of clarification. His exposition leaves it unclear as to whether Heidegger simply wants to criticize common philosophical positions and modes of argumentation or wants to do so with some larger purpose in mind. As I have argued previously (chapter 4), Heidegger's concerns with the dominant modes of intellectual discourse of the day are primarily motivated by their apparent complicity in an inauthentic way of life. Once again, it is only against the background of the ideal of authenticity and, *a forteriori*, of Heidegger's reading of Christian thought through the ages that one can make real sense of the program of destruction.

Jeffrey Barash notes how destruction represents Heidegger's alternative to widespread attempts by Weimar-era intellectuals to "save culture."[6] Barash claims that the real target of Heidegger's critical enterprise is "the groundlessness of historical methods in the human sciences in their attempt to elaborate objective, universally valid criteria of judgment as a basis for comparison of typical patterns of cultural expression."[7] Certainly, there can be no doubt that Heidegger was bitterly opposed to the prevailing obsession with providing an epistemological foundation for the sciences of culture, particularly history. The work of both Barash and Bambach has contributed to correcting the neglect of the problems of the historicist tradition in Heidegger's thought. However, Barash's account also partakes of the same difficulty. Why is Heidegger concerned with criticizing and exposing the flaws in historicist thinking? What is the ultimate purpose that animates the attempt to achieve this more proximate goal? This is a question that has remained too often unasked, and to which I think the answer is clear.

"Destruction" as the "How" of Philosophy

In the preceding chapter, I argued that Heidegger's commitment to the value of an authentic life, as well as his readings of Paul and Luther, led him to arrive at a particular conception of how philosophy ought to be practiced if it is to help in the cultivation of an authentic life. To put it as briefly as possible, the "duty" of philosophy in this regard is "making things hard" rather than offering more hiding places to a life that is on the run from itself. The record shows that around 1920, Heidegger began to tentatively employ the term "destruction [*Destruktion*]" as a designation for this way of doing philosophy. Given what I have already shown about the most plausible reading of Heidegger's motives, it follows that "destruction" is his term for a way of doing philosophy that is ultimately aimed at the cultivation and preservation of an authentic life.

During SS 1920, Heidegger tells us that "[t]he destruction will continue; it leaves no bitter aftertaste. *It is the expression of philosophy to the extent that the motive of philosophy lies in securing, or rather, in making insecure, one's own Dasein*" (G59 171, emphasis added). Here we are told that destruction is something that will continue; presumably, it leaves no "bitter aftertaste" because it is never over and done with. More important, however, is the second half of this passage. Heidegger explicitly asserts that (1) the "motive" of philosophy lies in "securing" something by making us "insecure," and that (2) "destruction" is a term that best "expresses" a philosophy that is motivated in this way. This suggests that by 1920, Heidegger had concluded that the term "destruction" best captures his own conception of the proper response of philosophy to the tyranny of inauthentic public discourse.

Two semesters later (SS 1921), Heidegger presents another clue about the ultimate meaning and motivation of destruction. In remarks connected with his lectures on Augustine's *Confessions*, Heidegger writes, "Existentiell motivation of destruction [. . .] from the basic experience of being concealed from oneself [*Sichselbstverborgenseins*] and the concealing of life itself—barricading [*Abriegelung*]" (G60 252). "Barricading," which Heidegger also calls "the elliptical," is a term he uses more extensively the following semester (WS 1921–1922) to refer to the tendency for life to erect "disguises" or "concealments" that allow its difficulty to be avoided (see chapter 3). Life hides behind self-erected "barricades" or "disguises," leading a kind of ghostly pseudo-existence that Heidegger terms "larvance." Concerned with maintaining these disguises, life tends to become set in its ways (G61 124f./91f.). This can be understood, Heidegger suggests, as a kind of "building," "forming," or "developing [*Bildung, Ausbildung*]" (G61 128/95). Life is carried out in accordance with a "pre-given, pre-offered, relucent image [*Bild*]." This, in turn, gives "structure [*Gebilde*]" to life. In Heidegger's account, "what is at issue is not primarily the figure of what has been formed but the temporalization as such—*struere* ['to construct']" (G61 128/95). That is, Heidegger is more concerned with the fugitive, dissembling way individuals hide from their lives by "constructing" them according to prearranged "plans" than with the content of the particular "images" themselves. In other words, life crafts "idols" so that it can avoid looking at itself in the face.

Particularly interesting here is that Heidegger makes reference to the Latin *'struere,'* "to build" or "to construct," in order to formally indicate this entire process. *'Struere'* is, of course, the root of *'de-struere,'* meaning to "destroy" or "dismantle." Luther, too, seems to draw this connection when he introduces the term *'destruere'* in his scholia on Romans. Having told us that the whole purpose of Romans is to "pluck up" and "destroy" the righteousness of the "flesh," Luther asserts that "[t]his is also the vision of Daniel concerning the stone that shattered the statue" (LW25 136). Luther is here making reference to the commentary of Lyra on Daniel 2:34, according to which it is Christ, the "cornerstone," who smashes the imperial idol. The biblical context of this interpretation is an episode usually referred to as "Nebuchadnezzar's Dream":

> You were looking, O king, and lo! there was a great statue. This statue was huge, its brilliance extraordinary; it was standing before you, and its appearance was frightening. The head of that statue was of fine gold, its chest and arms of silver, its middle and thighs of bronze, its legs of iron, its feet partly of iron and partly of clay. As you looked on, a stone was cut out, not by human hands, and it struck the statue on its feet of iron and clay and broke them in pieces. Then the iron, the clay, the bronze, the silver, and the gold were all broken in pieces and became like the chaff of the summer threshing floors; and the wind carried them away, so that not a trace of them could be found. But the stone that struck the statue became a great mountain and filled the whole earth. (Dan. 2:31–35)

In his own striking commentary, Luther develops this image of "dismantling" or "destroying [*destruere*]" the self-made idols of human conceit. So similarly, Heidegger conceives of the various modes of human self-deception as "idols" or "images [*Bilden*]," "constructions" that have been molded by a deeply rooted desire for security and which, like Nebuchadnezzar's statue, must be smashed and "destroyed." Heidegger's *'de-struere'* is meant to undo and break up this self-deceiving *"struere."* Hence, on his view, philosophy is meant to function in a way remarkably similar to those phenomena that he describes collectively as the "voice of conscience," i.e., those "graced" moments of special "intensity" that interrupt the humdrum course of a life, moments in which an individual's life reveals itself to her (chapter 6). Philosophy is meant, in this sense, to be the "conscience" of others. Heidegger's name for this function is "destruction [*Destruktion*]."

By breaking down and clearing away the "masks" and "constructions" that proliferate through the agency of "idle talk," Heidegger hopes to provoke a decisive encounter with the real needs of the present situation. He makes this clear in WS 1921–1922, where he writes that "the formative appropriation of the concrete situation of enactment of philosophizing is enacted in the manner of a destruction" (G61 67/51). In the Natorp Report from late 1922, Heidegger asserts that philosophy must "play its part in helping the contemporary situation with the possibility of its being appropriated in a radical manner" (NB 20/124). He goes on to provide the following gloss: "Hermeneutics carries out its tasks only on the path of destruction [. . .]" (NB 20/124).

As I have described previously (chapter 6), Heidegger conceives of the "situation" as a totality of concepts, problems, and tasks that are collectively faced by a particular "generation." The purpose of destruction, then, is to make it possible for this "situation" to be confronted with honesty and clarity. In Heidegger's mind, this is a marked departure from the usual, fugitive, self-dissembling way people avoid the burden of their "generation" by taking refuge behind accepted ways of thinking and acting. Destruction is a way of doing philosophy that places all this into question, or, to quote Heidegger, "destruction is the authentic path upon which the present needs to encounter itself in its own basic movements, doing this in such a way that what springs forth for it from its history is the permanent question of the extent to which it itself is worried about appropriating radical possibilities [. . .]" (NB 21/124). Or, more clearly, in another text Heidegger asserts that "destruction always remains inseparable from concrete, fully historical, anxious concern for one's own self" (G9 34/29 f.).

The "Pre-history" of Destruction: 1919–1920

It is clear, then, that "destruction" is a term Heidegger uses to describe not some "historical" appendage to his "systematic" work, but rather to describe a way of doing philosophy motivated by the value of authenticity. But what exactly does "destruction" mean? This is a question that has yet to be satisfactorily answered. Van Buren, for example, though he clearly recognizes the importance of this idea in Heidegger's thought, fails to provide any clarification of its sense. Similarly, Bambach "defines" "destruction" as "a curious appropriation/transformation of theological and phenomenological sources from within [Heidegger's] own historical situation [. . .]."[8] Part of the problem here is that the term "destruction" never receives an unequivocal definition from Heidegger himself. By now, we should be familiar with Heidegger's style of philosophizing, which more often uses suggestive intimations or "formal indications" than concepts. This situation holds for the term "destruction" as well. Heidegger uses this term to capture a whole way of doing philosophy, oriented toward the tradition and motivated by a concern with an authentic way of life.

At times, Heidegger does strive to present a relatively clear picture of what he means. At others, he is content to leave matters sketchy and to employ the term "destruction" without much determinacy. The latter holds in particular of Heidegger's earliest uses of this term, from WS 1919–1920. Indeed, it is not really until SS 1920 that he offers a truly detailed exposition of "destruction." This account, however, leaves out elements of his earlier discussions, and many of the ideas presented in it do not reappear in subsequent descriptions. Thus, in order to arrive at clarity regarding what Heidegger means by "destruction," it is necessary to examine the *development* of this usage. The hope is that some sense of the whole (what "destruction" means) can be achieved through a detailed examination of the parts (Heidegger's scattered remarks about "destruction"). This task will be facilitated by reference to what I have already said about the nature of Heidegger's conception of philosophy. More specifically, the aim of fostering an authentic way of life helps to unify Heidegger's scattered references to "destruction" into a more or less coherent picture.

Phenomenological Critique

I begin my examination with the lecture course from SS 1919, in which the term "destruction" does not appear at all. Instead, Heidegger describes what he calls "phenomenological critique." Why begin here, since the term under discussion is not even used until WS 1919–1920? The reasonableness of this approach will become much more apparent later. For now, it is sufficient to note that many of the features of what Heidegger calls "phenomenological critique," e.g., its orientation toward history and its critical perspective on contemporary philosophical positions, reappear later on as features of "destruction." "Phenomenological critique" refers to the direct ancestor of the practice Heidegger later calls "destruction." These sorts of terminological shifts are common in Heidegger's work. I have already discussed several of them; for example, Heidegger employs a whole medley of terms like "genuineness," "truthfulness," and "wakefulness" to refer to authenticity. Similarly, in the early 1920s, he designates the interrelated contexts or "worlds" of immediate life by the terms "self-world," "with-world," and "environing-world." By *Being and Time* (1927), "self-world" has been replaced by the "who of Dasein," and "with-world" is rarely used. The situation is much the same with regard to "phenomenological critique" and "destruction." The referent of the former is a practice that clearly has a great deal in common with that of the latter.

The topic of the 1919 course is neo-Kantian philosophy of value [*Wertphilosophie*], which Heidegger proposes to examine in connection with three main problematics: (1) the problem of "value," (2) the problem of "form," and (3) the problem of "system" (G56/57 121/103).[9] Heidegger had begun his confrontation with the neo-Kantianism of Rickert, Windelband, and others during the preceding semester. There he suggested that the whole problem of value is ultimately motivated by the dominance of the "theoretical attitude" and the consequent alienation of philosophical research from its sources in life. In SS 1919, he takes a different approach to criticizing neo-Kantianism. Right at the beginning of the course, Heidegger announces his plans for a "*Historical introduction*: motivation and tendency of the three problem-ideas in intellectual history" (G56/57 121/103). Heidegger's intentions here seem

clear enough; he hopes to gain some understanding of neo-Kantian philosophy of value by exploring the development of its principal concepts and problematics. It is only later, however, that we get some hint of the importance of
this project when he writes *"Phenomenological and historical method;* their
absolute unity in the purity of the understanding of life in and for itself (cf. by
contrast the Marburg conception of the history of philosophy, or Hönigswald,
Ancient Philosophy)" (G56/57 125/106).

Here Heidegger suggests that "historical" investigations are not secondary
to the larger task of critically examining neo-Kantianism or of gaining an
"understanding of life." Instead, historical research is, in some sense, one of
the primary ways these other goals can be accomplished. At this point in his
thinking, Heidegger has only just begun to intimate why this might be the
case. The previous semester, he had told his students that "[e]very history and
history of philosophy *constitutes* itself in life in and for itself, life which is itself
historical in an absolute sense" (G56/57 21/18). Later he makes passing reference to the "historical I" that is "de-historicized [*ent-geschichtlicht*]" by the
"theoretical attitude" (G56/57 74/62, 89/75). Heidegger holds that philosophy belongs to life, and life is, in a deep sense, *historical*. The history of
philosophy itself belongs to life and shapes the forms of expression that one
uses to talk about life. Thus, investigating the history of philosophy gives one a
window on the ways life expresses itself. This approach is contrasted here with
that of neo-Kantians like the "Marburg School" and Hönigswald. These philosophers approached the history of philosophy as a "history of problems," i.e.,
as a history of attempts to solve individual philosophical puzzles, rather than as
a succession of all-embracing systems.

In SS 1919, one finds Heidegger presenting the implication of these ideas
for his present investigations. He writes:

> Phenomenological-scientific confrontation with a philosophy that has al-
> ready achieved its expression in intellectual history must, in order to secure
> real understanding, embrace two kinds of task. First, it must understand the
> motives in intellectual history for the historical factual expression of this
> type of philosophy; second, it must understand this type of philosophy in
> the genuineness of its own problematic. (G56/57 125/106)

This description of "phenomenological critique" shows the strong influence of Dilthey on Heidegger's thought at this time. The concept of "expression" is used by Dilthey to describe the way phenomena like social arrange-
ments, philosophical theories, and poetry articulate the meanings embedded
within the immediate stream of "lived-experience." This way of thinking is
particularly characteristic of the later period of Dilthey's work from about 1900
till his death in 1911. This period was inaugurated by several essays on hermeneutics and also saw the completion of a draft of a work called *The Formation
of the Historical World in the Human Sciences.* As he puts it here, the basic
project is "to relate human life, and the objective spirit realized by it, back to a

creative, evaluative, and active source, something that expresses and objec-
tifies itself" (GS7 87f./109). This is, in turn, motivated by Dilthey's basic
conviction that "[t]he givens of history are always manifestations of life"
(GS7 205/226).

In the passage quoted here, Heidegger describes the project as a matter of
"understanding the motives" of a philosophical position. These motives are
said to lie in "spiritual" or "intellectual" history. That is, the concepts and
questions of a particular form of philosophy have been shaped, in one way or
another, by *tradition*. Tradition, in turn, is a repository of the manifold ways life
happens to "express" itself. Thus, given Heidegger's assumptions, a clear line
leads from contemporary philosophy, through traditional ideas, directly to life
as it is lived. Understanding the "motives" of a particular position, however,
does not imply that one simply rejects the position in question. Instead, Heidegger seems to be envisioning a sort of "sifting" procedure premised on the
idea that a clearer picture of the motives of a particular viewpoint gives one a
more certain basis for evaluating what might be "genuine" about it. Heidegger
is clearly trying to articulate an alternative to the ahistorical "history of problems" approach associated with the neo-Kantians. Philosophical assertions and
theories are, on his view, *expressions* of life as it has unfolded at a particular
time and place.

Heidegger once again reiterates his repudiation of the common distinction between "historical" research and "systematic" philosophy (G56/57
125/107). He does not present any detailed argument as to why this distinction
is worthy of rejection. However, his use of Dilthey's language of "expression"
and "spiritual history" suggests that he shares the latter's views about history. If
indeed history is a "manifestation" or "expression" of life, then historical research can itself also be a kind of investigation of life. Clearly, this version of
historical research will ultimately be something quite different from pure
scholarship. It is important to note, however, that nothing Heidegger says here
excludes the possibility of scholarship being a justifiable and valid enterprise.

Heidegger also contends that "phenomenological critique," as this kind of
idiosyncratic examination of history, is not "negative," in the sense that it is not
concerned with relativizing particular positions or pointing out flaws in particular arguments (G56/57 125f./107). Instead, the analysis of a position takes
its cue from "its origin, from *where* its meaning derives." Such a critical examination is "a positive sounding out of genuine motivations" (G56/57 126/107).
This is emphasized again a bit later on:

> Genuine critique is always positive—and phenomenological critique espe-
> cially, given that it is phenomenological, can as such *only* be positive. It
> overcomes and rejects confused, half-clarified false problematics only through
> *demonstration* of the genuine sphere of problems. (G56/57 127/108)

Heidegger holds that while a particular philosophical position such as neo-
Kantianism is worthy of criticism, the point of criticism is not simply to prove a

position wrong but rather to clarify the genuine concepts, questions, and general motivations at work in it. "Phenomenological critique" articulates these foundational elements of a position in order to judge that position by the standard implicit in these elements. This means that one sifts out what is "ungenuine" in order to make positive use of the remainder. That is, these "true and genuine origins of spiritual life," once they have been brought to light through a critical examination of particular philosophical theories, can then point the way toward new questions and possibilities of research (G56/57 127/108).

A good example of what a "phenomenological critique" looks like is Heidegger's approach to Husserl's phenomenology. While Heidegger nowhere uses the phrase "phenomenological critique" to describe this approach, and most of the relevant discussions occur several years after this phrase was current, Heidegger's remarks on Husserl nevertheless conform to the pattern laid out in SS 1919. During SS 1923, one of the sections of Heidegger's lecture is called "On the History of Phenomenology" (G63 67ff./53ff.). Heidegger traces this history all the way back to the Greek usage of the term '*phainomenon*,' then follows its usage out through the history of the natural sciences and nineteenth-century psychology right up to Husserl. The explicit purpose of this exercise is to sift out the prejudices of his predecessors in order to clarify phenomenology as a "possibility" for future research. As such it is "not simply to be picked up as a theme and treated in a businesslike fashion—taking up a possibility means rather: taking it up in its being and developing it, i.e., what is sketched out in advance in it regarding possibilities" (G63 74/58).

In the following semester, WS 1923–1924, Heidegger presents a much more detailed exposition of the Greek terms '*phainomenon*' and '*logos*' that lie at the root of the modern notion of "phenomenology." This account makes particular reference to Aristotle (G17 6ff.). A few years later, in his lectures at Kassel, Heidegger takes up the phenomenological motto "to the things themselves," but also demands that the "historical motives" which are "alive" in phenomenology be thoroughly examined, especially as these pertain to the "framework of the older psychological tradition" (S 160ff.). In each case, Heidegger is clearly engaged in a project that is at once *critical* and *positive*. By self-consciously examining the history of an idea (or group of ideas), Heidegger hopes to both (1) overcome flaws in the traditional presentation and (2) uncover "genuine," useful elements that have been hidden away.

WS 1919–1920: "Destruction" Makes an Appearance

During WS 1919–1920, instead of exclusively examining the philosophical positions of his contemporaries, Heidegger turns toward the explication of "factical life-experience" itself. He also revisits the issue of the origins of science in life in order to work out in greater detail his conception of phenomenology as a "primordial science." In a later portion of the course, mostly preserved for us in student transcripts, Heidegger introduces a new term into his philosophical vocabulary, i.e., "destruction." The term appears in a brief note regarding phenomenological method: "Method [. . .]: 1. destruction and the possible steps, 2. pure understanding, 3. interpretation, 4. reconstruction" (G58 139).[10] There is no hint here as to what Heidegger means by "destruction," nor is there any indication of what needs to be "destroyed." It is clear, however, that something called "destruction" plays in integral role in his way of doing philosophy. At the same time, it is not the sum total of this "method."[11]

In order to understand what "destruction" means and what it is supposed to accomplish, it is necessary to look to other remarks in this lecture course. Taking Heidegger's brief and scattered remarks all together, one can reconstruct his inchoate views on the motives, targets, and nature of phenomenological destruction. In one passage, he links together two claims: (1) philosophical research involves a *negative* or critical element, and (2) this is necessitated by a particular feature of life itself.

> Because life, in all its forms, somehow or other expresses itself and thereby undergoes a deformation, and in this way actually experiences its own living actuality, its questionableness, its tension, etc., the basic sense of phenomenological method and of philosophical method in general is nay-saying, the *productivity of the not* (sense of the Hegelian dialectic). (G58 148)

Life, Heidegger contends, tends to be "distorted" or "deformed" under the influence of the ways it has "expressed" itself. This observation looks ahead to his later, more developed views about the role of tradition, public discourse, and "idle talk" in shaping an inauthentic way of life that is "barricaded" off from life itself. The proper philosophical response to this tendency is *critical* or *negative*. Heidegger clearly regards Hegel's much-discussed "dialectic" as a practice that approaches this negative moment in phenomenology. Indeed, a later remark again refers to the "dialectical method of negation, of which the first stage is *destructive*" (G58 241). Here Heidegger explicitly uses the term "destruction" to describe part of the negative or critical element of philosophical research. From this it can be inferred that destruction is a philosophical practice that is called for by the questionable tendencies that belong to life itself. Heidegger is, as I have already pointed out, much more explicit about this connection in SS 1921. There he states that life's tendency toward "barricading [*Abriegelung*]" is the "existentiell motive" for destruction.

This connection reappears in a later note entitled "Stages of Phenomenological Understanding" (G58 254ff.). Here Heidegger writes:

> During the course (of "accompanying" or) of "articulation," phenomenological method already works with the aid of a *critical destruction* of objectifications which are always ready to accumulate on the phenomenon. [. . .]. Indeed, before all else I say that the phenomenon is not such and such. But this can only be carried out after the fashion of an *argumentation* that is in a certain sense *dialectical.* (G58 255)

This passage clarifies, to a certain degree, the nature of the "target" for destruction. This negative way of doing philosophy is called for because of the "objectifications" or "deformations" that accumulate on the object of study and distort it. Hence, before positive work can begin, these distortions must be cleared away. Heidegger seems to have not quite settled on the term that describes this process. On the one hand, he makes reference to dialectic, in the specifically Hegelian sense. On the other, he uses a curious new term, one that he had gleaned from his readings of Luther: "destruction." A final relevant remark seems to favor the former: "Dialectic in philosophy, as a form of expression, is not dialectic in the sense of a synthetic confrontation of concepts; rather, philosophical dialectical is '*diahermeneutic*' " (G58 262 f.).

These brief, sketchy notes provide little to go on with regard to the meaning of this new word "destruction." However, the explicit analogy Heidegger draws between his method and Hegel's dialectic does give some help. For Hegel, "dialectic" is a negative process, but one that culminates in something positive. Hegel's most well-known presentation of the dialectic is in the introduction to *Phenomenology of Spirit*. There he draws a suggestive analogy between the course of his projected study and "way of the cross." Just as the latter led, through something painful and negative, to something new and eternal, so too the "dialectic" traverses "the pathway of doubt" or the "highway of despair" in order to arrive at "the realization of the concept." More specifically, Hegel wants to present us with the story of "the detailed history of the *education* of consciousness itself to the standpoint of science." For "natural knowledge," i.e., any naïve claim to certainty, this is a necessarily painful process. Hegel writes:

> Natural consciousness will show itself to be only the concept of knowledge, or, in other words, not to be real knowledge. But since it directly takes itself to be real knowledge, this path has a negative significance for it, and what is in fact the realization of the concept, counts for it rather as the loss of its own self; for it does lose its truth on this path.[12]

To put it another way, dialectic is a kind of skeptical argumentation which, perhaps unlike other forms of skepticism, aims at something positive:

> The skepticism that is directed against the whole range of phenomenal consciousness, on the other hand, renders the spirit for the first time competent to examine what truth is. For it brings about a state of despair about all the so-called natural ideas, thoughts, and opinions, regardless of whether they are called one's own or someone else's, ideas with which consciousness that sets about the examination [of truth] *straight away* is still filled and hampered, so that it is, in fact, incapable of carrying out what it wants to undertake.[13]

Hegelian dialectic has as its goal the liberation of consciousness from the uncritical opinions that keep it from achieving the standpoint from which it can make a plausible claim to possess objective knowledge of the truth. This is what Heidegger alludes to when he mentions the so-called "productivity of the not." In other words, uncritical ideas are certainly negated or rejected through the dialectical method, and yet this negation ultimately points to something positive. Hegel's use of Christian metaphors to describe this process is striking. Luther, too, describes how the apparently negative process of *destructio* ultimately leads to the justification of sinners. One of his favorite passages from the Bible captures this idea graphically: "The LORD kills and brings to life" (1 Sam. 2:6). Heidegger seems to have appreciated Dilthey's work on the "young Hegel," which made clear for the first time the extent to which theological problems motivated a great deal of Hegel's work (see S 154, NB 22/125). Indeed, Heidegger liked to say of Hegel that he was really a theologian (see G61 7/7). It is no wonder, then, that Heidegger finds it natural to slide back and forth between Luther's '*destructio*' and Hegel's "dialectic."

Ultimately, however, Heidegger was unsatisfied with a Hegelian approach to phenomenology. This is suggested above, when he coins the odd term "diahermeneutic" to indicate the differences between his own method and that of Hegel. Just what "diahermeneutic" means, however, is not apparent. Clarity can be gained by looking ahead several years, to SS 1923, where Heidegger once again discusses dialectic. In this later lecture course, Heidegger expresses his concern that there is some "already constructed context" or "external framework of classification" at work in Hegel's dialectic (G63 44ff./35f.). In *Phenomenology of Spirit*, Hegel does indeed base his entire discussion around the "concept of knowledge" or of "science." It is the "inner logic" of this concept that compels the dialectic onward by providing the standard or "criterion [*Maßtab*]" against which each of the "forms of consciousness" is measured. From Heidegger's point of view, this does irreparable violence to the subject matter, in this case "consciousness" or "life." By uncritically taking over a normative conception of "science," Hegel only perpetuates the "deformation" of life that is brought on by the rigidified tradition. In place of this approach, Heidegger rejects any independent criteria in his "reading" of "factical life-experience." Hence, he calls his project "diahermeneutic."

Up to this point, I have depicted Heidegger as presenting two distinct ideas, neither of which seems to have any obvious connection with the other. The first, "phenomenological critique," refers to a way of critically analyzing particular philosophical positions (e.g., neo-Kantian value theory) by tracing out their basic concepts and problematics in intellectual history. The ultimate aim of this procedure seems to be to salvage what is "genuine" about these positions. The second idea, called "destruction," is presented as an integral element of phenomenological method. While the exact nature of "destruction" is unclear, it is evident that Heidegger holds it to be warranted by the presence of "deformations" or "objectifications" that obscure the immediacy of "factical life-experience." Just what these "deformations" are is left unclear. Heidegger does attempt to clarify this procedure of "destruction" by drawing an analogy between it and Hegelian dialectic. As in the case of Hegel's "high-way of despair," the negative or critical character of "destruction" is ultimately supposed to issue in something positive. Unlike dialectic, phenomenological destruction does not employ concepts or criteria that are alien to "factical life-experience."

SS 1920: Defining "Destruction"

Having introduced the term "destruction" in WS 1919–1920, Heidegger attempts to clarify it in the lecture for the following semester. His basic argument during this lecture course is that, in one way or another, "life" is the central problem of contemporary philosophy (G59 12f.). This interest in "life," however, results from a complex interplay of disparate motives, which, according to Heidegger, remain unclarified (G59 14f.). "Life" is central to problems in the contemporary philosophy of history and of culture, as well as the "logic of the sciences," i.e., theories regarding concept formation in the sciences. The task that Heidegger gives himself, then, is to gain a deeper appreciation for the problem of "life" by confronting the "concrete, contemporary situation" (G59 29). We must, he says, learn to "speak the language" that motivates this sphere of problems. It is particularly important to achieve clarity regarding the all-important word "life," to disentangle the various conflicting motivations that have resulted in the central position of "life" in the contemporary philosophical situation (G59 29).

This can be achieved, Heidegger asserts, only through a procedure called "phenomenological-critical destruction" (G59 29). By means of this procedure, some "philosophical settlement [*Austrag*]" can be reached regarding the "moments of sense" that are "concealed" in contemporary discourse about life, with the hope that this may "lead into [*hindrängen*] something decisive" (G59 29). This last remark suggests that Heidegger is here using the term "destruction" in a way similar to his earlier talk of "phenomenological critique." It will be recalled that the aim of the latter was to critically examine the motives of contemporary philosophical positions in order to arrive at something "genuine" and fruitful for future positive research. Here, during SS 1920, Heidegger is outlining a practice that bears philosophical fruit by *clarifying* the haphazard welter of motives, ideas, and historical viewpoints clustered around a particular term such as "life."

The similarity between "phenomenological critique" and "destruction" becomes even more clear in light of Heidegger's contention, expressed during SS 1920, that "it is naïve to think that one could today, or ever, begin from scratch in philosophy, or that one could be so radical that one can dispose of so-called tradition" (G59 29). In other words, part of the motivation for this "phenomenological-critical destruction" is a sober recognition that concepts and problems are, more often than not, rooted in the intellectual *tradition*. Heidegger castigates those who are blind to this fact, whose position ultimately amounts to a "retreat into one's own common sense, which always presents itself as rationalistically more watered down and 'universalized' than the contingent spiritual horizon, and which must always be mistrusted in philosophy"

(G59 30). "Destruction" is a procedure that is demanded by the realization that the so-called self-evidence of "common sense" conceals a rich web of traditional concepts and questions, all of which are, on Heidegger's view, worthy of question. In SS 1919, "phenomenological critique" also targeted the sources of contemporary viewpoints in intellectual history in the hopes of unearthing something positive and fruitful for future work.

Heidegger also maintains, as he had done in WS 1919–1920, that destruction belongs to the very meaning of a phenomenological approach to philosophy (G59 30). This might not, however, be immediately evident. On the surface, it seems as though the concern of destruction is with "poking around [*Herumstochern*]" particular concepts or terms, or with correcting how language is used. At worst, then, "destruction" would seem to be a distracting detour that leads away from the proper (i.e., Husserlian) phenomenological project of describing the transcendental structures of "pure consciousness." Playing games with words seems like an unnecessary addition to productive philosophical research in this case. Heidegger suggests that this worry is rooted in the quest to transform philosophy, through phenomenological method, into a "rigorous science" (G59 31 f.). Husserl had argued that this goal could only be accomplished by "bracketing" the so-called "natural attitude" and focusing instead on pure consciousness. Any deviation from this program seemed bound to strike its defenders as "unscientific." Heidegger, however, is suggesting that this invocation of "science" is itself something worthy of question, and that it might be necessary to explore in more detail its questionable past. This, of course, is precisely the sort of things that Heidegger calls "destruction."

Heidegger is willing to admit, however, that there is some truth in the idea that destruction is concerned with the meaning of words. He admits that he finds this "business of clarifying words" somewhat "questionable" (G59 33). At the same time, it seems, at least at this stage, to be the best way to articulate what destruction is all about. Destruction deals with terms which refer to allegedly "fundamental" concepts, such as "representation [*Vorstellung*]" or "life." The necessity of it lies in that they are "unclear," that they are "permeated" by "distinct meanings," because the words themselves are "ambiguous [*vieldeutig*]." This "ambiguity" refers to a "multiplicity [*Vielheit*] of directions of meaning" which are themselves derived from different "contexts of meaning" (G59 33). The task of "destruction," then, is to "follow up on the directions of sense that run counter to one another" (G59 33). This "following up on" is supposed to lead back to the contexts of meaning from which the particular "directions of sense" emanate. Here Heidegger does not clearly indicate what these "contexts of meaning" are, or where they might be located. He does, however, mention that the "clarification" involved here requires that one "go back to the philosophically original basis of enactment" (G59 34). This "basis of enactment" is, no doubt, "factical life-experience" itself, which, as Heidegger often points out, is the genuine "origin" of all philosophy.

The procedure of "destruction" begins, Heidegger tells us, with "rudimentary, partially clear moments of meaning" (G59 33). He stresses the importance of beginning cautiously and circumspectly, so as to avoid "blindly catching hold of [*Aufgreifen*]" particular ideas or hints of ideas (G59 34). To avoid this kind of haphazard approach, one requires a "preliminary sketch" that outlines in advance the "context of sense" in which a particular usage is to be understood (G59 35). This is what keeps destruction from being "directionless," from degenerating into some mere "smashing into pieces [*Zerstrümmern*]" (G59 35).

After outlining the basic procedure of "destruction" in this very general way, Heidegger goes on to describe in more detail its motives. This section of the discussion is particularly important. Destruction is not, he holds, simply an optional appendage to philosophical research, but belongs to its very nature. This is because philosophical research is itself "always an element of *factical life-experience*" (G59 36). This observation becomes relevant once a particular phenomenon belonging to factical life-experience is brought into view, i.e., the "fading of meaning" (G59 37f.). This is a phenomenon I have already discussed at length (chapter 4). The basic idea is that, once meaning has been expressed, it tends to be reduced to the level of something self-evident, something merely "available" and hence "usable." On Heidegger's view, once this occurs, the "meaning" that has thus "faded" is simply passed along in the public discourse of "idle talk." As I have argued previously, "idle talk" feeds nicely into the tendency to seek unworried security, which Heidegger regards as a hallmark of an inauthentic way of life.

This discussion anticipates Heidegger's claim in SS 1921 that "destruction" is motivated by life's tendency to "barricade" itself. The primary instrument for the realization of this tendency is the *tradition*, the cultural inheritance that provides the initial and pervasive context of meaning in which individuals make sense of their lives. The concepts, practices, and ideals that make up this inheritance are, according to Heidegger, subjected to a "fading of meaning." That is, they become trivialized, taking on a false veneer of self-evidence. This trivialization process is fueled by public discourse, which, as "idle talk," involves a tendency to simply pass things along without any real attempt at understanding. The pervasive tendencies of individuals to avoid self-responsibility then fits into this overall structure like a hand in a glove.

An example of the sort of procedure Heidegger is recommending here can be found in his discussions of the term "world" from the late 1920s. In his course for SS 1928, he begins his examination with the ancient Greek (i.e., pre-Socratic) term '*kosmos*,' which, as Heidegger observes, does not mean "what is usually believed," i.e., "extant beings as such" (G26 219/171). He next moves to early Christian usages of this term, showing how once again it does not refer to the totality of what exists but rather to the "condition" or "situation" of human beings (G26 222/173). Heidegger contends that these usages express the "pre-philosophical" experience of the "world" in practical life (G26 232f./181).

He recapitulates these claims in his essay "On the Essence of Ground," which appeared in 1929. The premise of his examination of the term "world" is expressed as follows: "In the case of such elementary concepts, the ordinary meaning is usually not the originary and essential one. The latter is repeatedly covered over, and attains its conceptual articulation only rarely and with difficulty" (G9 142/111). In both the lecture course of SS 1928 and the essay from 1929, Heidegger argues that Augustine bequeathed the usual understanding of the term "world" by offering a particular interpretation of the doctrine of creation. This whole account illustrates how Heidegger attempts to separate the different origins of a commonly used term in an attempt to trace these usages back to those he takes to give more adequate expression to the phenomena of immediate "factical life-experience."

An example from the early 1920s is found in the Natorp Report from late 1922. There Heidegger offers a brief examination of the "Graeco-Christian interpretation of life" (NB 21/125). This requires taking a hard look at the "theological anthropology" of the Middle Ages in particular (NB 22f./125). Heidegger calls this whole procedure "phenomenological destruction" (NB 23/126). Yet another example can be found in the lecture course for SS 1923. There Heidegger's theme is the term "man." He traces out the development of the usage of this term in biblical texts, patristic and medieval theology, Reformation thought, and modern personalism (G63 22ff./17ff.). All these examples give one a more or less clear idea of the procedure Heidegger recommends in SS 1920.

The discussion in SS 1920 is important for a number of reasons. Most important is that here Heidegger connects what he had called "phenomenological critique" (SS 1919) with what he later called "destruction" (WS 1919–1920). The former is best understood as a critical engagement with contemporary philosophical positions with a view toward tracing out the origins of the concepts used by their proponents. The latter is a bit more mysterious, but seems to be clearly motivated by the fact that discourse can conceal the immediacy of "factical life-experience." Here, in SS 1920, Heidegger links these two together, proposing a "destruction" of contemporary philosophical discourse about "life" which, he suggests, is rooted in an uncritical use of ideas and concepts drawn from a variety of disparate sources. I have previously argued that the ultimate targets of "destruction" are the "idols" that "barricade" human life from itself. Beginning in WS 1919–1920, Heidegger articulates the view that public discourse, particularly in intellectual circles, both erects and perpetuates these kinds of idols. The aim of "destruction," then, is twofold: (1) to strip commonly used concepts and expressions of the veneer of self-evidence that they have acquired, and (2) to uncover once again what is "genuine" about these expressions as a possibility for the future.

Destruction and History

The discussion up to this point has established several things about Heidegger's conception of philosophy as "destruction." First and most important, I have shown that Heidegger's foray into philosophy is motivated, at the deepest level, by his commitment to the ideal of an authentic life. Second, I have presented a strong case for the view that "destruction" is the term Heidegger uses to describe the way philosophical research contributes to fostering an authentic way of life. This case rests not only on Heidegger's own explicit comments, but also on a consideration of Luther's idea of "*destructio*" which inspired Heidegger's work. Finally, I have reconstructed Heidegger's earliest discussions of "destruction," showing in detail how this idea developed over the course of 1919 and 1920. By 1920, Heidegger has arrived at a conception of "destruction" that unites the project of a "phenomenological critique" of prevailing philosophical positions with a critical assessment of the role of public discourse in blocking access to "factical life-experience."

Heidegger's conception of "destruction," however, only achieves full maturity in the years after 1920. It was during these years that he finally articulated his views on the complex relation between history, identity, and philosophy that ultimately appear in *Being and Time*. His views on history, in particular, provided Heidegger with the resources necessary to articulate more fully his conception of philosophy as "destruction." I have already explained (chapter 4) some of Heidegger's views on history, but it is worthwhile to briefly reiterate the primary components of his settled opinions in order to ground the present discussion. One of Heidegger's principal convictions is that life encounters us as already meaningful, even on the most immediate level. Part of this meaningfulness rests upon the fact that life as a whole has already been interpreted and expressed in discourse prior to any individual's own attempts to arrive at some understanding. This "having-been-interpreted [*Ausgelegtheit*]" can be understood as *tradition*, as the totality of practices, concepts, and tacit agreements about meaning that ground every individual act of interpretation. This includes, above all, self-interpretation. In this case, tradition gives shape and content to our identities.

At the same time, as I have more thoroughly discussed elsewhere (chapter 4), tradition tends to get passed along as something self-evident. That is, individual acts of interpretation tend to involve simply taking over what "one" says or does, without any effort toward a deeper or more "original" understanding. On Heidegger's analysis, this is largely due to a pervasive urge to seek security, to avoid the difficulty of having to live one's own life in one's own way by genuinely making some part of a cultural inheritance into one's own. This drive, and the superficial mode of discourse Heidegger calls "idle talk," tend to reinforce one another. Heidegger is especially critical of the way educated discourse, in the realms of philosophy, historiography, and theology contribute to self-abdication by perpetuating a kind of superficial understanding. Tradition, operating in the mode of the "idle talk" of the "one," comes to exercise a sort of tyranny over individuals.

A number of passages in Heidegger's writings clearly show that "destruction" is, in some sense, designed to address this situation. To put it another way, destruction is concerned with tradition, with the "history that we are," to use one of Heidegger's more dramatic phrases. For example, as early as SS 1920, Heidegger tells us that his plan is to deal with both "Greek philosophy" and "modern philosophy since Descartes" in a "destructive way [*im den destruktiven Aspekt*]," a project which is itself supposed to contribute to the "positive decisive destruction of Christian philosophy and theology" (G59 12). In his SS 1921 lectures on Augustine, there are further sketchy remarks that indicate some link between the activity of "destruction" and tradition. "Tradition—not in certain respects, but rather completely destroyed!" (G60 193). "Here, the basic tendency is still Greek, as is that of philosophy up to the present, and it does not arrive at a destruction" (G60 257). Again, in WS 1921–1922, after rejecting the common distinction between "systematic" and "historical" ways of doing philosophy, Heidegger adds a note: "Basic sense of phenomenology. Carrying out a destruction in the history of the spirit [*Geistesgeschichtlich destruktiv führend*]" (G61 132/98).

Clearly after about 1920, Heidegger began to link the project of destruction with his growing convictions about tradition and history. Heidegger was certainly not alone, however, in occupying himself with the problem of history. A host of thinkers as diverse as Dilthey, the neo-Kantians, and Spengler all made "history" one of the watchwords of contemporary philosophy in the late nineteenth and early twentieth centuries. Heidegger's interest in the problems of history, however, was of a different sort. What all the above-named thinkers had in common was a dual concern with (1) the epistemological grounding of the new sciences of history and of human nature (i.e., historiography, anthropology, psychology), and (2) combating the specter of "relativism" that stemmed from the growing historical consciousness of the age. While Heidegger certainly has something to say about both of these issues, the principal reason behind his concern with history is none other than the principal reason behind most of his philosophical endeavors, i.e., a deep concern with the value of an authentic way of life.

The Problem of History

Recent commentaries on Heidegger's early work have done a great deal to illuminate the hitherto overlooked relationship between his work and the debates about historical meaning and the status of history as a science that occupied German philosophy after Hegel.[14] Moreover, there has also been a recognition that the meaning of "destruction" can be worked out by examining this context in more detail. Despite this important achievement, some of these commentators nevertheless make an important mistake. Both Charles R.

Bambach and Jeffrey Barash argue that Heidegger's signature conception of the "history that we are" is the *result* of carrying out a "destruction" on prevailing views about historical meaning. The opposite is in fact the case; Heidegger's conception of human "historicality [*Geschichtlichkeit*]" actually forms the presupposition against which the project of "destruction," in its mature form, makes sense.

Bambach, for example, states that the real target of Heidegger's "destruction" is the "research-oriented mode of traditional hermeneutics" with its "critical-exegetical method of inquiry."[15] He goes on to suggest that this destruction produces a "new way of conceiving the tradition freed from the metaphysical notions of 'objectivity,' 'scientific rigor,' 'historical erudition,' and 'history of concepts' (*Begriffsgeschichte*) spawned by *Wissenschaft/Weltanschauung* philosophy."[16] It is not clear, however, that the "notions" listed by Bambach are *metaphysical*. "Objectivity," "scientific rigor," and "historical erudition" are all notions belonging to the kind of epistemological discipline that was known at the time as the "logic of the sciences." Moreover, it is not clear how "history of concepts" fits with these other examples of a "metaphysical" approach to history. Nor is it obvious what is meant by "*Wissenschaft/ Weltanschauung* philosophy," since these terms refer to two rival ways of conceiving the nature and tasks of philosophical research. The most problematic element of this assertion, however, is that it places Heidegger's own conception of history at the *end* of a "destruction." That this is Bambach's view is also clear from his later claim that destruction reveals the "genuine meaning of history."[17]

Jeffrey Barash presents a similar view. He claims that the "central target" of "Heidegger's deconstruction" is "the historical and historicist orientations responsible for the elaboration of these ideas [culture, value, etc.] since the late nineteenth century."[18] The problem, allegedly, with these "orientations" is that they "obstructed the approach to the past requisite for the reformulation of the originary question of Being."[19] Both Bambach and Barash maintain, then, that Heidegger's revolutionary way of viewing history not as objective data for historiographical analysis, but rather as the transmission of meaning that determines the possibilities of human identity, is the *result* of something called "destruction." It is clear, however, that the project of "destruction" ultimately only makes sense against the background of this view of history. Why, after all, should Heidegger care about "destroying" the history of ontology if he did not already view history as more than just a record of facts?

In this regard, Robert Bernasconi's view comes much closer to the truth. He points out that Heidegger explicitly asserts that the notion of "historicality" is meant to lay the groundwork for the whole project of "destroying" the history of Western thought.[20] Bernasconi refers to a passage from §75 of *Being and Time*, in which Heidegger explains the purpose of attempting to trace the origins of historical research back to "historicality": "This projection will serve to prepare us for the clarification of the task of destroying the history of philosophy in a historical way [. . .]" (SZ 392/444). Heidegger had already made much the same point in §6, where, after briefly explaining what "historicality" means, he asserts that "[h]istorical science—or more precisely, historicity—is possible as a kind of being which the inquiring Dasein may possess, only because historicality is a determining characteristic for Dasein in the very basis of its being" (SZ 20/41 f.). In other words, any kind of explicit attempt to understand history is predicated on the idea that we are "historical" beings. Moreover, the project of "destruction" in particular rests upon a whole view of history and of tradition which assumes that we have already rejected the concern with "objective" historical science (SZ 21/43). In §77 of *Being and Time*, Heidegger concedes that Dilthey's friend Count Paul Yorck von Wartenburg can be viewed as a pioneer of this conception of history. As Heidegger points out, Yorck castigates the detached objectivism of the Historical School, whose concern with objectivity and impartiality led to an allegedly distorted view of history (see SZ 400 f./451 f.). Hence Barash and Bambach are both incorrect in their contention that the notion of "historicality [*Geschichtlichkeit*]" is the *result* of a destruction.

While Bernasconi avoids the problems of Barash and Bambach's view, he nonetheless fails to recognize the real import of his own insight into the connection between "historicality" and destruction. "Historicality [*Geschichtlichkeit*]" is a term Heidegger uses in *Being and Time* to capture the idea that history is *not* merely an assemblage of facts and entertaining personalities, but rather is integral to our own identities, both on the individual and communal levels. Heidegger holds that through our own acts of self-interpretation and self-determination, we participate in the transmission of meaning through time. We "are" history [*Geschichte*], or the "happening [*Geschehen*]" of the tradition. But, as Heidegger never tires in pointing out, we "are" history in an inauthentic way. That is, we too often fail to make our history *our own* through clear-sighted vocational commitment, instead opting for the easy path of superficiality and conformity. At issue, then, in the relation between historicality and destruction is that the inauthentic condition of the former is precisely what calls for the critical activity of the latter.

A look at Heidegger's explicit discussions of the problem of history justifies this contention. Heidegger's first extensive treatment of contemporary debates regarding history and historicism is during the lecture course for WS 1920–1921. Heidegger announces here that his purposes is to examine and to understand "the historical [*Historische*] as it encounters us in life, not in the science of history" (G60 32). To put it another way, the theme here is the "historical" as "an immediate living reality" (G60 33). On his view, the common philosophical approaches to the "historical" are such that it has in some sense become "homeless," i.e., it has "lost its systematic place" (G60 34). This is something that can only be regained, says Heidegger, by returning to the meaning that history has in "factical life-experience." For most philosophers, history is only an issue insofar as it bears on the question of the validity of scientific propositions. "One says that the validity of these propositions is independent of the historical, it is 'supratemporal'; reflection on the historical serves only to throw this into relief. But this would assign a more secondary role to the historical [. . .]" (G60 35). Heidegger, however, asserts "the importance of the historical for the meaning of philosophy *prior to* all questions of validity" (G60 35).

Heidegger proposes to correct the flaws of this one-sided approach by exploring the "historical consciousness" of the age (G60 33). He begins by noting that "historical consciousness" is something that "disturbs" people in one of two senses: "first, it provokes, incites, and stimulates; second, it obstructs [*es hemmt*]" (G60 33). He goes on to elaborate these responses in more detail. The first is bound up with what he calls the "worldliness and self-satisfaction of factical life," which leads one to a "tolerance of foreign conceptions by means of which one wants to achieve a new security" (G60 33). How does "historical consciousness" contribute to the security of a self-satisfied culture? The "mania" for understanding the different forms and periods of culture "leads to the belief that one has arrived at the ultimate stage [of culture]" (G60 33). He describes this response again in a later remark, noting that "the multiplicity of historical forms gives life *fulfillment* and lets it rest [. . .]" (G60 37).

Here historical consciousness functions in two interrelated ways. First, it feeds into the self-congratulatory sentiment of an age that views itself as the culmination of human civilization. The past can be surveyed to provide justification for the belief that the present age has finally transcended the barbarism of the past and of more "primitive" peoples. Second, the "mania" for typology allows one to appreciate history in an aesthetic way, without having to confront its meaning for the present or the future. In both cases, the pervasive drive for security, which as I have already shown (chapter 3) fuels an inauthentic way of life, can be satisfied.

Heidegger characterizes the second reaction differently. Here the historical is viewed *not* as a guarantee of cultural supremacy, but rather as an obstruction. The problem, on this view, is that "the historical averts the gaze of the present, it destroys the naïveté of creation and thus immobilizes it" (G60 33f.). Or, as he puts it later, "the historical is a *burden* for us, an obstacle" (G60 37). Historical consciousness "accompanies every attempt at a new creation like a shadow. The consciousness of the past makes itself felt to such a degree that it robs us of enthusiasm for the absolute" (G60 38). Here one can recognize the complaint of the avant-garde in every age against the tyranny of the traditional. In Heidegger's day, Nietzsche was a sort of spokesman for this iconoclasm. Groups like the futurists in Italy offered shrill denunciations of sterile academic art, as well as of social conventions. For these people, history was a burden that thwarted true creativity by threatening to relativize it. For example, the "Manifesto of Futurist Dramatists" from 1911 urged that "[e]very day we must spit on the altar of art."[21] Similarly, Marinetti's "Manifesto of Futurism" likewise announced that "[w]e will destroy the museums, libraries, academies of every kind [. . .]."[22]

For Heidegger, what is significant about both of these reactions is that (1) they have little or nothing to do with contemporary philosophy of history, and (2) they express the fact that history is something that disturbs *life*. History is either appropriated for the sake of complacent self-satisfaction or it is something one must "struggle" against to create something truly new. In either case, according to Heidegger, it is life itself that is "disturbed" by history. It is here, then, that one can catch a glimpse of "the historical" as it encounters us in factical life-experience, rather than in the rarefied debates about historicism.

Heidegger does, however, present a case for the claim that this same concern can be discerned beneath the surface of various philosophical approaches to questions about history. He describes three basic approaches: (1) a "platonic" approach, which attempts to escape from the specter of relativism by positing eternal, *a priori* values, (2) a "self-surrendering" approach that rejects this specious apriorism in the name of embracing the flux of historical reality, and (3) an approach that attempts to mediate between these two (G60 38 ff.). The details of these three approaches are not important to the present discussion. What is important is the conclusion that Heidegger draws regarding the deeper motives of these various positions. "Today's confrontation with history," he asserts, "is essentially revealed as a struggle against skepticism and relativism" (G60 47). The latter are not merely academic problems, but rather point to something deeper: "The struggle against history—indirectly and unconsciously—is the struggle over a new culture" (G60 47). These various philosophical positions attempt to address the underlying "disquiet" of life by theorizing about how one can achieve objective knowledge of values in the face of the reality of historical consciousness. Heidegger, for his part, totally repudiates these attempts to appease life:

> That which is disturbed is the reality of life, human Dasein in its anxious worry about its own security, taken not as it is in itself, but rather viewed as an *object* and placed as an object within *objective* historical reality. No answer to the anxious worry is forthcoming; instead, it is simply objectified. (G60 51)

Here Heidegger contends that academic worries about skepticism and relativism only serve to mask or conceal the real worry, which belongs to life itself. Instead of confronting life, these common approaches to history simply objectify it in a formal, aesthetic manner, exemplified by concepts like "type" (Dilthey) and "soul of a culture" (Spengler). The phenomenon of the historical must be kept separate from historical science, which, with its guiding orientation toward epistemology or the "logic of the sciences," places the whole problem into the wrong context (G60 52). These approaches fail to clarify the "anxious worry" that really motivates contemporary attitudes toward history. Heidegger characterizes this worry as follows: "One's own present Dasein desires not just *meaning* in general, but *concrete* meaning: namely, a *different* meaning than it had in past cultures, a *new* meaning that surmounts that of earlier life. It wants to be a new creation [*Neuschöpfung*], to be something totally original [. . .]" (G60 52). Philosophy can, however, only make a real contribution to addressing the "anxious worry" of life if a new understanding of history is achieved.

Several years later, Heidegger returns to the issue of history and life. Here, however, he focuses more on the specific talk of "university reform" rather than on "culture" in general. While all agree that the "past" has some part to play in assessing and transforming the current situation of the universities, many tend to view it as a "burden" (G61 65/49; 72f./54f.). In other words, opinions differ as to the *normativity* of the past with respect to the future. Some hope to look at the history of the university "objectively," and so "read off criteria and goals" (G61 73/55). Others, however, repudiate the idea that history has any normative force at all (G61 75/56f.). According to Heidegger, what is missing from all these discussions is any real attempt "to clarify the meaning and the rights of the tradition" (G61 75/57). As he argued in WS 1920–1921, he once again claims that this can only be corrected by taking on the "problematic of the historical itself" and showing how "the meaning of the historical is, in turn, rooted in the facticity of factical life" (G61 76/57).

Clearly Heidegger does not expect much progress to be made on this front by approaching history the way most of his contemporaries did. For the neo-Kantians, Husserl, and even for Dilthey, the primary issue was *epistemological*. The guiding question was "how can historical science claim to have objective validity like that enjoyed by the mathematical sciences?" For Heidegger, this rests on the assumption that "history" primarily designates an object of knowledge. Instead, he suggests, "history" might be meaningful on the level of practical life, of "anxious worry" about one's individual and cultural identity. This is clear from a passage in his review of Karl Jaspers's *Psychology of Worldviews*:

> The historical today is almost exclusively something objective, i.e., an object of knowledge and curiosity, a locus providing the opportunity to glean instructions for future action, an object for critique and rejection as something antiquated, a fund of materials and examples to be collected, a conglomeration of "instances" for systematic observations dealing with the universal. Since we are unable to see the phenomenon of existence today in an authentic manner, we no longer experience the meaning of conscience and responsibility that lies in the historical itself (the historical is not merely something of which we have knowledge and about which we write books; rather, we ourselves are it, and have it as a task). (G9 33/29)

History is too often viewed as simply an "irretrievable busyness" (BZ 19). It then becomes just a kind of aesthetic spectacle. "The contemplation of what was going on is inexhaustible. It loses itself in its material" (BZ 19). This sort of approach simply fails to really address the practical questions involved in history. "The present generation," Heidegger observes, "thinks that it has found history, it thinks that it is even overburdened by history" (BZ 19). Again, he refers to the "platonizing" approach of the neo-Kantians who attempt to overcome the relativistic implications of historical consciousness by attaining "the supra-historical," for it is "on this fantastical path to supra-historicity that we are supposed to find the world-view" (BZ 19). What such views completely overlook, according to Heidegger, is that "[t]he enigma of history lies in what it means to *be* historical" (BZ 19).

Similar claims can be found in Heidegger's contemporaneous lectures on Dilthey at Kassel. The ostensive theme of these lectures is the "struggle [*Kampf*] for a historical world-view." More precisely, a "historical world-view" is "one in which knowledge of history determines one's understanding of the world and of Dasein" (S 149). Here Heidegger goes into more detail regarding the origins of this problem in modern German philosophy, particularly as it developed after Hegel. Following the nadir of the grand systems of idealism, however, the focus shifted to the allegedly more "scientific" concern with the epistemology of historical science. Heidegger, however, contends that the "struggle for a historical world-view is not played out in debates about the historical conception of the world, but rather in those about the sense of historical being itself" (S 150).

Clearly, Barash and Bambach are correct in maintaining that Heidegger rejects the dominant philosophical approaches to history. What they are mistaken about is the view that his own conception of the "history that we are," or "historicality," is the *result* of some (undefined) procedure called "destruction." Instead, Heidegger's views about the meaning of history for life *ground* his views about both the nature and necessity for destruction. He rejects the prevailing tone of most philosophy of history because it blocks the way to seeing what is really at issue, i.e., "factical life" in its "anxious worry." History, on Heidegger's view, is not to be regarded as a cabinet of antiquities. To the contrary, we "are" history, in a literal sense. Each individual's life involves acts of self-interpretation as well as the interpretation of other people, things, and events. These acts of interpretation are all made possible by the fact that life has always already been interpreted, in both language and practice. Tradition transmits this totality of meaning to us, and we take it over in our own acts of interpretation. The act of interpretation Heidegger is most concerned with is the one that shapes our identities as individuals. This can occur either by abdicating self-responsibility to the anonymous public discourse of the "one" or by facing up to the task of living one's own unique life and making a vocational commitment. As Heidegger says, what is needed is the recognition that we have a *responsibility* for our own histories, that we *are* history, and have it as a "task."

Dismantling the Idols

Heidegger's conception of "historicality [*Geschichtlichkeit*]" is aimed at clarifying the meaning that history has for life. To put it another way, Heidegger wants to show that each individual has a responsibility with respect to history. This is something, he contends, that is completely ignored by the prevailing approaches to the philosophy of history. Taking responsibility for the history that we "are" is one way of understanding what it means to live an authentic life (chapter 6). Destruction is a way of doing philosophy that aims to assist in this process.

There are two sides to the practice of destruction which, when taken together, articulate a conception of philosophy that is ultimately motivated by a concern with authenticity. At the risk of oversimplification, these two aspects can be categorized as "negative" and "positive."[23] The "negative" side of destruction is something Heidegger had emphasized in his first halting discussions of this term during WS 1919–1920. Like Hegelian dialectic, Heidegger's destruction drags the "common sense" and "idle talk" of public discourse along a figurative "highway of despair." Like Lutheran *destructio*, it smashes the idols of self-satisfaction and fugitive self-abdication that have accumulated on life like tumors. On the "positive" side, however, destruction frees what is "genuine" in the past so that this might challenge the self-conception of the present and so point forward toward a new future.

What is the target of the "negative" side of destruction? Heidegger makes it clear in a number of places that it is not the tradition *per se* that is the object of critique, but rather the public discourse of the present, insofar as it perpetuates a kind of superficiality that lends itself to inauthentic tendencies. To put it another way, the object of destruction is the "tradition" as it operates in a given generation through the agency of educated discourse in particular. "Critique of history," Heidegger writes in 1922, "is always only critique of the present [. . .]. History gets negated not because it is 'false,' but because it sill remains effective in the present without, however, being able to be an authentically appropriated present (NB 4f./114). Heidegger's settled view of much intellectual discourse is that it simply serves to erect "masks" and "barricades" behind which life can hide, presenting it with illusory "metaphysical tranquilizers" so that "business as usual" can proceed smoothly (chapter 4). For Heidegger, this hampers the ability of individuals to face up to the challenge of having to live their own lives in their own ways. Furthermore, it can even tranquilize an entire "generation" by directing attention away from the real problems and tasks it faces. The real function of philosophy, Heidegger contends, is to "play its part in helping the contemporary situation with the possibility of its being appropriated in a radical manner" (NB 20/124).

Heidegger suggests that this can be realized by attacking the veneer of self-evidence that attaches to the "common sense" of an age. Philosophy has the task of

> loosening up the reigning state of traditional interpretation today with respect to its hidden motives and its unexpressed tendencies and modes of interpreting so that it can, by way of a *deconstructive regress*, penetrate to the

original motivational sources of these explications. *Hermeneutics carries out its tasks only on the path of destruction.* (NB 20/124)

To carry out this project, there has to be a recognition of what he elsewhere calls the "responsibility" that lies in the historical. That is, the usual goals and procedures that are connected with the study of history must be cast aside. Heidegger has no interest in "illustrating how things stood in earlier times" (NB 20/124). In other words, like Dilthey's friend Count Yorck, Heidegger feels no compulsion to obey the allegedly normative dictates regarding objectivity that were first formulated by Ranke and the "Historical School." Moreover, Heidegger does not wish to provide "an occasional overview of what others before us 'came up with,'" as if "historical research" were simply an entertaining appendage to real "scientific" work (NB 20f./124). "Rather," he asserts, "destruction is the authentic path upon which the present needs to encounter itself in its own basic movements [. . .]" (NB 21/124). The real issue here is presented in unmistakable language:

> Here, the sort of critique already arising precisely through the concrete actualization of destruction is thereby centered not on the fact *that* we always stand within a tradition, but rather on the *how* of our standing within a tradition. (NB 21/124)

The "how" of our belonging to a tradition is either a matter of conformity and superficiality (inauthenticity) or of clear-sightedness and self-critical resolve (authenticity). Hence the real *issue* in destroying the tradition is the struggle to live an authentic life. In his lecture course for SS 1923, Heidegger attempts to clarify in more detail just what the project outlined above would really look like. He first of all argues for the necessity of a genuine "historical critique," something which, he maintains, is generally absent from other philosophers of the phenomenological school (G63 75/59). Such a critique would require that the "tradition of philosophical questioning must be pursued all the way back to the original sources of its subject matter. The tradition must be dismantled [*abgebaut*]" (G63 75/59). It is important to note that this "dismantling [*Abbau*]" begins with "today's situation" (G63 75/59). Indeed, it is the "today," the public discourse of the present, which is the real target of critical "dismantling."

The following semester, WS 1923–1924, includes the most lengthy discussion of destruction since SS 1920. Here Heidegger elaborates more fully on this project of "dismantling" the tradition, indicating why this is necessary and sketching out how it might proceed. The contemporary philosophical scene, he claims, is dominated by "ancient ontology and logic, all of which today holds as self-evident [. . .]" (G17 113). For this reason

> the task of freely giving Dasein to itself and achieving an explication of it is bound up with the task of unsettling [*erschüttern*] contemporary Dasein [. . .]. This is carried out in the manner of a dismantling [*abzubauen*], in

which the basic categories of consciousness, person, and subject are led back to their original meaning, in the sense that one shows, through insight into the origin of these categories, that they arise from a totally different basis of ontological experience and that their conceptual tendencies are unsuitable for what we want to bring into view as Dasein. (G17 113)

This discussion certainly harks back to Heidegger's first attempt to define "destruction" during the SS 1920 lecture. As I have already shown, the idea there seems to be that certain forms of expression have lost any real meaning and are simply passed along. Heidegger proposes that the different "directions of meaning" involved in terms like "representation," "person," and the like be followed up on to strip away their self-evidence. Here, in WS 1923–1924, Heidegger adds a new element to this project, i.e., that of showing how, when looked at from the perspective of their origins in intellectual history, many common concepts are actually not fit to do the work they are meant to do. Another notable element of this passage is Heidegger's talk of "unsettling contemporary Dasein." I have already pointed out (chapter 5) how this sort of "unsettling" interruption of the everyday way of things is one of the main features Heidegger attributes to the primitive Christian proclamation. Similarly, in *Being and Time*, the sudden, unexpected "voice of conscience" shakes one up and disturbs the complacent blindness of inauthenticity. Philosophy too, as I have already shown, is meant to play a similar role. "Destruction" is the name for the practice that accomplishes this "unsettling."

The purpose here is "to set [Dasein] free from this conceptual overgrowth [*Überwucherungen*] that Dasein itself has developed for the purpose of its own authentic explication, but in which a peculiar tendency shows up today: self-obstruction [*Sich-selbst-verbauen*]" (G17 117). The point here is similar to the one Heidegger first made during WS 1919–1920, where he argued that due to life's tendency to be "expressed," it often shows up as somehow or other "deformed." Even more to the point is a comment from SS 1921, which I have also alluded to previously, in which Heidegger explicitly locates the motivation for "destruction" in a tendency that he calls "barricading [*Abriegelung*]." Here in WS 1923–1924, Heidegger observes how these "obstructions," "masks," and "barricades" were oftentimes originally developed with the intention of providing some kind of genuine expression of the meaning of human life. However, due to the way discourse naturally "fades in meaning" and becomes mere "idle talk," these original productions of the human spirit become refuges for superficial understanding and self-abdication. The "setting free" or "freeing up" Heidegger envisions "occurs in the manner of a dismantling [*Abbauens*], a destruction, in which concepts are led back to their particular origins" (G17 117f.).

The recognition that what now functions as a "mask" or a "barricade" was once genuine only serves to drive home the point, constantly reiterated by Heidegger, that the real target of critical destruction is the public discourse of the "today" which passes along superficial understandings. He makes this clear in later remarks from this same lecture course (WS 1923–1924):

> In point of fact, destruction is critical. But what is criticized is not the past, which is opened up through destruction. Rather, the critique falls upon the present, upon our contemporary Dasein, to the extent that it is concealed by a past that has become inauthentic. Aristotle or Augustine are not criticized, but rather the present. [. . .]. Thus, destruction as critique is critique of the today, which makes visible that which is authentically, originally positive in the past. (G17 119; cf. G17 122)

Heidegger makes it clear that (1) destruction *is critical*, and (2) that it is critical of the public discourse of the present, the "today." During lectures from 1923–1924, he often describes this critical project as one of "dismantling" the tradition. The goal of doing so is to strip away the veneer of self-evidence and "common sense" that has accrued on basic terms, concepts, and ways of asking philosophical questions. The tradition only becomes problematic for Heidegger when it becomes "master" (SZ 21/42). The routines and superficially available ways of thinking and acting that are passed along by public discourse effectively block the possibility that a person might try to form an original, uniquely individual way of life for herself. Instead, they throw up "masks" behind which one can hide. The goal of "dismantling" the tradition is to disrupt these tendencies by calling into question the ideas and practices that are superficially available in this way.

This is one of the ways a philosopher can "have an effect on the world of others," as Heidegger puts it. I have previously described how a person committed to the value of authenticity forswears moralistic pronouncements and the guiding hand of paternalism (chapter 6). This attitude is entirely consistent with one that places the highest value on individuality. For a philosopher motivated by this same value, these paternalistic activities are also clearly inconsistent with her deeply held commitments. This does not, however, mean that a philosopher should do nothing to foster authentic ways of life. Indeed, it would be odd to hold a value and do nothing to promote it. Hence, on Heidegger's conception, the philosopher can function as the "conscience" of other people. The "voice of conscience," it will be recalled (see chapter 6), operates by interrupting the routine of everyday life, thereby opening up the possibility of an authentic vocational commitment. Philosophical "destruction" attempts to play a similar role by unsettling the quotidian patterns of thought and action that prevail at a particular time.

Heidegger generally gives a relatively uniform account of how this can be accomplished. Destruction "dismantles" the traditional ideas and practices of a particular time by tracing them back to their roots in "spiritual history." This can have the effect of showing that these ideas and practices, when considered in light of their origination, are unsuitable for the purposes they are intended to fulfill. Alternatively, it might be shown that the commonsense interpretation these ideas and practices have received actually falsifies that which is "genuine" about them. In either case, destruction has the effect of bringing uncritically accepted practices and ideas to the light, placing them in the forefront of reflective consciousness.

Another element of the critical side of destruction also involves tracing out the roots of widely accepted ideas, but in a slightly different way. Like Lutheran *destructio*, Heideggerian destruction also exposes the darker motivations behind prevailing ideas and practices. For example, Heidegger articulates an unflattering picture of the real motive for much public discourse, i.e., a drive for security. Heidegger traces out the roots of the hegemony of "theory" in Western thought and culture, exposing its alleged origins in the idle "curiosity" of an inauthentic life. This has the effect of calling into question the hegemony of certain other practices and ideas.

In all these ways, then, destruction is a philosophical practice that attempts to cultivate a specific way of belonging to a tradition. On the one hand, one might be "pushed around" by the tradition, i.e., one might abdicate self-responsibility to the routinized practices and ideas circulating about in the public discourse of the "one." On the other hand, one might confront the reality of having to determine one's own identity, thereby choosing to make some aspect of one's cultural inheritance one's "own." Destruction, by way of a critical "dismantling" of the tradition as it operates at any given time, makes it more difficult to simply settle in to common ways of thinking and acting by calling these into question, bringing them to one's awareness, and tracing out their origins in one's cultural history. Carrying out this sort of a project clearly does *not* involve making any sort of positive recommendations about which aspects of one's cultural inheritance are worth choosing as the focal points of one's identity. Heidegger makes this clear in *Being and Time*, when he writes that "[t]he existential analytic is not in a position to discuss that upon which Dasein *factically* resolves in each case" (SZ 383/434).

Destruction as the Liberation of the Past

There is a sense in which destruction is clearly a *negative* or *critical* practice for Heidegger. Yet, like Luther's *destructio*, the ultimate purpose of destruction is *positive*. Authenticity, as I have argued at length, is ultimately to be understood as a kind of vocational commitment. Since authenticity is the value that motivates the practice of destruction, it would be odd for Heidegger to make no reference to the relation between destruction and vocational commitment. While the proximal function of destruction is to break down the hegemony of what passes for "common sense" at a particular time, this is only part of the story. The other part, which I have not examined in detail up to this point but which is nonetheless a vital element in Heidegger's overall conception of philosophy as destruction, involves the attempt to *liberate* or *free up* [*überliefern*] possibilities from the past for the sake of the future.

This liberation of the past for a new future is, as I have argued, the heart of

Heidegger's notion of "repetition [*Wiederholung*]." This is by no means a kind of uncritical imitation, nor is it radical iconoclasm. Instead, it is best understood as a way of responding to the possibilities of the past, making them one's own, and thereby achieving a distinctive position with regard to the present situation. There is a sense in which "repetition" is Heidegger's name for a kind of authentic historical consciousness. This is a historical consciousness that is distinct from either the self-congratulatory triumphalism that surveys the past in order to secure its own superiority, just as much as it is distinct from the vitalistic protest against the burden that the past places on all creativity. Heidegger describes this authentic historical consciousness at the close of §76 of *Being and Time*. There he invokes Nietzsche's famous views about the "use and liability of history for life," especially his views about the three different ways the past can be approached.

In §76, Heidegger presents what he fully admits is an idealized picture of historical understanding, which he calls the "existential" idea of history (SZ 392 f./445). For this reason, this portion of *Being and Time* shares a number of similarities with Heidegger's idealization of theology in his 1927 essay "Phenomenology and Theology." There, too, Heidegger stresses that theology is a *historical* discipline. This does not mean, however, that it is an objective consideration of "something that has come about in world history," for it *belongs* to the special "history" that constitutes what it means to be a Christian (G9 54/45). As I have already described, Heidegger views being a Christian as a participation in the "history" that begins with the cross (G9 53 f./44 f.). Theology, then, is the self-interpretation of Christian existence in which the sources of the latter are "appropriated ever anew" as the "possibilities of a faithful existence" (G9 58 f./48). I have already shown (chapter 1) how Heidegger's "idealization" of theology in this essay shares a great deal with his conception of philosophy as the "hermeneutics of facticity." In §76 of *Being and Time*, the sort of authentic historical consciousness envisioned by Heidegger is also strikingly similar to this idealization of theology. The only substantial difference between the two accounts is that in *Being and Time*, Heidegger does not mark off the range of the "possibilities" that historical understanding appropriates, whereas in "Phenomenology and Theology" it is clear that the range of possibilities is limited by reference to the content of revelation.

According to the "existential" idea of history, the real subject matter of historical science is to be identified neither with individual facts nor with some universal pattern, but rather with "the possibility that is already factically existent" (SZ 395/447). Grasping this subject matter requires a special approach, one that clearly deviates from other philosophical approaches to history, most notably the "metaphysical" approaches that were characteristic of nineteenth-century thought:

> This possibility does not get repeated as such—that is to say, understood in an authentically historical manner—if it becomes perverted into the color-

lessness of a supratemporal model. Only by historicality which is factical and authentic can the history of what already is, as a resolute fate, be disclosed in such a manner that in repetition the "force" of the possible gets struck home into one's factical existence—in other words, that it comes towards that existence in its futural character. (SZ 395/447)

The three kinds of historical consciousness described by Nietzsche, "monumental," "antiquarian," and "critical," are all unified by the sort of authentic historical consciousness that Heidegger envisions here. First of all, in repetition, one is open to what is "monumental," i.e., great, challenging, and stimulating, in one's cultural inheritance. At the same time, because one is explicitly looking to the past, there is also the possibility of having "reverence" for the tradition. Finally, on Heidegger's view, the process of making a possibility from the past one's own provides one with a vantage point from which the shortcomings of the present are thrown into relief. He writes:

> But, insofar as this "today" has been interpreted in terms of understanding a possibility of existence which has been seized upon—an understanding which is repetitive in a futural manner—authentic history becomes a way in which the "today" gets deprived of its character as present; in other words, it becomes a way of painfully detaching oneself from the falling publicness of the "today." (SZ 395/449)

Crucial to authentic historical consciousness of this kind, then, is the ability to see the past not as the manifestation of eternal, *a priori* values or as a supply of individual facts, but rather as a "definite task that is sketched out in advance [*vorgezeichnet*]" (G17 113f.). Through dismantling the obviousness of what passes for "common sense," the past "first becomes visible as our authentic being already [*Gewesensein*], and as our ability to be again [*Wiederseinkönnen*]" (G17 119). In other words, the past is "freed" as a *possibility* for the future, as an exemplar or model in terms of which individuals can define their own futures.

Destruction, Heidegger maintains, is most definitely a "struggle with the past." Yet it possesses a strange kind of "objectivity":

> The objectivity of destruction is of such a kind that it brings the past back to its authentic being, i.e. to its appropriateness [*Eignung*] for striking back [*Rückstoß*] at the present. (G17 119)

The "objectivity" of destruction does not lie in some specious claim to be free of all prejudice. Instead, on Heidegger's view, destruction is *objective* because it allows for the possibility that a person's current beliefs and practices might be *challenged* by the past. As a critique of the "today," destruction helps the present achieve a new level of self-criticism. The past "strikes back" at the present, on Heidegger's view, only when it is taken as a model or exemplar for the *future*. The positive aim of destruction is to make this possible. "Phenomenology needs," says Heidegger, "to enter more and more into the possibility of extricating itself from the tradition in order to free up past philosophy for a genuine appropriation" (S 160). Here in his lectures on Dilthey at Kassel, Heidegger makes it clear that this is the ultimate dividend of destruction, insofar as destruction is best conceived of as a critique of the present age. He writes:

> What is required of philosophical research is that it be a critique of the present. In disclosing the past in an original manner, the past is no longer seen to be merely a present that preceded our own present. Rather, it is possible to emancipate the past so that we can find in it the authentic roots of our existence and bring it into our own present as a vital force. Historical consciousness liberates the past for the future, and it is then that the past gains force and becomes productive. (S 174f.)

In this passage, Heidegger explicitly links "historical consciousness" with the "critique of the present." As I have already shown, "critique of the present" is the best way to understand the *negative* side of what Heidegger calls "destruction." The hope expressed here is that by means of critically "dismantling" the "common sense" of the present age, the past might become the "root" or "anchor" of a new way of life. This is clearly a way of life that is not beholden to the common ways "one" thinks or acts, but rather is a genuine attempt to confront one's cultural inheritance, freed from the constraining hegemony of the "idle talk" of the "today."

Heidegger expresses similar ideas in the Natorp Report from late 1922. The history of philosophy, he maintains, is only ultimately relevant when it is taken to contain "radically simple *monuments which evoke thinking* [*Denkwürdigkeiten*]" (NB 4/113). This comment looks ahead to Heidegger's discussion of historical consciousness in §76 of *Being and Time*, where, as I have already mentioned, he argues that the past should be viewed as a *possibility* for the future rather than as a collection of individual facts. Here, in 1922, Heidegger makes a similar claim, arguing that present-day research in philosophy ought not to "divert understanding" toward the task of "merely enlarging knowledge about the past," but should instead, by confronting the intellectual tradition, force "the present back upon itself in order to intensify its questionability" (NB 4/113).

"Understanding," says Heidegger, "consists not merely in taking up the past for the sake of a knowledge that merely takes note of it, but rather in *repeating* [*wiederholen*] in an original manner what is understood in the past in terms of and for the sake of one's very own situation" (NB 4/114). Again, this passage is striking in its anticipation of Heidegger's comments in §76 of *Being and Time*. There he explicitly connects an authentic kind of historical consciousness with "repetition." This term is introduced in §75, where it describes one particular form an authentic existence can take. "Repetition" means the "struggling imitation" of some particular model or exemplar derived from one's own cultural inheritance. "Repetition" is an active participation in the unfolding history of one's own tradition in the form of a personal commitment to some exemplar or model one finds valuable (chapter 6). "Repetition" is not slavish imitation, but instead a "response [*Erwiderung*]" to the past as a possibility, a way of taking the past as a challenge for the future. Similar claims can be found in Heidegger's lecture course for SS 1928. There he argues that his way of doing philosophy is "always only a repetition [*Wiederholung*] of the ancient, the early" (G26 197/155). This can be "freed up [*überliefert sich*] for repetition only when it is granted the possibility of being transformed [*sich zu verwandeln*]." The way things get handed down in "fixed ways of questioning and of discussing" actually blocks the possibility of "transforming" the past as a reality for the future. Heidegger makes this same point in the Natorp Report:

> The use of models that understands [*Verstehende Vorbildnahme*], which is concerned with itself, subjects these models [*Vorbilde*] from the ground up to the sharpest critique, and develops them for a possibly fruitful opposition [*Gegnerschaft*]. (NB 4/114)

Heidegger does not indicate here what these models "oppose." If, however, we look ahead to the concluding portion of §75 of *Being and Time*, the situation becomes clearer. There Heidegger asserts that "repetition," as an authentic way of belonging to a tradition, "deprives the 'today' of its character as something that is present, and weans one from the conventionalities of the 'one'" (SZ 391/443 f.). "Repetition" is an activity that gives the past a *new* future, one that relativizes the conventional routines of contemporary life. In both *Being and Time* and in other texts, like the Natorp Report, Heidegger makes it clear that philosophy can function in the same way. When it does so, Heidegger calls it "destruction." Destruction is an activity that "breaks into [*einschlägt*]" the present and "unsettles [*erschüttert*]" it, freeing individuals from the burden of what passes itself off as "common sense" at a particular time, and thus making possible a new confrontation with one's intellectual and cultural heritage that may ultimately lead to genuine vocational commitment.

At this point, it is useful to recall Heidegger's intimations of what a philosopher can do to effect some kind of renewal in the cultural, social, and political life of his or her "generation." Earlier, in chapter 7, I described how Heidegger frequently uses the language of "exemplary living [*vorleben*]" to capture his vision of the practical efficacy of philosophical labor. In contrast to those who chatter on about "world-views" or *a priori* values, Heidegger maintains that the philosophical revolutionary is a quiet one, a person whose philosophical activity in the classroom and on paper "exemplifies" what it means to be an authentic person. This view coheres with Heidegger's overall commitment to a kind of Romantic personalism. For someone who values uniqueness and individuality, and who sees conformity, anonymity, and self-abdication as the roots of many of the ills of society, the only plausible way to bring about a realization of these values is to eschew "sermonizing" attempts to relieve other people of the burden of having to determine their own lives, and instead to "exemplify" the ideal that one holds.

Destruction is a way of doing philosophy that clearly embodies, in almost every detail, Heidegger's vision of an authentic way of life. Carrying out a philosophical destruction of the public discourse of the time breaks down its claims to obviousness or self-evidence by revealing the way it passes off superficial understandings as gospel. Thus, it "interrupts" the normal course of life, much in the way the "voice of conscience" does. Moreover, destruction attempts to clear away obstacles to seeing what is "genuine" about one's cultural and intellectual inheritance. Having done so, the philosopher is then able to appropriate these "genuine" possibilities as live options for the future. Doing so further calls into question the prevailing tendencies of thought and action at a particular time. By linking destruction with "repetition" and authentic historical consciousness, Heidegger means to convey a conception of philosophy that "exemplifies" what it means to live an authentic life.

NOTES

1. See, for example, Van Buren 1994a, pp. 143f., 165ff., 201f.; Kisiel 1993, pp. 104, 126, 249ff., 311f., 347f.; McNeill 1999, pp. 53f.; Barash 1994, pp. 111–122; Bambach 1995, pp. 31, 33, 54, 197ff., 210ff.

2. Of course, I make reference at a number of points to works that do not date from the period under consideration. This only shows that it is extremely difficult to erect any clear-cut distinctions between different "periods" in Heidegger's work and that later material is often relevant to the exposition of earlier material, and vice versa.

3. Sheehan 2001, pp. 184f.

4. Van Buren 1994a, pp. 17–18.

5. Ibid., pp. 28, 38.

6. Sheehan 2001, p. 88.

7. Kisiel 2002b, p. 130.

1. HEIDEGGER'S "RELIGION"

1. See Gadamer 1987. Among commentators on Heidegger's work, I find that Gadamer comes closest to actually appreciating the importance of the "religious dimension." As Jean Grondin relates, Gadamer maintained that the primary questions driving Heidegger's thought were theological. Grondin 2003, p. 101.

2. See Heidegger's letter to Father Engelbert Krebs (S 69f).

3. See especially Jonas 1963, Jonas 1964, and Löwith 1942.

4. See, among other places, Bultmann 1987, pp. 313–331. Barash's comments can be found in his insightful study of Heidegger's philosophy of history. See Barash 1988, pp. 174, 183.

5. In his recent essay on Heidegger's "atheism," István M. Fehér explicitly challenges what I am here calling the "disciplinary" account of Heidegger's "religious dimension." See Fehér 1995. Fehér is particularly critical of the views of Richard Schaeffler (p. 104).

6. For a discussion of Heidegger's theological education, see Casper 1980.

7. Fehér 1995, pp. 201–202.

8. Remarks to this effect can be found throughout Heidegger's early lecture courses. During SS 1920 Heidegger describes the "disfigurement [*Verunstaltung*]" of Christian existence by Greek ontology (G59 91). During WS 1923–1924, he points out that theology "lives hand to mouth" from philosophy (G17 118). Much later, in his "Introduction" to "What Is Metaphysics?" Heidegger revisits this theme of the "on-

totheological" disfigurement of Christianity, citing the Pauline-Lutheran *topos* of the "foolishness" of philosophy (G9 378/287–8). He asks, "Will Christian theology one day resolve to take seriously the word of the apostle and thus also the conception of philosophy as foolishness?" Heidegger's view on intellectual history will receive a more complete treatment in chapter 5 below.

9. See for example Heidegger's "grateful indication of sources" in the text for WS 1921–1922 (G61 182) and the foreword to the text of SS 1923 (G63 5–6/4).

10. Van Buren 1994a, p. 151.

11. Cf. Gadamer 1989.

12. Van Buren 1994a, p. 157.

13. Ibid., p. 189.

14. Ibid., pp. 389ff.

15. Kisiel 1993, pp. 112ff. See also Kisiel 1988.

16. Kisiel 1993, pp. 424ff.

17. Van Buren himself argues that the misleading impression of "universality" or "scientificity" in Heidegger's work stems from the privileging of *Being and Time,* which is characterized by the quasi-Kantian language of transcendental philosophy. See Van Buren 1994a, pp. 363–367.

18. Thomas Sheehan suggests such skepticism in his essay on Heidegger's WS 1920–1921 course, in which he attributes a deflationary view of primitive Christian eschatology to Heidegger. Heidegger's view is that the proper attitude toward the future advent of Christ is not detached observation, and this does not entail in any obvious way any doubts about the objective reality of the event in question. See Sheehan 1979.

19. In a letter of December 28, 1945, to a Professor von Dietze, Heidegger endorses a Kierkegaardian distinction between "Christianness [*Christlichkeit*]" as "the faithfulness of the individual," and "Christendom [*Christentum*]," as "the historical, cultural, and political manifestation of Christianness" (G16 416).

20. For an example of Bultmann's "de-mythologizing," see Bultmann 1987, pp. 165–183.

21. Merold Westphal has offered a clear and cogent articulation of this aspect of Heidegger's thought. See Westphal 2001.

22. Stout 1981, p. 170.

23. See Kisiel 1993, pp. 38–59.

24. Heidegger elsewhere charges his phenomenological mentor with a neglect of "history" and of "life" (cf. G58 146; G17 85–86) and with a bias toward the "theoretical" (e.g., S 160f.).

25. "Facticity" is one of several terms Heidegger uses throughout the 1920s to designate what he takes to be the principal subject matter of philosophy. For a formal indication of the sense of this term, see G63 7/5. Other terms Heidegger uses include "life" or "factical life" (e.g., G58 59, 173, 104–110), "life-experience" (G60 9–14), "experience" (G56/57 66; G 59 23–29), and, of course, Dasein (G60 52–4; NB 4ff./114ff.; G63 15ff.; etc.).

26. Cf. NB 4/113, etc.

27. This is true even in the case of something "unfamiliar" in the usual sense of the word. In the course of KNS 1919, Heidegger illustrates this through the example of a lectern. He contrasts the "meaning" it has for students and professors with that which a farmer from deep in the Black Forest or a native from Senegal might "see" (G56/57 71–73).

28. Heidegger had already alluded to the circularity of science during WS 1919–1920, arguing that its "idea" always emerges from its "object-domain," and yet the latter is still determined by the idea (G58 210).

29. Heidegger addresses objections to the "hermeneutical circle" once again later in the book, in §63.

30. This remark is also interesting in that it seems to be an explicit acknowledgment of Heidegger's "theological" starting point. As his references in *Being and Time* demonstrate, some of the core concepts involved in the idea of authenticity, such as conscience, being-toward-death, and the "moment of vision," had been treated long before in theology. Theodore Kisiel is mildly critical of this element of Heidegger's methodology, as it seems to involve presupposing some world-view or other. See Kisiel 1993, pp. 430 ff. This criticism only seems viable if one ignores Heidegger's frequent avowal of the necessity of presuppositions and of the incompleteness and provisionality of philosophy.

31. These qualitatively distinctive moments of insight will receive a more complete treatment in chapter 6 below.

32. Blochmann was a philosopher of education who had earlier elicited Heidegger's assistance with her dissertation on Schleiermacher (cf. HB 11–12).

33. He had introduced this idea briefly during KNS 1919 in connection with the possibility of experiencing the "pre-worldly something of life" (G56/57 115 f./97 f.).

34. Kisiel quotes an undated note from sometime around 1917 in which Heidegger seems to make this point for the first time. See Kisiel 1993, pp. 73–74.

35. See Ogden 1991.

36. Quoted in Kisiel 1993, p. 80.

37. This letter is quoted in Kisiel 1993, p. 452.

38. Kisiel 1993, p. 72.

39. Ibid., p. 100.

40. Ibid., p. 112.

41. This, too, is a thesis that shows the influence of Dilthey on Heidegger. See for example the following remark: "Rather, each metaphysics has had to contend with the protest of religious experience, which is clearly rooted in the will, from the first Christian mystics who opposed medieval metaphysics—and were no poorer Christians on that account—to Tauler and Luther" (GS1 385/218).

42. In the debate over the extent of the influence of German mysticism on Luther, Heidegger clearly falls into the camp of those who would emphasize the experiential, personal dimension of Luther's theology and its kinship with mystics such as Tauler. For an interesting treatment of this debate, see Hoffman 1976, pp. 25–123.

43. It is important to note here that an appreciation of the central significance of Luther's work in Heidegger's intellectual development does not entail any claim that other influences were less significant, any more that my thesis about the importance of religious life in Heidegger's "hermeneutics of facticity" entails that poetry, art, politics, or even daily life were somehow "less" important to him.

44. Wilfried Joest argues that Luther regarded the proper sphere of the object of faith as the history of salvation. See Joest 1967, pp. 98 f. This claim serves to lend further support to the idea that Heidegger owes his "ideal construction" of faith to Luther.

45. See Van Buren 1994b and 1994a, Chapter 8.

2. LUTHER'S *THEOLOGIA CRUCIS*

1. On the relation between Lutheran *"destructio"* and Heideggerean *"Destruktion,"* see Van Buren 1994b, p. 159. Van Buren has laid out the fundamental contours of this issue. What is still lacking is a detailed, systematic treatment of the actual concept of *destructio* in Luther's work and a comparison of this concept with Heidegger's destruction.

2. Van Buren 1994a, p. 189.

3. Luther at times gave a positive evaluation of Aristotle's work, though his vitriolic ravings are more well-known. See Gerrish 1962, pp. 34f.

4. Ibid., pp. 9, 58. See also zur Mühlen 1980, p. 6, and Eckermann 1978.

5. For a more general account of the place of *ratio* in the anthropology of high scholasticism, see Joest 1967, p. 151.

6. Zur Mühlen 1980, pp. 6–7. Another contentious part of medieval soteriology concerned the interpretation of Christ's "dwelling in" the souls of the just. There were two basic positions: (1) the Thomistic theory of "created habits" and (2) the Augustinian view that justification is a direct, personal act of God. See McGrath 1985, pp. 81ff.

7. See McGrath 1985, pp. 55–63.

8. Ibid., pp. 137f.

9. See his "Disputation Against Scholastic Theology," in LW31, pp. 3–16.

10. See Ebeling 1979, pp. 99f.

11. See zur Mühlen 1981, pp. 60ff.

12. Ebeling 1979, p. 101.

13. Zur Mühlen 1981, pp. 58f.

14. See Bernasconi 1994; Ijsseling 1986.

15. The complex issue of the dating of Luther's "breakthrough," as well as the related debate about the famous *Turmerlebnis*, lies beyond the scope of the present discussion. For an interesting analysis, see McGrath 1985, pp. 95ff.

16. In a supplement to the main text of his WS 1919–1920 lecture course *Die Grundprobleme der Phänomenologie*, based on the transcript by Oskar Becker, Heidegger refers directly to the recent publication of these lectures by Ficker (G58 204). Moreover, in the surviving notes for his projected course on medieval mysticism, Heidegger refers directly to Ficker's introduction to his edition of Luther's lectures (G60 308f.).

17. References are to the "American edition" of Luther's works. For terminological clarity, occasional reference is made to Luther's Latin, according to the collected works published by Böhlaus at Weimar.

18. See Gerrish 1962, p. 71.

19. John Calvin seems to have held a similar view about the corruptibility of "natural" knowledge of God. Calvin's views on this issue have recently been defended by Alvin Plantinga as part of a more general apologetic strategy. See Plantinga 2000.

20. See Westphal 2001.

21. Rosenzweig 2000a, p. 19.

22. The injustice is that all these theologians, upholding orthodoxy, regard grace as a necessary condition for salvation.

23. Luther elsewhere emphasizes the necessity of a radical transformation, pp. 324ff.

24. See Ozment 1969, pp. 202, 207 f.

25. Cf. Hoffman 1976, pp. 151 f. See also Beintker 1954.

26. Pinomaa 1940, p. 8.

27. Ibid., p. 11.

28. Ibid., pp. 84 f.

29. Cf. the marginal gloss on Romans 1:1, "The whole purpose and intention of the apostle in this epistle is to break down [*destruere*] all righteousness and wisdom of our own. . . ." LW25 3/WA56 3. Cf. also the scholion to Romans 2:21: "the whole task of the apostle and of his Lord is to humiliate the proud and to bring them to a realization of this condition, to teach them that they need grace, to destroy their own righteousness [*iustitiam propriam destruat*] so that in humility they will seek Christ and confess that they are sinners and thus receive grace and be saved" LW25 191 f./WA56 200.

30. For an excellent discussion of this series of lectures, see Ellwein 1936.

31. See Ellwein 1936, pp. 383 f.

32. Ibid., p. 395.

33. Ibid., pp. 394 f.

34. The classic study of Luther's *theologia crucis* is von Loewenich 1976. Von Loewenich argues that this theological position is central to Luther's thought throughout his career, and not merely in 1518. A more recent study is McGrath 1985. McGrath traces the development of Luther's thought from his earliest works up through 1519. Both of these works are invaluable to the study of Luther.

35. For an interesting discussion of this work, see zur Mühlen 1981.

36. There are numerous scholarly investigations of Luther's concept of the "hidden God." For just one interesting discussion, see Adam 1963.

37. See McGrath 1985, pp. 162 f., 169 ff., 173.

38. See Pinomaa 1940, pp. 8 ff.

39. It is puzzling that more attention has not been given to this concept by scholars. This is all the more surprising in light of the volume of research on closely related topics such as *theologia crucis*, Luther's critique of philosophy, and *Anfechtung*.

3. INAUTHENTICITY

1. Nietzsche 1995, p. 7. This remark comes from the essay "David Strauss the Confessor and Writer."

2. This is my rendering of a passage from HL 27–32. For a description of Löwith's letter, to which Heidegger responds, see Kisiel 1993, pp. 77 f.

3. The reader is directed to Kaes, et al., 1994, pp. 330 ff., for exemplary texts from this broad movement of political and cultural critique. Some recent discussions include Breuer 1993 and Woods 1996. Needless to say, Heidegger's affinities for the Conservative Revolution can certainly be cast in a more troubling light given his later political activities on behalf of the Third Reich. For an interesting and judicious treatment of this issue, see Kisiel 2002a, pp. 1–35. The reader should recall, however, that the aim of this study is not to arrive at moral or political evaluations of Heidegger's views, but rather simply to get clear about what these views *are*.

4. For a comprehensive treatment of inauthenticity, see Zimmerman 1981. A more recent discussion can be found in Rickey 2002. On inauthenticity in the young Heidegger, see Van Buren 1994a. Van Buren briefly discusses the idea of inauthenticity in connection with the influence of Christianity on Heidegger (pp. 177 ff.), and he also

examines Heidegger's critiques of ideology and the issue of university reform (pp. 320ff., 352ff.). While I agree with a substantial part of Van Buren's discussion of this topic, there is need for a more focused analysis of Heidegger's views.

5. Heidegger remarks that "[w]hat we called the inauthenticity of Dasein now experiences a sharper definition through the interpretation of falling [*Verfallens*]" (SZ 175f./220).

6. Dreyfus 1991, p. 334. Dreyfus's analysis has sparked a debate among scholars regarding the cogency of his reading of Heidegger. See Ewing 1995; MacAvoy 2001; and Carman 2000.

7. Dreyfus refers throughout his book to the "essential structures" of Dasein while at the same time recognizing that Heidegger's commitment to the centrality of interpretation successfully undermines the possibility of robust metaphysics (see Dreyfus 1991, p. 37).

8. See "The Problem of Sin in Luther" (S 105ff.). Cf. also Heidegger's brief, though very "Lutheran," discussion of "Pharisaism" and the misuse of the concept of conscience (SZ 291).

9. This eschatological reading of the "righteousness of God" has also been employed by Jürgen Moltmann, specifically in connection with a "messianic Christology" that works toward overcoming the anti-Judaism implied in older, metaphysical Christologies. See Moltmann 1993, pp. 21ff.

10. Heidegger also seems to have thought that these theologians were not *radical enough* in their reassertion of the basic tenets of Protestantism (S 110).

11. A similar point is made with respect to authentic discourse and "idle talk" (SZ 169/213).

12. Heidegger makes this clear in connection with the notion of "resoluteness [*Entschlossenheit*]" (SZ 289f./345).

13. Cf. also Heidegger's discussion of the concept of *molestia* in Augustine (G60 242ff.).

14. While I agree in part with this element of Löwith's assessment, I think he is mistaken in viewing authenticity as "decisionistic." See Crowe 2001.

15. My discussion at this point is indebted to Van Buren 1995.

16. I have not been able to determine any significant *conceptual* difference that corresponds to this *terminological* variance.

17. It is difficult to adequately capture the sense of '*zerfallen*' and its cognates in English in a precise way. The root '*zer-*,' which appears in many verbs, connotes something like "asunder" or "into pieces." It also has the connotation of "decadence." '*Zerfallen*' means something like "to disintegrate" or "to decompose."

Note should also be taken of Heidegger's play, in this passage, between '*Hang*' and '*Verhängnis*,' which cannot be captured by the English equivalents "propensity" and "fate."

18. Here again one can detect something of the distinctiveness of Heidegger's position vis-à-vis both leftist-modernist critics of industrial society and neo-Romantic, *völkisch* idealizers of the past.

19. For a discussion of Heidegger's conception of the intentional "senses" of factical life, see Van Buren 1994a, pp. 29–47.

20. I have chosen to render '*Neigung*' as "conative inclination" to bring out the connotation of "desire" or "lust," which played such an important role in Kant's use of this term in his critique of hedonism.

21. For a discussion of this cultural context, see Rowland 1982.

22. Cf. Van Buren 1994b.

23. "Furthermore, there are many ways to be mistaken (for evil belongs to the unlimited, as the Pythagoreans judge, but the good belongs to the limited), but there is only one way to act correctly (because of this the one is easy, the other difficult; it is easy to miss the mark and difficult to hit it). Accordingly, excess and deficiency are bad, and the mean is excellent."

24. In his subsequent discussion of anxiety, in §40, Heidegger elaborates on this feature of existence. In our primary, *de facto* way of existing, everything is "familiar" (SZ 188/233). Falling aggravates this mode of existing in such a way that it becomes "tranquil self-assurance" or a kind of "self-evident being at home [*Zuhause-sein*]" (SZ 188f./233). This, of course, conceals the basic situation of the unrest of life, "uncanniness [*Unheimlichkeit*]," "not being at home [*das Nicht-zu-Hause-sein*]," or "unhomeliness [*Un-zuhause*]" (SZ 188f./233).

25. William P. Alston has recently pointed out that a negative "evaluative orientation" vis-à-vis human existence on the part of potential converts can lead to receptivity to the Christian proclamation. See Alston 2001. Classics of apologetics, like Pascal's *Pensées*, often involve extended elaborations of this sort of "evaluative orientation." It is not unreasonable to read Heidegger's own extensive discussions of "inauthenticity," and his suggestive "formal indications" of "authenticity," as instances of this sort of apologetic strategy.

26. Augustine of Hippo 2000, p. 102.

27. Ibid., p. 104.

28. Ibid., p. 106.

29. Ibid., p. 263.

30. It is worth pointing out here that a similar view of the aimlessness of everyday life can be found in the writings of Conservative Revolutionaries like Ernst Jünger and Franz Schauwecker. For these ideologues, the "aimless and unclear" quality of everyday life was temporarily effaced by the "simplified and disciplined" life of the *Frontsoldat*. See Woods 1996, p. 9. Needless to say, this idealization of trench warfare soon gave way to disillusionment. Heidegger himself also seems to have found the "primitive Dasein" of life at the front strangely exhilarating (HB 9–12). See Kisiel's discussion of this in Kisiel 2002a, p. 27. It is important to recognize, however, that Heidegger most often alludes to peasant life, to the isolation of Todtnauberg, to monastic retreat, and to intensive academic labor as examples of such a simplified existence.

31. See Heidegger's remark in the review of Jaspers's *Psychology of Worldviews*: "[The] past is not like an appendage that the 'I' drags along with itself; rather, it is experienced as the past of an 'I' that experiences it historically within a horizon of expectations placed in advance of itself and for itself" (G9 31/27).

32. Pannenberg 1968, p. 152.

33. Pannenberg 1963. Pannenberg has used these ideas to develop a view regarding the historical problem of the resurrection of Christ, which has been further developed by Jürgen Moltmann. See Pannenberg 1977, pp. 88ff.; Moltmann 1993, pp. 227–245.

34. In *Being and Time*, this idea is developed much more thoroughly in terms of the idea of "projection [*Entwurf*]" (§31), Dasein's being "ahead" of itself or "beyond" itself (§41), and the primacy of the "futural" or "adventive [*zukünftig*]" in Dasein's temporality (§65).

35. This lack of proper "measure" in the hustle and bustle of everyday life is something Heidegger examines again much later in his career, in a 1951 essay "Dichterisch wohnet der Mensch" (G7 199–203). What is particularly notable about this later discussion is that it has an explicitly *theological* cast.

36. See Kisiel 1994.

37. Among contemporary theologians, I think Moltmann best captures the "unrest" at the core of Christian life. See Moltmann 1993, pp. 153 f.

38. In a remark that will eventually prove significant to the overall structure of the present discussion, Heidegger places the motivation for philosophy as *Destruktion* firmly within the self-concealment of life: "Existentiell motivation of destruction [...] from out of the basic experience of being concealed from oneself [*Sichselbstverborgenseins*], and the concealing within life itself—barricading [*Abriegelung*]" (G60 252).

39. This image of life's "constructing" itself presents an interesting counter-image to the philosophical project of "dismantling [*Abbau* (literally, "un-building")]" or "destruction." Recall Luther's employment of the graven image as a metaphor for our self-conception in his *Lectures on Romans*. Indeed, Heidegger goes on to say that phenomenological interpretation is a "counter-movedness" against the movement that is here conceived of as construction (G61 132/98). See chapter 8.

40. The influence of this idea can be found throughout Herbert Marcuse's *One Dimensional Man* (Boston: Beacon Press, 1964). It also appears, not surprisingly, in some of Rudolf Bultmann's work, e.g., 1969, pp. 165–183.

41. Recent theoretical literature in psychology has contributed to our understanding of the way totalitarian regimes and oppressive social orders operate through the complicity of those they dominate. See Sidanius and Pratto 1999 and Jost and Major 2001.

42. For a discussion of the idea of *confrontation* in Heidegger's work from the late 1920s through World War II, see Fried 2000.

4. The Language of Inauthenticity

1. The *locus classicus* for Kierkegaard's views on mass culture and intellectual discourse is in Kierkegaard 1978. This aspect of Kierkegaard's thought has received extensive treatment in secondary literature. Two studies of this material are Westphal 1987 and Elrod 1981.

2. Indeed, Heidegger professes allegiance to a "free Christianity," after the manner of the liberal Ernst Troeltsch, as early as 1917, in a letter to Heinrich Rickert (HR 42).

3. For an overview of this discussion, and of Heidegger's position in it, see Bambach 1995.

4. On the concept of "meaning" in Heidegger, see Dahlstrom 1994b and 1995. In the latter, Dahlstrom succinctly captures Heidegger's concept of meaning as "what sustains a level of understandability, without necessarily becoming explicit" (p. 108).

5. Van Buren 1994a, pp. 320 f.

6. For a discussion of Heidegger's pessimistic, Spenglerian view of Western history, see Zimmerman 2001.

7. Cf. also Heidegger's earlier discussion of these ideas during WS 1923–1924, his first semester at Marburg (G17 112 f.).

8. The notion of a *Fragestellung* is one that is difficult to capture in English. It signifies, loosely, a "way of posing questions." As such, it encompasses the fundamental

concepts and the methodological paradigms available at a particular time for positive research. A *Fragestellung* is the basis upon which intellectual inquiry is grounded. This allows, of course, for different directions of research and for different answers to particular questions, but always within the limits of a pre-established set of assumptions.

9. Strictly speaking, for Heidegger, it is not appropriate to label elements of the "environmental experience" as "things" at all. However, I have slightly altered his usage in the interests of ease of exposition.

10. For an extensive treatment of Heidegger's story about the genesis of the theoretical attitude, see McNeill 1999.

11. For a good overview of Heidegger's synthesis of neo-scholasticism and neo-Kantianism during the "student years" see Van Buren 1994a, pp. 49–130.

12. I will revisit some of this material in my later discussion of Heidegger's position vis-à-vis contemporary debates about historical science (chapter 8).

13. This term has a long history in German polemics, having been made famous by Luther in his invectives against various radical Protestants such as Thomas Müntzer and the Anabaptists.

14. See Gadamer 1996, pp. 55 ff.; 81 ff.

15. Unfortunately, the editors of the *Gesamtausgabe* give us no information about where in the text Heidegger intended this insertion to be. As it stands, these remarks must be read in isolation from their intended context.

16. Heidegger's critique of Spengler's "typologizing" approach to history is significant. Woods has pointed out that a tendency toward abstraction and historical determinism is characteristic of the ideology of many Conservative Revolutionaries in the Weimar era. See Woods 1996, pp. 21–24. Many moved in this direction to find meaning in the horrors of World War I and the ignominy of defeat in 1918. By explicitly and vociferously rejecting this tendency, Heidegger has clearly separated himself from one of the significant trends in the right-wing ideology of the time.

17. For a discussion of Heidegger's early anti-modernism, see Van Buren 1994a, pp. 122–129.

18. Quoted in Van Buren 1994a, p. 349.

19. See Kisiel 1988, pp. 73–75.

20. Nietzsche 1995, pp. 17 f.

21. Overbeck 1974, p. 50.

22. Ibid., p. 51.

23. Ibid., p. 10.

5. The Roots of Authenticity

1. A typical aphorism from Novalis. Stoljar 1997, p. 32.

2. Recent years have seen a number of detailed examinations of Heidegger's critique of neo-Kantianism. Some good examples include Kovacs 1994, Farin 1998, and Kisiel 1993, pp. 13 ff. On life-philosophy, see, for example, Fehér 1994.

3. An issue is raised, of course, by Heidegger's disavowals of moral theory *per se* in many of his works from this period and later. I have dealt with this issue in the previous chapter, focusing on the notion of "formal indication" as a way of minimizing the awkwardness these disavowals entail, without necessarily eliminating all the problems.

4. Taylor 1991, p. 29.

5. Ibid., pp. 25 ff.

6. For a recent discussion of Schleiermacher's moral philosophy, see Scholtz 1995.

7. See Van Buren 1994a, pp. 264 ff., etc.

8. Schleiermacher 1926, p. 31.

9. Stachura 1981, p. 15.

10. Taylor 1991, pp. 26 f.

11. "Forensic" justification is the idea that people are *accounted righteous* by God in virtue of Christ's atoning sacrifice. The Pietists wanted to emphasize the actual *experience* of being made righteous while at the same time maintaining the essential Lutheran idea of God's prevenience.

12. Van Buren 1994a, pp. 310 ff.

13. Ibid., p. 343.

14. Ibid., pp. 345 f.

15. Part of this may be due to the seemingly inexplicable fact that scholars have by and large ignored the moral and religious aspects of Dilthey's thought, focusing instead on Dilthey as the "theorist of the human sciences." None of the more recent book-length studies of Dilthey devote any significant space to the moral or the religious even though Dilthey had a good deal to say about these sorts of issues.

16. Kisiel has convincingly illustrated Dilthey's importance in Heidegger's work from the mid-1920s. See Kisiel 1993, pp. 315 ff. More recently, Charles Bambach has drawn attention to the importance of the historicist tradition in general, and Dilthey in particular, for Heidegger's early philosophy of history.

17. The earlier lecture course from WS 1919–1920 betrays, on virtually every page, the profound influence Dilthey had on Heidegger during these years (see G58). The difference is that in SS 1920, Dilthey's work is more a matter of explicit critical concern, whereas the previous semester Dilthey was something of a silent conversation partner.

18. From some of the aphorisms of Novalis we can extract mottos for the Romantic personalist tradition: (1) "Only the individual is interesting"; (2) "The artist stands on the human being as a statue does on a pedestal"; (3) "Genius in general is poetic. Where genius has been active it has been poetically active. The truly moral person is a poet." See Stoljar 1997, pp. 32, 55, 57.

19. Cf. GS1 96/145.

20. Ibid., pp. 81/270; 91/280 f.; 206/376.

21. Van Buren 1994a, pp. 292 f.

22. That Heidegger places so much emphasis on these points serves to further distinguish his thought from the broader trends of proto-fascist Conservative Revolutionary thought. Ideologues like Jünger, Schauwecker, and von Schramm tended to explicitly privilege the collective over the individual. See Woods 1996, p. 24.

23. Sheehan 1979. More recently, Theodore Kisiel has also documented Heidegger's unpublished notes on theology, mystical and devotional literature, and philosophy of religion. See Kisiel 1993, pp. 71 ff. My account here is deeply indebted to both.

24. Neither of these renderings of '*Gewordensein*' is entirely accurate. However, I think the sense of what Heidegger is getting at is best captured by talking about "being-already."

25. Moltmann 1996, p. 22.

26. Ibid., p. 24.

27. To use more technical theological language, one can say that the revelation of God in the word of the cross is *proleptic*. See Pannenberg 1968.

28. Augustine of Hippo 2000, p. 270.

29. LW31, p. 89.

30. Notably absent from Heidegger's account, at least during WS 1920–1921, is *love*. John D. Caputo has made this the linchpin of some of his recent critiques of Heidegger. See, for example, Caputo 1994. To the extent Caputo is faulting Heidegger for the incompleteness of his rendition of Christian life, his point is well-taken. My discussion, however, is in no way aimed at evaluating Heidegger's work during WS 1920–1921 as a piece of biblical scholarship or dogmatics, but simply with coming to grips with his ideal of authenticity.

6. AUTHENTICITY

1. A few examples of explicit statements to this effect can be found in Grondin 1994; Habermas 1987 and 1992; and Wolin 1990.

2. Zimmerman 1981, p. xx.

3. Ibid., p. 41.

4. Ibid., p. 55.

5. Ibid., p. 58.

6. Sheehan 1979, p. 624.

7. Ibid., p. 632.

8. Zimmerman 1981, p. 53.

9. Ibid., p. 49.

10. To be completely fair to the proponents of the "ontological" reading, some of this material has only recently become available to scholars.

11. Guignon 1983, p. 135.

12. See Guignon 1993, pp. 215 ff. See also Guignon 1992.

13. Guignon 1983, p. 135.

14. Guignon 1993, p. 229.

15. Van Buren 1994a, p. 291.

16. Ibid., p. 267.

17. Ibid., pp. 320 f.

18. Ibid., pp. 346 ff.

19. See Stachura 1981, pp. 15 ff.

20. This esteem for the paradigmatic status of the artist is also characteristic of the neo-Romantic George Circle. The difference between this version of Romanticism and Heidegger's is that, for George, the poet-artist is a quasi-messianic *Führer*, while for Heidegger, the artist (e.g., Van Gogh) is an exemplar of personal self-responsibility. On the George Circle, see Travers 2001, pp. 51–86.

21. *Confessions* X, 3,3. Heidegger quotes the original Latin, while I have made use of an English translation: Augustine of Hippo 2000, p. 238.

22. It is worth noting that '*abgesetzt*' is also a musical term, the German equivalent of "staccato." The sense is of an event that interrupts the "rhythm" of life, a term that Heidegger also employed in the early 1920s. That this connection is not accidental is indicated by one of Heidegger's own handwritten notes on this passage, in which he glosses '*abgesetzten*' as "*aber auch das anhaltende*," or "but also unremitting" or "sustained."

23. Like many German intellectuals in the 1920s, Heidegger employs military-sounding rhetoric to convey his message. One of the best examples of this is Karl Barth's

Der Römerbrief. Johannes Fritsche, in his study of §74 of *Being and Time,* argues that the use of such language uncovers inherently "fascist" tendencies in Heidegger's early work. Given that Christian theologians, Marxists, and anti-war writers used the same sort of rhetoric, this claim ultimately only serves to accentuate the limitations of Fritsche's interpretation. See Fritsche 1999. Besides the fact that the rhetoric of *Kampf* was all-pervasive in Weimar politics, it is also worth noting that "fascism," as Fritsche uses it, is far too general a category to really shed any light on a particular thinker's ideas. Furthermore, Heidegger nowhere endorses *political* violence. Even in 1934, in an address to his former classmates from Konstanz, Heidegger makes it clear that, for him, *Kampf* and *Krieg* are not synonymous with war or storm trooper street fights, but with "the *inner law* of our Dasein" (G16 283).

24. It is worth noting that Heidegger had earlier used the verb '*einschlagen*' in WS 1920–1921 to describe the intrusive and disturbing effect of the Christian proclamation of the crucified God.

25. In this passage we can detect Heidegger's critical position with respect to Dilthey's early methodology of "self-reflection [*Selbstbesinnung*]," which Dilthey places at the very core of his "descriptive" and "analytic" psychology as the foundational discipline of the "human sciences [*Geisteswissenschaften*]."

26. Richardson 1963, p. 81.

27. Taminiaux 1991, p. 67.

28. Blitz 1981, p. 131.

29. See Zimmerman 1981, pp. 74f.; Kaelin 1988, p. 170; Sikka 1997, p. 205; King 2001, pp. 164ff.; Haar 1993, p. 19; Hyde 1994; Frings 1992.

30. See KNS 1919, where Heidegger uses the curious expression "it worlds [*es weltet*]" as a way of formally indicating the factical life-experience of living within a meaningful world (G56/57 73/61).

31. Sheehan and Painter 1999.

32. Ibid., p. 74. The texts they refer to are *Der Satz vom Grund* (Pfullingen: Neske, 1957), p. 171 and *Was ist das—die Philosophie?* (Pfullingen: Neske, 1966), 34, 70.

33. Kluge and Seebold 2002.

34. Ibid., p. 248.

35. Ibid., p. 810. These cognates are words in which the "s-" has clearly been dropped.

36. Johannes Fritsche misreads Heidegger in a parallel fashion when he asserts that authenticity requires that one "realize that [one] owes [one's] eigentliches [*sic*] ethos and identity to the past." See Fritsche 1999, p. 132.

37. Guignon 1992, p, 135.

38. While Heidegger uses the word '*erschließen*' in the technical sense of "to disclose," the passage may be using a more colloquial sense of "to derive from." If the latter is the case, then the passage would run "derives temporally particular factical possibilities from the heritage [. . .]." In either case, there is no suggestion that explicit historical consciousness is a necessary condition, or even an important part, of resoluteness.

39. Fritsche 1999, p. 132; cf. pp. 16f. The ideology of at least *some* Conservative Revolutionaries, e.g., Oswald Spengler, certainly did include this sort of determinism or fatalism. See Woods 1996, pp. 21–24. Such a notion is entirely absent from Heidegger's work. Even in *Besinnung,* an unpublished work from the late 1930s, Heidegger attacks Spengler's fatalism and the so-called "heroic realism" of a Nietzschean *amor fati*

(G66 19, 29). In particular, Heidegger objects to fatalistic readings of *his own* conception of fate.

40. Indeed, '*Nachfolge*' can mean "discipleship," as in the phrase '*Nachfolge Christi.*' Compare, for example, the title of Dietrich Bonhoeffer's most famous work, *Nachfolge*.

41. LW29, 117, 131f., 216.

42. Moltmann 1993, pp. 240f.

43. Sluga 2001, pp. 223f.

44. Vogel 1994, p. 59.

45. For a recent analysis of this side of Heidegger's work, see Bambach 2003. Cf. Van Buren's discussion of what he calls the "Greek-German axis" in Heidegger's thought in Van Buren 1994a, pp. 382ff.

46. Again, this critique of George is telling. The George Circle, and at times George himself, advocated a number of values that have a striking and disturbing affinity with some central elements of Nazism: (1) amoralism, (2) the cult of the quasi-messianic *Führer*, (3) the privileging of the aesthetic over the moral or religious, (4) a Nietzschean aristocratic disdain for the masses, and (5) the celebration of grand rituals. At least during the 1920s, Heidegger is contemptuous of such ideas. See Travers 2001.

47. Vogel 1994, p. 67.

48. For Husserl's discussion of this problem, see Husserl 1960, §§42–62.

49. "Novalis" is the pseudonym for Georg Friedrich Philip, Freiherr von Hardenberg (1772–1801), a Romantic poet and contemporary of Hölderlin, Schelling, and Hegel. Heidegger discusses Novalis's aphorism "[p]hilosophy is really homesickness, an urge to be at home everywhere" at length in his lecture course for WS 1929–1930 (G29/30 7ff./5ff.).

50. Wilhelm Dilthey, *Das Erlebnis und die Dichtung: Lessing, Goethe, Novalis, Hölderlin*, 10th ed. (Leipzig: B.G. Teubner, 1929): p. 269.

51. Ibid., p. 270.

52. Ibid., p. 271.

53. Cf. Van Buren 1994a, pp. 346ff. This point, too, tells against any precipitous assimilation of Heidegger to the Conservative Revolutionaries, many of whom explicitly advocated a subordination of the individual to the collective and mythologized the *Fronterlebnis* as an instantiation of this ideal. See Woods 1996, 24.

54. On Vogel's view, this amounts to a concern for the "freedom" of the other person. It would be more correct to say that the concern is with the *possibility* of that person being an authentic individual. See Vogel 1994, p. 74.

55. Vogel articulates this anti-paternalism clearly and uses the examples of a teacher-student relation or a therapist-patient relation. See ibid., pp. 75f. Unfortunately, these examples still suggest some superior insight into the good of the other on behalf of one of the parties involved, an idea that is notably absent from Heidegger's discussions.

56. Vogel 1994, p. 70.

7. HEIDEGGER ON THE "HOW" OF PHILOSOPHY

1. Charles R. Bambach has provided an excellent summary of this feature of nineteenth-century German philosophy. See Bambach 1995, pp. 22ff.

2. Heidegger himself describes the development of this particular stream in German philosophy. See G20 13ff./13ff.

3. Bambach 1995, p. 26.

4. Heidegger describes this idea in KNS 1919. See G56/57 9f./7ff.

5. See Kovacs 1994.

6. For a recent discussion of Heidegger's position vis-à-vis both, "life-philosophy" in particular, see Fehér 1994.

7. Jeffrey Barash has discussed Heidegger's critical stance with respect to the project of creating "culture." Barash convincingly articulates Heidegger's rejection of all projects aimed at "saving" culture. See Barash 1994, pp. 113f.

8. Charles R. Bambach discusses Heidegger's "blood and soil" views in a recent study; see Bambach 2003. Bambach's motives in this study are made explicit in a note, where he suggests that Heidegger's work from the 1930s has influenced the agenda of "contemporary continental philosophy" such that Jewish thinkers like Löwith, Bloch, and Rosenzweig are "marginalized" (see p. 136, note 53). One can, of course, only applaud the attempt to grant these figures their rightful place in modern thought. At the same time, however, one can only think that the cause would better be served by thorough and innovative study of these thinkers, and not by a limited critique of Heidegger. One might also note, in passing, that these figures have not been marginalized at all in *theology*. See, for example, Moltmann 1996, pp. 29–43, where all three are discussed.

9. Bambach 1995, p. 201. It is not immediately clear what it means to think of the "phenomenological meaning" of crisis, since we are not told what it is for something to have "phenomenological meaning."

10. Cf. Heidegger's remarks at the very beginning of KNS 1919: "The idea of science, therefore—and every element of its genuine realization—means a transforming intervention in the immediate consciousness of life; it involves a transition to a new attitude of consciousness, and thus its own form of the movement of spiritual life" (G56/57 3/3).

11. Charles R. Bambach describes some of the parallels between Heidegger's own philosophical development and the neo-orthodox assault on liberal *Kulturprotestantismus*. See Bambach 1995, pp. 189ff.

12. See Kisiel 1988.

13. Van Buren 1994a, pp. 188ff.

14. Ibid., p. 167.

8. Destruction

1. Bernasconi 1994.

2. Bambach 1995, p. 198.

3. Ibid., p. 199.

4. Ibid., p. 209.

5. Ibid., p. 209.

6. Barash 1994, p. 112.

7. Ibid., p. 114.

8. Bambach 1995, p. 197.

9. Heidegger goes on to explain in more detail what these "problem areas" are: (1) The problem of "value" refers to the sphere of questions that arose through the neo-Kantian attempt to overcome naturalism without recourse to speculative metaphysics by positing *a priori* values as ways to account for normativity in logic, epistemology, and

ethics; (2) The problem of "form" develops out of (1) and involves the transcendental problem of trying to clarify the way concepts and categories function; (3) Finally, the problem of "system" represents the attempt by Rickert, Lask, and others to formulate a "system" of transcendental values that provides an exhaustive, unifying account of objective knowledge. See G56/57 122 ff./103 ff.

10. In a similar vein, Heidegger later observes that the first step in phenomenology is always a "critical destruction of objectifying enclosure [*Objektivierungseinschlüsse*]" (G58 164).

11. Bambach claims at one point that "destruction" is a kind of shorthand term for the totality of Heidegger's philosophical method. See Bambach 1995, p. 197. In light of the passage quoted here, this is a misleading claim. Bernasconi, on the other hand, correctly recognizes that "destruction" is only *part* of Heidegger's overall project. See Bernasconi 1994, p. 123.

12. Hegel 1977, p. 49. Translation modified.

13. Ibid., p. 50. Translation modified.

14. To be more accurate, this connection had been largely overlooked by *American* commentators on Heidegger's work. This is not quite the case in Germany. Hans-Georg Gadamer's discussion of Heidegger in *Truth and Method* is a clear example of the recognition that Heidegger's views on interpretation emerged from his own confrontation with the debates sparked by historicism in the nineteenth century.

15. Bambach 1995, p. 201.

16. Ibid., p. 211.

17. Ibid., p. 219.

18. Barash 1994, p. 113.

19. Ibid., p. 113.

20. Bernasconi 1994, pp. 133f.

21. Tisdale and Bozzolla 1977, p. 89.

22. Flint and Coppotelli 1969, p. 42.

23. Robert Bernasconi has pointed out how many commentators overlook completely the "positive" side of destruction. His own examination of the idea goes a long way toward correcting this flaw. See Bernasconi 1994.

REFERENCES

SECONDARY LITERATURE ON HEIDEGGER

Bambach, Charles R. 1995. *Heidegger, Dilthey, and the Crisis of Historicism*. Ithaca, N.Y.: Cornell University Press.

———. 2003. *Heidegger's Roots: Nietzsche, National Socialism, and the Greeks*. Ithaca, N.Y.: Cornell University Press.

Barash, Jeffrey A. 1988. *Martin Heidegger and the Problem of Historical Meaning*. Dordrecht: Martinus Nijhoff.

———. 1994. "Heidegger's Ontological 'Destruction' of Western Intellectual Traditions." In *Reading Heidegger From the Start: Essays in His Earliest Thought*. Edited by Theodore Kisiel and John Van Buren. Albany: State University of New York Press, 111–122.

Bernasconi, Robert. 1994. "Repitition and Tradition: Heidegger's Destructuring of the Distinction Between Essence and Existence in *Basic Problems of Phenomenology*." In *Reading Heidegger from the Start: Essays in His Earliest Thought*. Edited by Theodore Kisiel and John Van Buren. Albany: State University of New York Press, 123–136.

Blitz, Mark. 1981. *Heidegger's "Being and Time" and the Possibility of Political Philosophy*. Ithaca, N.Y.: Cornell University Press.

Caputo, John D. 1978. *The Mystical Element in Heidegger's Thought*. Athens: Ohio University Press.

———. 1994. "*Sorge* and *Kardia*: The Hermeneutics of Factical Life and the Categories of the Heart." In *Reading Heidegger From the Start: Essays in His Earliest Thought*. Edited by Theodore Kisiel and John Van Buren. Albany: State University of New York Press, 327–344.

Carman, Taylor. 2000. "Must We Be Inauthentic?" In *Heidegger, Authenticity, and Modernity: Essays in Honor of Hubert L. Dreyfus, Vol. 1*. Cambridge, Mass.: MIT Press, 13–28.

Casper, Bernhard. 1980. "Martin Heidegger und die Theologische Fakultät Freiburg, 1909–1923." In *Kirche am Oberrhein: Beiträge zur Geschichte der Bistümer Konstanz und Freiburg*. Edited by Remigius Bäumer, Karl Suso Frank, and Heinrich Ott. Freiburg: Verlag Herder, 534–541.

Crowe, Benjamin D. 2001. "Resoluteness in the Middle Voice: On the Ethical Dimensions of Heidegger's *Being and Time*." *Philosophy Today* 45 (3): 225–241.

Crowell, Steven G. 1994. "Making Logic Philosophical Again (1912–1916)." In *Reading Heidegger From the Start: Essays in His Earliest Thought*. Edited by Theodore Kisiel and John Van Buren. Albany: State University of New York Press, 55–72.

References

Dahlstrom, Daniel O. 1994a. "Heidegger's Method: Philosophical Concepts as Formal Indications." *Review of Metaphysics* 47: 775–795.

———. 1994b. *Das logische Vorurteil: Untersuchungen zur Wahrheitstheorie des frühen Heidegger.* Wien: Passagen.

———. 1995. "Heidegger's Concept of Temporality: Reflections on a Recent Criticism." *Review of Metaphysics* 49: 95–115.

Dreyfus, Hubert L. 1991. *Being-in-the-World: A Commentary on Heidegger's "Being and Time," Division I.* Cambridge, Mass.: MIT Press.

Ewing, Elizabeth. 1995. "Authenticity in Heidegger: A Response to Dreyfus." *Inquiry* 38 (4): 469–487.

Farin, Ingo. 1998. "Heidegger's Critique of Value Philosophy." *Journal of the British Society for Phenomenology* 29 (3): 268–280.

Fehér, István M. 1994. "Phenomenology, Hermeneutics, *Lebensphilosophie*: Heidegger's Confrontation with Husserl, Dilthey, and Jaspers." In *Reading Heidegger from the Start: Essays in His Earliest Thought.* Edited by Theodore Kisiel and John Van Buren. Albany: State University of New York Press, 73–90.

———. 1995. "Heidegger's Understanding of the 'Atheism' of Philosophy: Philosophy, Theology, and Religion in His Early Lectures up to *Being and Time*." *American Catholic Philosophical Quarterly* 69: 189–228.

Fried, Gregory. 2000. *Heidegger's Polemos: From Being to Politics.* New Haven, Conn.: Yale University Press.

Frings, Manfred S. 1992. "The Background of Max Scheler's 1927 Reading of *Being and Time*: A Critique of a Critique through Ethics." *Philosophy Today* 36: 99–113.

Fritsche, Johannes. 1999. *Historical Destiny and National Socialism in Heidegger's "Being and Time."* Berkeley: University of California Press.

Gadamer, Hans-Georg. 1987. "Die Religiöse Dimension." In *Gesammelte Werke,* vol. 3: *Neuere Philosophie: Hegel, Husserl, Heidegger.* Tübingen: J.C.B. Mohr.

———. 1989. "Heidegger's 'theologische' Jugendschrift." *Dilthey Jahrbuch für Philosophie und Geschichte der Geisteswissenschaften* 6: 228–234.

Grondin, Jean. 1994. "The Ethical and Young Hegelian Motives in Heidegger's Hermeneutics of Facticity." In *Reading Heidegger from the Start: Essays in His Earliest Thought.* Edited by Theodore Kisiel and John Van Buren. Albany: State University of New York Press, 345–360.

Guignon, Charles B. 1983. *Heidegger and the Problem of Knowledge.* Indianapolis, Ind.: Hackett Publishing Company.

———. 1992. "History and Commitment in the Early Heidegger." In *Heidegger: A Critical Reader.* Edited by Hubert Dreyfus and Harrison Hall. Cambridge: Blackwell, 130–142.

———. 1993. "Authenticity, moral values, and psychotherapy." In *The Cambridge Companion to Heidegger.* Edited by Charles B. Guignon. Cambridge: Cambridge University Press, 215–239.

———. 2001. "Being as Appearing: Retrieving the Greek Experience of *Phusis*." In *A Companion to Heidegger's* Introduction to Metaphysics. Edited by Richard Polt and Gregory Fried. New Haven, Conn.: Yale University Press, 34–57.

Haar, Michel. 1993. *Heidegger and the Essence of Man.* Translated by William Mc-Neill. Albany: State University of New York Press.

Habermas, Jürgen. 1987. *The Philosophical Discourse of Modernity: Twelve Lectures.* Translated by F. Lawrence. Cambridge, Mass.: MIT Press.

———. 1992. "Work and *Weltanschauung*: The Heidegger Controversy from a German Perspective." In *Heidegger: A Critical Reader*. Edited by Hubert Dreyfus and Harrison Hall. Cambridge: Blackwell, 186–208.

Hyde, J. 1994. "The Call of Conscience: Heidegger and the Question of Rhetoric." *Philosophy and Rhetoric* 27 (4): 374–396.

Ijsseling, Samuel. 1986. "Heidegger and the Destruction of Ontology." In *A Companion to Heidegger's "Being and Time."* Edited by Joseph J. Kockelmans. Washington, D.C.: University Press of America, 127–144.

Jonas, Hans. 1963. *The Gnostic Religion: The Message of the Alien God and the Beginnings of Christianity.* Boston: Beacon Press.

———. 1964. "Heidegger and Theology." *Review of Metaphysics* 18: 207–233.

Kaelin, E. F. 1988. *Heidegger's "Being and Time": A Reading for Readers.* Tallahassee: Florida State University Press.

King, Magda. 2001. *A Guide to Heidegger's "Being and Time."* Edited by John Llewelyn. Albany: State University of New York Press.

Kisiel, Theodore. 1988. "War der frühe Heidegger tatsächliche ein 'christlicher Theologe'?" In *Philosophie und Poesie: Otto Pöggeler zum 60. Geburstag.* Edited by Annemarie Gethmann-Siefert. Stuttgart: Frommann-Holzboog. 59–75.

———. 1993. *The Genesis of Heidegger's Being and Time.* Berkeley: University of California Press.

———. 1994. "Heidegger (1920–1921) on Becoming a Christian: A Conceptual Picture Show." In *Reading Heidegger From the Start: Essays in His Earliest Thought.* Edited by Theodore Kisiel and John Van Buren. Albany: State University of New York Press, 175–192.

———. 2002a. "Heidegger's Apology: Biography as Philosophy and Ideology." In *Heidegger's Way of Thought: Critical and Interpretive Signposts.* Edited by Alfred Denker and Marion Heinz. New York: Continuum, 1–35.

———. 2002b. "Why Students of Heidegger Will Have to Read Emil Lask." In *Heidegger's Way of Thought: Critical and Interpretive Signposts.* Edited by Alfred Denker and Marion Heinz. New York: Continuum, 101–136.

Kovacs, George. 1994. "Philosophy as Primordial Science in Heidegger's Courses of 1919." In *Reading Heidegger from the Start: Essays in His Earliest Thought.* Edited by Theodore Kisiel and John Van Buren. Albany: State University of New York Press, 91–110.

Löwith, Karl. 1942. "Martin Heidegger and Franz Rosenzweig, or Temporality and Eternity." *Philosophy and Phenomenological Research* 3: 53–77.

MacAvoy, Leslie. 2001. "Overturning Cartesianism and the Hermeneutics of Suspicion: Rethinking Dreyfus on Heidegger." *Inquiry* 44 (4): 455–480.

McNeill, William. 1999. *The Glance of the Eye: Heidegger, Aristotle, and the Ends of Theory.* Albany: State University of New York Press.

Raffoul, François. 1998. *Heidegger and the Subject.* Translated by David Pettigrew and Gregory Recco. Atlantic Highlands, N.J.: Humanities Press.

Richardson, William J. 1963. *From Phenomenology to Thought.* The Hague: Martinus Nijhoff.

Rickey, Christopher. 2002. *Revolutionary Saints: Heidegger, National Socialism, and Antinomian Politics.* University Park: Pennsylvania State University Press.

Sheehan, Thomas. 1979. "Heidegger's 'Introduction to the Phenomenology of Religion,' 1920–1921." *The Personalist* 60 (3): 312–324.

References

———. 2001. "A Paradigm Shift in Heidegger Research." *Continental Philosophy Review* 34: 183–202.

Sheehan, Thomas, and Corinne Painter. 1999. "Choosing One's Fate: A Re-reading of *Sein und Zeit* §74." *Research in Phenomenology* 29: 63–82.

Sikka, Sonya. 1997. *Forms of Transcendence: Heidegger and Medieval Mystical Theology*. Albany: State University of New York Press.

Sluga, Hans. 1993. *Heidegger's Crisis: Philosophy and Politics in Nazi Germany* Cambridge, Mass.: Harvard University Press.

———. 2001. "Conflict is the Father of All Things: Heidegger's Polemical Conception of Politics." In *A Companion to Heidegger's* Introduction to Metaphysics. Edited by Richard Polt and Gregory Fried. New Haven, Conn.: Yale University Press, 205–225.

Streeter, Ryan. 1997. "Heidegger's Formal Indication: A Question of Method in *Being and Time*." *Man and World* 30 (4): 413–430.

Taminiaux, Jacques. 1991. *Heidegger and the Project of Fundamental Ontology*. Translated by Michael Gerdre. Albany: State University of New York Press.

Van Buren, John. 1994a. *The Young Heidegger: Rumor of the Hidden King*. Bloomington: Indiana University Press.

———. 1994b. "Martin Heidegger, Martin Luther." In *Reading Heidegger from the Start: Essays in His Earliest Thought*. Edited by Theodore Kisiel and John Van Buren. Albany: State University of New York Press, 159–174.

———. 1995. "The Ethics of *Formale Anzeige* in Heidegger." *American Catholic Philosophical Quarterly* 69 (2): 157–170.

Vogel, Lawrence. 1994. *The Fragile "We": Ethical Implications of Heidegger's "Being and Time"*. Evanston, Ill.: Northwestern University Press.

Wolin, Richard. 1990. *The Politics of Being: The Political Thought of Martin Heidegger*. New York: Columbia University Press.

Zimmerman, Michael E. 1981. *Eclipse of the Self: The Development of Heidegger's Concept of Authenticity*. Athens: Ohio University Press.

———. 1990. *Heidegger's Confrontation with Modernity: Technology, Politics, Art*. Bloomington: Indiana University Press.

———. 2001. "The Ontological Decline of the West." In *A Companion to Heidegger's* Introduction to Metaphysics. Edited by Richard Polt and Gregory Fried. New Haven, Conn.: Yale University Press, 185–204.

Secondary Literature on Luther

Adam, Alfred. 1963. "Der Begriff 'Deus absconditus' bei Luther nach Herkunft und Bedeutung." *Lutherjahrbuch* 30: 97–106.

Beintker, Horst. 1954. *Die Überwindung der Anfechtung bei Luther: Eine Studie zu seiner Theologie nach den Operationes in Psalmos, 1519–1521*. Berlin: Evangelische Verlagsanstalt.

Ebeling, Gerhard. 1970. *Luther: An Introduction to His Thought*. Translated by R. A. Wilson. London: Collins.

———. 1979. "Fides occidet rationem: Ein Aspekt der theologia crucis in Luthers Auslegung von Gal 3,6." In *Theologia Crucis—Signum Crucis: Festschrift für Erick Dinkler zum 70. Geburstag*. Edited by Carl Andresen and Günter Klein. Tübingen: J.C.B. Mohr (Paul Siebeck), 97–136.

Eckermann, Willigis. 1978. "Die Aristoteleskritik Luthers: Ihre Bedeutung für Seine Theologie." *Catholica* 32: 114–130.

Ellwein, Eduard. 1936. "Die Entfaltung der theologia crucis in Luthers Hebräerbriefvorlesung." In *Theologische Aufsätze: Karl Barth zum 50. Geburstag.* Edited by E. Wolf. (München: Chr. Kaiser Verlag, 382–404.

Gerrish, B.A. 1962. *Grace and Reason.* Oxford: Clarendon Press.

Hoffman, Bengt R. 1976. *Luther and the Mystics.* Minneapolis, Minn.: Augsburg Publishing House.

Joest, Wilfried. 1967. *Ontologie der Person bei Luther.* Göttingen: Vandenhoeck and Ruprecht.

McGrath, Alister E. 1985. *Luther's Theology of the Cross: Martin Luther's Theological Breakthrough.* Oxford: Blackwell.

Ozment, Steven E. 1969. *Homo Spiritualis: A Comparative Study of the Anthropology of Johannes Tauler, Jean Gerson and Martin Luther (1509–1516) in the Context of Their Theological Thought.* Leiden: E. J. Brill.

Pinomaa, Lennart. 1940. *Der Existentielle Charakter der Theologie Luthers: Das Hervorbrechen der Theologie der Anfechtung und Ihre Bedeutung für das Lutherverständnis.* Helsinki: Finnish Academy of the Sciences.

Ringleben, Joachim. 1990. "Die Einheit von Gotteserkenntnis und Selbsterkenntnis: Beobachtung anhand von Luther's Römerbrief-Vorlesung." *Neue Zeitschrift für systematische Theologie und Religionsphilosophie* 32 (2): 125–133.

Von Loewenich, Walther. 1976. *Luther's Theology of the Cross.* Translated by Herbert J. A. Bouman. Minneapolis, Minn.: Augsburg Publishing House.

Zur Mühlen, Karl-Heinz. 1980. "Luthers Kritik der Vernunft im Mittelalterlichen und Neuzeitlichen Kontext." *Lutheriana: zum 500. Geburstag Martin Luthers:* 3–15.

———. 1981. "Luthers Kritik am scholastischen Aristotelismus in der 25. These der 'Heidelberger Disputation' von 1518." *Lutherjahrbuch:* 54–79.

OTHER SOURCES

Alston, William P. 2001. "Religious Beliefs and Values." *Faith and Philosophy* 18 (1): 36–49.

Augustine of Hippo. 2000. *The Confessions.* Translated by Maria Boulding, O.S.B. Hyde Park, N.Y.: New City Press.

Breuer, Stefan. 1993. *Anatomie der Konservativen Revolution.* Darmstadt: Wissenschaftliche Buchgesellschaft.

Bultmann, Rudolf. 1987. *Faith and Understanding.* Translated by Louise P. Smith. Philadelphia: Fortress Press.

Elrod, John W. 1981. *Kierkegaard and Christendom.* Princeton, N.J.: Princeton University Press.

Ermarth, Michael. 1978. *Wilhelm Dilthey: The Critique of Historical Reason.* Chicago: University of Chicago Press.

Flint, R. W., and Arthur A. Coppotelli, eds. 1969. *Marinetti: Selected Writings.* New York: Farrar, Strauss, and Giroux.

Gadamer, Hans-Georg. 1996. *Truth and Method.* Translated by Joel Weinsheimer and Donald G. Marshall. New York: Continuum.

Grondin, Jean. 2003. *Hans-Georg Gadamer: A Biography.* Translated by Joel Weinsheimer. New Haven, Conn.: Yale University Press.

References

Hegel, G. W. F. 1977. *Phenomenology of Spirit*. Translated by A. V. Miller. Oxford: Oxford University Press.

Husserl, Edmund. 1960. *Cartesian Meditations: An Introduction to Phenomenology*. Translated by Dorion Cairns. The Hague: Martinus Nijhoff.

———. 1982. *Collected Works, Vol. 2: Ideas Pertaining to a Pure Phenomenology and to a Phenomenological Philosophy, First Book: General Introduction to Pure Phenomenology*. Translated by F. Kersten. The Hague: Martinus Nijhoff.

Jost, John T., and Brenda Major, eds. 2001. *The Psychology of Legitimacy: Emerging Perspectives on Ideology, Justice, and Intergroup Relations*. Cambridge, Mass.: Cambridge University Press.

Jüngel, Eberhard. 1983. *God as the Mystery of the World: On the Foundation of the Theology of the Crucified One in the Dispute between Theism and Atheism*. Translated by Darrell L. Guder. Grand Rapids, Mich.: William B. Eerdmans Publishing Company.

Kaes, Anton, et al., eds. 1994. *The Weimar Republic Sourcebook*. Berkeley: University of California Press.

Kierkegaard, Søren. 1978. *Two Ages*. Translated by Howard V. Hong and Edna H. Hong. Princeton, N.J.: Princeton University Press.

Kluge, Friedrich, and Elmar Seebold. 2002. *Etymologisches Wörterbuch der deutschen Sprache*. 24th ed. Berlin: Walter de Gruyter.

Marcuse, Herbert. 1964. *One-Dimensional Man*. Boston: Beacon Press.

Moltmann, Jürgen. 1993. *The Way of Jesus Christ: Christology in Messianic Dimensions*. Translated by Margaret Kohl. Minneapolis, Minn.: Fortress Press.

———. 1996. *The Coming of God: Christian Eschatology*. Translated by Margaret Kohl. Minneapolis, Minn.: Fortress Press.

Nietzsche, Friedrich. 1995. *Unfashionable Observations*. Translated by Richard T. Gray. Stanford, Calif.: Stanford University Press.

Ogden, Mark. 1991. *The Problem of Christ in the Works of Friedrich Hölderlin*. London: Modern Humanities Research Association and the Institute of Germanic Studies.

Overbeck, Franz. 1974. *Über die Christlichkeit unserer heutigen Theologie. Streit- und Friedensschrift*. Darmstadt: Wissenschaftlicher Buchgesellschaft.

Pannenberg, Wolfhart. 1963. "Hermeneutik und Universalgeschichte." *Zeitschrift für Theologie und Kirche* 60: 90–121.

———. 1968. "Dogmatic Theses on the Doctrine of Revelation." In *Revelation as History*. Edited by Wolfhart Pannenberg. Translated by David Granskou. New York: Macmillan, 123–158.

———. 1977. *Jesus: God and Man*. Translated by Lewis L. Wilkins and Duane A. Priebe. Philadelphia: Westminster Press.

———. 1985. *Anthropology in Theological Perspective*. Translated by Matthew J. O'Connell. Philadelphia: Westminster Press.

Plantinga, Alvin. 2000. *Warranted Christian Belief*. Oxford: Oxford University Press.

Rosenzweig, Franz. 1999. *Understanding the Sick and the Healthy: A View of World, Man, and God*. Translated by Nahum Glatzer. Cambridge, Mass.: Harvard University Press.

———. 2000a. "Atheistic Theology." In *Franz Rosenzweig: Philosophical and Theological Writings*. Edited by Paul W. Franks and Michael L. Morgan. Indianapolis, Ind.: Hackett Publishing, 10–24.

———. 2000b. " '*Urzelle*' to the *Star of Redemption*." In *Franz Rosenzweig: Philosophical and Theological Writings*. Edited by Paul W. Franks and Michael L. Morgan. Indianapolis, Ind.: Hackett Publishing, 48–72.

Rowland, Christopher. 1982. *The Open Heaven: A Study of Apocalyptic in Judaism and Early Christianity*. New York: Crossroads.

Schleiermacher, Friedrich. 1926. *Soliloquies*. Translated by H. L. Friess. Chicago: Open Court Publishing.

Scholtz, Gunter. 1995. *Ethik und Hermeneutik: Schleiermachers Grundlegung der Geisteswissenschaften*. Frankfurt am Main: Suhrkamp Verlag.

Sidanius, Jim, and Felicia Pratto. 1999. *Social Dominance: An Intergroup Theory of Social Hierarchy and Oppression*. Cambridge: Cambridge University Press.

Stachura, Peter D. 1981. *The German Youth Movement, 1900–1945: An Interpretive and Documentary History*. London: Macmillan.

Stoljar, Margaret Mahony, ed. and trans. 1997. *Novalis: Philosophical Writings*. Albany: State University of New York Press.

Stout, Jeffrey. 1981. *The Flight from Authority: Religion, Morality, and the Quest for Autonomy*. Notre Dame, Ind.: University of Notre Dame Press.

Taylor, Charles. 1991. *The Ethics of Authenticity*. Cambridge, Mass.: Harvard University Press.

Tisdale, Caroline, and Angelo Bozzolla. 1977. *Futurism*. London: Thames and Hudson.

Travers, Martin. 2001. *Critics of Modernity: The Literature of the Conservative Revolution in Germany, 1890–1933*. New York: Peter Lang.

Westphal, Merold. 1987. *Kierkegaard's Critique of Reason and Society*. Macon, Ga.: Mercer University Press, 1987.

———. 2001. *Overcoming Onto-theology: Toward a Postmodern Christian Faith*. New York: Fordham University Press.

Woods, Roger. 1996. *The Conservative Revolution in the Weimar Republic*. London: Macmillan.

INDEX

alienation, 26, 98–99, 135, 165, 167, 174, 223, 237

Alston, William P., 273n25:3

Anfechtung, 45, 57, 229, 271n39:2

anthropology, theological, 44, 66, 152–54, 178, 270n5:2

anxiety [*Angst*], 42, 57, 65, 95, 119, 165, 185, 273n24:3

anxious worry [*Bekümmerung*], 10, 38, 70, 79, 82, 92, 99, 100, 113, 156, 158, 161, 172–76, 180–81, 212, 214, 222–25, 227, 253–54, 255

Aristotle, 24, 25, 77, 113, 136, 240, 259; influence on medieval theology, 46–48; Luther's reaction to, 15, 46–47, 64, 66, 118–19; on "the easy," 83

atheism, 16, 20, 267n5:1

Augustine of Hippo, 35, 36, 41, 62, 63, 83, 88, 89, 92, 93, 100, 113, 152, 182, 247, 259, 272n13:3, 273n26:3, 277n28:5, 277n21:6; on *ambitio saeculi*, 88–89; on continence, 86–87; on *molestia*, 92, 172

authenticity [*Eigentlichkeit*], 3, 4, 8, 9–10, 11, 12, 32, 74, 76–78, 93, 94, 132, 139, 163, 169, 176, 180, 217, 221, 224, 233, 237, 257, 269n30:1, 272n14:3, 273n25:3, 277n30:5, 278n36:6; artists as paradigms of, 70, 140, 170, 177, 178, 220, 276n18:5, 277n20:6; basic contours of, 70, 78, 142, 160–61, 171–72, 177, 180, 181, 260; "emancipatory" interpretation, 10, 168–69; as focused life, 190–91; individual nature of, 189; "narrative" interpretation, 10, 167–68; "ontological" interpretation, 10, 164–67; religious people as paradigms of, 140–41, 149, 170, 177–78, 220; and Romantic personalism, 135, 136–38, 154, 162, 178, 179; social aspects of, 11, 195–203, 226, 259

Bambach, Charles R., 209, 217, 233, 236, 250, 251, 267n1:Introduction, 274n3:4, 276n16:5, 279n45:6, 279n1:7, 280n3:7, 280n8:7, 280n9:7, 280n11:7, 280n2:8, 280n8:8, 281n11:8, 281n15:8

Barash, Jeffrey A., 17, 233, 250, 251, 255, 267n1:Introduction, 267n4:1, 280n7:7, 280n6:8, 281n18:8

barricading [*Abriegelung*], 93–94, 96, 234, 241, 246–47, 258, 274n38:3. *See also* larvance; "one," the; self-abdication

Barth, Karl, 1, 50, 56, 63, 75, 117, 161, 176

basic experience [*Grunderfahrung*], 7, 15, 16, 21, 29–32, 39, 42, 186, 222, 234, 274n38:3; authenticity as, 15, 29, 37; primitive Christianity as, 22, 32–37, 41, 222

Becker, Oskar, 30, 69–70, 270n16:2

"Being," 6, 17, 20

being-in-the-world [*In-der-Welt-Sein*], 6, 98, 196. *See also* Dasein; factical life-experience; facticity; life

Bernard of Clairvaux, 32, 36, 152

Bernasconi, Robert, 232–33, 251, 270n14:2, 280n1:8, 281n11:8, 281n20:8, 281n23:8

Blochmann, Elisabeth, 16, 30, 31, 33, 142, 169, 171, 172, 175, 180, 183, 189, 202, 203, 217, 269n32:1

Bousset, Wilhelm, 131

Bultmann, Rudolf, 1, 17, 20, 35, 62, 267n4:1, 268n20:1, 274n40:3

Calvin, John, 270n19:2

Caputo, John D., 277n30:5

categories, 6, 23–25, 74, 94, 98, 144, 155, 167, 185, 258, 281n9:8. *See also* life

categories of "fallen" life, 8, 71, 78–79, 80, 83, 84, 85, 93. *See also* inauthenticity

Christianity, 7, 15, 17, 75, 91, 130–31; as paradigm of authenticity, 9, 135, 143, 149–54, 154–61, 162, 191, 200, 271n4:3; Greek philosophy and, 18, 33–34, 36, 112–14, 268n8:1; Heidegger's view of, 18–21, 34–35, 103, 130, 274n2:4; "primitive" [*Urchristentum*], 9, 12, 20, 32–37, 41, 76, 82, 140, 171

clearing [*die Lichtung*], 6

Cohen, Hermann, 33

community of struggle [*Kampfgemeinschaft*], 11, 164, 168, 179, 200, 203, 226; modeled on friendship with K. Jaspers, 199–200; modeled on "primitive Christianity," 92, 97, 140, 154, 158, 199. *See also* authenticity, social aspects of

concupiscence, 48–49, 50, 51, 53, 58, 59, 89, 92

conscience [*Gewissen*], 32, 56, 165–66, 176, 179, 185–88, 191, 235, 258, 272n8:3; being the conscience of another person, 200–202, 235, 259, 265 (*see also* authenticity, social aspects of); in *Being and Time*, 10, 163, 179–80, 182–84; Heidegger's early views on, 10, 180–82

Conservative Revolution, 70, 71, 117, 170–71, 184, 273n30:3, 275n16:4, 276n22:5, 279n53:6

culture, 10, 33–34, 56, 73, 75, 79, 81–82, 103, 112, 119, 120, 121–29, 130, 132, 142, 172, 181, 194–95, 197–98, 203, 208, 213–15, 217, 222, 233, 244, 250–54, 274n1:4, 280n7:7. *See also* historical consciousness; tradition

Dahlstrom, Daniel, 4, 274n4:4

Dasein, 6, 26, 35, 71–72, 80, 82, 95, 97, 103, 104, 119, 120, 126, 132–33, 138–39, 166–67, 176, 177, 181, 184–85, 186, 196, 212, 237, 251. *See also* being-in-the-world; factical life-experience; facticity; life

decline [*Abfall*], 8, 36, 71, 92, 83, 102, 106–12, 128

de-historicizing, 22, 112, 238

destiny [*Geschick*], 155, 192, 196, 199. *See also* authenticity, social aspects of

destructio [and cognate terms], 2, 7, 38, 45; as act of God, 54–55, 57–58, 61–62, 63–65; as part of theology, 38, 48, 58–59

destruction [*Destruktion*], 2, 12, 232–34, 236, 248, 281n11:8; as core practice of philosophy, 3, 208, 232, 234, 281n10:8; defini-

tion of, in SS 1920, 244–47; earliest uses of, 3, 240–44; modeled on Lutheran *destructio*, 7, 230, 270n1:2, 274n39:3; motives for, 3, 9, 16, 107, 224, 232, 234–36, 274n38:3; negative sense of, 255–60; positive sense of, 260–65, 281n23:8; and repetition, 261–62; and tradition, 248–49, 250–51; usage after *Being and Time*, 3–4

dialectic, Hegelian, 12, 125, 232, 241–43, 256

Dilthey, Wilhelm, 9, 34, 82, 125, 127, 150, 221, 238–39, 249, 253, 276n15:5, 276n16:5, 276n17:5; concept of "generation," 196–98; influence on Heidegger's views of tradition, 102–103; on "primitive Christianity," 36, 135, 147–49, 152, 154, 179, 220; and Romantic personalism, 135, 138, 140, 143–46

dismantling [*Abbau*], 235, 255–60, 274n39:3. *See also* destruction, negative sense of

dispersion [*Zerstreuung*], 78, 85–88, 142. *See also* categories of "fallen" life; inauthenticity

distantiality [*Abständigkeit*], 90

Dostoyevsky, Fyodor, 10, 118, 170, 184

Dreyfus, Hubert, 4, 73–76, 272n6:3, 272n7:3

Ebbinghaus, Julius, 42

Ebeling, Gerhard, 47, 270n10:2, 270n12:2

Eckhart, Meister, 18, 36, 150, 152

Ellwein, Eduard, 61, 271n30:2, 271n31:2

Enlightenment (historical period), 98, 126, 139–40, 148, 154

Ereignis, 6, 150, 165

eschatology, 114, 130, 131, 135, 157–58, 161, 162, 268n18:1

exemplification [*Vorleben*], 202–203, 219–20, 226, 229, 264. *See also* authenticity, social aspects of

existentialism, 167

Existenz, 10, 172–76, 177, 178, 179, 198, 202, 228. *See also* authenticity

factical life-experience, 6, 16, 35, 37, 38, 42, 47, 104, 123, 138, 149, 211, 223, 226, 243, 246–47, 251. *See also* being-in-the-world; Dasein; facticity; life

facticity, 26, 34, 38, 70, 72, 80, 119, 124, 138, 155, 172, 173, 174, 177, 178, 185–86, 223, 227, 254, 268n25:1. *See also* being-in-the-world; Dasein; factical life-experience; life

fading of significance, 88, 107–109. *See also* idle talk; public discourse

faith, 19–21, 35, 40–41, 47, 65, 131–32, 156, 159, 192–93, 222; Luther's views on, 40–41, 52, 54, 57, 60–62, 64, 66, 75, 192, 269n44:2

falling [*Verfallen*], 18, 71, 72, 78, 79, 84, 98, 99, 110, 173, 174, 272n5:3. *See also* inauthenticity

fanaticism [*Schwärmerei*], 19, 83, 121–22, 215

fatalism, 278n39:6

fate [*Schicksal*], 87, 149, 190–91, 211, 212, 262, 279n39:6. *See also* authenticity

formal indication [*formale Anzeige*], 32, 77–78, 94, 101, 135, 186, 187, 188, 190, 201, 208, 226–27, 268n25:1, 275n3:5

free Christianity, 19, 103, 130, 274n2:4

fundamental ontology, 26. *See also* hermeneutics of facticity

futurism, 1, 252

Gadamer, Hans-Georg, 3, 228, 267n1:1, 268n11:1

generation, 11, 109, 115, 141, 195–98, 203, 208, 221, 226, 236, 254, 256, 264. *See also* authenticity, social aspects of

genuineness, 30, 35, 85, 97, 99, 135, 140, 142, 170, 172, 176, 189, 217, 218, 220, 221, 237. *See also* authenticity

George, Stefan, 145, 194, 277n20:6, 279n46:6

Gerrish, B. A., 46, 270n3:2, 270n18:2

God, 2, 7, 17, 35, 42, 45, 46, 47, 49, 50, 53, 56, 57, 61, 75, 89, 153, 229, 270n6:2; "Crucified," 40, 66, 119, 192, 278n24:6; "hidden" [*deus absconditus*], 58, 60, 63–64, 66, 271n36:2; righteousness of, 49, 55, 272n9:2; word of, 56–57, 156–58, 230 (*see also* proclamation)

Gogarten, Friedrich, 56, 161

graced moments, 30, 142, 171, 183, 188, 235. *See also* conscience; interruption; life-intensification

Guignon, Charles B., 167–68, 190, 277n11:6, 277n12:6, 277n13:6, 277n14:6, 278n37:6

guilt, 186–87, 188, 191

Gunkel, Hermann, 131

Habermas, Jürgen, 277n1:6

Hegel, Georg Wilhelm Friedrich, 24, 34, 152, 197, 242–43, 255, 281n12:8

Heidegger, Martin: later assessments of *Being and Time*, 5; theological education, 16–17, 131

Heitmüller, Josef, 228

Herder, J. G., 126, 137, 139–40, 145, 146, 154, 176

hermeneutic circle, 27–29

hermeneutical intuition, 22

hermeneutics of facticity, 7, 21–22, 26–27, 28, 30–32, 37, 44, 71, 77, 81, 119, 120, 124, 132, 143, 185, 223, 261

historical consciousness, 9, 36, 82, 94, 102–103, 139, 263; and authenticity, 190–93, 262, 265, 278n38:6; in the early 1920s, 232, 249–55; and public discourse, 120, 126–29, 228; Nietzsche's views on, 261–62

historical I, 22, 23, 30. *See also* self-world

Historical School, 251, 257

historicality [*Geschichtlichkeit*], 126, 189–93, 196, 250–51, 255, 262; Christian model of, 191–93

history, philosophy of, 140, 244, 253, 255, 256, 267n4:1, 276n16:5

History of Religions School, 131

Hölderlin, Friedrich, 16, 33, 144, 183, 197, 279n49:6

Husserl, Edmund, 25, 39, 82, 121–22, 209, 210, 212, 240, 245, 254, 279n48:6

hyperbolic life, 53, 78, 88–91, 99, 142, 167. *See also* categories of "fallen" life; inauthenticity

idle talk [*Gerede*], 8, 72, 102, 107, 114–17, 119, 132, 133, 182, 203, 219, 222, 235, 241, 246, 248–49, 256, 258, 263, 272n11:3. *See also* public discourse

imitation [*Nachfolge*], 191–93, 263

inauthenticity [*Uneigentlichkeit*], 4, 8, 12, 69, 71–73, 73–75, 78–79, 80, 93, 99–100, 119–21, 125, 133, 139, 167, 168, 257, 258, 271n4:3. *See also* categories of "fallen" life; falling

intellectual discourse, 8, 12, 53, 118–33, 215–16, 228, 233, 256, 274n1:4. *See also* idle talk; public discourse; "today," the

interpretation, 25, 27–29, 40, 87, 101, 104–106, 109, 112, 115, 120, 126, 128, 147, 227, 247, 248, 251, 255, 261, 281n14:8

interruption, 32, 80, 156–60, 171, 176, 180–83, 201, 235, 258–59. *See also* authenticity; conscience; graced moments; life-intensification

inwardness, 143, 147–48, 175
"it worlds," 6, 278n30:6

Jaspers, Karl, 23, 130, 180, 194, 199–200,
    218–19
Jemeinigkeit, 138–39, 151, 174, 195
Jesus Christ, 28, 55, 58, 60, 61–62, 64, 65, 69,
    73, 92, 128, 131, 144, 156–57, 160, 178,
    192, 230, 235, 268n18:1, 271n29:2,
    273n33:3
Jeweiligkeit, 97, 119, 138–39, 176, 278n38:6
Joest, Wilfried, 269n44:1, 270n5:2
Jonas, Hans, 17, 267n3:1
Jünger, Ernst, 273n30:3

Kant, Immanuel, 19, 23, 24, 25, 34, 75,
    152–53
Kierkegaard, Søren, 1, 10, 18–19, 35, 70, 77,
    102, 114, 118, 131, 139, 152, 153, 175,
    178, 207, 228, 274n1:4
Kisiel, Theodore, 6, 18–19, 35, 71, 130, 228,
    267n1:Introduction, 267n7:Introduction,
    268n15:1, 268n16:1, 268n23:1, 269n30:1,
    269n36:1, 269n37:1, 269n38:1, 271n2:3,
    273n30:3, 274n36:3, 275n19:4, 275n2:5,
    276n16:5, 276n23:5, 280n12:7
Krebs, Engelbert, 2, 33, 102, 129, 142, 175,
    214, 218, 267n2:1

larvance [*Larvanz*], 93, 234. *See also* barricad-
    ing; "one," the; self-abdication
Lask, Emil, 6, 217
Left Hegelians, 223
life, 6, 9, 11, 15, 21, 22, 23, 25–27, 29, 30, 31,
    32, 34, 38–39, 71, 73, 77, 79. *See also*
    being-in-the-world; Dasein; factical life-
    experience; facticity
life-intensification, 10, 140, 154, 169, 170,
    177, 184. *See also* conscience; graced
    moments; interruption
life-world, 22–23, 32, 33, 140, 184, 214
Löwith, Karl, 33, 35, 69–70, 77, 198, 200, 218,
    267n3:1, 280n8:7
Luther, Martin, 2, 4, 33, 48, 59, 61, 69, 88, 91,
    92, 143, 148–49, 175, 176, 207, 234,
    270n3:2, 271n34:2, 275n13:4; criticism
    of scholastic theology, 45–48, 49, 153,
    272n8:2; Heidegger's 1924 lectures on,
    42–43, 44, 153, 272n8:2; his influence
    on Heidegger, 2–3, 7, 12, 18, 35, 38–43,
    45, 54, 56, 62, 66, 73, 75, 102, 114, 118–
    19, 125, 132, 134, 152–53, 161, 222, 228,

230–31, 232, 234–35, 242; relation to
    mysticism, 65, 152, 269n41:1, 269n44:1;
    views on sin and salvation, 48–54, 57, 58,
    59–60, 65, 270n23:2

Marcuse, Herbert, 227
McGrath, Alistair, 47, 270n6:2, 270n7:2,
    270n15:2
metaphysics, 18, 20, 23–25, 39, 41, 45, 46, 50,
    52, 62, 114, 124, 132, 144–47, 149, 153,
    167, 269n41:1, 272n7:3, 280n9:7
militarism, 141, 183, 278n23:6
Moltmann, Jürgen, 157–58, 161, 272n9:3,
    273n33:3, 274n37:3

National Socialism, 76, 141, 164, 215,
    279n46:6
nationalism, 141, 194
Natorp, Paul, 33, 144, 213, 221
Neo-Kantianism, 11, 12, 22, 24, 39, 46, 66, 77,
    81, 121, 125, 134, 186, 208, 212, 217,
    232–33, 237–38, 239, 243, 275n2:5,
    280n9:7
Neo-orthodox theology, 75, 161, 228, 280n11:7
New Testament, 16, 20, 32, 56, 153, 154, 156,
    229
Nietzsche, Friedrich, 1, 11, 16, 20, 33, 34, 70,
    103, 118, 127, 130, 252, 262, 271n1:3,
    275n20:4
nihilism, 193–94
Novalis (Georg Philipp Friedrich Freiherr von
    Hardenberg), 144, 148, 196, 197,
    275n1:5, 276n18:5, 279n49:6

"one," the [*das Man*], 72, 84, 94–99, 101,
    119–20, 139, 168, 193, 201, 248, 255,
    263. *See also* barricading; larvance; self-
    abdication
onto-theology, 20, 49
Overbeck, Franz, 56, 130–31, 275n21:4

Pannenberg, Wolfhart, 87, 161, 273n32:3,
    273n33:3, 276n27:5
Pascal, Blaise, 10, 178
Paul, 8, 10, 17, 34–35, 36, 37, 42, 45, 50, 54,
    58, 62, 63, 82–83, 84, 86, 91, 102, 153,
    155–57, 158–59, 160, 175, 178, 180,
    183, 199, 207, 222, 224, 228–30, 234
Pelagianism, 52, 59, 65
perfectionism, 8, 76–77, 136
phenomenological critique, 232, 237–40,
    244, 247, 248. *See also* destruction

phenomenology, 23, 25, 30, 96, 111, 121, 125, 131–32, 134–35, 156, 210, 212–13, 240, 241, 243, 249, 262

philosophy, 1, 2, 3, 7, 16–18, 20, 21, 22, 25, 26, 29, 33, 38–39, 46–47, 51, 54, 69, 74, 77, 81, 104, 112, 130, 138, 144, 145, 153, 185, 208, 241, 250, 267n8:1, 268n25:1, 269n30:1; crisis of legitimacy in, 39–40, 208–209; as "making things hard," 38–39, 227–30, 234, 258; motives for, 8, 9, 12, 44, 66, 134, 135, 216–19, 222–23, 234, 236, 248; practice of, 73, 96, 107, 132, 163, 219–23, 226–27, 235, 254; as public discourse, 12, 34, 82, 94, 102, 117, 118–26, 207; "scientific," 11, 122, 209–12; and tradition, 108–11, 114, 139, 236, 238–39, 249, 264; as a vocation, 2, 38, 70, 142–43, 199–200, 265; "world-view," 11, 77, 121–22, 212–16

Pietism, 143, 148

Platonism, 86, 125, 127, 128

proclamation [Verkündigung], 20, 21, 56, 86, 92, 113–14, 130, 155–60, 172, 187–88, 192, 199, 224, 228, 229, 258, 273n25:3. See also Christianity; God, word of

public discourse, 8, 53, 101, 114–16, 119, 120, 126, 129, 133, 189, 207, 222, 225, 228, 231, 234, 241, 246–48, 255, 257, 258–59, 260, 265. See also idle talk; intellectual discourse; "today," the

Reitzenstein, Richard, 131

Relativism, 12, 82, 129, 144, 194–95, 202, 232, 249, 253

religion, 2, 7, 15, 16, 25, 34, 36, 40, 81, 114, 141, 147–49, 178, 276n23:5; Heidegger's critique of, 19–21, 83, 128; as public discourse, 119, 129–33

repetition [Wiederholung], 10, 163, 181, 190–93, 261–64, 265. See also authenticity; historical consciousness

resoluteness [Entschlossenheit], 10, 173, 181, 187–89, 190, 191, 196, 272n12:3. See also authenticity; vocational commitment

Rickert, Heinrich, 19, 24, 122, 125, 129, 217, 237, 274n2:4, 281n9:8

Ritschl, Albrecht, 36

Roman Catholicism, 82, 171; anti-modernist controversy in, 1, 129, 214, 275n17:4; Heidegger's relationship with, 16–17, 19, 102, 129, 214, 218

Romantic personalism, 9, 10, 70, 135, 137–38, 138–43, 146, 154, 161, 169, 171, 177, 195, 220, 264

Romanticism, 70, 170, 277n20:6

Rosenzweig, Franz, 50, 70, 114, 270n21:2, 280n8:7

ruinance [Ruinanz], 71, 78, 99, 227. See also falling; inauthenticity

Schauwecker, Franz, 273n30:3, 276n22:5

Scheler, Max, 153

Schelling, Friedrich, 34, 152, 197, 279n49:6

Schleiermacher, F. D. E., 9, 35, 137, 138, 140, 143–44, 146, 148, 149, 168, 175, 197, 220, 269n32:1, 276n8:5

scholasticism, 22, 24, 40, 42, 46, 47–53, 59, 61–62, 64, 66, 69, 113, 117–19, 148, 161, 192, 270n5:2, 275n11:4

Schweitzer, Albert, 1, 56, 131

self-abdication, 12, 53, 91–99, 117, 167, 203, 256, 258, 264. See also barricading; larvance; "one," the

self-knowledge, 91–92, 159–61, 162, 177, 180, 188, 222, 224, 225. See also authenticity

self-world, 30, 31, 36, 80, 88, 149, 152, 195, 222, 237 (see also historical I); intensifying concentration toward [Zugespitztheit], 31, 150–51, 169 (see also authenticity)

Sheehan, Thomas, 4, 6, 155, 164–65, 166, 189, 267n3:Introduction, 267n6:Introduction, 268n18:1, 276n23:5, 277n6:6

Sluga, Hans, 193, 279n43:6

solicitude [Fürsorge], 200–202. See also authenticity, social aspects of

soteriology, 17, 65, 113; as context for destructio in Luther's early thought, 47, 54, 57–58, 59, 61; late scholastic views of, 45–47, 50, 51, 59, 66, 270n6:2

Spengler, Oswald, 118, 127–28, 249, 253, 278n39:6

struggle [Kampf], 40, 54–55, 59, 66, 70, 90, 92, 102, 116, 118–19, 125, 132, 159–60, 189, 192, 199–203, 208, 224, 226, 227, 228, 253, 255, 262, 278n23:6

taking it easy, 81–85. See also categories of "fallen" life; inauthenticity

Tauler, Johannes, 36, 147, 150, 152, 269n41:1, 269n42:1

Taylor, Charles, 9, 137, 275n4:5, 276n10:5

temptation, 79–81. *See also* categories of "fallen" life; inauthenticity

theology, 1, 2, 4, 7, 21, 34, 36, 46, 47, 53, 54, 56, 66, 75, 149, 152–53, 156, 157, 161, 211, 261, 280n8:7; Heidegger's criticisms of, 19, 114, 129–32, 267n8:1; Heidegger's relationship to, 3, 16, 17–18, 20, 37, 38–43, 70, 269n30:1; of the cross, 7, 41–42, 54, 58, 62, 65, 69, 231, 232

today, the [*das Heute*], 119–20, 126, 193, 259. *See also* idle talk; intellectual discourse; public discourse

tradition, 8, 10, 35, 87, 101, 102–106, 115, 120, 126, 139, 167, 180, 193–95, 196, 232, 239, 246, 248–49, 255; decline of, 8, 106–108, 110–11, 133, 159; influence on contemporary philosophical views, 26, 34, 108–10, 118, 211, 212, 231, 241, 244, 256, 263; outlines of Western philosophy, 112–14

Trakl, Georg, 33

Troeltsch, Ernst, 274n2:4

truthfulness, 142, 154, 179, 183, 198, 217, 219, 220, 224, 237

Van Buren, John, 5, 6, 18–19, 20, 41, 45, 48, 71, 107, 138, 143–44, 150, 168–69, 229, 236, 267n1:Introduction, 267n4:Introduction, 268n10:1, 268n12:1, 268n17:1, 269n45:1, 270n1:2, 270n2:2, 271n4:3, 272n14:3, 272n19:3, 273n22:3, 274n5:4, 275n11:4, 275n17:4, 275n18:4, 276n7:5, 276n12:5, 276n21:5, 277n15:6, 279n45:6, 279n53:6, 280n13:7

Van Gogh, Vincent, 95, 118, 178, 277n20:6

vocational commitment, 10, 32, 162, 167, 171, 175, 180, 188, 190, 194, 195, 198, 203, 219, 227, 251, 255, 259, 260. *See also* authenticity; resoluteness

Vogel, Lawrence, 193–94, 202, 279n44:6, 279n47:6, 279n54:6, 279n55:6

wakefulness, 10, 18, 133, 142, 158, 176–78, 179, 222–24, 237. *See also* authenticity

Weimar Republic, 141, 194, 198, 200, 275n16:4

Wendland, Johannes, 131

Westphal, Merold, 268n21:1, 270n20:2, 274n1:4

Windelband, Wilhelm, 24, 237

with-world [*Mitwelt*], 80, 88, 149, 195, 237

world, 6, 24, 25, 27, 71, 73, 77, 79, 80–81, 82, 85, 86, 98, 104–105, 112, 119, 138, 145, 186–87, 188, 195, 278n30:6; as example of "destruction," 246–47

World War I, 1, 11, 16, 35, 82, 169, 198, 203, 214, 217, 218, 275n16:4

Yorck von Wartenburg, Count Paul, 251, 257

Youth Movement, 70, 138, 140–41, 163, 170–72, 203

Zimmerman, Michael E., 164–67, 277n8:6

zur Mühlen, Karl-Heinz, 46, 47, 270n11:2

Benjamin D. Crowe is adjunct assistant professor in the Department of Philosophy at the University of Utah, Salt Lake City. His current research focuses on Heidegger, neo-Kantian theories of religion, and early German Romanticism.